OPEN MIKE

Also by Michael Eric Dyson

Why I Love Black Women
Holler If You Hear Me
I May Not Get There with You
Race Rules
Between God and Gangsta Rap
Making Malcolm
Reflecting Black

OPEN MIKE

Reflections on Philosophy,
Race, Sex, Culture and Religion

Michael Eric Dyson

A Member of the
Perseus Books Group

Published by Basic *Civitas* Books,
A Member of the Perseus Books Group

Designed by Jeff Williams
Typeset in 10.5-point Giovanni

Library of Congress Cataloging-in-Publication Data

Dyson, Michael Eric.
Open mike : reflections on philosophy, race, sex, culture and religion / Michael Eric Dyson.
p. cm.
Includes bibliography references and index.
ISBN 0-465-01765-7 (alk. paper)
1. African Americans—Race identity. 2. United States—Race relations. 3. African Americans—Intellectual life. 4. African American philosophy. 5. African Americans—Social conditions—1975- . 6. African Americans in popular culture. 7. Dyson, Michael Eric—Interviews. 8. African American intellectuals—Interviews. I. Title. II. Title.
E185.625.D97 2002
305.896'073—dc21 2002013467

03 04 05 / 10 9 8 7 6 5 4 3 2

To Precious Friends and Mentors

D. Soyini Madison

Brilliant performance studies scholar and ingenious teacher

James Melvin Washington

(1948–1997)

Major religious historian and gifted gospel preacher

Cornel West

Towering intellectual and courageous inspiration to a generation

Jeffrey Stout

Distinguished religious ethicist and devoted teacher

CONTENTS

II Cultural Studies

III Religious Beliefs, Theological Arguments

FOREWORD

"Teach the Bourgeois and Rock the Boulevard": Michael Eric Dyson as Celebrity Gramscian

> Reputation spreads, and eventually opportunities present themselves to cross over from the left intellectual ghetto to the status of Black Voice for the mainstream. . . . This is the path blazed so far by Gates and West, and Dyson, as usual, is bringing his best Pigmeat-Markham-Meets-Baudrillard act along behind.
>
> —Adolph Reed

Of course Adolph Reed meant the above epigraph as a "dis." It was just a small chunk of the flesh that Reed took from his more celebrated public intellectual contemporaries, in what may be the most widely circulated and cited diatribe against the so-called black public intellectual. What Reed didn't understand then (and apparently has no interest in understanding now) is that the "Pigmeat-Markham-Meets-Baudrillard act" was the whole reason a bunch of us were digging Michael Eric Dyson in the first place. When Dyson's *Reflecting Black: African-American Cultural Criticism* dropped in 1993, a whole new world was opened up for black cultural studies in the United States. I was one of those bright-eyed and hungry poststructuralist shorties who found his calling after reading *Reflecting Black: African-American Cultural Criticism*, and later sucking the bone marrow from Robin D.G. Kelley's *Race Rebels: Culture, Politics, and the Black Working Class* and Tricia Rose's *Black Noise: Rap Music and Black Culture in Contemporary America*, as these texts, and the thinkers behind them, provided a generation of black graduate students in the humanities and the social sciences the license to bring the diverse and competing realities of black life into conversation with contemporary cultural and critical theory. As Dyson himself admits, "I do want to make the life of the mind sexy for young people in the academy and beyond its reach. I want to have a mode of criticism that allows me to be mobile, to move from the academy to the streets to the world" (p. 127).

By the time Dyson's *Race Rules* (his fourth book in four years) was published in 1996, Dyson was regularly mentioned alongside Cornel West, Henry Louis Gates Jr., and bell hooks as a member of a generation of black public intellectuals who were worthy of intense praise (Robert Boynton and Michael Berube) and scrutiny (Reed and Leon Wieseltier). A few years before the hype hit the fan, Cornel West tried to make some sense of the functions of these yet to be ordained black public intellectuals, as he argued for an "insurgency model" of black intellectual activity. This model was in part inspired by the work of Antonio Gramsci, who posited the emergence of a class of "organic" intellectuals. According to West, the "central task of postmodern Black intellectuals is to stimulate, hasten, and enable alternative perceptions and practices by dislodging prevailing discourse and power. . . . Instead of the solitary hero, embattled exile, and isolated genius—the intellectual as star, celebrity, commodity—this model privileges collective intellectual work that contributes to communal resistance" (*Breaking Bread*, 144). These were the words of a man who had not yet become the very thing he critiqued after the publication of his bestseller *Race Matters* in 1993.

West's conflation of the postmodernist public intellectual, as well as the Gramscian organic intellectual, is really indebted to the Cultural Studies movement that emerged in Britain in the late 1950s and early 1960s. Speaking about that first generation of cultural theorists who worked out of Birmingham University's Centre for Contemporary Cultural Studies, Stuart Hall—generally regarded as the forefather of contemporary Black Cultural Studies—asserts that "we had to be at the very forefront of intellectual theoretical work because, as Gramsci says, it is the job of the organic intellectual to know more than the traditional intellectuals do" but adds that it was just as crucial that the "organic intellectual cannot absolve himself or herself from the responsibility of transmitting those ideas, that knowledge, through the intellectual function, to those who do not belong, professionally, in the intellectual class" (*Stuart Hall: Critical Dialogues in Cultural Studies*, 268). Not surprisingly, many of the so-called black public intellectuals of the 1990s emerged within the institutional rubric of American Cultural Studies, despite their very specific training in the fields of philosophy, theology, and literature.

If the point was to "speak truth to power" on behalf of the folks in the hood, or as Chuck D put it, to "Teach the bourgeois and rock the boulevard" ("Don't Believe the Hype"), then no doubt black public intellectuals were the hot hype that preceded them. *Nightline, The Today Show, Charlie Rose, TalkBack Live, BET Tonight,* "came arunnin'" looking for those fly, bespectacled, dressed-up spokespersons of the race who could put a "literate" spin ("Why they're so articulate") on issues such as the O.J. Simpson trial, the Dream Team (both the Michael Jordan–led Olympic team and Simpson's legal advisers), the deaths of Tupac Shakur and Biggie Smalls, and the Million Man March. Dyson himself became one of the brightest lights among black public intellectuals in the aftermath of the O.J. Simpson trial, providing commentary during the trial (and immediately after the jury decision) for NPR and appearing as the "color commentator" on BET, when Ed Gordon sat down with Simpson after his acquittal. Adolph Reed may be a "hater supreme," but he ain't crazy, so there's some legitimacy to his claims that the high visibility of black public intellectuals does not naturally correlate with the concerns and ambitions of the black masses these intellectuals ostensibly "speak" for. No amount of Apple computer ads with elite black intellectuals are getting black farmers the duckets that the federal government has thus far fronted on. Even Dyson admits "true dat," but in describing the political components of his own teaching, he submits, "we don't have to subscribe to such a literal view of the work of politics. Creating discursive spaces in hegemonic academic culture is a specific kind of work that should be valued, even if it is rightly not confused, better yet, conflated, with traditional politics. Such activity has an empirical effect on the concrete political interests of folk outside the academy" (p. 66).

The current generation of black public intellectuals has been thoughtfully, though mistakenly, aligned to the New York intellectuals of the 1950s. Stuart Hall, Raymond Williams, and the cadre of "Birmingham School" cultural theorists are more tangible influences, though truth be told, the very tradition of black public intellectuals can be traced back to figures like David Walker and Alexander Crummell (whom DuBois eulogized in *The Souls of Black Folk*) in the nineteenth century, and Hubert Harrison and Zora Neale Hurston in the early twentieth century. No doubt, David Walker's *Appeal* was a gangsterish takeover of the dominant media of the day, making him a prototype for Harlem Renaissance era figures like Wallace Thurman, Bruce Nugent, and a bunch of the other folks who were behind the "insurgent" periodical *Fire!* or early hip-hop purveyors like Kool Herc and Grand Wizard Theodore. But what if Walker would have had access to twenty-four-hour cable stations or had mounted a fifty-city book tour? As Nas said, "imagine that." I make this point only to suggest that Dyson, West, Gates, and all the usual suspects (can't name them all, though I must acknowledge the work of the late June Jordan) have really transcended the tradition of black public intellectuals, at least in the context that this tradition has flourished during the last century. Perhaps more apropos is the title "black celebrity intellectuals"—media stars, commodities in Ivy League battles to capture the "bigga nigga," and the postmodern "niggeratti" (as Hurston so poignantly called it seventy-five years ago), who floss alongside the anointed black political spokespersons, hip-hop moguls, Dream Team lawyers, and black Hollywood icons, with little distinction made among them, since they are all examples of "black star power." Dyson admits "celebrity is a temptation among scholars and especially among black intellectuals, given the relatively small numbers of us who are able to survive and thrive in the academy. . . we have to constantly resist that temptation by making relentless forays into those base communities for which we claim to speak" (p. 68–69).

It is in the guise of his celebrity that Michael Eric Dyson has distinguished himself among the cadre of black celebrities who happen to live a life of the mind. Sure, we can talk about his flow (a *real* black intellectual hip-hop CD would have Dyson and fellow Detroiter Todd Boyd flowin' lovely like a Biggie and 'Pac collabo), and how the "brotha" has found a comfort zone equally at home with the high-brow, starched collar of Brian Lamb's *Booknotes* or in "poppin' that collar" with Tavis Smiley on Smiley's NPR program. Although we all secretly harbor some desires to be *the* "head nigga in charge," Dyson's never been about becoming a black *entrepreneurial* intellectual, or the black "moral conscience of the nation" intellectual, and that's what made him "real" for us "thug nigga intellectuals" who actually hold it down in the academy, and the fo' real "thug niggas" surviving the triple Ps: penitentiaries, projects, and poverty.

But it goes a little deeper than what are essentially surface and stylistic distinctions among black intellectuals. Stuart Hall notes that Gramsci's concept of "organic" intellectuals "appears to align intellectuals with an emerging historical movement and we [Birmingham Cultural Theorists] couldn't tell then, and can hardly tell now, where that emerging historical movement was to be found. We were organic intellectuals without any organic point of reference" (*Stuart Hall*, 267). Though the current reparations movement will likely produce its own insurgent intellectual tradition, the emergence of black public intellectuals in the 1990s occurred outside of the kind of social movement (unless of course we consider the hypercommodification of black popular culture as such) that Hall, per Gramsci, suggests is necessary for the full realization of an organic intellectual tradition. Ironically, the one phenomenon that could be considered a legitimate social movement in the last two decades is the basis for what is arguably the most commodified form of black expression on the earth.

Despite intense commodification, hip-hop culture has produced its own tradition of insurgent and organic intellectuals, who have used the ghetto pulpit—now firmly situated in the mainstream—as a means to speak the essence of a "postworld" (postmodern, postsoul, post–civil rights, postindustrial, take your pick). There is little question that figures like Chuck D, Rakim Allah, Melle Mel, Sista Souljah, Mos Def, M–1 and Stic.man of Dead Prez, Talib Kweli, Sarah Jones, S. Craig Watkins, Ursula Rucker, Ice Cube, Bahamadia, Common, the late Lisa Sullivan, Kevin Powell, Raquel Cepeda, Paris, Davey D,

Yvonne Bynoe, Bakari Kitwana, Gwendolyn Pough, Danny Hoch, William Upski Wimsatt, and the often bombastic KRS-One (to name a few) are a formidable cadre of thinkers and artists who rightfully represent the organic intellectual voices of their generation. But as hip-hop has circulated around the globe, so have the images—more so than the deeds—of these hip-hop Gramscians. Mos Def appears in a Pulitzer Prize–winning Broadway play, while his music ("Umi Says") serves as the soundtrack for a Nike commercial. Sarah Jones, in battle with the FCC over the lyrics of her song "Your Revolution," has become the poster child for the ACLU and the left liberal press, recently appearing on the cover of *Utne Reader*. The fabulous "white boyz" Hoch and Wimsatt have become the celebrated icons of the "back packer" set. In every way, shape, and form, these figures are all celebrities. In many regards, these "celebrity Gramscians" are the progeny of the late Nigerian musician and activist Fela Kuti, who wedded his celebrity, proclivity for hedonistic practices, and hatred for corrupt Nigerian leaders, including the late Sunni Abacha, into the global musical movement known as Afro-beat. This was the proverbial "party and bullshit," with a trenchant and critical political message.

Less the sellouts that they would have been defined as a generation ago, this generation of what can only be called celebrity Gramscians, speaks to the ironies of hip-hop itself—an art form that seeks to neither delegitimize nor undermine the logics of late-stage capitalism, but rather to reorient those logics to serve the interests of its constituents. It's not a perfect science—I'm not at all suggesting that a CD, or book, or spoken word program broadcast on an AOL-Time Warner network replace the real work in the trenches. But hip-hop, in concert with advances in technology such as the Internet, mp3s, CD burners, and so on, has facilitated a unique moment in which "cultures of resistance" can circulate quickly and widely in ways unknown to previous generations. It is these celebrity Gramscians who are the talking heads—MTV's *TRL* and BET's *106th and Park* notwithstanding—of this moment.

For more than a decade, Michael Eric Dyson has been referred to as the "hip-hop intellectual." Speaking of his earlier years as a teen father and welfare recipient, Dyson notes "to many onlookers, I suppose I looked like a loser, a typical, pathological, self-defeating young black male. That may help explain why I empathize with such youth in the hip-hop generation; because I was one of those brothers that many social scientists and cultural critics easily dismiss and effortlessly, perhaps, literally, write off" (p. 10). Dyson has more than "empathized" with the hip-hop generation; he has *represented* for them, in the academy, in the pulpit, on the tube, within the lily-whiteness of mainstream America, arguably, more effectively than any of his peers within the higher echelons of "black public intellectual–dom." While many of his peers have been well positioned to talk about and interpret hip-hop culture for the lily-white masses, dating back to a well-known case involving a bunch of "booty-ass" rappers known as the 2 Live Crew, Dyson has been "organically" connected to hip-hop in ways that many of his peers neither understood nor desired. Dyson has been fond of remarking during his public talks that if he had to choose between high-falutin' Ivy League Negroes or the "niggas," he was "representin' fo' the niggas."

The best testament of Dyson's importance in this regard is the runaway success of his book, *Holler If You Hear Me: Searching for Tupac Shakur,* which had its roots in Dyson's previous book, *I May Not Get There with You: The True Martin Luther King Jr.* Many critics have taken Dyson to task for suggesting that King had much in common with the likes of the late Tupac Shakur or Christopher Wallace, also known as Notorious B.I.G. Dyson responds, "We do not have to deny the huge differences between King and many contemporary black youth, but both have good and bad things in common: how they view women, how they borrow and piece together intellectual sources, how they view sex, and how they confront the evils of racism and ghetto oppression." Even if Dyson's claims are not legitimate (I for one think that they are), what is the harm in attempting to build some kind of intellectual or ideological bridge between the civil rights generation and "generation hip-hop"? The possibilities of the bridge were realized with the publication of *Holler If You Hear Me,* as Dyson understood, better than most, that Jesse Jackson, Al Sharpton, Louis Farrakhan, Hugh Price, and the contingent of initialized, acronymed organizations (NAACP, SCLC, CBC, etc.) cannot compete with a "dead" Tupac Shakur for the attention and devotion of the hip-hop generation. By tapping into the myth and symbol of Tupac Shakur—this generation's most fetishized Gramscian intellectual—Dyson has been the most influential of his generation of black public intellectuals among the hip-hop and post–hip-hop generations.

America has never really taken seriously the intellectual capacity of the folks of African descent spread out across its terrain. Despite their successes and their visibility, black thinkers and artists are rarely allowed a "public complexity," but are reduced to the smallest possible "racial box" in order to sell them and their ideas to a mainstream audience, black and nonblack, who have never thought of "blackness" as being complex at all. Among mainstream audiences who have very little familiarity with the black intellectual tradition and its complexity, a book like John McWhorter's largely anecdotal *Losing the Race: Self-Sabotage in Black America*, for example, is hailed as a "brave intellectual achievement," instead of just a collection of uncritical and often misinformed perceptions about black life. Though Skip Gates and Cornel West have produced groundbreaking scholarship in literary theory and religious philosophy (Gates's *Signifying Monkey* is the most accomplished piece of scholarship of his generation), the two are likely more well known, respectively, for narrating a PBS series, *Africa*, and the "pithy little book" that made West a media star. Though these are folks who are now clearly writing for general, nonscholarly audiences, the mode of authority that they derive in these spaces often anchors them to work that, by definition, is not meant to overly challenge its readers. The small space allowed black public intellectuals was made painfully clear recently when Dyson appeared on C-SPAN's *Booknotes* with Brian Lamb to promote *Holler If You Hear Me*. Admittedly, Lamb's audience is not the type that would be familiar with Shakur, or Dyson for that matter. But rather than let Dyson do his thing, Lamb reduced him to answering inane questions like, "What's a homie? . . . Okay, then what's a ho (whore)? Then what's a bitch?" These questions reflect a general disregard for the complexity of black life and culture, as well as the intellectual acumen of those who survey and scrutinize it for a living.

Since the publication of his third book, *Between God and Gangsta Rap*, Dyson has primarily written for general audiences. It is in the context of writing for such audiences that Dyson has been able to have the widest impact on American culture, though he has been subject to often mean-spirited critiques suggesting that intellectually he was "soft." In the pages of *Open Mike: Reflections on Philosophy, Race, Sex, Culture, and Religion*, Dyson admits that it is "unavoidable that an academic surrenders depth for breadth in making many public forays into television, radio, or the popular press. But that doesn't automatically overrule the usefulness of such pursuits. . . . in a word we have to respect the genre" (p. 63). Indeed, some of the missives aimed at Dyson from, say, the likes of Adolph Reed, are informed by "hostility" toward the folks who are able to "take the knowledge, to take the profound rigor that is often suggested in such exercises, and make them available to a broader audience" (p. 63). But Dyson does not need to be defended here. *Open Mike* stands on its own as a response to all those who suggest that Dyson isn't erudite enough to represent at the big table. In the discourse of one of the many rhetorical communities in which Dyson flows, *Open Mike* is a "critical beat-down."

Scholars who do work in cultural studies are often dismissed by some who believe that "everyday life" is not worthy of scholarly inquiry. But they are also attacked because of old-school, conservative notions about "interdisciplinary scholarship." Dyson argues that at its core, "interdisciplinarity threatens academics who construe their interests narrowly and seek to preserve their intellectual bailiwick" (p. 66). Like so many of us in the field of cultural studies, Dyson was likely born an "interdisciplinarian." Describing the early development of his intellectual project, Dyson asserts that "there are tensions, and, in fact, these multiple tensions define my intellectual projects and existential identities: tensions between sacred and secular, tensions between the intellectual and the religious, tensions between radical politics and mainstream institutions, tensions between preaching and teaching" (p. 12).

Open Mike speaks to the legitimacy of Dyson's project, as the book is structured to represent the distinct spheres of Dyson's intellectual engagement. The opening section features Dyson in the mode of the critical race theorist, while the following sections find Dyson in his well-known guises of cultural critic and religious philosopher. *Open Mike* is Michael Eric Dyson "unplugged." In the chapter entitled "Is It Something I Said? Dissident Speech, Plantation Negro Syndrome, and the Politics of Self-Respect," Dyson announces, "I am an unadulterated black man, ain't got no shame about it, I'm gon' represent the African American interests *while being critical of them*. I'm going to speak to the larger, universal themes of black American culture while being critical of the ways that we fail to live up to our obligation to defend our own people—AND—I'm going to hit themes that the larger American culture can resonate with, because black folk are not orangutans living outside the arch of human experience" (p. 135).

In the words of the pure playas, "Respect the Game."

Mark Anthony Neal
Assistant Professor, English
State University of New York at Albany

PREFACE

In my career as a scholar and preacher, I have had the good fortune to encounter journalists and intellectuals who gave me the opportunity to air my views on a wide range of subjects through interviews. I conceive of the interviewer as an intellectual midwife, coaxing his subject to deliver thoughts and ideas in the clearest way possible. But that metaphor may not walk on all fours. The interviewer is even more active in the process of creation through the questions she asks, the clarifications she demands, and the new formulations she inspires.

At its dynamic best, the interview is characterized by at least three keywords: explanation, expansion, and experimentation. One may explain ideas that were stated—or poorly stated, maybe misstated—on another occasion. Or, one may illumine thoughts that may have been difficult to digest, controversial, or perhaps misunderstood, even misinterpreted. As a result, one expands on themes declared in other forms; one enlarges on motifs touched on in passing, but which beg for more comment and critical examination. The interview, therefore, is tailor-made for experimentation with new impressions and new expressions. The interview showcases rhetorical improvisation in its purest incarnation: as an elaboration of previous reflections where one is free to try out novel concepts and to try on fresh critical gear in the spontaneity of intellectual exchange.

I am especially fond of the interview because it combines my deep devotion to critical engagement and my love of language in its various modes and genres, whether on page or stage. Lectures and sermons allow one to engage a specific topic where one's content is in part shaped by the interaction with a live audience. Articles and essays permit an author to tackle a finite subject within a necessarily narrow scope. And books permit one to carve out an intellectual territory and explore it with depth and rigor. The interview blends the virtues of the written and spoken word. In this form, one may freestyle on ideas while entertaining questions of one's work. In the most electrifying moments of the interview, one is invited, sometimes begged, at other times cajoled, to dig deeply into one's intellectual resources to respond.

I have been blessed over the last decade by some great interviewers who have thoroughly engaged my work. They have often inspired me to probe my thoughts more innovatively and intensely. They have come to the interview well prepared, which stoked my own creative fire to blaze new paths in my thinking on philosophy, black identity, gender conflicts, basketball, intellectuals, modernism and postmodernism, the Olympics, preaching, hip-hop culture, television, comedy, homosexuality, the Bible, morality and ethics, whiteness studies, Christian theology, jazz music, postcolonial theory, rhetoric, critical race theory, multiculturalism, semiotics, technology, writing, reading, social justice, Islamic thought, cultural studies, liberalism, religious beliefs, capitalism, Marxism, politics, the academy, literary theory, the civil rights movement, black nationalism, white supremacy, self-esteem and self-hatred, boxing, social theory, public education, psychological theory, death, stereotypes, cyberspace, and a great deal more. Many of my students and colleagues have urged me to collect the best of these encounters in one place. You hold the result in your hands.

With a few exceptions, these interviews are seeing the light of published day for the first time. My exchange with the composition scholar Sidney Dobrin occurred in a marathon session one crisp spring day in Durham, North Carolina, a very shortened version of which was published in *JAC: A Journal of Composition Theory*, and later, in the book, *Race, Rhetoric, and the Postcolonial*, edited by Gary A. Olson and Lynn

Worsham. My interview on whiteness with educational scholar Ronald E. Chennault was published in the book, *White Reign*, and my interview on preaching and social justice with homiletics professor and pastor Frank Thomas appeared in briefer form in *The African American Pulpit*. My interview with English professor Laura Winkiel on Malcolm X appeared in the journal, *Religion & Literature*, and my interview with freelance writer and graduate student Hisham Aidi on Martin Luther King Jr., appeared on *Africana.com*. My interview with Marc Vogl on self-criticism and comedy was excerpted on *Citysearch.com*, and the interview with Kheven LaGrone on homosexuality and religion will appear in a volume on black homosexuality.

In many cases, the interviews in *Open Mike* are rescued words from a larger project—television and film documentaries, newspaper or magazine stories—that excerpted small portions of my speech in their finished products. The writers and producers often sent me the entire transcripts of our encounters, which, understandably, couldn't be reasonably fit into their films, essays, interviews, or stories. If they had not passed them along to me, these interviews might have wasted into oblivion. I hope you will agree that they are worth preserving and that they might serve a useful function to readers who wrestle with the issues they engage.

part one

Philosophy, Theory, and Race

1

Not from Some Racial Zeus's Head

My Intellectual Development

Michael, let's talk a little about your self-perception. I've seen articles describing you as an intellectual giant, a person who has created a rather unique niche, as having one foot in the scholarly world and the other "on the block," and somehow synthesizing the two. When I've seen you, you've been very vocal in your opinions on issues or themes outside of yourself. But the little I've heard about you as a man, a person . . . how did you pull this off? That "raising up from the bootstraps" thing is cool, but where we're from, a lot of us have had to do that. Yet you are special and unique and obviously on a distinct path that, on the one hand, you're carving, but on the other, seems like it was laid out there for you. How did you have the good sense to follow it, to take that dive? How'd you do that?

There's no question that nobody is self-made in America. All this mythology of the rugged individual has to be deconstructed. We've got to get at the heart of the essential lie that America was founded on this ethic of personal and private individual achievement. That has to be scrapped because a form of American Protestant communalism is the basis of discourse about American democracy. Recent studies in American political history evince a strong philosophical disagreement with the underlying principles of this American mythology—that we came here as solo artists and that we developed as individuals articulating ourselves against the wilderness of the collective. That's really not the case. People are produced by cultures and communities, by larger networks of association, love, kin, affection, and so on. And the same is true for me. I was produced, first of all, in the womb of a family that loved me, with my mother and father in the house. My father adopted me when I was two years old. I called him daddy because I didn't know any other man in my life. He was my daddy and my father. I'm one of five boys who grew up together in our immediate family. There were four older brothers and sisters, all of whom now are deceased.

When were you born?

October 23, 1958. Being born in what we would call the ghetto of Detroit had a decisive influence on my life and an impact on how I understand the relationship between scholarship and the street, between the world of the mind and the world of concrete outside of the academy. I think being born in the ghetto and being reared there, and dealing with the inner-city black community, connected me to other African American people who were doing extraordinarily important things. Detroit was a vibrant, vital black world teeming with possibility beyond the ballyhooed violence that stalked poor and working-class blacks. It was a wonderfully rich experience seeing black folk who lived meaningful lives, who ran their own businesses, and who eventually ran the city. When I was still in my teens, Coleman Young was elected the first black mayor of Detroit. I encountered in the political landscape powerful figures like Kenneth Cockrel, a Marxist black lawyer who was very important in my own rhetorical development, especially the stylistic etiquette of joining black radical discourse to a powerful social criticism of the forces of oppression.

My pastor, Dr. Frederick Sampson, came to my church when I was twelve years old. He was the decisive intellectual influence in my life, with his fusion in his rhetorical repertoire of metaphysical poetry, racial uplift, and classical learning. Another pastor, Dr. Charles Adams, also thrilled us with his brilliant preaching and his exploration of the radical social implications of the Bible and theology. My fifth-grade teacher, Mrs. James, was extraordinarily important in my understanding of black people. She taught us about black history when folks didn't want to hear that, even other black teachers at Wingert Elementary School, which I attended from kindergarten through sixth grade. My Sunday school teachers in church appreciated black history and black culture and exposed us to the broad outlines of our people's sojourn in America, which gave us a sense of somebodyness as black children. It wasn't done so much by my teachers deploying a formal didacticism or a pedagogy geared toward instilling pride, but as they took for granted that black folk could achieve and love each other. That had a huge influence on me. They gave us a sense of helping ourselves while not harming others. We could love ourselves without hating anyone else, including white brothers and sisters. It wasn't about them, it was about us. They taught us to take for granted the existence of a black universe rooted in a black psychic infrastructure that had no need to pay deference to white culture, embracing all folk while defending black humanity and interests in the face of inimical forces.

That was the kind of world in which I was reared. This framework of existential and spiritual nurture provided a rich background for me—Sampson with this attention to the spiritual needs of African American people, Cockrel with his black Marxist discourse, Adams with this attention to the social ramifications of the gospel, and Mrs. James with her attention to the need for black history and memory as a resource to stabilize the black present and to secure the black future. They were among the folk who gave me a sense of self, who helped to create Michael Eric Dyson, who helped me understand the different bricks that must be laid at the foundation of my head and heart in order to have a healthy identity. So, I didn't spring fully formed out of some racial Zeus's head; I was shaped and molded in an environment where black achievement was taken for granted, where black excellence was expected, where black aspiration was crucial, and where black intellectual engagement was the norm of the day—on every level. And I'm not primarily referring to formal education in school. I'm referring largely to everyday life with brothers and sisters who were playing the numbers and playing the dozens. They were trying to use their linguistic and rhetorical capacity to defend their interests and worldviews.

That's just what I was going to ask, if you had that duality even then, where on the one hand, you were already processing what you were being given, and exposed to, from your elders, but I was thinking—what were you doing with the fellas on the street, your peers? That's what you're talking about.

Oh yeah. There was at least a duality going on. I felt I belonged to many worlds. I kicked it with the fellas on the street and spent a lot of time engaging the Motown curriculum: Smokey Robinson, Stevie Wonder, Marvin Gaye, and so on. And at the same time, I learned to engage Paul Laurence Dunbar, W.E.B. Du Bois, Paul Robeson, and other great figures. Those interests didn't develop automatically, but were encouraged by teachers like Mrs. James, who wanted to make sure we knew about Jan Metzeliger and the shoe-lasting machine; Deadwood Dick and Wild Bill Pickett and the hidden tradition of black cowboys; Garrett T. Morgan and the invention of the traffic signal; Daniel Hale Williams and open heart surgery; Charles Drew and blood plasma; and Elijah McCoy and the lubricating cup. Her interest in black life was contagious. At Webber Junior High School, I was fortunate to encounter teachers who were instrumental in my further development. My seventh-grade English teacher, Mr. Burdette, enhanced my speaking skills by encouraging me to become involved in oratorical contests sponsored by the Detroit Optimist Club. And Mrs. Click taught me to type quickly and accurately, and besides that, gave me tremendous affection as a growing young man who had a huge crush on her. To tell the truth, I had crushes on many of my female teachers, starting with Mrs. Jefferson in kindergarten, to Mrs. Stewart and Mrs. Williams at Webber, and Mrs. Ray and Mrs. Carter at Northwestern, almost all of them English teachers. In my mind, love, language, and learning were profoundly linked in what may be termed an erotics of epistemology.

When I got to Northwestern High School, I had a crush on yet another teacher, Madame Black, who taught me French and so much more. She gave me a sense of my burgeoning intellectual power and encouraged me to tutor other students in French. She also gave me a sense that I should use language as a doorway into further investigation of American and African American culture. So did her husband, Dr. Cordell Black, whom I perceived then as my friendly competition! Dr. Black was a professor at Oakland University who often came to pick up Madame Black after school, and I'd still be there, and he'd see me trying to read Jean Paul Sartre's masterly philosophical tome, *L'etre et Le Neant,* in its original French, a book that, in English, translates to *Being and Nothingness*. He'd laugh a laugh of wonder and encouragement and say, "Look at him, look at his aspiration and ambition." But most important, he also encouraged me to read Du Bois and Fanon and other classics in black letters. These figures gave important direction to my scholarly inclinations.

But I can't romanticize things. At the same time, there was quite a bit of pain and conflict going on as well. There was the pain of being called by some of my peers "brainiac," "Poindexter," and "Professor." Of course, it was their way of slyly, sometimes harshly, complimenting what they thought of as my smarts. But recognition and resentment were, in that beautiful phrase of Ralph Bunche's, "ineluctably concomitant." To be sure, there was also a hierarchy of virtues established, one that comedian Chris Rock refers to when he jokes in a routine that black folk who get out of prison get much more "dap," or respect, from other blacks than those who've just graduated with a master's degree from college. I faced a version of that phenomenon, something that is termed in pedagogical theory as "rival epistemologies," or competing schemes of understanding how the world operates and the place of knowledge and formal training in its orbit. Some blacks think you can't be simultaneously cool and smart, at least in the sense of formal education. But I also experienced strong support in my peer group. Some of my peers said, "This brother's destined for a different world than we are." Others said, "He's in the ghetto, he's with us, but he's got something different. We don't always understand it, we tease him about it, but we admire him too." Some of my male peers—I'm thinking especially of a young man named Michael Squirewell—sought to protect me from some of the worst elements in our neighborhood. Unfortunately, that doesn't happen as often today as it did then.

I grew up in Detroit during the restructuring of the automobile industry. My father worked at Kelsey Hayes Wheel-Brake & Drum Company, which I call his alma mater, a place where I "matriculated" as well between the ages of nineteen and twenty. I didn't go to college until I was twenty-one years old. I had been a teen father, lived on welfare, and hustled several years before furthering my formal education. I had gotten off track from the enabling tradition and heritage handed on to me by my teachers. I had gone to Cranbrook, one of the mostly highly esteemed private schools in the country, located in Bloomfield Hills, a suburb of Detroit. I was dating a young lady from my church, whose father, Damon Keith, was a deacon there, as well as a federal judge and one of the city's most prominent citizens. Judge Keith arranged for me to take the IQ and entry exams, and when I scored well, I was admitted, even though I couldn't afford the $11,000 annual tuition, which was damned near my father's yearly salary. Judge Keith arranged for me to receive a partial scholarship from New Detroit, a local civic and leadership organization, and to work for the other part of my tuition by traveling the forty or so miles from what was then the second richest suburb in the country to one of the bleakest neighborhoods in America, on the East Side of Detroit, to fill bags with food items, and to do maintenance work, for a group that aided the poor, Operation Hope, run by Bernard Parker. Two of Judge Keith's daughters, including the young lady I dated, attended Kingswood, the female complement to the all-boys Cranbrook. The schools have since merged.

I went to Cranbrook—where I agreed to repeat the eleventh grade in order to get sufficient academic grounding and to get at least two years at this prestigious institution under my belt, with an eye to getting into a quality college or university—and in some ways, I had a tremendous experience, and in other ways, it was a very painful one. I was seventeen years old, and I had never gone to school with white kids before. Now here I was going to school with kids who were extremely rich, many of them the sons and daughters of some of the wealthiest parents in the country. I remember, for instance, doing a report with Bill Taubman, the son of Alfred Taubman, one of the richest men in the nation. I was also the classmate of an heir apparent to Rockwell International, and the half-brother, Robert Zimmerman, of director Steven Spielberg. And at Kingswood, where we sometimes took classes, things were no different, and I remember Ford Motor Company head Lee Iaccoca's daughter, Kathy, was a student at the time. When I got out to Cranbrook, which rested on over three hundred acres of verdant, prosperous geography, nestled in a city of extraordinary material blessing, I felt like the Jimmy Stewart character in Hitchcock's *Vertigo*. My head began to spin.

As if that wasn't enough, there were strains of overt racism poisoning the common good. This was during the time that *Roots* was being televised. I came home to my dorm room one evening to find a newspaper cartoon of one of the *Roots* characters tacked to my door, with the words scribbled on it: "Nigger, go home." Some students also anonymously circulated a cassette tape about the black students that we got hold of. On the tape, a voice says in exaggerated southern cadence, "We're going cigar fishing today. No we're not, we're going 'nigar' fishing. What's the bait? Hominy grits!" On another occasion, a white student expressed the wish to place a bottle of sickle-cell anemia in the school's quadrangle to "kill off all the undesirables." So it was very tough for me. I got lost, did some crazy stuff—like helping to devise a system to dial out of the dorm on a phone without a face, allowing me and some friends to call our girlfriends and run up huge bills, which I had to get a second job to pay for while their parents ponied up—didn't do well in school, got expelled, and went back to Detroit a failure after being a golden boy. That was tough to handle. Then I finished night school, which I don't think they have any more, and got my diploma from Northwestern High School.

Almost immediately after I graduated, I met a woman, got her pregnant, married her, and then divorced her. It was a very trying period in my life. I was eighteen years old, she was twenty-six. She eventually had to give up her job as a waitress when she started to show—she had one of those jobs where the waitresses wore hot pants and tiny tops—and I was eventually fired from a job at Chrysler that my wife's uncle helped me to secure (an unjust firing, I might add, as I'll never forget my boss's words, "It had to be somebody's ass, and I'd rather it be yours than mine"). We were forced to live on welfare, since I lost my job a little more than a month before my son was to be born. We got food stamps and government medical assistance to pay the costs of delivering our baby. My wife was enrolled in WIC, or Women, Infants, and Children, and I stood many a day in those long lines and collected packets of powdered milk and artificial eggs—just as I did at the welfare office, where the civil servants were often rude and loud, making the experience that much more degrading.

Why did you marry her, Michael?

I married her because she was pregnant. I suppose those southern values were in effect—my parents were from Alabama and Georgia—and I was, after all, a church boy who believed that if you got a woman pregnant, you should marry her. I didn't want my son to be born out of wedlock. Of course, that was a narrow, naive view, but I suppose I had to learn the hard way. But I really did love Terrie, the woman I got pregnant. I just discovered too late that she didn't love me. She told me two months into our marriage that she didn't love me and should have never married me. I was devastated.

By that time, however, she was well into her pregnancy. So we made as good a go of it as possible for young people who were poor, stressed, often unemployed, on welfare, and unequally yoked in affection. We had our son, a wonderful, beautiful boy who is now nineteen years old. I spent quite a bit of time attending to him. I did much of the night duty. I loved my son and wanted to bond with him.

That's a startling contrast to many black fathers today.

I don't know. I think many more black men than are given credit want to love and nurture their children. It is true that I lived in a moral universe with an ethical framework that dictated that one should acknowledge one's responsibility, and in my case, the obligation to marry in the belief that marriage itself would protect and preserve the family. At this time in my life, I think such a belief can be downright wrong. Still, I suppose there's something to be said for wanting to assume responsibility for what one does. But that couldn't prevent our almost inevitable breakup, so after working in a factory, hustling, cutting grass, shoveling snow and painting houses, working as an emergency substitute janitor for the public school system, working as a maintenance man in a suburban hotel, doing construction jobs, getting laid off, getting fired, going on welfare, and seeing my marriage dissolve, I decided right before my twenty-first birthday that I'd had enough, and I wanted to go to college. I had in my late teens felt a call to ministry, and that call, in tandem with my desire to better provide for my son's future, sent me to school. Plus, my desire to fulfill my early promise, which had been greatly tarnished by the events of my life after being kicked out of Cranbrook, goaded me to take my destiny into my own hands.

To many onlookers, I suppose I looked like a loser, a typical, pathological, self-defeating young black male. That may help explain why I empathize with such youth in the hip-hop generation; I was one of those brothers that many social scientists and cultural critics easily dismiss and effortlessly, perhaps literally, write off. In any regard, there were two people in my church who had gone to Knoxville College, a historically black college in Knoxville, Tennessee. I called the college and asked the dean if they had space for a young black man from Detroit. When he replied in the affirmative, the next day I "grabbed me an arm full of Greyhound," as Sam Cooke once sang, and took the fifteen-hour bus trip from Detroit to Knoxville. I went to college there and initially worked in a factory, then pastored three different churches as I completed my undergraduate studies at Carson-Newman, a small, white southern Baptist school. I transferred from Knoxville College because I wanted to study philosophy, and they didn't offer but a few courses in the subject. Carson-Newman was a true baptism in Southern Baptist theology and worldviews, many of which were problematic and sometimes racist, even as members of the academic community encouraged students to nurture their spiritual faculties. But my time in east Tennessee was crucial to my intellectual development, and taught me to navigate some perilous racial and cultural waters.

During the time frame you became a Baptist minister, it seems like there again you were operating on a number of levels. You were obviously fascinated by theology and philosophy, but I detect something else stirred you to commit yourself to that course of study.

No question. I was influenced to enter the ministry by having a pastor who was broadly learned and extremely erudite, who reflected critically on social and spiritual issues and who had read widely and deeply in philosophy and theology. Later on, as a burgeoning scholar, I was also influenced by scholars such as religious historian James Melvin Washington, a renowned bibliophile whom I met in the early '80s in Knoxville, and the great Cornel West, Washington's colleague at New York's Union Theological Seminary, whom I met in early 1984 at Kalamazoo College in Michigan, during a lecture series West was giving at the college. I had driven there from Tennessee, when I was an undergraduate student at Carson-Newman, a junior I believe, and he was a professor of philosophy of religion on his way to teach at Yale Divinity School. Within African American religious studies and theology, I was also influenced by the work and example of scholars like James Cone, Charles Long, J. Deotis Roberts, William R. Jones, Cecil Cone, Jacqueline Grant, and Riggins Earl. These are figures whose commitment to black theology and, to a lesser degree, to black philosophy, had whetted my appetite to study philosophy and religion.

At Carson-Newman, I experienced a growing desire to wed the life of the mind to the life of the heart. As an undergraduate, I was getting quite an introduction to the ministry in pastoring three different churches, and addressing the issues of life and death: I was preaching to my congregation, counseling them, and marrying and burying them. It was exciting, and at times quite stressful, but I increasingly sought a stronger academic vocabulary to express my intellectual goals and interests. Hence my sharpened focus on philosophy, social theory, literary criticism, and what would later be termed critical race theory. But I have never been one to think that religion dulled one's cutting edge or critical capacities. Of course, if one is honest, there are some tremendous difficulties in maintaining one's commitment to a religious tradition that says, "We know by faith and not by sight," while maintaining habits of critical inquiry that rest on relentless interrogation of the warrants, grounds, bases, and assertions of truth put forth in all sorts of intellectual communities, including religious ones. So there are tensions and, in fact, these multiple tensions define my intellectual projects and existential identities: tensions between sacred and secular, tensions between the intellectual and the religious, tensions between radical politics and mainstream institutions, tensions between preaching and teaching, and so on. But I think they are useful, edifying tensions, tensions that help reshape my ongoing evolution as a thinker, writer, teacher, preacher, and activist.

In many ways, I see myself as a rhetorical acrobat, navigating through varied communities of intellectual interest and pivoting around multiple centers of linguistic engagement, since all of these commitments have their own languages, rhetorics, and vocabularies. I view myself as a work in progress, an improvised expression of identity that is constantly evolving through stages and vistas of self-understanding. Such language owes several debts and has many sources, including my religious tradition's plea to, as the James Cleveland song goes, "Please be patient with me, God is not through with me yet"; my musical roots in jazz, and now in hip-hop, where relentless improvisation and restless experimentation are artistic hallmarks; and postmodern philosophical ruminations on the fluidity of identity. Plus, openness to new experience is critical, but you can't be so open that you lose sight of the crucial references, the haunting paths, the transforming traces, and the grounding marks of your identity. But one has got to constantly evolve and regenerate, stretching the boundaries of identity in a way that permits you to integrate new strains, new molds, new themes, and new ideas into the evolving self-awareness that occupies your heart and mind.

When did you know, finally recognize that your star was rising? When did all this start to take shape for you, Michael?

Good question. Throughout my college years, I struggled financially. Early on, I had to live in my car for almost a month because I didn't have a place to live. My pastor would dig into his pocket to help me out. My father was able to give me a used station wagon after my raggedy old car died, but he had no money to give me. For the most part, I paid for my own education. I borrowed money and had loans that I only recently paid back because I was deep in debt as a result of supporting myself through college. I had to make it on my own, which wasn't new since I'd basically been living away from my parent's home after starting boarding school at sixteen. I knew I'd come a long way when I got to Knoxville and, after working in a factory, I was able to get some acclaim for my preaching and began to pastor. But in my third church, I was booted out for attempting to ordain three women as deacons in the male supremacist black Baptist church, so I went back to school. I had, ironically enough, been kicked out of Carson-Newman because I refused to attend chapel, a mandatory assignment every Tuesday morning. I was protesting the dearth of black scholars and preachers who were invited to campus, especially after it was explained to me by an administrator that, based on the small number of blacks, one speaker a year was all we could expect.

But after my church let me go—and isn't this more than a little ironic, since it was named Thankful Baptist Church?—with a month's severance pay, and with nowhere to land to support my family, since I had remarried and got temporary custody of my son, I headed back to Carson-Newman in 1983 to finish my studies. I received no scholarship money from the school, despite maintaining a straight-A average in philosophy, so I borrowed more money and graduated magna cum laude, and as outstanding graduate in philosophy, in 1985. I applied and got into Vanderbilt University's Ph.D. department of philosophy, and into Brown and Princeton's departments of religion. I was interested in Vanderbilt because of Robert Williams, a respected philosopher of black experience, and because I wanted to study with Alisdair MacIntyre, a renowned philosopher whose book, *After Virtue,* had recently made a huge splash in moral philosophy. I remember meeting with him on my visit to Vanderbilt, and I remember him asking me why anyone who had gotten into Princeton wanted to come to Vanderbilt to study. I told him I was wrestling with whether to become a philosopher with an interest in religion, or a scholar of religion who took philosophy seriously. His eyes lit up, and he uttered, "That's precisely the question you must answer."

I decided on the latter course, and after visiting Brown and Princeton, I chose to attend Princeton. But there was a snag: Carson-Newman refused to release my final transcript to Princeton because I owed them money, a little more than $7,000, a sum that I knew wouldn't exist if they had given me the scholarship help I thought I deserved. I was quite nervous until a dean at Princeton's graduate school told me that I could come to Princeton without my final grades, since they had already accepted me on my documented performance. It was the closing of a widely gyrating circle of promise that had begun in the ghetto of Detroit where my teachers, my pastor, and some of my peers had foreseen, and in many cases, through their contributions, had assured my success. I realized at Princeton, as great a school as it is, that my being there was nothing less than what I should be doing in living out the early promise that they—my teachers, pastor, and peers—detected in me.

As a second-year graduate student at Princeton in 1987, I began to write professionally, if by that it is meant that one is compensated for one's work. I wrote for religious journals of opinion, for newspapers, for scholarly journals, and for mass-market magazines, much of this before completing my master's degree in 1991 and my Ph.D. in 1993. In fact, I wrote the lead review essay in the *New York Times Book Review,* which ran longer than five thousand words, when they had such a feature in the book review back in 1992. I had begun to write book reviews for the *New York Times* in 1990, along with reviews for the *Chicago Tribune* book review. I wrote the "Black America" column for the left-wing *Z Magazine* in the late '80s and early '90s, which I inherited from Cornel West, and during this time, I also wrote op-eds for *The Nation* and later for the *New York Times, Washington Post, Chicago Tribune, Los Angeles Times,* and other papers. I also wrote essays and chapters for several books. So I guess I took off pretty quickly after hitting graduate school, which, while not unique, I suppose was nonetheless rare enough. Interestingly enough, I ended up writing my first book, *Reflecting Black,* before I wrote my Ph.D. thesis. That fact encouraged me to complete my degree before my book was published in 1993. In fact, I received my Ph.D. from Princeton in June 1993, and my book was printed in late May 1993, and published later in June. I just made it!

But weren't there some highly unusual circumstances surrounding your dissertation, particularly the fashion in which you completed it? Rumor has it that your legend still lives at Princeton because of how you finished.

Well, I don't know if legend is quite the word; infamy may be more like it. The usual process of completing one's dissertation is the submission to one's doctoral committee of a prospectus, a document that details and outlines one's proposed thesis, which can run up to twenty, thirty, or sometimes forty pages. After one is subject to a long, maybe three-hour, oral examination by one's committee members, other professors, and one's peers, one is asked to step out of the room while the committee votes to accept or reject one's prospectus. If it is accepted, often with recommendations for changes, you are then permitted to go about the business of working on the dissertation, which might take anywhere from two to ten years to complete. You then submit the thesis to your committee (which responds with challenges and changes that are integrated into your work), sit for a final oral examination, and, hopefully, your dissertation is approved.

My committee included Cornel West, whose name I had submitted to a search committee to direct the Afro-American Studies program at Princeton before I left to run an antipoverty project and teach at Hartford Seminary in 1988; Jeffrey Stout, a well-respected religious ethicist, and the teacher with whom I spent the most time in the rigors of writing and rewriting papers, taking courses, and critically reading challenging books; and Albert Raboteau, the well-regarded religious historian and author of the classic work *Slave Religion*. Well, I submitted my prospectus in April 1993, and after a three-hour public oral examination, consisting of close questioning by my committee members and a few others in attendance, I was asked to leave the room. Upon being invited back in and taking my seat at the head of the examining table, I was informed that I had passed and that my prospectus had been approved.

Needless to say, I was quite happy, but for more than the usual reasons of having one's intellectual work approved by one's teachers. I had an even bigger investment than usual because of a big risk I had taken. As my teachers, and the others in attendance, verbally congratulated me from where they sat, I reached under the table and pulled out my completed dissertation, handed copies to my committee members, and said, "Here it is." It is true that that was an electrifying moment. There was a collective gasp that was articulated, an "ah" that reverberated through the room, with some of the folk, including members of my committee, clearly stunned. I realized that it was a big risk to do what I had done. After all, they could have rejected my prospectus or asked for huge changes that would have necessitated significant revision of my work. Fortunately, it was approved, and after I submitted my thesis, I responded to the criticisms, integrated them into the final version of my dissertation, sat for my final oral examination, and was awarded my doctoral degree. And it is true that after my prospectus performance, some of my colleagues cornered me and said, "Day-am," in the black vernacular, "that was unbelievable." And when I came back to defend my dissertation in my final oral examination, some of my peers said that I had become a legend in the department. I'm just glad that things turned out the way they did.

But your legend doesn't stop there. You also had a meteoric rise in academe for one so young. Didn't you get your Ph.D. in 1993, and in the very next year, you received tenure at Brown, also an Ivy League university, and became a full professor at the University of North Carolina? That's almost unheard of in conservative academic circles, where promotion through the ranks often takes years and years.

Yes, that's true. I had been pretty much teaching full time since 1989, when I left Hartford Seminary to become an instructor of ethics, philosophy, and cultural criticism at Chicago Theological Seminary. I taught at CTS for three years, two as an instructor, and when I completed my master's degree in 1991, I got promoted to an assistant professor. I left CTS in 1992 to become an assistant professor of American civilization and Afro-American Studies at Brown. In 1993, as you know, I received my Ph.D. from Princeton, and my first book, *Reflecting Black,* was published and received favorable critical attention from both the academy and the broader public, and I was offered several teaching positions, including offers from Northwestern and Chapel Hill. Because of those offers, Brown sped up my tenure decision by about six years, since one normally receives tenure in one's seventh year.

I was extremely gratified to be awarded tenure at Brown and, as it turns out, at Chapel Hill. (Northwestern offered me tenure too, but the president intervened and told me I could come to the university and essentially "try out" for two years; and if after that time I fulfilled my promise, then I would be awarded tenure. He based his decision, he said, on the fact that he had never known a scholar to be awarded tenure less than a year after he completed his Ph.D., with one exception—a scholar who would go on to win a Nobel Prize in economics. I shot back that, first, no one knew at the time the scholar was awarded tenure that he would receive the Nobel Prize, so the decision to grant him tenure was, by those terms at least, a risk, and second, since the president couldn't be sure that I wouldn't achieve equal prominence in my field, it made no sense to deny me tenure either. Needless to say, I rejected Northwestern's offer.) Chapel Hill made the extraordinary step of offering me tenure and a full professorship, in light of the fact that I had completed my next book, which would be published shortly, a study of Malcolm X.

Wait. If it normally takes seven years to get tenure in the first place, it must take at least another seven years, if not longer, to become a full professor, right?

Well, it certainly can. After seven years, a scholar who successfully obtains tenure is usually made an associate professor. When you write the next book or two, depending on where you teach, you can be granted full professorship. And that may take seven to ten years, or in some cases not quite as long, and in other cases, significantly longer. So yes, it's safe to say that I was fortunate enough to do in a year what can in other circumstances take as long as seventeen to more than twenty years to achieve. In a way, I have been driven by the sense that I have to make up for lost time, which, ironically enough, has put me ahead of the pace of some of my peers. Plus, I felt a sense of responsibility to my peers from my old neighborhood who will never be able to achieve at the levels I have enjoyed, not because they aren't talented, but because they lack opportunity. Or, on my block, most of them are either in prison or dead. I felt blessed by God, and I didn't want to blow it. Plus, a lot of the early writing and speaking I did—which, as it turns out, helped me to climb the academic ladder rapidly—was not only driven by a sense of vocation, but was done as well in the desperate attempt to raise funds for my brother Everett's defense against the charge, and later the conviction, of second-degree murder. Almost the month after I landed in Chicago to teach at CTS, Everett was accused of murdering a young black man in Detroit. I believe he is innocent, and I have expended quite a few resources in trying to prove his innocence, and to free him from prison. He's been there now for eight years. That has given me great incentive to work as hard as I can, and of course, I'm sure there's a good bit of survivor guilt involved as well.

Have you ever talked with John Edgar Wideman? He crossed my mind; as you know, he's had a similar circumstance with his brother.

We've talked, but not about our brothers. Yes, he too has had to deal with that strange and haunting reality that often morphs into a tragic trope of black existence: one brother a prisoner, the other a professor. One of you free to move, the other one caged like an animal. The effect of that thought on one's psyche is like an enormous downward gravitational pull. But I'm grateful to God for the ability to be able to do what I do, because I know it's a tremendous gift and pleasure and leisure to be able to write and think. And I work hard, traveling around the country giving lectures, speeches, and sermons, writing books, articles, and essays, just trying, as the hip-hoppers say, "to represent." So I spend long hours at what I do, but I'm not complaining. I'm a well-paid, highly visible black public intellectual who is grateful for what God has done for him and who wants to pass it on to somebody else. I don't want to keep it for myself. I want to make sure that other people get a chance to express their talents and their visions. I have no desire to be the HNIC, or the "head nigger in charge."

Do you get a sense of that . . . when you are in your flow . . . do you know the impact you're having on a room?

That's a good question. Let's not have any false modesty: I'm a public speaker and I've been trained from a very young age in the art of verbal articulation. I've been seasoned to engage at the highest level of oral expression. So, I'm experienced enough to know when I'm hitting my target and when I'm missing it. There are times when I can feel the electricity of getting things right, because I've known when I failed [laughs]. I know what that feels like. And even when other people think I've done well, I often feel a great need for improvement. There have been very few times when I feel like I absolutely nailed it. There are some moments when I know I'm "representin'" because I know I'm a vehicle. I'm a vessel. My religion teaches me that the gift is not in the vehicle, but in the giver of the gift. I honestly hope to be an instrument of the Lord. I hope that I'm an instrument of God. And I hope, therefore, that I work hard to stimulate the gift God gave me. I'm constantly striving to get better, to get clearer, sharper, and more eloquent. I think one of the ways that occurs is through testing ourselves in situations where people are unpersuaded by our beliefs and we have to make a case for them with as much passion and precision as possible. Crossing swords rhetorically is a great joy to me, and often a great learning experience.

At the same time, I'm attempting to excel at the height of my profession and at the top of my game, like Michael Jordan. I have no bones about that. I want to represent on that level where people go, "DAMN, did you hear what that brother said?" 'Cause I want young people to say it ain't just got to be about sport, it doesn't just have to be about some athletic achievement—as great as that may be—or about Oprah or Bill Cosby, as great and ingenious as they are at what they do. I want young people to say the same thing about intellectual engagement. I want them to have a desire to deploy a variety of jargons, grammars, rhetorics, languages, and vocabularies to articulate views in defense of African American or marginalized identities, as I attempt to do. I want young people to say, as the folk in the '60s and '70s used to say, "Got to be mo' careful," in admiration of such linguistic and intellectual skill. Not for show, but for war, against ignorance, misery, and oppression. I want young folk to say, "I wish I could do that, I wish I could be like Mike!" I have no qualms in hoping for that, because I want to seduce young people into excellence, since they've often been sabotaged by mediocrity. I have no reservations in seeking to inspire young people to do what I do, only better. So I constantly strive to deepen my vision, broaden my intellectual reach, and expand my repertoire of verbal skills. And at times, you feel the pleasures of the palpable responses you evoke in those who hear or read you.

On the other hand, you're always surprised by people who claim you have influenced them, because you can never accurately or adequately measure such a thing. We are prevented by circumstance and environment and context from knowing the true nature of our own influence, which is why we should really remain structurally humble. Not falsely modest, but structurally humble. For me that means if I am wielding influence, it is because I have tried to be faithful to the gifts God has given to me. Structural humility means that as a matter of principle, we remain cognizant of the need to check our arrogance and bridle our vanity. This recognition must be the very foundation, the very structure, of our public activity, to keep us from taking credit for what only God can give. To be sure, we never know the full extent of our influence, which is why we should also attempt to be vigilant in exercising our gifts. As the rapper Guru says, we never know when someone is watching or listening. I've had people around the country, folk who read my books, articles, and essays, or hear my sermons, lectures, or commentary on radio or television, tell me that something I've said or done has changed their lives. That's a huge responsibility, and we've got to accept it as part of our duties as public intellectuals. And such responsibility doesn't stop at our national borders. I just got a letter from Japan, and some intellectuals want me to come there because they think I'm doing important cultural criticism. And I've just fielded an invitation from London to speak on religion, and from Italy to speak on politics, and from Cuba to talk about African American culture and politics.

In light of all of this, structural humility is surely in order. The best we can do is to represent the truth as honestly and clearly as we understand it, with all the skills at our disposal. Of course, nothing I'm saying means we can't feel good about our achievements, or about the influence we might wield. From my perspective, if we truly believe that our vocations are manifestations of ultimate purpose, we'll want to do our level best to stay at the top of our games as an acknowledgment of the gifts God has given us.

One last thing that ties in is how you'll be able to do that. I can see very clearly your intellectual path. But how are you going to be able to keep your hand on the pulse of the street, because by necessity . . . it doesn't have anything to do with your commitment . . . but, like you said, Japan, Italy, universities, busy . . . How do you maintain that connection? I know that's vital to you.

It is vital. That's one reason I still spend so much of my time on Sunday mornings preaching, and going into communities as a public intellectual and political activist.

You ever just go walk through the neighborhoods?

Lord yes. When I go to neighborhoods all over this country, I'm trying to find the barbecue shack. I'm trying to find where the Negroes hang out. I hang with the bloods. I want the local color, the local flavor, what Geertz calls local knowledge, because black folks are so diverse and profoundly complex, even if we have similarities that bind us together. Black folks fascinate me. I want to continue to learn about us: the different vernaculars we have in different regions; the different ideological and political subcultures we generate; the varied contexts that shape our cultural identities; the varied sexualities we express, especially beneath the radar of racial correctness or mainstream propriety; and the inflections of the black diaspora in our food, fashion, and faith. So, I'm constantly trying to learn more wherever I go. Of course, one of the critiques of intellectuals I often hear is that we're out of touch with "the folk." Well, when I preach, I'm reaching "the folk." Those critics who say that intellectuals per se—not particular intellectuals, mind you, but intellectuals as a category—are out of touch, have often stereotyped "the folk." Further, they feel free to speak for, and identify with, "the folk," and they feel free to attack intellectuals in the name of "the folk." But I've often discovered that "the folk"—these very souls whom critics seek to protect through claims of our irrelevance—are hungry for intellectual engagement.

In the meantime, "the folk" are out-reading, out-thinking, and out-intellectualizing the very people who quite defensively and condescendingly argue in their name that they won't get what we're doing, won't understand what we're up to, or will be automatically suspicious of our aspirations. Now don't get me wrong; there is more than enough warrant for the skepticism, perhaps even the cynicism, which some folk harbor toward intellectuals who've earned the titles Irrelevant, Pedantic, Didactic, or Condescending. On the other hand, when intellectuals prove that they're serious about helping people think deeply and clearly about the problems they confront, their advice, insight, and analysis is more than welcomed by "the folk." I think we have to stop essentializing the folk, as if it's some mythic community. Well, I'm the folk. They're the folk. So my preservation of connection is through the immediate context of preaching, teaching, and activist politics, as well as hanging out in the 'hood and going to the barber shop and the barbecue joint and hanging with "the niggas." And not for ethnographic titillation or anthropological voyeurism, but as a legitimate participant in vibrant black folk culture, the kind from which I sprang and in which I feel most comfortable.

I can't tell you how many black folk I've met who've said, "Brother, we read your book, keep on writing," or, "We saw you on TV, keep on speaking." And these are ordinary, average people, the so-called folk from whom ostensible grassroots gatekeepers attempt to divide us, almost by ontological fiat, as if we're a different species of people. These black folk say to me, "Man, you're speaking to white folk, you're speaking to black folk, you're keeping it real on a level we often don't see." That makes me feel good, when black folk say I'm speaking brilliantly, insightfully, intelligently. But that doesn't mean I can't disagree with what the majority of black folk think, that I'm somehow locked into a rigid perspective because I am committed to their amelioration. I love black folk, which is why I ain't afraid of them. I'm not afraid to disagree with mass black opinion, to call into question beliefs, habits, dispositions, traditions, and practices that I think need to be criticized. I seek to speak truth to power in love, as the Bible suggests. I seek to address the high and low, those on the inside and those locked out. That's my obligation and lifelong objective.

Interview by Lana Williams
Durham, North Carolina, 1997

2

Textual Acts and Semiotic Gestures

Race, Writing, and Technotopia

Recently, conversations regarding what role universities play in larger communities have become prolific. Some scholars have argued that the walls dividing academics from the "real world" are false and that the university is as much the real world as any other site. Others have adamantly sought ways to maintain and strengthen the protective walls of the ivory tower, insisting that what gets done in the academy is somehow more virtuous because it is cerebral. Michael Eric Dyson, known as the "hip-hop public intellectual," has emerged as a vocal radical who seeks to bring the intellectual work of the academy to mass culture in ways that not only encourage political action but also maintain academic integrity. For Dyson, doing this involves getting one's hands dirty and taking one's work to sites outside the academy. He says, "A geography of destiny is shaped by parochial views of the appropriate intellectual terrain one occupies, and that usually means valorizing the university as the exclusive site of legitimate academic work. We in the academy, especially on the left, love to talk about transgression, speaking of it in intellectual and symbolic terms, but we don't want to engage in such transgression literally or epistemologically."

Dyson is by trade a preacher and teacher. His books and articles appear in scholarly forums, religious forums, and the popular press; they address issues that range from critiques of rap music to critical readings of Malcolm X to cultural theory to the examination of religious values. His voice is heard by many in the academy and many more outside its walls. It is to this end that Dyson works. He is clear: "I want to speak to the academy in very powerful and interesting ways, but I don't want to be limited to the academy." For Dyson, what goes on outside of the academy is of tremendous consequence, and in the conversation that follows, he's adamant about our need to talk about how race and discussions of race affect people on both sides of the academic wall.

What many will find interesting about Dyson's relational view of the university and the outside world is that he sees great importance in the kinds of theoretical work that get done in the university. For Dyson, theory becomes the avenue by which important questions get asked; yet, he contends that those questions do not need to be asked in ways that deny nonacademics access to the answers. At the forefront of Dyson's agenda is a push for academic and mass-cultural discussions to better inform each other. This gets done, he argues, through public intellectualism. For Dyson, the job of the public intellectual—the black public intellectual, in particular—is to be a "paid pest" whose function is to disrupt and intervene in conversations in ways that are disturbing and that force people to ask "why they frame the questions in the way that they do or why they make the analysis they do."

For Dyson, disrupting notions of race and multiculturalism helps us understand how issues of race, gender, class, and culture get constructed. He is critical of the "market multiculturalism" that inhabits American universities, contending that the rough edges and discomforting moments of race and multiculturalism are smoothed over in the versions universities promote; they lack the raw vitality and danger that should be associated with issues of conflict. However, he makes plain that the ways in which multiculturalism and issues of race are safely broached in classrooms are critically important. Dyson is clear that he would rather see conflicts of race break out in safe contestations in classrooms than not be discussed at all, and that he would rather see classroom approaches to race and multiculturalism than many of the violent ways in which race gets "debated" in the street. When he talks of the conflict of race and culture, his metaphors reflect this violence and his wish for race to break out in classrooms so that it "wounds our most cherished expectations" of the safety of classroom multiculturalism.

What compositionists will notice immediately about Dyson is his acute awareness of how language comes to the fore in matters of race. He is self-conscious of the language he uses and the ways in which he addresses different audiences. But he is also cognizant of how theoretical approaches to understanding discourse and writing affect the epistemological ways in which race, gender, class, and ideology get constructed. Dyson identifies this intellectual engagement with language as having powerful implications in redefining the relationship between the work that gets done in the academy and the lives of people outside of its borders. Dyson seeks to make the intellectual projects of the academy available to the masses in accessible ways in order to enact change and to reenvision how the world views race, class, gender, and the other constructs that shape our thinking about difference.

In Reflecting Black *you write: "The desire for literacy has characterized the culture of African Americans since their arrival here under the myriad brutalities of slavery. Although reading and writing were legally prohibited, black folk developed a resourceful oral tradition that had cultural precedence in African societies . . . black folk generated an oral tradition that expressed and reinforced their cultural values, social norms, and religious beliefs. . . . Even with the subsequent development of literate intellectual traditions, a resonant orality continues to shape and influence cultural expression" (31). You are a prolific writer; your work appears in scholarly forums, major newspapers, popular magazines, religious forums, and so on. How important has writing become in the tradition of black storytelling, in shaping and influencing black cultural expression? How do you think of writing in the larger scopes of black narrative?*

I think that writing has become extraordinarily important in terms of black storytelling, and in shaping and influencing black cultural expression, especially because of the centrality of narrative. The narrativity of black experience—the way that stories shape self-understanding and enable self-revelation—is powerfully glimpsed in creative forms, particularly autobiographical narratives, which constitute the attempt of the race to state, and then move forward to, its goal of survival through the individual literacy of representative figures. That goal is enhanced and revealed in stories of "overcoming odds," of rising "up from slavery," and of coming "out of the ghetto." Narrativity is an extraordinarily important component of self-understanding. It plays a crucial role in how African Americans form their identities, especially in the postmodern moment.

I think that writing per se—the capacity of people to reflect critically upon their experiences and then filter those experiences through the lens of a composed text—certainly shapes self-expression in a way different from, say, oral expression. In other words, as Ali Mazrui, the Africanist scholar, says, there is, strictly speaking, something deeply conservative about the oral form because it only preserves what people remember, and more important, what they've chosen to weave into the fabric of their collective memory. The oral form is crucial to the cultural and racial identity of the tribe, the group, and the polis, and preserves the political and ethnic imagination that grounds communal existence. On the other hand, the written form contests certain limitations of the oral form because it situates the writer and the reader at a critical discursive juncture that encourages the articulation of conflicting memories. It makes a big difference to have a body of writing to appeal to, and against which to contrast our self-understanding, our self-revelation, and our self-invention. It makes a huge difference to think about our ideas in relation to written words that anger us, that inspire us, that cajole us to agree or argue with what's being communicated, whether it's the writings of Ellison, or the writings of Foucault, or the writings of Baldwin, or the writings of Hurston. With writing, there's a different—and I want to stress different, not superior—moment of textual possibility than with orality, because the written narrative opens up space within its seams for the alternate reading, the alternative interpretation, a subject to which I'll return later.

As a result, you've got essays, articles, poems, short stories, and so on that constitute a rhetoric of resistance: they forge a discursive stream that flows against established truths. You can get multiple, contested readings of the same events, histories, and beliefs. But let's not kid ourselves; whether we're talking about orality or writing, those in power have used either, or both, to repress black speech, to cloak black voices, to squelch black dissent, or to enforce a stultifying ideological consensus. So I'm not romanticizing writing. Neither am I saying that you can't get any variation of perspective in oral traditions. It's just that the functions of oral traditions in black culture are inherently more conservative because of the material conditions that give rise to them. For instance, a big problem that black slaves confronted was how do you survive having your own literacy—and the forms of intellectual life that it nurtured—attacked, even outlawed, for God's sake, by the state? The oral tradition became a powerful way for black folk to preserve dangerous memories of their beauty and intelligence in a hostile white world that thought of them as beasts and morons. It's a hell of a hard thing to have textual variation, or to encourage different traditions of interpretation, when white supremacy is winnowing your thoughts and banishing your body from the precincts of cultural appreciation.

So I'm by no means suggesting a vicious hierarchy of the written word over its verbal complement. There is a historically and politically problematic, even racist, cast to many debates about orality and literacy that seek to privilege Eurocentric biases about the superiority of the written word—and its various modalities, technes, and textualities—against the "inferior" spoken word and its myriad oral articulations. I have no truck with these theories, especially since so much of my life is literally lived in the oral moment, entrenched in narrative foxholes doing ideological battle with intellectual and cultural hegemonies, deploying rhetorical weapons shaped in the black church, radical politics, and in the crucible of ghetto-centric cosmologies. Rather, what I mean to do is to rescue, ratify, and reinscribe a largely hidden tradition—that is, to those outside the arc of black letters—of what might be termed indigenous *Afrecriture*, a black history of writing ourselves into existence. If it is racist to subordinate orality to literacy in the embrace of European hegemony, and in the dismissal of the ingenuity of black diasporic oral traditions, it is equally opprobrious to slight the will to literacy that has motivated black folk to leave written records of our existence. In fact, the mechanisms of literacy, of *Afrecriture*, have been strategically deployed by griots, intellectuals, and artists to expand the influence of black oral traditions through written stories, tales, and folklore, and through the body of criticism that follows in its wake. The collective articulation of black identity through written narratives is of huge consequence in the black interventions on—and if the truth be told, of the black inventions of—modernity. I simply want to specify the intellectual and, unavoidably, the political utility of orality and literacy and to inventory, in the Gramscian sense, the various registers and effects of each pole of expression in black culture.

In regard to the creation of the self through narrative, it is much different when you have an oral community where people are relying upon the circuits of memory to mediate their self-understanding. Orality carries ontological weight, impressed as it is through the sensuous, esthetic, tactile dimensions of communication, through tongue and mouth, as its bearers speak meaning and identity into existence. Writing is differently ordered, perceived, and nuanced. To be sure, orality is embodied, but in a different way than is the case for literacy. Still, writing possesses, in Donna Haraway's term, material density. In my mind, writing finesses a certain crude physicality—the act of putting pen to paper, or in our day, of hammering words into a computer keyboard—into an epistemological weight, a material witness against amnesia because you can refer *to* the text. On the other hand, oral traditions certainly have a kind of genealogical effect: they index how a group passes history and culture over to the next group or down to the next generation. And of course, it's not a static process; folk transform what they inherit. In that sense, I suspect that what's going on in such oral traditions is not entirely divorced from what Nietzsche and Foucault meant by genealogy, either: that we try to account for how and when ideas, beliefs, and practices emerge and flourish. What these oral traditions help us to see is that all cultural practices rely, to a degree, on the force of invented memory, that is, memory that is shaped by the intellectual parameters, social circumstances, historical energies, and existential needs of a particular group or society.

So I think that writing is very important in terms of the negotiation by African peoples of modernist and postmodernist cultural forms. Writing is enormously important to try to figure out what the past is about, and what the present is about in relationship to the past. It is also important to understand how writing becomes a bridge of communication and connection between previous cultures and contemporary ones—*and* a way of reinventing the very character of experience by means of critical reflection and articulation. Writing, of course, is as much about revelation as it is about invention. I'm not suggesting an appeal to authority here, where revelation signifies a Leibnizian view of reality *sub species aeternatatis*, opposed to what we might term a Wes Montgomery epistemology, since, as the famed jazz guitarist played, we're "down here on the ground," suggesting a grassroots deconstruction of an ahistorical metaphysics. I'm speaking of the sense of revelation that comes when one agrees with Dr. Johnson that one doesn't know what one is thinking until one begins to write. When one is writing, one is literally *writing into* and *writing from*, which I'll return to later. These poles of writing into and writing from—inscribing and reinscribing—situate the writer in an interpretive and performative moment where the writer becomes the mediator between these two poles of creation. Writing becomes a crucial avenue of both revealing and inventing the future of the race, especially for African American people who are preoccupied with literacy and the articulation of a self through narrative.

In many ways, the debate over writing and other narrative forms taps into an ancient debate about black intelligence. The debate over black writing also sheds light on the constitution of different forms of self-understanding that are critical if we're to move beyond the *mere* fixation on the oral—or for that matter, the *mere* fixation on the cinematic—to talk about the legitimate concern of literate expression. Black people have been torn in at least two directions here. On the one hand, some have defensively said about literacy, in light of how it has been deployed against black intelligence, "That's about white folk and what they do; that's about mainstream society and culture. Black folks' abilities to articulate self-identity, and revelation and culture, are about orality, so writing is not a central part of our project." On the other hand, some have reflexively said, in a damaging capitulation to European standards of culture, achievement, and intelligence, "Only when we begin to write with a certain level of mastery—with the patriarchal codes implicit in such a statement left in place—will we be able to exemplify our specific forms of intelligence. Then we will be able, in a large sense, to enter the modern world and prove that we are worthy of participation in American democracy and worthy bearers of culture."

I think there's a way to avoid the extremes of both views. We can embrace the genius of our oral traditions without downplaying *Afrecriture*. We can celebrate black orality and literacy without feeling that the mastery of the latter eradicates the necessity for the former. It is not an either/or proposition. We need not feel that black culture should engage in uncritical mimesis of hegemonic conceptions of literacy that degrade the already significant, even Herculean, achievements of black folk. After all, the unpaid labor of black slaves provided the elite of Western culture the leisure to write and think, and to remonstrate against the ignorant and lazy black, which included demeaning our orally based culture. What's important to me is not to discard writing as a central project of African and African American peoples. There have been all kinds of writings embedded in black culture from the get-go. One of the things we have to see is that it's a deeply racist moment to suggest that writing (as opposed to orality) is about a tradition external to African American culture. I see myself as a speaker *and* writer: an articulator of speech and an articulator of ideas, believing that such ideas are not only mediated through speech but are constituted through the very act of writing, through the epistemological weight of writing, through the intellectual and ontological self-revelation that are expressed in writing.

We have to figure out a way to highlight the link between writing and the articulation of black culture, which is where, for me, questions of authenticity are introduced. And right away, one comes up against the bulwark of racist assumptions about black being and intelligence: "It's not authentic for blacks to speak articulately. It's not authentic for them to engage in intellectual performances." As a result, there is a *reductio ad absurdum* argument made that rests on white supremacist beliefs which, ironically enough, attempt to name the narrowly conceived strengths of black culture: it's about the articulation of the self through the body. Therefore, the black savage is naturalized as the ideal projection of white beliefs about contact with primal passions in the state of nature. As a result, some critics ignore how the racial contexts of the evolution of black cultural forms exerted a profound material effect on what gained priority in black life. So many of the narrative forms that prevailed in black life, especially oral and musical cultures, have precedence in African American culture because, as Hortense Spillers points out, these are forms that were demanded during slavery. Slave masters didn't say, "Come and perform a trope for us; come and perform an allegory." They said, "Come and perform a song for us, and come engage in physical activity." We have to refocus attention on narrative forms that became a way for black people to extend and investigate a tradition of black cultural expression and survival. I'm not suggesting that black cultural forms developed exclusively or primarily in response to white supremacy. What I am saying is that the disproportionate emphasis on certain cultural forms, and the neglect of others, owes a great deal to the priorities and prejudices of white hegemonic culture. The best black cultural and literary scholars have begun to force us to rethink these issues in light of notions of multiple literacies, inviting us to see how these literacies are connected to varied forms of cultural expression within black society.

The same forces are at work in writing, too, even if they manifest themselves in different ways. In fact, writing is a symptom of the restless quest for literacy that began with orality, an orality that continues to surface in black writing and other narrative practices. In one sense, we've come full circle, not only in black culture but in Western culture in general, because writing has supposedly given way—in this cinematic, so-called postliterate culture—to the dominance of the visual and the oral. The latter is best seen, of course, in hip-hop culture, although rap has increasingly experimented as well with visual innovation and technique. But what's interesting in hip-hop is the lyrical ingenuity and inventiveness that shape oral expression. The different styles in rap music are not simply determined by forms of linguistic expression and aesthetic articulation; they're shaped as well by the lyrical flow of its greatest artists. We see this in figures like Rakim from earlier hip-hop. We glimpse it more recently in an artist like Nas, who raps about living in the shadow of cliché, randomness, and absurdity, and while there, trying to turn up the light of pleasure to negate their force, as his mate AZ raps on Nas's debut album, *Illmatic*: "Life's a bitch, and then you die, That's why we puff lie, Cause ya never know/when ya gonna go." Or when Nas shrewdly reconfigures Shakespeare as he justifies the frenetic pace of black youth culture in its attempt to evade death's irresistible pursuit: "I never sleep, Cause sleep's the cousin of death." You also see it in Lauryn Hill, a rapper from the Fugees group, who gives a brilliantly pithy lesson in how to adapt political sophistication to rhetorical strategy in exposing hardcore rap's thuggish pretensions, as she raps: "So even after all my logic and my theory, I add a 'mother fucker' so you ignorant niggers hear me."

For me, hip-hop is not simply the oral articulation of a specific moment of black cultural expression among young people. It's also a profound lesson in how verbal creativity is joined to, perhaps even revealed in, the lyrical imagination that *under*writes rap music. I think that lyrical imagination is a powerful form of the narrativity that is crucial to the construction of black identities in postmodernity. Writing, as art and artifact—and as the process of critical assertion that French intellectuals call *ecriture*, and you see my debt to this concept in my term, *Afrecriture*—becomes a bridge of articulation among and between cultures. It's also a way, of course, of reinventing the very shape and texture of life experience in the crucible of textuality, that is, in the unavoidably semiotic character of what Socrates thought of as the examined life. As I said earlier, I think that writing is both *writing into* and *writing from*. Of course, there's a *jouissance,* an edifying playfulness, that we can experience in coming up with all sorts of prepositions to signify different intensities, and intentions, of writing: writing onto, writing under, writing within, and so forth. *Writing into* captures the utter utility of writing, how there's a world to be written into existence, as well as a material surface on which we inscribe our meanings, aims, interpretations, and ultimately our lives. *Writing from* is done in the opposite direction: it assumes—partly because it has helped to create it—a world of meaning and signification that is the springboard for textual acts and semiotic gestures. Writing—the process of scribing, or even scribbling—involves all sorts of *in*scriptions, *de*scriptions, *sub*scriptions, and *tran*scriptions. In this vein, writing is ultimately about rewriting. It's about the making and unmaking, the coding and decoding, the mythologizing and demythologizing of signs, symbols, and meanings through which we narrate our existence. As a result, the writer is situated in the performative moment of narrativity, functioning as an acrobat of interpretation who mediates between the various poles of invention. I think that especially for African American people, who are obsessed with literacy, who are consumed with the articulation of a self through narrative forms, writing becomes a most important avenue of both revealing and inventing the identity of the race.

In terms of writing within the larger scopes of black narratives, I think that hip-hop culture and black cinema are two black narrative styles that fuse, to a degree, traditional forms of orality and new forms of literacy. I see the written word as only one form of literacy; I think we have to talk about multiple literacies. The form of literacy we're dealing with—cinematic, visual, literary, musical, and so on—will determine how we judge its effectiveness. But we've got to remember that in black communities created in a white supremacist world, those who claim literacy carry a double burden: they have had to justify the particular form of literacy they value to the white world, and they have had to justify themselves as worthy bearers of literacy. In both cases, what's being asked of black folk is proof of their intelligence, which, paradoxically, rarely if ever satisfies those who disbelieve that black folk possess intelligence to begin with. That's why, of course, even when poet Phillis Wheatley "mastered" Greek—which was supposed to have been the critical proof that a black person was truly intelligent—and wrote poetry that showcased her sophisticated use of technical literary devices, her critics, including Thomas Jefferson, only grudgingly acknowledged her competence. I'll come back to this issue of the link between literacy and proof of intelligence shortly.

In speaking about multiple literacies, it's crucial to emphasize that reading and writing—traditional literacy—still supplies the grounding metaphor for how such extraliterary enterprises are assessed. For instance, few would deny that John Singleton's critically acclaimed movie *Boyz N The Hood* worked so magnificently *as a film* because of its literate treatment of the complex issues that thwart or enable a healthy black masculine identity. The film's literacy was judged in large part on how well it was written—on the quality of its script—and on how well it narrated its themes through a variety of vocabularies—visual, cinematic, characterological, and the like. Whatever media are employed to express literacy refer back, either literally or symbolically, to writing.

What's fascinating about writing, too, is how it relates to the varied uses of speech, of articulateness, in black communities, proving how modes of oral and written communication are sutured in black culture. In many ways, orality and literacy, in Walter J. Ong's memorable phrase, are flip sides of the same coin of rhetorical articulation that is at the heart of fierce debates in American life over the value and status of black identity and intelligence. It all boils down to whether or not black folk are able to read, write, or speak in ways that prove their facility with language and, hence, prove their identity as true Americans and their status as intelligent beings. That's why there's still a great deal of white cultural energy focused on the fact that a figure like Colin Powell is so *articulate,* an observation that captures at once surprise and relief.

So often, however, such beliefs about black folk—about how intelligence and identity are marked by literacy and speech—are rarely engaged in an explicit manner that reveals their ideological stakes and political predicates. In this light, it makes sense to think of black writing—and indeed black narratives and literacies in general—in two ways. First, they assault the dominant culture's ideological inarticulation—the suppressed features and unspoken dimensions of its hegemony over black culture. Second, they are fashioned to resist the overarticulation of negative readings and distorted images of black life in the dominant culture's political economy of representation.

When thinking about the roles of black writing, narrative, and literacy, I have in the back of my mind T.S. Eliot's notion of speech as a "raid on the inarticulate," although my meaning of it is quite different from Eliot's. Eliot's statement is backed by a modernist conception of speech as a relatively stable content with a fixed referent that is thrust into the homogeneous space of inarticulation. In my thinking, speech is a much more fluid, changeable feature of linguisticality. And the inarticulate is both noun and verb, both a way to name silenced speech and the processes by which that silence is managed. If Robert Farris Thompson, Peter Linebaugh, and Paul Gilroy are right about the black Atlantic—that black cultural meanings are, at the very least, triangulated in the intersection of disaporic cultures in the Caribbean, the United Kingdom, and the United States—then black rhetorical practices are likewise polyvocal and multiarticulative: they register the accents of a variety of simultaneous, mutually reinforcing cultural voicings in a transnational zone of exchange, appropriation, and emulation.

What this emphasizes is the radical mobility of black writing, narrative, and literacy. The meanings, and mediators, of black rhetoric move back and forth along—and certainly across—an ever enlarging circumference of racial experience and racial identity. This entire black rhetorical network—including books, articles, films, speeches, plays, and so on—is often mobilized against the ideology of white supremacy. White supremacy is shorthand for the institutional and cultural practices of white racial dominance that are intellectually justified by its exponents as normal and natural. In such a cultural milieu, black rhetorical acts are unavoidable gestures of political contestation.

This social circumstance has given black writing, narrative, and literacy a surplus utility: supplying empirical verification of black humanity while enabling the struggle for black identity and liberation. That's why literacy is such a powerful subject in black communities; the surplus utility of black literacy also explains why many black folk are hypersensitive about getting, and being perceived as possessing, the "right" sorts of literacy. Beyond black literacy's surplus utility, it provides for its bearers a more fundamental function that accords with more traditional uses of literacy: the ability to secure gainful employment and to become a useful citizen of one's nation.

The issues attached to black writing—including identity, liberation, citizenship, intelligence, humanity—are even more important as we move into the world of hypertextuality and cyberspace. Cyberliteracy compounds the complexity of writing in black communities. We're not simply talking of forms of articulation that are mediated through literary or oral narratives. We're speaking about a revolutionary reconceptualization of the act of writing where, for instance, the consolidation or collaboration of narratives through communal interaction alter the possibility of defining authorship vis-à-vis a written text. In cyberwriting, there's a different character to the ontological risk of self-revelation than the sort implied in traditional writing. And of course the issue of agency is considerably more muddied. For instance, how do we account for individual, or personal, responsibility of the text in cyberspace? But there is still, so far, despite poststructuralist ruminations about the "death of the author," a mediating agent—the writer, who not only stands in for a larger narrative community but also intervenes with his or her own viewpoints about what constitutes, for present purposes, authentic black identity. It's ironic, in a century marked by radical technological innovation, that there already seems to be a backlash against cyberwriting and a nostalgic move to recover writing as we've known it for a few centuries now. Such factors will most certainly have a profound effect on black communities as we continue our struggle with the relation of literacy to identity, and with how technology is a burden or blessing to our progress.

You've begun to discuss technology, and recently in contemporary composition scholarship there has been a lot of conversation regarding how technology affects writers. But there hasn't been much written about how technology specifically affects African American writers. There are some who see cyberwriting and publishing as closer to oral communication than traditional writing and publication. Do you see this as a potential advantage for blacks and others? That is, how do you see the role of technology and writing being affected by or affecting matters of language and race?

I think that new technologies can certainly enhance black cultural expression. In this area, we're immediately confronted with the argument that black people are scared off by science and technology. But a more accurate reading of how black folk relate to technology must factor in the perception among some blacks that new technologies are controlled by white technical elites who are indifferent to technology's often negative effects in black communities. For instance, many blacks believe that white technical elites have no interest in making sure that the superinformation highway has an off-ramp into the inner city. There is also a concern that white technical elites evoke notions of technical proficiency, indeed technical literacy, to stigmatize black people because of their alleged exclusion from the regime of scientific intelligence that technology represents.

Still, technology can be extremely useful to black communities. New technologies can increase the "global" experience of blacks—although global is a contested term that deserves scare quotes because one meaning of globalization operates through reproducing narratives of totalization and mastery that control and channel information in destructive ways. But if what is meant by global is access to an international network of artists, cultural workers, activists, professionals, government officials, dissidents, entrepreneurs, and everyday people whose intellectual labor is magnified in the virtual domains of cyberspace, then there's tremendous good in new technology, beyond the cell phones, pagers, video games, and other forms of urban technology that blacks popularize, stylize, and disproportionately consume. Such a view encourages us to link technology to concerns about the global village that reinforce the internationalism of great political figures and thinkers in our culture, including W.E.B. Du Bois, Ida B. Wells-Barnett, Paul Robeson, Ella Baker, Martin Luther King Jr., and Malcolm X.

Any discussion of black culture and technology must also grapple with black cultural skepticism—some would argue paranoia—about technological development and scientific discourse, since the former has sometimes been deployed against black bodies and the latter has been used in arguments against black intelligence. The criminal trial of O.J. Simpson provided a powerful lens on how such skepticism functions in black communities. One of the reasons many black folk were willing to believe that Simpson was innocent (well, that's not quite true; they simply believed he wasn't guilty, and that's a legal, not a moral, distinction), despite expert testimony about sophisticated DNA testing that all but assured Simpson's imprisonment, was the history of abusive applications of medical technology to black bodies. The infamous Tuskegee experiment—where nearly three hundred black men were used as guinea pigs to test the biological and psychological effects of fully developed syphilis—provides a rhetorical framework and ideological shadow within which medical practices and scientific technologies are interpreted in many black communities. The hostility to certain technologies is historically and culturally inbred.

There is a Foucaultian dimension to these debates as well: many blacks perceive themselves as living in a state of biological surveillance, where medical procedures, new technologies, and artificially induced diseases are mobilized to contain, and to contaminate, the black body. One thinks here of the belief in some black quarters that AIDS was created in a scientific laboratory to kill off black populations. In this sense, the black body becomes a technological spectacle: it is the site of medical fetishization and experimentation through which the practices of white racial dominance are evoked and extended. We must devise strategies to uncouple the relationship between technological advance and racial repression. Once we find ways to interrupt unjust uses of scientific procedures, I think black folk will feel safer, and more empowered, to seize the communicative opportunities presented by new information technologies. One of the more democratic results of blacks "getting wired" is the heightened level of civic literacy and political participation it might encourage. There are few things more liberating than being equipped with information that empowers one to think critically and to act strategically in one's self-interest.

In a larger theoretical and philosophical sense, there is some merit to the argument that oral communication is closer to information technology than is traditional writing and publication. For instance, if one is on-line and responding to a question posed by a cyberlocutor through "instant messaging," for example, the interactive, spontaneous character of one's rhetorical exchange, its densely textured immediacy, is quite like an oral encounter. Traditional writing, on the other hand, depends upon deferred spontaneity; it is the effort to discipline the immediate thought into the protracted reflection. Traditional writing reconceives the object of its examination through a process of relentless revision, even though the Bakhtinian dialogical moment of cyberwriting is quite clear. When orality is conceived as the rhetorical medium through which spontaneous dialogic encounters occur, there's little doubt that it closely resembles a particular variety of cyberwriting. Certain modes of traditional writing, for instance, nonfiction forms, involve tracking ideas through their logical progression on to their resolution, or at least their conclusion. And you can constantly revise, playing with an idea before it appears in print. But the immediacy of imprint and trace in cyberwriting give it a different phenomenological value. It's not that one can't revise cyberwriting, but one does so with a potentially extended community of interlocutors, even if it is only the single person on the other end of one's communication. The immediacy of the potential response livens the spontaneity but limits the process of critical reflection. In traditional writing, one writes, rewrites, and revises before delivering a provisionally characteristic, or, paradoxically, a situationally definitive, statement of what one thinks. (After all, one can always revise an essay written for a journal or magazine for publication in a subsequent book.) In one sense, such a process of creation is being interrupted by new technologies where one commits oneself to a belief more immediately. One has a more quickly determined linguistic or textual loyalty than is the case with traditional writing. In this sense, cyberwriting is certainly closer to oral communication, where orality includes the spontaneous articulation of beliefs and not simply the recirculation of well-honed cultural and ethnic ideas.

But there's a different sense of orality to which I've briefly referred: the way that an oral tradition has already weeded out alternative visions of a particular story to become that oral tradition. I think it makes sense to distinguish between oral tradition and orality. The former suggests a more conservative view, as I've indicated, of what can survive transmission from one generation to another. New technologies explode that kind of oral tradition. New technologies entail a subversive sense of orality that can be seen in some instances as more egalitarian, more democratic. As with orality, cyberwriting creates a more immediate discursive community than the one created through traditional writing. For instance, if I make a statement on-line that I think that Michael Jackson's experimentation with a hyperbaric chamber was a desperately symbolic attempt to preserve what had already disappeared—his face as a signifier for his racial identity—there may be a hundred participants gathered in a chat room in cyberspace who will immediately augment, amend, agree with, or argue against what I've written. While traditional writing certainly draws from a discursive community composed of interlocutors and texts, the act of artistic creation or textual production is more strictly solitary than in cyberwriting. Perhaps the trope that best captures the highly individualized conception of traditional modes of rhetorical invention is the Lone Ranger: the writer as a solo narrative gun sling, her technical devices masked beneath literary style, her sentences riding a gleaming white horse of authorial intentionality, her writing voice as singular as a silver bullet. At its best, cyberwriting has the potential to challenge the illusory individualism and atomizing impulses of American identity by constituting narrative interactions across a global cyberscape that is deeply inflected with every species of difference one might imagine.

Finally, new information technologies can enhance the black struggle for democratic participation in national politics. When black folk get wired, it expands our capacity to access a global information base whose data may be employed to sharpen our arguments against social inequality and racial injustice. We can more easily tap into the research of local activist groups fighting against welfare reform or supporting the reproductive rights of poor mothers. The possibilities are literally limitless.

One of the most promising features of cyberspace technology—a feature surely not envisioned by Norbert Wiener and Warren McCullough when they laid the intellectual groundwork for communication science in the 1950s—is that it extends the capacity of blacks to exercise personal and political agency. Blacks can increasingly become subjects of techno-scientific culture and not merely its objects. For instance, with the resources we can glean from the Internet, we can actively intervene in debates about black intelligence, especially those most recently sparked by Herrnstein and Murray's infamous pseudotome *The Bell Curve*. On the other hand, to the degree that African American people are excluded from technology's advance, there will be the rearticulation of a vicious hierarchy that subordinates black people to whites, and others, in the technological order. Black folk are not afraid of science or technology. We are afraid of *technicians* and *scientists* who use their knowledge to harm our culture, distort our identities, and minimize our humanity and intelligence. Hence, participation in new information technologies might also bring to bear historic black reservations about the unfettered narcissism and ethical insularity that often attend techno-scientific discourse and practices. So I don't think there should be an unquestioning acceptance of science and technology among black folk. One of the real advantages we bring to the realm of technology and science is a cautionary tale rooted in our experience of oppression about the ethical ends, and limits, of scientific inquiry and technological advancement. Historically informed, technically sophisticated, socially conscientious blacks engaging science and technology might be able to caution us against the waves of uncritical celebration that often wash over exponents of new technologies.

You mentioned access, briefly. Could you speak to how class intersects matters of race when we talk about technology?

There's no question that the bulk of blacks who gain access to new information technologies are middle class, upper middle class, and upper class. There have been attempts to get some of this technology into the inner city, where many ghetto residents are just now using computers in ways that suburban children have been doing for nearly twenty years. Class intersects race powerfully in techno-scientific culture precisely because those African Americans who get wired already understand the nature of the game: the reproduction of national identity and class status through techno-scientific narratives that enable the manipulation, dissemination, and commodification of information, and, of course, the accumulation of capital.

The connection between capital and technology is obvious, especially when it involves cybercaptains of the information industry such as Bill Gates and Steve Jobs, a fact that should make us skeptical when we are told of the ostensibly democratic exchange of information among participants in what can only be termed a *technotopia*. The truth is that the use of new information technologies often reflects, facilitates, and reproduces the class stratification that existed prior to the forging of the cyberspace frontier.

One of the barriers to getting poor communities to use information technology is convincing its inhabitants of technology's relevance to their lives. Of course, some of the political uses that I've described are not usually evoked as selling points of such technology. Still, technical and ruling elites haven't aggressively marketed information technologies in economically immiserated communities. We must make greater efforts to explain the importance of this technology for poor and working folk—especially in light of how information technology has increasingly come to dominate the entrepreneurial and employment landscape. We must help educate poor and working people about the link between technical literacy and upward mobility, a link that has been mastered for years by technical and ruling elites.

It's fascinating that both Newt Gingrich and Al Gore—the far political right and the weak political center—view wiring communities as a medium to enhance democracy in our nation, including black communities. What Gingrich and Gore lack is a profound commitment to the sort of materialist analysis that their desire to bring technology to the ghetto most certainly entails. Although there is some agreement that the poor and the working class need to be wired, we don't have a great deal of emphasis on how they should be wired. Class antagonisms are refracted through the prism of race, gender, and ethnicity in disturbing, indeed destructive, ways. In light of this reality, class and race work against many African Americans and Latinos who really deserve to take fuller advantage of the *cybertopia* being touted by technical and political elites. What we've got to do is figure out how to color cyberspace black and brown, and how to deploy its considerable influence and reach, to help the working class and the poor.

Interview by Sidney Dobrin
Durham, North Carolina, 1997

3

Baptizing Theory, Representing Truth

Religious Discourse, Poststructuralist Theory, and Multiculturalism

You're very conscious of language. You seem to enjoy words; you play with them when you write. You refer to your "color commentary" on BET about the O.J. case; you pun with phrases like "Crossing over Jordan" in reference to Michael Jordan and "what a difference a Dre makes." You even use racial tension in the sounds of words when you play with alliterations like the "charm and chutzpa" of your son. You've also written that it is clear that "language is crucial to understanding, perhaps solving, though at other times even intensifying, the quandaries of identity that vex most blacks." You argue that "black culture lives and dies by language" (Between God and Gangsta Rap, *122–123). It's a big question to ask about the relationship between race and language—an inquiry that your work regularly explores in depth. But could you talk about how language affects your own coming to terms with race?*

That's a very intriguing question. There's a passage in the Hebrew Bible, what Christians call the Old Testament, in Psalm 51, that says: "Behold, I was shapen in iniquity; and in sin did my mother conceive me." I feel that I was born in language; I feel that I was nurtured in a rhetorical womb. My mother, who is a highly intelligent black woman, appreciates literacy. But she was prevented from pursuing higher education because she was a female and the youngest of a family of five children born to farmers in Alabama. But that didn't hinder her from bathing us in a stream of linguistic appreciation. My mother talked and read to her five children. And I went to church, which was, and remains, a very important narrative community for me because of the moral norms it advocated through stories about human identity and divine destiny, and also because those stories encouraged us to understand the relationship between politics and spirituality, a strong feature of many black churches.

My church was full of resplendent rhetorical resonances. I heard the prophetic articulations of black preachers and the linguistic and stylistic innovations of black singers. I was transfixed by the rhetorical skill of a revivalist who came to town trying to paint for us the picture of God-as-Jesus dying on a cross and helping us understand the cosmic consequences of Jesus' death. The preacher did not simply tell us about a theology of atonement or speak to us in dry, arcane, esoteric language about the dispensations of God; neither did he simply parrot theological beliefs about human creation in the *imago Dei*, or about the world being created *ex nihilo*. Instead, he wanted us to feel religious truth beyond cant, doctrine, or dogma; he wanted us to vibrate to our existential depths with the Word of God traumatizing and then rescuing us.

I learned in my church about at least four features of black religious discourse: its *ontological mediation*, its *performative epistemology*, its *hermeneutical ubiquity*, and its *dense materiality*. Ontological mediation stresses how black religious narratives help structure relations between beings: horizontal relations between human beings and vertical relations between human beings and God. Black religious discourse helps define, and mediate, the moral status of human existence. It also helps clarify the ethical ends human beings should adopt in forming human community, and the moral means they should employ in its defense. Black religious narratives define a relationship of human subordination to divine authority as the linchpin of personal redemption, while asserting moral transformation as the consequence of spiritual rebirth. Black religious narratives support the claim that human emancipation is rooted in observation of, and obedience to, divine imperatives of justice and equality.

The performative epistemology of black religious narratives underscores the intimate relation between religious knowledge and social practice, and secondarily the link between belief and behavior. In black sacred rhetoric, a crucial distinction is made between *knowing about* God and *knowing* God. The former represents a strictly intellectual exercise devoid of fideistic commitments; the latter is rooted in the faithful assertion of a cognitive and personal relationship with the supreme supernatural being. The consequence of such cognition is the *performance of faith*, the *dramatization of devotion*, and the *behaving of belief*. In black religious discourse, there is little substance or benefit to knowing God without *doing*, or performing, one's knowledge of God. Further, performative epistemology emphasizes that knowledge is not produced by having an accurate account of the relationship between truth and its representation, but by the relation of knowing to a grounding ideal of truth whose justification depends in part upon an appeal to human praxis. Finally, performative epistemology accents the engaged, humane, and political character of religious curiosity, linking the experience of knowing and loving God to knowing and loving human beings. Black religious discourse suggests that it is difficult, and indeed morally noxious, to know God and not do right in the world.

The hermeneutical ubiquity of black religious discourse highlights the fecund interpretive properties to be found in all forms of black sacred rhetoric, from homiletics to Sunday school pedagogy. I mean this in three ways. First, black sacred rhetoric gives religious believers vast opportunity and great variety in interpreting their religious experience. Black religious narratives secrete interpretation as a function of their justification of a sacred cosmology. Black sacred rhetoric encourages the interpretation of faith in the light of reasoned articulation of the grounds of belief. Second, hermeneutical ubiquity suggests how black religious narratives shape the interpretive activities of believers in secular intellectual and cultural environments. This encompasses two elements: the religious interpretation of ideas and events, including, for example, abortion, civil rights, the Million Man March, and feminism; and the interpretive strategies that believers adapt in the public square, including, for instance, the translation of religious passion into political language and the voicing of religious dissent to political policies and cultural practices in protest rallies.

Hermeneutical ubiquity also casts light on how black religious rhetoric seizes any event, crisis, idea, or movement as grist for its interpretive mill. Black sacred rhetoricians, especially black preachers, constantly view and interpret the world through the prism of moral narratives generated in black churches. Black religious narratives are relentlessly deployed by black sacred rhetoricians to carve an interpretive niche in political behaviors, social movements, cultural organizations, and institutional operations. Black sacred rhetoricians are interpretive cartographers as well: they map prophetic criticism onto social practice with an eye to reconstructing the geography of national identity.

Finally, black sacred rhetoric, especially black preaching, exhibits dense materiality, which refers to the rhythms, tones, lyricisms, and textures of black religious language. Many of my Sunday school teachers—including Mrs. Keene, Mrs. Bennett, and Mrs. Douglass—gave me and my fellow students a sense of the materiality of black language, instructing us in the arts of verbal articulation through performing plays, set pieces from larger works, and other oral works. Because the narrative generativity, semiotic strategies, and linguistic adaptability of black religious discourse has influenced black scholars, preachers, lawyers, doctors, scientists, and entertainers, black sacred rhetoric should be much more rigorously examined. I'll come back to the dense materiality of black sacred rhetoric in a moment, but first I want to speak about how crucial black linguistic practices have shaped my own intellectual development.

In my own life, language is very important because it created the possibility of my receiving reward and recognition for my verbal talents and oratorical gifts. I won my first blue ribbon in Mrs. James's fifth grade class for reciting Paul Laurence Dunbar's vernacular poem "Little Brown Baby." I can vividly recall the sense of reverie that I experienced in doing that well. Mrs. James had an extraordinary ability to make black history and black literary achievement come alive off the page. Mrs. James encouraged her students to imagine the direct connection between our fledgling attempts at self-expression and the great reservoir of rhetorical invention bequeathed to us by prior generations. Becoming excellent at oral recitations encouraged me to understand the work of those figures extraordinarily skilled in ancient black traditions of verbal expression—those who might now be unstylishly dubbed "the masters." Hence I eventually came to understand myself as part of a larger tradition of narrative self-recognition, which was the basis of collective racial enhancement. More immediately, my experiments in orality provided me a real tool for self-realization. I won several spelling bee contests in elementary school, and in junior high school—under the influence of my teacher Otis Burdette—I won several prizes and trophies for my oratorical abilities. The cumulative effect of my experiments in orality and literacy was a great appreciation for the narrative character of racial experience. If we acknowledge the unavoidable storyness of human experience, then narrative can be viewed as the dominant shape of black intelligence; speech and text can be seen as the crucial rhetorical surfaces on which black identity is inscribed.

My boyhood pastor, Frederick Sampson, was the greatest influence in my immediate environment on my understanding of the power of language to educate, uplift, and inspire survival. Here was a man who read widely and enthusiastically in what was then known simply, and uncontroversially, as "the classics." He came into the pulpit speaking about subjects ranging from metaphysical poetry to racial double-consciousness, quoting figures as diverse as Bertrand Russell, William Shakespeare, and W.E.B. Du Bois. Although he was the most sophisticated rhetorician with whom I had intimate contact, I had been seductively trapped in the brilliant rhetorical webs woven by Martin Luther King Jr. and Malcolm X.

Growing up in Detroit in the '60s and '70s, I had the opportunity to listen regularly to two other towering pulpiteers—C. L. Franklin and Charles Gilchrist Adams—who, while they possessed sharply contrasting styles, were formidable practitioners of black homiletical art. Franklin and Adams, and Sampson too, are superb examples of how the dense materiality—and, for that matter, the ontological mediation, the performative epistemology, and hermeneutical ubiquity—of black sacred rhetoric functions in dynamic, and diverse, fashion. Franklin, the father of soul music idol Aretha Franklin, was a legendary preacher and pastor who was uniquely gifted in the style of black preaching known technically as the "chanted sermon," and more colloquially as "whooping." As a species of black sacred rhetoric, whooping is characterized by the repetition of rhythmic patterns of speech whose effect is achieved by variation of pitch, speed, and rhythm. The "whooped" sermon climaxes in an artful enjambment or artificial elongation of syllables, a dramatic shift in meter, and often a coarsening of timbre, producing tuneful speech. In the sacred spaces of black worship, the performative dimension of black rhetoric is acutely accented in whooping.

Moreover, the antiphonal character of black ecclesiastical settings means that congregational participation is ritually sanctioned in the call and response between preacher and pew dweller. The interactive character of black worship exerts a profound rhetorical pressure on the preacher to integrate into her sermon hermeneutical gestures, semantic cues, and linguistic opportunities that evoke verbal response and vocal validation from the congregation. Franklin was a past master at deploying his vast rhetorical skills to orchestrate the religious rites and ecclesiastical practices of black Christendom with flair and drama.

Charles Adams, who pastored another of my neighborhood's landmark institutions, Hartford Avenue Baptist Church, is equally gifted. Adams was dubbed the "Harvard Whooper" because of his uncanny fusion of an intellectual acuity honed as a student at Harvard Divinity School and a charismatic quality of folk preaching gleaned from his immersion as a youth in the colorful cadences of black religious rhetoric. Adams's riveting sermonic style is characterized by a rapid-fire delivery, keen exegetical analyses of biblical texts, the merger of spiritual and political themes, a far-ranging exploration of the varied sources of African American identity, and a rhythmic, melodic tone that, at its height, is a piercing rhetorical ensemble composed of deliberately striated diction, staccato sentences, stressed syllabic construction, alliterative cultural allusion, and percussive phrasing.

Further, Adams sacralizes the inherent drama of black religious rhetoric by embodying its edifying theatrical dimensions. As preacher, he is both *shaman* and *showman*. In his brilliant pulpit oratory, Adams nurtures the sacrament of performance: the ritualized reinvestment of ordinary time and event with the theological utility of spectacle. Adams, for instance, not only preached a biblical story of a woman searching for a lost coin; he took a broom into the pulpit and dramatized the search for lost meaning in life and the need to reorder existential priorities. Besides his pulpit work, Adams also wrote a column for the black weekly *Michigan Chronicle* and was active in local politics (president of the NAACP) and later in national black religious life (president of the Progressive National Baptist Convention). Adams is one of the foremost examples of black preaching's polysemous power, and of the sanctification of language and imagination for salvific ends.

Finally, Kenneth Cockrel exerted significant influence on my understanding and use of language in the service of social resistance and racial emancipation. Cockrel was a self-styled Marxist lawyer and revolutionary Detroit activist who eventually served on Detroit's city council. Had he lived, he would surely have had a serious chance of succeeding Coleman Young as Detroit's mayor. In my adolescence, Cockrel made his reputation by successfully defending three black youth accused of murdering some Detroit policemen in the early '70s. That celebrated case was a crucial blow in black Detroiters' war against a repressive police agenda—appropriately named STRESS (Stop The Robberies Enjoy Safe Streets)—that had resulted in the killing of several black men. I was riveted by Cockrel's relentless, high-speed, and bravely loquacious appearances on local television, and by his colorful quotes in the local newspapers. Cockrel made verbal facility seductive; he shaped words into weapons to be wielded on behalf of the oppressed. By watching and reading Cockrel's daring assaults on the racism of elected officials and policemen, and by listening to his linguistic skill in defending black interests, I became convinced that race and rhetoric are indissoluble.

Keene, Bennett, Douglass, James, Burdette, Sampson, Franklin, Adams, and Cockrel all made me aware, in various ways, of the personal and social functions of eloquence, of the racial utility of articulation. These figures helped me understand the phenomenological merit of linguisticality—that language possesses a self-reflexive quality that allows its users to analyze its constitutive parts. But they also helped me see that words can lend ontological credence to a developing identity, that language can house an existential weight, a self-regenerating energy, that can be levied against the denials of black being expressed in racist sentiment and practice.

In theorizing the relation of race to language, we must pay attention to the important work of cultural studies figures, literary critics, and critical race theorists. I think we must come to terms with poststructuralist theory as well. While the contribution of cultural studies scholars, literary critics, and critical race theorists to debates about race and language is well established—although not without controversy—it is neither obvious nor acceptable to some black critics that they should employ European theories in explicating black culture. I think that French poststructuralist theory, for example, has a great deal to offer critics who interrogate the complex meanings of African American discursive practices. Of course, those French critics must not be fetishized or given undue deference. Nor should their thought be uncritically adapted to black life without acknowledging the complicated process by which European theory has historically been deployed to colonize the psychic, intellectual, and ideological spaces of black culture. Colonization as a corollary to European theoretical transgression against indigenous, native, and subaltern populations—or more precisely, theoretical transgression as an adjunct to European colonial expansion—is reason enough for a healthy skepticism about such matters. Still, the critical appropriation of poststructuralist theory by black intellectuals can prove beneficial.

For example, parts of Derrida's theory of deconstruction might help illumine the relation of black identity to linguistic expression. Derrida's critique of the conception of speech as expression independent of a transcendental object of inquiry rather than as a mode of articulation constitutive of its object of inquiry might strengthen the liberation of African American critical discourse from the quest for transcendental epistemic security within a framework of universal reason. This is helpful in at least two ways. First, it relieves the "burden of representation," so that African American culture is no longer viewed as an effort to suture the gaping theoretical wound produced by splitting truth (objectivity) from its discursive mode of expression (relativism).

Representational theories of truth are only relevant when one believes that accurate pictures of the world are possible. Once one dismisses the quest for such a transcendental basis of epistemic authority and representational accuracy, one clears discursive space for a new conception of truth as a function of justifying beliefs by referring to the contingent practices of human reason. Truth cannot be known apart from the linguistic resources and intellectual grounds at our disposal. Hence black critics need not fear that by contending for truth as produced and known by fallible human beings that they are fatefully departing from epistemic strategies and philosophical procedures that allow others to know with certainty the objective world. On the view I have discussed, *all* human efforts to discover truth are similarly circumscribed, despite the apparently authoritative character of many epistemological claims.

The second consequence flows from the first: the political fallout of such a theory of truth is that all linguistic assertions, and the grounds of reason and morality that support them, are provisional rhetorical practices subject to revision as the telos of the social order is transformed through conflict and struggle. Thus differential assertions about race are often predicated on conflicting social or group values within a hierarchy of racial perspectives that reflects a structural validation of certain views as more legitimate, hence more *reasonable*, than others. Since this conception of reason is widely viewed as the adjudicative force that resolves disputes (and restores a fictive view of balance) between rival claims to racial common sense, an artificial and contingent set of racial norms is made to appear natural and universal. In the process, supplying the necessary condition of the relative social and intellectual merits of racial claims is deceptively portrayed as the sufficient condition of such arguments. There is in turn a neat, even elegant, justification of the inherent superiority—the self-evident and logically appealing nature—of certain racial claims. By highlighting the logical means, rhetorical strategies, and political ends that structure hegemonic racial practices—showing how the contingent is rendered eternal—black critics help demystify the complex procedures by which racial hierarchy is maintained.

Another relevant feature of Derrida's theory of deconstruction is the accent on multiple meanings of sentential rationality and linguistic practice. This means that the horizon of meaning—and here, Gadamer's work is of paramount importance as well—is not closed by definitive hermeneutic acts or absolute notations of truth. In determining a text's *meanings*—already that's a polemical plural, suggesting a break of the powerful link between authorial intentionality and textual interpretation, while also suggesting that a text might be a book, a social convention, a rhetorical practice, a film, and so on—the emphasis is not on the singular meaning, the decisive reading, or the right interpretation, ideas premised on the belief that it is possible to exhaust the ways one might understand *(verstehen)* a text. The question one asks of a text is not, What does it mean? but How does it signify? This is linked to black critical reflections on signifying practices within black diasporic cultures. The simultaneous convergence of possible meanings underscores the multiple valences a text may generate. These valences index a political economy of expressive culture that is embedded in a thick network of flexible readings, which are an exercise in hermeneutical warfare.

Indeed, competing schemas of explaining and knowing the world are implicated in the readings, *re*readings, *mis*readings, *sur*readings, *un*readings, *ir*readings, and *anti*readings that flow from the irreverent jouissance of *a* poststructuralist ethic of reading, if the poststructuralists can be said to possess one or even any at all. It might be useful as well to remember Foucault's notion of the "insurrection of subjugated knowledges." Such a notion sheds light on how marginalized discourses, suppressed rhetorics, decentered voicings, and subaltern speech have erupted along a trajectory of political struggles and discursive quests for self-justification, since the search for other-validation is arrested in the recognition of truth's contingent borders. In short, all quests for truth are interested and biased. The rise of such knowledges—signifying in part what Althusser termed an "epistemic break" with previous epistemological conditions, positions, and authorities—enables the articulative possibilities of minority cultures.

But borrowing from my own theological tradition, I think we must baptize European cultural and social theories. It is not that Derrida, Foucault, Guattari, Deleuze, Lyotard, Kristeva, Irigaray, Baudrillard, and Barthes must be subject to a xenophobic rearticulation of American nationalist values. Neither is it the case that we should force them to show, as it were, their theoretical passports in order to traverse the semiotic or ideological borders of American theory. Rather, we should shape poststructuralist theory to the peculiar demands of American intellectual and social life. The translation of poststructuralist theorists with our rhetorical resonances, linguistic tics, and discursive habits challenges national biases and intellectual insularities on both sides of the Atlantic. We must gritty the smooth surface of poststructuralist theories—which often enjoy untroubled travel to our intellectual shores—with the specificities of our racial and political struggles. This is especially the case as we theorize the links between language and black identities. I think that, on a metanarrative level, language itself is a metaphor for the extraordinary elasticity of human identity. Race only compounds the metaphor's complexity.

In the preface to Between God and Gangsta Rap, *you write, "The recycling of tired debates about racial and cultural authenticity abound. These debates have taken many forms in many different forums, but they all come down to the same question: how can we define the Real Black Person?" (xii). Obviously, there is also no Real Black Writer, but do institutional, mass-read texts—such as multicultural readers—that depict particular black experience attempt to construct a "Real Black Person" and a "Real Black Writer" in the name of diversity and tolerance?*

To perfectly equivocate, in some senses yes, and in other senses no. Yes, in the sense that one of the hidden logics of a specific variety of multiculturalism is the effort to evade the rude heterogeneity and inconvenient diversity of black identity—or, for that matter, any minority identity. On this view, multiculturalism may be pictured as a concession to the demand to package black identity for a mainstream audience in a relatively painless fashion. That sort of multiculturalism is indivisible from our nation's commodity fetishism and consumptive appetites.

Something like the Epcot version of culture.

That's exactly right! On that view, multiculturalism expresses the desire to cross over black culture in acceptable mainstream forms under the impetus of asserting that the voices of at first racial but now sexual, ethnic, and gender "others" must be heard. What's problematic about this version of multiculturalism, however, is the leveling effect of its hidden premise: that there are interchangeable "others" whose perspectives and histories are being mobilized within multicultural discourse. In such a case, there is an empty slate of marginality whose contents are determined by the flavor of difference one seeks to accent in a given situation. "Black," "woman," or "Asian" become static categories of identity to be conveniently referenced when one needs to plug in a variety of otherness.

Equally troubling is the view that there is a relative equality of means to articulate difference within the ideological spaces of multiculturalism. All that anyone seeking to understand another race, culture, ethnicity, gender, or sexuality need do is select a species of otherness from a list of equally available options. This procedure ignores how class, gender, and racial forces create a hierarchy of difference within difference itself—that is, within difference generically conceived. It ignores, for instance, how, in the politicization of multicultural rhetoric through affirmative action, white women have fared far more successfully in employment and education opportunities than black women and men. It also ignores how, on the representational front created by multicultural struggles to combat stereotypes, blacks have done far better, especially on television and on the silver screen, than Latinos. It also ignores how, in the empirical terms of economic advantage and social status, gay white men have been able to leverage considerable clout within domains—particularly corporate life and Hollywood production—closed to most minorities. The point is simple: *social* differences within the *ideology* of difference make a *material* difference in how the *politics* of difference are conceived and expressed.

The material context of the politics of difference must be kept in mind as we untangle the ideological roots of multiculturalism. The version of multiculturalism about which I have been speaking—what you called the "Epcot version," or what might be usefully termed market multiculturalism—reifies difference as an ontological fusion of otherness. The effect of such reification is a conceptual confusion: not only is the hierarchy of difference obscured, but different racial, sexual, class, and gender identities are uniformly conceived as *different in the same way*. Difference, however, must be conceived not only in terms of its categorical distinctiveness—its unique elements of self-identification—but also in the relational definition of its constitutive properties.

It is important to acknowledge that conceptions of difference have been used in a variety of ways even before the emergence of multiculturalism and postmodernism. First, *ratio-spatial difference* is conceived as a dimension of otherness whose identity is located in a measure of rational and emotional distance from a defining social, racial, or sexual norm. Second, *taxonomic difference*, which builds on ratio-spatial difference, is conceived as a classificatory order of otherness mediated through a comparative analysis of identities defined in relation to each other. Third, *organic difference* is conceived as the process of individuation within a group dynamic where otherness is a function of the *character* of interaction between mutually constitutive—although often diametrically opposed—and evolving identities. And finally, *metaphysical difference* is conceived as a self-generated, hence self-justifying, identity whose otherness is defined by its roots in discursive grounds viewed as apart from (or antithetical to) universal, self-evident truth.

This truncated genealogy of difference—or, to shift metaphors, this political cartography of the variegated terrain of difference and the different ways it has been mapped, a map of the maps of difference, if you will—is a cautionary tale against liberal conceptions of conversation, civility, and tolerance that underlie even the progressive version of multiculturalism that I favor. To be sure, conversation, civility, and tolerance are crucial components in our efforts to accent the multicultural character of national identity and to acknowledge the political utility of discourses of difference, diversity, otherness, subalternity, alterity, and marginality. Still, it is essential to emphasize not only the benefits but also the limits of analogizing (or in some cases, blurring the real boundaries between) discursive argument and political practice. The way the metaphor of conversation has bled from intellectual to social practice illustrates what we gain and lose by such a process.

For instance, philosophical discourse was revolutionized in 1979 when Richard Rorty published *Philosophy and the Mirror of Nature*. Among many brilliant insights, Rorty argues that philosophy should no longer be conceived as a tribunal of pure reason before which other disciplines must appear in order to adjudicate competing claims of truth. Rorty also argues, with the support of Wittgenstein, Heidegger, and Dewey, that philosophy is neither transcendental nor objective but value-laden, language-derived, and theory-drenched. Contrary to the view that philosophy constitutes an objective mode of inquiry within a unique epistemological and disciplinary boundary, Rorty "blurs the genres" between philosophy and literary criticism in maintaining that philosophy, à la Derrida, is "a kind of writing."

All of these insights lead Rorty to conclude that philosophy, long considered the "queen bee" of the human sciences, is a narrative-laden intellectual pursuit whose grounds for truth are no more secure than, say, those of theology or sociology. Further, philosophy is part of an ongoing conversation about truth and other indispensable subjects of intellectual inquiry. But it has no more inherent power to settle disputes among rival versions of morality than say mathematics or psychology. As part *of* the conversation, and not as the ultimate rational ground *on which* the conversation takes place, philosophy has no greater power to resolve discursive conflicts than, say, economics or anthropology.

Rorty's view that philosophy is not a discursive practice whose technical superiority or foundational security mandates recognition of its epistemological authority, but a partner in conversation with other ways of thinking, speaking, and writing the world, is of profound importance in academic debates about the status and function of truth, objectivity, and reason. It is equally important in illuminating debates about truth, objectivity, and reason as they relate to, and are evoked in, various conceptions of multiculturalism.

Rorty's conception of conversation, adapted from the philosopher Michael Oakeshott, suggests that no single disciplinary habit of organizing knowledge, pursuing questions of truth, or intervening in intellectual or moral disagreements can exhaust the myriad ways of interpreting the world we constitute through language and social practice. Therefore defenders of "the canon" and "the tradition" who lambast the insurgent rhetorical and discursive practices of intellectuals who advocate multiculturalism have from the beginning a distorted picture of how knowledge and truth are produced.

In a way, the conservative defenders of "the canon" and "the tradition" have got things backward. Conservative defenders of traditional ways of knowing the world often mask their discursive anxieties and theoretical contradictions behind a veiled attack on multiculturalism's political agenda. All the while, conservatives refuse to acknowledge the political pressures that bear on their own work while denying the crisis of explanation that besieges their own disciplines. It is easier for conservatives to blame multiculturalism's political agenda for their hermeneutical crises than to address the theoretical leakages of their own discursive paradigms. The greatest risk of such a venture is *not* that it might lead the conservatives to embrace the insights of the multiculturalists; it is that they might have to confront the defective elements of their own intellectual enterprise, none of which have been caused by the "scourge" of multiculturalism. It is easier to attack Toni Morrison than to face up to Richard Rorty.

On the other hand, too often liberal advocates of multiculturalism—or of the rigorous disciplinary self-examination which is its intellectual predicate—don't have a political analysis of how arguments over disciplinary boundaries and conceptions of conversation play out in the quotidian world of academic policy and intellectual life. The irony of such a situation is heightened when we recall that multiculturalists are accused by conservatives, and many liberals, of *politicizing* knowledge. Still, many advocates of multiculturalism lack a sophisticated materialist analysis of how intellectual and financial resources are distributed within even their own circles to support or stifle the work of "minority" scholars. In other words, even when mainstream scholars are committed to multiculturalism in principle—and to the notion of conversation as a regulative ideal of intellectual interrogation and as a means to broaden the basis of interracial dialogue—they often fail to question the political economy of racial discourse in the American academy. Not enough structural questions are raised about who participates in the conversation, when and under what conditions such dialogue should take place, and who sets the agenda to determine what's important to know or do.

Given this situation, an ironic consequence follows: inequality is reinscribed in the very discourse of multiculturalism that should relieve, or at least reveal, such conditions. Because many liberal scholars don't account for the social and political conditions that make possible the practice of liberal multicultural conversation, the arguments to which they sometimes resort to explain such inequality often mimic conservative responses. In sum, converting conversation from an intellectual ideal in academic circles to a regulative ideal of social practice gains and loses in the translation.

A further sign of the unequal means by which participants are engaged in the conversation of multiculturalism is the prevalence of market multiculturalism over progressive multiculturalism. I have already been discussing the definition and effects of the former. The latter argues against the notion that there is a single thing called multiculturalism from which extends a single line of interpretation or meaning to a single, static thing called "the mainstream." That is why I have tried to challenge a simple, reductionist conception, a singular formulation, of multiculturalism. Rather, there are *multiculturalisms*, including the varieties I have discussed: market and liberal multiculturalism. Progressive, or complex, multiculturalism maintains that there are incredible intellectual and ideological diversities within a "minority" group, and that radiating out from its various epicenters are simultaneous lines of relation to a range of dynamic elements that constitute the mainstream. In some cases, "the mainstream" is extraordinarily different from "marginal" cultures; in others, marginal cultures are equally mainstream. Both multiculturalism and the mainstream, the margin, and the center are more complexly rendered in progressive multiculturalism. The differences between margins and centers depend on just such an analysis as I have been trying to give of the social, moral, intellectual, and political stakes involved in arguments over the ideology of difference and, in this case, their embodiment in academic institutions.

As for the practices of market multiculturalism, the various inequalities of opportunity for participants to converse are often overlooked. Indeed, one could argue that the advocates of market multiculturalism depend on such inequalities to ensure their success in diluting and distributing marginal cultures. This is where your notion of the Real Black Writer or my view of the Real Black Person presented in such a discourse of mutliculturalism is most evident. The advocates of market multiculturalism appropriate marginalized minority discourses for the purposes of packaging and reproducing a hegemonic conception of what is authentically black. Those who challenge market multiculturalism by naming its social functions and political intents are often disciplined, disavowed, or, as the hip-hoppers say, just plain "dissed."

Further, progressive multicultural articulations of a complex blackness that opposes singular, simplistic racial identities expressed within market multiculturalism are silenced or marginalized. Market multiculturalism, more precisely corporate multiculturalism, doesn't often pay attention to the radical particularity and the vibrant heterogeneity of black identities. In that sense, the Real Black Person is being constituted within the logic of market multiculturalism against dissenting forms of blackness. Such alternative views of blackness are expressed, ironically enough, on the margins of this hegemonic ideology of multiculturalism. Thus multiculturalism, which in principle is an expression of marginal identity, becomes commodified by the market interests of dominant society. Thus the peripheral is literally *brought* front and center and thus severed from its resistive function and its potential to disrupt. Within the cultural zone penetrated by such market forces, expressions of blackness that resist the values and visions of dominant culture are quickly deflected or defeated. Moreover, the Real Black Person is put forth—whether through literary text, popular song, or television character—in response to cultural desires to mass-produce and to consume and, to a degree, control the meaning of black identity. Arguably, then, the racially authentic takes a backseat to a mass-produced racial authenticity tailored to the interests and tastes of mainstream society.

While the academy is certainly not impervious to market multiculturalism, universities and colleges are more likely the sites for promoting an easily accessible and untroubling version of liberal multiculturalism. Moreover, discourses of tolerance and civility within higher education, strangely enough, are deployed to restrict the powerful expression of more raw, less muted, occasionally rage-filled visions of marginal racial existence. Of course, one would expect that groups which have been systematically denied access to the goods and resources of American educational and political life might have bruised feelings about such unfair denials. To a certain degree, such anger is anticipated and thus deflected within elite academic circles, especially as it concerns minority students. For instance, there are minority and multicultural affairs offices established on many campuses to counsel minority students and to facilitate their adjustment to academic life before anti–affirmative action backlashes made the administrators of higher education nervous about extending even informal help to minority students who are often alienated on majority culture campuses.

The hostility against affirmative action—and therefore against the presence and interests of minority students throughout higher education—and the backlash against the so-called rise of identity politics among students and faculty of color, has led to a strange collusion between conservatives and (neo)liberals. Both sides have implicitly agreed, if for different reasons, that an aggressive minority presence on campuses must be held in check by liberal conceptions of civility and tolerance. One must not act ugly (i.e. outlandish, angry, diffident, surly, rage-filled, standoffish, etc.) if one is a minority because the minority's very presence in academia was secured by the observance of civility and tolerance. Thus proprietary behavior, the logic continues, is the least thing a minority should observe in gratitude for the privilege of being present in the academy—though it is rarely ever thought of, much less, stated, in such an explicit fashion.

In practical terms, it would be hard to argue against such powerful principles as civility and tolerance. In many ways, these virtues make possible the peaceful resolution of differences of opinion and belief about race in society. To some degree, civility and tolerance function on university campuses as the social predicates to an idealized, Leibnizian best of all possible linguistic worlds where dissident speech is protected, where all views are aired, and where all points of view are equally considered and debated. But such parity is rarely the fact, although blacks and other minorities are blamed for deploying political correctness to drown out or close down undesirable opinions. It is often forgotten that blacks practiced these principles in abundance when they were manifestly absent in those folk who were most uncivil and intolerant in their denial of black rights, even as they insisted on the essential inferiority of black humanity.

Still, present liberal multicultural arbiters of civility and tolerance often forget two things. First, it was not the exercise of civility and tolerance that brought blacks into the mainstreams of American privilege. Rather, it was civil disobedience and a studied intolerance for second-class citizenship on the parts of black activists that finally brought institutional white supremacy, including that of higher education, to its knees. Second, views of civility and tolerance have been crafted largely out of a liberal preconception of the legitimacy of representational articulation: that is, in cases where the state or social forces prevent the speech of minorities from being heard, their voices will be represented by proxy.

Thus civility and tolerance preserve a social fabric that excluded black—and Native American, Latino, and Asian—rhetoric from being woven into the national dialogue on most subjects. This is not to suggest that black or Native American or Latino or Asian views would necessarily depart from all views held by white Americans; it simply accents the unjust process by which minority voices were considered illegitimate and hence eliminated from national debates. As a result, the easy resort now to discourses of civility and tolerance in racial or national debates, without accounting for the complex social impact of the systematic exclusion of those voices, merely preserves the status quo with the *appearance* of fairness and justice because black bodies are now at the table. In short, we have phenotypical inclusion, but we are nonetheless saddled with the metaphysical exclusion of diverse black points of view.

What this means in regard to the present-day academy is clear: minorities are fine as long as they don't raise ruckus or make aggressive arguments about, or respond angrily to, the presence of social or racial injustice; as long as they act civilly and tolerantly, especially of poisonous perspectives that in the past advocated their exclusion from the academy and in the present attack their intelligence and their very being. Perhaps one of the most difficult aspects of promoting these liberal versions of civility and tolerance as the proper forces to adjudicate racial disputes is the fact that, as with market multiculturalism, there is little interrogation within liberal multiculturalism about the unequal access of minorities to resources to publicize their views or to amplify their pain. Inevitably, then, in the political economy of racial representation, well-meaning white allies sometimes have greater freedom to speak for minorities or about the issues that are crucial to their survival.

Many liberal whites failed to anticipate that once excluded minorities for whom they spoke actually began to speak for themselves, substantive, structural changes would be demanded. That is, the very rhetorical edifice of civility and tolerance that liberal whites had helped to construct and that had allowed them to defend minority interests, was viewed by some minorities as a crucial part of the problem, a structure in need of dismantling and reconstruction. The very devices that allowed white representatives of black interests to survive—calm, cool argument and rational explication—are often viewed by those whites as the only, or the best, way to secure racial advance. But blacks whose primary weapons in the struggle for equality have been defensive speech (against the verbal and physical attacks of whites) have a different experiential base for articulating racial pain and securing racial benefit. As minorities speak for themselves—in tones, perhaps, more harsh, more insistent, or less patient, less *civil* or less *tolerant*—their views are seen, sometimes even by those who have formerly spoken for them, as unacceptable. Thus the competition of racial virtues at times appears inevitable: civility and tolerance as the highest priority for even liberal whites, agitation and disobedience as the means to liberation deployed by excluded blacks.

The benefit of progressive multiculturalism is that it highlights, in this case, the complexity of black identity. It also refutes the template of ontological essentialism that is used to reproduce market multiculturalism's characterizations of authentic blackness. Further, it contests the awkwardly apolitical versions of difference that fail to account for social differences in the ideology of difference. And it contests the dehistoricization of regulative ideals like civility and tolerance in the American academy. In the final analysis, multiculturalism is too important a concept to be left to well-meaning but restrictive liberal advocates with beliefs about proprietary behavior. Nor can multiculturalism be left to the machinations of a market culture that seeks to package and distribute notions of blackness without accounting for the profound diversity of black culture.

Interview by Sidney Dobrin
Durham, North Carolina, 1997

4

More Than Academic

Seamless Theory, Racial Disruptions, and Public Intellectuals in the Ebony Tower

Many people argue that the jargon-rich language of the academy is more obfuscating than illuminating for those outside of the specialized area of academic work. Yet you write in Between God and Gangsta Rap, *"The language of the academy is crucial because it allows me to communicate within a community of scholars whose work contributes to the intellectual strength of our culture. . . . The language of the academy is most important to me because it provides a critical vocabulary to explore the complex features of American and African American life. The language of the academy should never divorce itself from the politics of crisis, social problems, cultural circumstances, moral dilemmas, or intellectual questions of the world in which we live." You continue, "As a public intellectual, I am motivated to translate my religious, academic, and political ideas into a language that is accessible without being simplistic." How do you see the transition between academic discourse and more public discourses affecting your work? Are there problems of translation when moving between discourses?*

I see the transition from the academic world to the world outside of the academy as a self-conscious decision to intervene in debates and conversations that occur in public spheres (a different public sphere from the academy because I consider the academy a public sphere) and have enormous impact on everyday people's lives. The transition, however, is not smooth. The demands for rigorous debate within the academy are much different from those demands in the public sphere beyond the academy. There are huge and heated debates going on right now about the function of academic language. I'm not one who, for obvious reasons—self-interest being the primary one (laughter)—jumps on academics because they don't speak for a public audience or because they cannot speak in ways that are deemed "clear" and "articulate." Those are loaded terms: *clear, articulate.* Scholars like Henry Giroux and Donna Haraway have reminded us that language has multiple functions, even within a limited context. To understand that is to acknowledge that there are a variety of fronts upon which we must launch our linguistic resistance to political destruction and moral misery on the one hand, and to narrow conceptions of what language does and how it functions, on the other hand.

Because I was reared in a black church in a "minority" linguistic community that had rich resources that were concealed, and obscured, for a variety of reasons, I think that I'm sensitive to the claims against academics that their languages are simply incomprehensible, impenetrable, perhaps even ineffable. I empathize to a degree with academics who are defensive about such matters, who say, "We're writing for a specific audience." That to my mind is a perfectly legitimate, though not exhaustive, mode of self-defense. If an academic writes an article that will be read by a thousand people, and those thousand people gain something from it—if there's an exchange of information and ideas, if there's a sharpening of debate and a deepening of understanding of a particular subject—that's a marvelous, worthy achievement. There's no reason to be apologetic for that because that's a very specific function within a larger academic enterprise that needs to be undertaken.

If, for instance, somebody writes an essay on a specific aspect of Foucault's appropriation of Benthamite conceptions of the prison that first clarifies the exact relationship between Bentham and Foucault, and then rearticulates and historicizes our conceptions of the panopticon, and how surveillance operates as it is extended into the black ghetto, that's all for the good, even if only a thousand people understand the language and ideas of the essay. That means that some advance in understanding and exchange of information has occurred, and that's wholly defensible on many grounds, from the intrinsic value of knowledge to its application to contemporary social problems involving the justice system and the prison-industrial complex. Think about it; we don't have a problem with brain surgeons who speak a language that only a handful of people, mainly other experts, can understand. Our attitude is—and, I think, rightfully so—if the man or woman can save your life, speak the jargon, do what you've got to do, operate! So I don't have a problem with a similar kind of precise, rigorous use of language that occurs in academic circles. But a major problem often arises when hostility is directed against those who are able to take the information, to take the knowledge, to take the profound rigor that is often suggested in such exercises, and make them available to a broader audience.

It is unavoidable that an academic surrenders depth for breadth in making many public forays into television, radio, or the popular press. But that doesn't automatically overrule the usefulness of such pursuits. I've written for venues such as *Cultural Studies* and *Cultural Critique*, journals that four to five thousand people may read, and I have found it intellectually rewarding. On the other hand, I've written for newspapers and magazines where millions of people have read my words. And that has been extremely satisfying. In a word, we have to respect the genre. The academic community, generally speaking, has a deep hostility to those who are aggressively public. Those scholars who are labeled public intellectuals are viewed as sellouts. We have our own version in the academy of the hip-hop mantra, "keeping it real," which in this case means the authentic scholar who is strictly concerned about academic matters, betraying a claustrophobic view of the life of the mind.

Interestingly enough, despite the sketchy, almost nonexistent treatment found in books like Russell Jacoby's influential *The Last Intellectuals*, the recent debate about academic authenticity has largely centered in the plight and predicament of black public intellectuals. Some of that hostility may be racially coded, but a lot of it has to do with rigid visions of academic propriety grounded in territorial disputes. A geography of destiny is shaped by parochial views of the appropriate intellectual terrain one occupies, and that usually means valorizing the university as the exclusive site of legitimate academic work. We in the academy, especially on the left, love to talk about transgression, speaking of it in intellectual and symbolic terms, but we don't want to engage in such transgression literally or epistemologically.

We resist the critique of being in an ivory tower, but then we're the ones who insist on putting ourselves there.

That's right. We want to attack the ivory tower *from* the ivory tower. What's interesting is that these assaults resonate with a punishing paradox. We celebrate transgression, hybridity, migration, and mobility, but when people actually *do* these things, there is incredible resentment against such movement.

In Professional Correctness, *Stanley Fish argues that as academics we cannot be public intellectuals, and as public intellectuals we give up our roles as university scholars. In essence, he argues that Michael Eric Dyson cannot simultaneously be an academic and a public intellectual. Your critique of the university sees the academy as inseparable from the "real world" and that our roles in the university are as important as any other vocation outside of the academy. How do you respond to Fish's critique? As the university becomes more interdisciplinary, do you see (as Fish does) interdisciplinarity as a threat to universities or as having potential to intervene in public policy and the larger culture?*

Stanley Fish is a really smart guy. I always listen carefully to what he says. Many of his criticisms are right on target, but on this point, I will disagree. He's right to challenge academics to rethink the relationship between what we do and what we say. Even more poignantly, he's forcing us to take seriously the idea that serving on a committee in the academy where you deploy Marxist language to demythologize class relationships is not the same as being involved in a labor dispute in the local AFL-CIO, or engaging the interests of black workers on the assembly line in Detroit. There's little doubt that he's absolutely right. But we've got to avoid a logical fallacy here: Just because Fish is right doesn't mean, therefore, that the function of the intellectual deploying Marxist language to demythologize class relations is not an important one. It simply possesses a different kind of importance. As a black person in the academy, I don't have the luxury of deciding that one kind of importance is more crucial than the other, or that one kind of work—say, rigorous academic analysis—excludes the necessity for its complement, the application of knowledge to ordinary folk and circumstances. To phrase it differently, there are multiple sites of intervention in academic and public spheres in defense of various, even competing, political interests. In the Fishian cosmology, there's a radical bifurcation between the "real" world—in which people operate with political interests at hand and deploy specific vocabularies to defend those interests—and the academy, which is a different sphere of knowledge production and consumption, with its own political interests.

However, the academy and the public sphere beyond it are both defined by interests that need to be taken seriously. I say this as a member of a group—African Americans—who have often been the object of intellectual inquiry within the hallowed, and often biased, halls of the academy. So most blacks have always known that, protestations to the contrary, what goes on in the academy always spills beyond its ostensibly hermetic seal, bleeding into everyday life with languages, grammars, and vocabularies that have often done great harm to black life. Even when blacks were closed out of the mainstream academy through segregated practices, we understood that what was going on there was important. For instance, Charles Murray and Richard Herrnstein—although they were dealing with reductionist and racialist scientific theories of the genetic inheritance of intelligence, ideas that were deconstructed by reputable scientists twenty years ago—sold 400,000 copies of their book, *The Bell Curve,* in hardback alone. We can safely say, without great fear of contradiction, that most people didn't read the entire book. The very existence of that book was a phenomenological weight to systematically justify cultural prejudices about the inherent inferiority of black intelligence. But the ensuing and bitter public debate occasioned by the book's publication reflected in part the belief held by many blacks that academic debates profoundly impact the material interests of black culture. We already see the connection between the academy and the "real" world because the real world looks to the academy to justify its prejudices, to dress them up in scientific discourse that grants them legitimacy and power. We have understood all along that even though twelve people may be reading a book, one of the twelve could end up being a congressman, a policy maker, or the director of an institute or governmental department with the ability to distribute or divert resources for black people. We have to deconstruct and demythologize this radical bifurcation between the academy and the real world, since both are defined and driven by ideological and intellectual interests. Truth and politics are deeply united in a fashion to which Fish, in this case, has not paid sufficient attention.

To my mind, Fish gives eloquent but problematic expression to a more narrow vision of the life of the mind than I favor. He warns us that thinkers who make Marxist or progressive analyses of forms of oppression are substituting such analyses for the real work of political action. But we don't have to subscribe to such a literal view of the work of politics. Creating discursive space in hegemonic academic culture is a specific kind of work that should be valued, even if it is rightly not confused, better yet, conflated, with traditional politics. Such activity has an empirical effect on the concrete political interests of folk outside the academy. Before I entered the academy, I was a teen father who lived on welfare, hustled on the streets of Detroit, and later worked full time in two factories. Scholars and intellectuals at the University of Detroit and Wayne State University who were thinking about the relationship between labor and commodity and wage alienation encouraged us autoworkers to engage in political resistance and to take intellectual work seriously as a weapon to defend our interests.

At its core, interdisciplinarity threatens academics who construe their interests narrowly and seek to preserve their intellectual bailiwick. Interdisciplinarity is not merely an index of the postmodern moment when we acknowledge the multiplicity of ethical ideals and claims to knowledge. More heady questions are engaged, such as who gets to control knowledge, for what purposes is it being deployed, and whose interests are being protected in the defense of narrowly conceived academic disciplines that pay no attention to what other thinkers are doing beyond the pale of one's intellectual orientation. To a large extent, the segregation of knowledge along disciplinary boundaries is an artificial division of intellectual inquiry that counters the most liberating traditions of African American studies in particular, and Western learning in general. Such academic segregation, like the social policy it mimics, should be corrected by the integration of intellectual inquiry that rests on robust interdisciplinary impulses.

In Race Rules *you write, "The anointing of a few voices to represent The Race is an old, abiding problem. For much of our history, blacks have had to rely on spokespersons to express our views and air our grievances to a white majority that controlled access to everything from education to employment." You discuss who gets to be black public intellectuals, who chooses them, and why they receive the attention they do. In contemporary America, there are relatively few black intellectuals. This suggests that the intellectual/academic world—which is still made up primarily of middle-class Anglo males—has constructed methods of gatekeeping (for example, graduate school entrance requirements, hiring practices, tenure, publication, speaking engagements) that "select" particular leaders to serve as "representative" voices. More exactly, having only a few black intellectuals is a product of the kind of oppressive strategies of management and containment maintained by the academy. What does this say about the small numbers of black public intellectuals and the possibility of the "radicalness" of public intellectuals such as yourself? Can you really be radical and effect change from the inside when the institution has in fact sanctioned your radicalness? After all, you are a high-profile, well-paid member of the academy.*

You're exactly right. It's a very difficult circumstance in which black intellectuals discover ourselves. I think that it's necessary to not only acknowledge the accuracy of the critique but also extend its political efficacy by being self-critical. There's always a dimension of hubris in self-criticism because when you're pointing to how self-critical you can be, you appear to be saying, "Look how critically engaging I can be about my own position even as I consolidate my interest as a high-profile, well-paid black intellectual." I face that problem head-on, even though it's very difficult. And you're absolutely correct about how the radicalism that we express is sanctioned: such radicalism is being deployed within a larger narrative of cooptation promoted by the American academy that we criticize, and, paradoxically, it is from that base that we articulate our conceptions of the world. But this is the present condition under which we live and labor as we fight for change from within and beyond the academy. Black public intellectuals must certainly question our subject positions and our professional status within the hierarchy of privilege and visibility that we presently enjoy. The trick is to scrutinize the ethics of our participation in the academy as a part of the regime of anointed black intellectuals while maintaining enough visibility and influence to have our voices and work make a difference.

As a practical but principled matter, black public intellectuals must examine whom we refer to in our work. It is telling to me, in reading the interviews of high-profile black intellectuals, that we repeatedly get the same names. There's a narrative re-inscription of notoriety, and a hierarchy of citation among public black intellectuals, where praise is heaped on a narrow range of novelists, artists, scholars, and intellectuals, who, although certainly deserving of the acclaim they receive, are increasingly viewed as the only important voices that merit attention. One of the most just and egalitarian gestures we can make as highly visible black public intellectuals is to throw light on figures whose work is important but not widely known.

You're leading into my next question. You write, "We don't speak for The Race. We speak as representatives of the ideological strands of blackness, and for those kinships we possess outside of black communities, that we think most healthy . . . We ain't messiahs." At the same time, though, you also write, "Equally worrisome, too many black public intellectuals hog the ball and refuse to pass it to others on their team. Many times I've been invited on a television program, a prestigious panel, or a national radio program because a white critic or intellectual recommended me. Later I often discover that another prominent black intellectual, when consulted, had conveniently forgotten to mention my name or that of other qualified black intellectuals. Ugly indeed." Do you think this is because those black public intellectuals who now have the spotlight actually do want to be anointed as spokesperson to represent "The Race"? Does the cult of celebrity, the protection of position as black intellectuals, work against a sort of "hand up for someone on the rung below" attitude?

There is no question that many black intellectuals do want to be what is known among blacks as the HNIC, or the "head nigger in charge." We do want to be the most visible, or as I say in my book, *Race Rules*, the "hottest Negro in the country." It is dizzying to attain a certain form of visibility in American culture as an intellectual. There is undeniably a narcotic effect. When people like Oprah or Charlie Rose or Montel Williams call you up, or when you are invited to write op-eds for the *Washington Post* or the *New York Times,* or when you're referred to as one of the leading voices of your generation, or in my case as the leading young black intellectual, that is very seductive. It can be a powerful trap. First, it encourages us to read our own press. Second, it encourages us to believe our own press. Third, it encourages us to reproduce our own press—even if we consciously deflect our self-anointment through the rhetoric of humility, or if we assign our coronation to onlookers or sycophants who believe in the absolute integrity of our intellectual celebration. Celebrity is a temptation among scholars and especially among black intellectuals, given the relatively small numbers of us who are able to survive and thrive in the academy. There is a barely suppressed impulse among some to be *the person,* or as Zora Neale Hurston said, "the pet Negro." We have to constantly resist that temptation by making relentless forays into those base communities for which we claim to speak.

There is no question that one of the most dispiriting things that I've witnessed among black intellectuals, and not just those who are publicly inclined, is cruel verbal sniping and behind-the-scenes pettiness, none of which, of course, are endemic to black culture. I have in mind Henry Kissinger's quip that the politics of the academy are so vicious because there is so little at stake. The topography of black intellectual space in the academy is so constricted that we are indeed fighting over a narrow terrain of resources and interests. The consequences of such infighting are not good for those moral and intellectual constituencies we claim to represent. The unregulated pursuit of visibility blocks the moral imperative that has circulated among various black communities of "each one teach one" or "each one reach one" or "lifting as we climb." There ain't much lifting as we climb, unless you count our self-promoting career ascension. We do not often lift others or carry them on our rhetorical and intellectual backs. Our failure to do so creates a multitiered hierarchy of black intellectuals.

You're critically conscious of your role as black public intellectual. In Race Rules *you offer a critical series of awards you call the "Envys." Your purpose is both to critique black public intellectuals and to answer critiques leveled by black public intellectuals. Though many of these critiques are unrelenting in their criticism, you don't leave yourself out of your own attack, and you award yourself "The Spike Lee/Terry McMillan Award for Shameless Self Promotion" for your lobbying for publicity for your work. Nonetheless, you are critical of how other black public intellectuals use the role of public intellectual and what they promote in that role. In light of your comments regarding the "lone black leader, and the "ugliness of not nurturing other black intellectuals'" careers, is such criticism helpful?*

It certainly can be construed as self-congratulatory self-flagellation in public view that only reinforces the visibility that I claim has been unequally cast on some intellectuals, including myself. More charitably, my remarks and awards can be taken as tongue-in-cheek. Partly what I'm saying is "lighten up," and that the world's progress doesn't depend on our individual flourishing as black public intellectuals. As intellectuals, we talk about being critical, and I was attempting to cast some of that critical light on ourselves. In effect, I was saying, "let's raise questions about the nature of our work, about its limits, and about how and why we make the political and rhetorical interventions that we do." At the least, we should be more conscious about the need to include other qualified but overlooked intellectuals in the debates we engage. The positive effect of my prodding black intellectuals to be self-critical can be that it will create a larger discourse space, with critics saying of my awards, "That was funny, but . . ." Or they can say, "That wasn't so funny because these charges are on target for the following reasons. . . ." Or they can say, "Well, even though Dyson is trying to promote himself *again,* what's important about his critique is that it does raise very important issues, such as how we confer the 'voice of the Negro' to a very few black figures, even as the bulk of intellectuals and academicians have no access to the media or publishing outlets."

Thus my bestowing of awards, and my critical inventory of black intellectual life, can prove helpful if black intellectuals interrogate our own practices, especially the cultural habit of anointing and saluting a few voices in the enterprise of examining and representing the race. If nothing else, I want to question why a select few political and intellectual figures are empowered to determine what other black people receive. One of the propitious consequences of the rise of black public intellectuals is the questioning of cultural and racial gatekeepers. One of the benefits of a class of public intellectuals gaining visibility and voice—which is why such a class must be as democratic and diverse as possible while providing opportunity to those who are skilled to take up the role—is the ability to thwart the rule of academic Booker T. Washingtons who are able to dole out punishment or reward based upon their often narrow understanding of the political efficacy of a particular work or a particular career. We must relentlessly resist such gatekeeping if we are to enliven the prospects of egalitarianism, excellence, and expansion among black public intellectuals.

In April 1996, Harper's *published a conversation on race between Jorge Klor De Alva, Earl Shorris, and Cornel West. In this discussion, West argues, "When we talk about identity, it's really important to define it. Identity has to do with protection, association, and recognition. People protect their bodies, their labor, their communities, their way of life; in order to be associated with people who ascribe value to them, who take them seriously, who respect them; and for purposes of recognition; to be acknowledged, to feel as if one actually belongs to a group over time and space, we have to be very specific about what the credible options are for them at any given moment." De Alva later says, "All identities are up for grabs. But black intellectuals in the United States, unlike Latino intellectuals in the United States, have an enormous media space within which to shape the politics of naming and to affect the symbols and meanings associated with certain terms. Thus, practically overnight, they convinced the media that they were an ethnic group and shifted over to the model of African American, hyphenated American, as opposed to being named by color. Knowing what we know about the negative aspects of naming, it would be better for all of us, regardless of color, if those who consider themselves, and are seen as, black intellectuals were to stop participating in the insidious one-drop-rule game of identifying themselves as black." You've written quite a bit about identity politics. How do you respond to this exchange between West and De Alva?*

West is absolutely right to focus on protection, association, and recognition, especially as these three modes of response to the formation of black identity have played themselves out within historically constituted black communities. It is an implicit rebuttal of Paul Gilroy's belief that any notion of ethnic solidarity means the hard purchase of a backward view of black identity. Gilroy has been especially critical of black American intellectuals for what he considers our essentialist treatments of racial identity. Interestingly enough, many of these same intellectuals have written powerfully about hybridity and transgression in black culture, and the need to pull into full view what Stuart Hall calls postmodern identity, which is a very complex navigation of a variety of possibilities and subject positions within a narrative of racial recognition. So West's notion that black identity includes protection, association, and recognition is, in part, an attempt to root black identity in the specific context of how African Americans have contested the erosion of, and attack on, their identities. It is also a political acknowledgment of how identity politics, at a crucial level, is a response to the vicious stereotypes imposed on black culture from outside its cultural authority.

Jorge's belief that, by considering themselves black, African Americans are surrendering to the "one-drop rule" misses the point of history and the context of culture. History suggests that there are criteria that are objective—if by objective we mean actually existing material, cultural and political forces independent of the subjective perceptions, wishes, or views of individuals or groups—that shape the lives and destinies of black life. There are socially constructed norms—which, contrary to popular misperception, makes them no less concrete or influential in their impact than if they are conceived to be permanent, necessary features of the social landscape—that mediate the relations of race, norms that help determine how black people are seen and judged. So even if black identity is up for grabs—a statement with which I largely agree, although with decidedly different political resonance, since I've argued in my work about the fluidity of the boundaries of black identity—it has real historical and cultural limitations.

Jorge is extricating a phenomenological analysis of race from its genealogical roots in politics and history. He is also entangled, perhaps, in a naively literal interpretation of the symbolic power of identity's flexibility argued by postmodernists. Saying that identity is a moveable feast of self-reinvention is not to say that there are no backdrops or hard grounds. To paraphrase the poet and essayist Elizabeth Alexander, one may subscribe to the nonessentialist racial politics of identity, but there has got to be a bottom line. The bottom line is composed of the material effects of historically constituted notions of blackness, both within and beyond African American culture. To give a brief example, you can tell the policeman that race is a trope, but if he's beating your head, such behavior won't be stopped by you proclaiming: "Listen, sir, this is a historically constituted, socially constructed reality that has no basis beyond our intellectual assent to its existence, and without our ideological agreement, there can be no consensus about its social effect in American culture." That's a deft bit of ideological maneuvering, but your head will still be bloodied by the battering you endure. So the concrete effects of the association of race with black identity or, more viscerally, with black skin has to be acknowledged as a material factor in the social perception of blackness, and in shaping our views of how race signifies and operates.

In the exchange between West and Jorge, West understands the need to ground the politics of black identity in cultural specificity, and in racial particularities that acknowledge the force of kinship, psychology, and sociology, even if we seek to question just how determinative they are in constructing blackness. Jorge appeals to a language that, on the surface, is more inviting of the postmodern interrogation of blackness as a socially constructed reality. Ironically, however, he does not pay sufficient attention to how blackness signifies in multiple ways in the public sphere. One of the most powerful and determining ways it signifies, however, is as a descriptive term to name people of color who have been historically constituted as black, and whose identities are invested at once in protecting and probing the boundaries of blackness.

Composition, like many intellectual disciplines, has been engaged in its own version of the "theory wars." You are very careful in your writing to acknowledge the importance of academic theories—particularly postmodernisms. You write, "At its best, theory should help us unmask the barbarous practices associated with some traditions of eloquent expression. But like a good sermon or a well-tailored suit, theory shouldn't show its seams." You write in Between God and Gangsta Rap, *"With some adjustments, I think theory may help to explain black culture." What role do you see theory playing in race issues? And would you describe the "seamless" theory?*

There are several roles for theory in black culture. First, theory should help us clarify the relationship between theory and practice. All practices are in some way theorized, and many theories are practiced at a certain level, even if it's not always apparent. The first function of theory in the hands of seasoned critics is to help us see that practices are shot through with intellectual and theoretical elements that are sometimes obfuscated or concealed. Theory is sometimes obfuscated because attention is paid by the advocates of one practice or another to how such practices are rooted in experience, underplaying the role of critical scrutiny in shaping and understanding the practice. Theory is sometimes concealed for no other reason than some advocates of a given practice shun the stigma of abstraction and irrelevance that a priority on theory has sometimes brought. Second, theory helps critics make the point that black culture is much more difficult, much more complex and densely layered, and much more combative, even within its own boundaries, than has sometimes been acknowledged. Theory is needed to name the various elements that constitute such a difficult, dense, and combative culture.

For instance, theory helps a critic like Henry Louis Gates talk about how signifying practices are glimpsed in rhetorical devices that have been deployed in black culture, ranging from blues music to literary expressions. But theory might also help us imagine the relations and discontinuities between the signifying practices of agrarian and urban blues, and those of hip-hop culture.

Theory, then, can help us identify cognates and contradictions in black cultural expression, even as it helps us isolate structures and registers of articulation that evoke the broad reinterpretation of received ideas about black life. Theory in the hands of a cutting-edge critic can help us pay attention to historically and socially neglected elements of black culture, and to how ordinary views of black life are already theory laden. We never begin in a pretheoretical density in the interpretation of black culture. We are already theorizing, even if we do not have the official language, the academic prose, to express that theory. Everyday people who interpret, analyze, and reflect on black culture are already working with a theoretical base, no matter how inchoate, poorly conceived, or unclearly stated. Theory simply forces the process of critical scrutiny to become explicit, and at times, systematic. Whenever people make the attempt to understand themselves, especially in relation to their culture, they are engaging, at even the most basic level with the most elementary vocabulary, the larger concerns of theory. Theory simply takes such questions to their most sophisticated expressions and to their logical, if surprising, conclusions.

For me a seamless theory is one that does not always have to display the most egregious forms of jargon-ridden discourse to make the critic's point. The occasion should determine usage. If one is engaging interlocutors with commensurate interests, training, and vocabularies, as I am in this interview, then by all means one must stretch the seams of the discourse to its breaking points, forging new discursive combinations out of the rhetorical shards and linguistic fragments that break along theory's ends—in terms of both its purposes and its limits. But for secular audiences, so to speak—those who do not belong to one's community of discourse, even if they belong to professions with their own rhetoric—and for civilians in the theory wars, one must employ a seamless theory. I think seamless theory permits one to intelligently express complex ideas in language that is easily accessible to a general audience. Of course, I can hear someone asking why can't we just do that in general, even for members of one's own profession? Of course, one should often make the attempt. It is a necessity if one regularly teaches undergraduates. But there are trade-offs: depth for breadth, complexity for comprehensiveness, and clarity for certain kinds of rigor that demand difficult ideas to be parsed in the languages of their theoretical birth. Still, it is good to have to translate one's ideas to a public beyond one's normal pitch—and the pun there is deliberate—and to rearticulate one's theoretical musings.

A seamless theory may at times have minimal jargon, but only when absolutely necessary; even then, one must provide context clues that help bring the message home. Some concepts are simply hard to express. Sometimes, as when translating words or phrases from one language to another (for instance, is there a French word for the hip-hop term "phat," a word that might take a couple of tries in English to clarify its meaning to those outside of the linguistic limits of rap culture?), one must keep the word in the original language but provide enough surrounding verbiage to clarify its meaning. The beauty and advantage of a seamless theory is that we cannot rely exclusively on the old habits of thought that jargon signifies, forcing us to break new ground by saying what we say in ways that a geologist may understand, as well as a literary theorist who has training in the field. However one speaks, whether in the theoretical cadences one learns from one's field, or in a tongue for the noninitiated, one gives up something of importance to either the expert or the layperson. For me, the effort to be as theoretically sophisticated as one can and to be as clear as one can is determined by the audiences to which you speak and the purposes for which your work exists in a given moment. The best use of seamless theory is to show people things they did not know before in ways that they understand.

For many theorists, notions of disruption become critical in the critique of traditional power structures. You write of black public intellectuals that they are "leaders of a particular kind. We stir up trouble in broad daylight so that the pieties by which we live and the principles for which we die, both as a people and a nation, are subject to critical conversation." However, in many of your discussions of black political figures and movements you are also critical of how disruption gets used. For instance, you juxtapose the militant disruptiveness of Malcolm X and the assimilative nondisruptiveness of Colin Powell. Would you speak to the idea of disruption in the role of racial matters?

Disruption is a primary prerogative of those of us, especially cultural critics and black intellectuals, who are paid pests. We are not only trying to point to the emperor who has no clothes, but we are also trying, through theory and rhetoric, to disrobe well-dressed imperialisms. I think our function, in part, is to intervene in conversations in disturbing ways, a disturbance that forces people to reflect on why they ask the questions and make the analyses they do. Disruption as I mean it is not simply chaotic interruption for its own sake; it is not intellectual anarchy that has no substantive effect. Disruption has a political goal: to force us to evaluate beliefs and social practices through a new lens, or to see these beliefs and practices differently through the same lens. For instance, race may be the lens through which many of us view reality, but if the folk who read or hear us begin to see race differently because of the questions we raise, we have exercised a crucial function of the paid pest, or, as it were, the critical disrupter. We don't always have to destroy the lens through which our readers view the world, a point eruditely and exhaustively made by Martin Jay in *Downcast Eyes*, his encyclopedic 1993 tome that provided an analytic genealogy and defense of ocularcentrism.

At other times, we must shatter both the lens and the very conception of knowledge through a visual, or ocularcentric metaphor, a project, for instance, that Richard Rorty has been eagerly pursuing since he published *Philosophy and the Mirror of Nature* in 1979. Rorty's work has in part attempted to historicize the regulative metaphors that ground epistemological claims within philosophical discourse, including what Dewey termed the "spectator theory of knowledge." In short, we must provide a moral psychology of the linguistic choices of interlocutors in the debate over what constitutes authentic and appropriate knowledge. The disruption of business as usual within the epistemic order can have a profound impact on racial claims: what can be said, by whom, under what conditions, and with what authority. Thus other metaphors within racial epistemologies may be placed in the foreground, so that, taking a cue form feminist theory, we can speak of hearing, for instance, or listening, as crucial means to knowing the world. What we have to do is create a string of metaphors that give us a different interventional possibility into the terrain of knowledge, politics, and culture. Such disruption is crucial to expanding our understanding of the fully embodied—or, better yet, full-bodied—ways of knowing the world that privilege experience, struggle, and religious belief as the structuring processes, perhaps even the catalytic agents, of epistemic quests in historically constituted black communities. In such communities, questions of morality often fused with epistemic interests: one's understanding of the world, especially its necessary composition, was in large part driven by what was good and just to know.

Questions of racial justice, then, were never completely divorced from questions of how and why we know the world we do. That is a critical disruption of Kantian or Cartesian epistemological claims that rest on the belief in transcendental grounds, mediated, as Rorty argues, through the metaphor of a mirror or glassy essence. In black religious cosmologies, for instance, epistemic warrants are grounded in the social and moral telos of knowledge: what will we do with what we know, and how do we know it is true, apart from its rooting in the social meanings we inherit, and the kind of world in which they make sense? Thus pragmatic interests, which ground knowledge and truth claims in explicit evocations of community, open up vistas of interpreting the world that are different in important ways from the interpretations generated in many white mainstreams. I am not arguing on behalf of a racial ontology or skin epistemology that rests on an essentialist conception of identity, truth, and knowledge. Rather, I'm referring to historically constructed and culturally mediated ways of knowing the world that generate their own discursive and ethical formations. There is little question that the very existence of such an alternative to business as usual disrupts the epistemologies and moral psychologies of hegemonic culture.

Intellectually speaking, disruption is not only important for resisting the paradigms, metaphors, and theories of the dominant culture, but it applies as well to thinking critically in-house, so to speak, and freeing ourselves from restrictive orthodoxies that police innovative thought within black culture. In many ways, disruption is quite unsettling because we can never be finally settled in a position from which we would defend certain visions, or attack certain versions, of black identity for the rest of our intellectual lives. Disruption concerns the perennial possibility of migration and mobility in black culture and identity, which is why the responsibility for its enactment can never rest in the hands of one set of intellectuals, whose definitions and defenses of black culture are hegemonic. It has to be constantly changing hands. It's not that one can't have a career in disruption, in its most edifying sense, or in interrogating the meanings, significations, and practices of race. It simply means that there must always be other voices that disrupt our paradigms and practices of disruption.

Interview by Sidney Dobrin
Durham, North Carolina, 1997

5

Trump Cards

Racial Paradigms, Postcolonial Theory, and Feminist Thought

There's a Xeroxed poster on a colleague's door in my department of a photograph of an old wooden sign that reads, "We Serve Whites Only. No Spanish or Mexicans." The sign was posted in 1949 to enforce the Jim Crow laws in San Antonio. On the copy, someone has written, "History is not just black and white." Though you make an effort to discuss races—particularly when you discuss issues of violence in terms of Latino/as, Koreans, Asians, and so on—your work on race deals mostly (as the preponderance of work on race does) with issues of black and white. Would you discuss the black and white depictions of race in America and speak to the (fewer than black) "other" race intellectuals?

If we are asking what it means if the narrative frame of race is black and white, when there are other racial realties that are ignored in such a formulation, there can be little argument. It is undeniably a specific, even narrow in some senses, understanding of race, but a very real one for diasporic Africans in America. The black-white disjunction was one that curtailed our economic and social mobility, contained the greatest potential to destroy our material interests, and constructed the symbiotic relationship of dominant and minority in which we've had to survive. This is why the work of theorists like James Scott, who writes about infrapolitics, which have to do with the hidden dimensions of political negotiation, and about everyday forms of resistance among the relatively powerless, is important to blacks. It helps us theorize the relationship of black to white and how such negotiations of station play out in our culture. Ralph Ellison, among many others, had already thought about how black folk have had to exist in relationship to dominant white culture. But Ellison flips the script and argues that we can't even imagine America without black Americans, without the contours and contexts of blackness traced through the anatomy of American identity, although white Americans have not always taken that seriously.

Scott's work is critical in figuring how to situate oneself as a degraded subject in relationship to the overarching objectification of one's existence in hegemonic cultures, which in the case of blacks includes much of the white mainstream. Much of the reflexive, defensive traits of black culture—and the survival techniques marshaled in the face of oppression—has developed in response to the need of blacks to preserve their identities vis-à-vis this dominant other. Scott's views of infrapolitics and everyday forms of resistance are quite imaginatively applied to black life in the work of historian Robin D.G. Kelley. In his book *Race Rebels,* Kelley writes about black folk riding the bus in Jim Crow Birmingham, Alabama, and how, even though they were not explicitly involved in racial politics, they were actively engaged in renegotiating the terms of segregated public space by transgressive, resistive behavior—including throwing their cursing voices beyond the segregated limits their bodies were prohibited from invading. Thus these folk were enacting the hidden dimensions of political resistance and refusing the racial meanings ascribed to them through manipulating the everyday cultural symbols of segregation that cluttered the racial landscape.

All of this suggests that perceiving and mastering the ethics and politics of the black-white divide has been a crucial plank in the agenda of black survival in America. It would not be overstating the case to say that our very existence depended on how well black folk knew the machinations and moralities of whiteness. As Fannie Lou Hamer said, the mistake that white folk made is that they put black people behind them and not in front of them. If whites had put black people in front of them, they could have surveyed and controlled their cultures. Instead, in their subjected, inferior social position, black folk looked up from their degraded status at the internal contradictions and fierce disruptions of white culture to learn the secrets and strategies of whiteness. They learned to survive within the politics of domination—and here Scott and Kelley are crucial—and to work the situation to their advantage, or, in the vernacular of black opportunism, to "get over" on the dominant white society. From the perspective of many blacks, the black-white bifurcation is an objective condition of domination that had to be met by the political negotiations, social manipulations, and cultural ingenuities of the minority. A key to deconstructing blackness in America consists in comprehending the epistemology of the epidermis and the ontology of security: *knowing* whiteness in its variegated and complex manifestations as the predicate for *being* safe, as much as possible, by reducing the likelihood of being ambushed by the unexpected meanings of whiteness.

One of the real liabilities of seeing race exclusively in black and white terms is that we overlook how race is being constructed around a number of axes that go beyond the black-white divide. Even certain debates about black-white relations are also shaped by factors other than race. For instance, black-Jewish conflicts are geographical at a certain level. Such conflicts are much more likely to occur in New York, which includes a significant population of Jews and blacks, than in Nebraska, where either population is much lower. In California, the black-white divide is challenged by the black-brown divide or the black-Korean divide—not only in terms of black-Korean and black-Latino conflicts, but also in terms of Latinos who are white and those who are black or nonwhite. These facts alone should force us to rethink how we understand the black-white divide. It does not mean that the divide is not important or that it has not been crucial, even as an analogy or inspiration for other minorities who have fought for inclusion in the larger circle of American identity and privilege. What it does suggest is that the black-white divide in its narrowest forms may lead dominant and black America to comprehend the experience of other racial minorities by imposing on them a substitute black status, instead of interrogating the particularities of their identities, movements, and ideologies.

In the Harper's *interview that I mentioned earlier, Klor De Alva claims that "with the exception of black-white relations, the racial perspective is not the critical one for most folks. The cultural perspective was, at one time, very sharply drawn, including the religious line between Catholics and Protestants, Jews and Protestants, Jews and Catholics, Jews and Christians. But in the course of the twentieth century, we have seen in the United States a phenomenon that we do not see any place else in the world—the capacity to blur the differences between these cultural groups, to construct them in such a way that they became insignificant and to fuse them into a new group called whites, which didn't exist before." If this is true, why has "difference" in America been reduced, at least publicly, to matters of color?*

Difference has been reduced to matters of color, but it's not a matter of mere color. For instance, as I argue in my book *Race Rules*, color alludes to the social processes of what I term pigmentification and pigmentosis. Pigmentification suggests that one gets adopted within the dominant order of the pigmentocracy, the regime of color that's associated with white skin. But pigmentosis suggests that one is excluded from the dominant white regime of color. In this sense, color is never self-referential but always indexes racial meanings that reveal cultural assumptions and biases that are the basis for the distribution of political and economic resources. Jorge is right that whiteness became a blurred distinction in America. Whiteness became a self-sufficient, or all-sufficient, racial category that wiped out ethnic distinctions: German, Polish, Irish, Italian, Lithuanian, Serbian, and in some cases, Jewish. Still, powerful subcultures organized around ethnic practices and identities have thrived, so I disagree with Jorge's analysis. But the process of racialization in America is undeniably predicated on pigmentocracy, so that goods like education, employment, and even health care are often dispersed according to one's own relationship to an ideal of color.

Color never has simply referred to skin tone. It has always been about the intellectual, ideological, and political dimensions of American identity and whether we would embrace Europe—which we have—and spurn Africa, a well-established fact of our culture. If we are racial literalists about color, we overlook, even underplay, how a complex range of conflicting social meanings have been mobilized and mediated through the sociology of skin and the politics of pigment. Skin and pigment became the visible index of a regime of political favor and a hierarchy of social privilege and status that are associated with a specific conception of racial species—a racial ontology—where blackness is stigmatized as an entirely different order of being. What I think Jorge is overlooking here is what Edward Shils, who was not a radical intellectual by any stretch of the imagination, called *pseudospeciation*—a concept deployed in hegemonic intellectual circles to ontologically segregate black people from the dominant, desirable qualities of human identity. The European ethnic groups that *came* to America—following John Ogbu's distinction between immigrants and involuntary minorities, a distinction that might save us a great deal of the facile, condescending parallelism between blacks and white immigrants to which conservative intellectuals appeal—did not get pseudospeciated. They did not get written out of the dominant narrative of humanity that included all white ethnics—even if there was a hierarchy of visibility, influence, and privilege among them—whereas with black people there was an attempt to rule them out of the *human* race, to expel them from the species.

In the preface to Making Malcolm, *you discuss an uncomfortable incident that occurred in one of your classes when tension between students about racial divisions erupted. Where does race belong in the classroom?*

Everywhere and nowhere. Race is an inevitable feature of the classroom; it is the ineluctable product of the racialization of American society. To expect that the classroom will somehow be exempt from the racialized meanings that circulate, even explode, in our culture is to have a pedagogical perspective that is not only naive and insular but in some cases destructive. Race should have the same place in the classroom that it has in society, if not with the same moral intents or philosophical goals. In fact, the classroom is the place where we should examine the intents, affects, goals, ideals, norms, privileges, practices, and so on, of race. I think about race in the same sense that Foucault thinks about power: it's not simply about structures of domination or hierarchies of privilege, although it obviously includes all of these. For Foucault, power breaks out everywhere, even between people who are themselves oppressed or marginalized. The philosophy of race, at the very least, fuses the traditional, perhaps Weberian, and Foucauldian approaches to power. There certainly is a hierarchy of race where power is associated with being white and *not black*, white and *not brown*, white and *not red*. These are objective conditions of race that we would do well to heed.

On the other hand, race breaks out in all kinds of interesting and unfastidious ways. It breaks out in uncomfortable and disruptive ways. Race can always surprise us. Like a camel on the loose, race has the capacity to do greater injury when we attempt to coop it up as opposed to when we let it run free. A classroom is an artificial cage for the animal of race, and race breaks out everywhere. That is powerful and productive because it wounds our most cherished expectations of what I have termed "market multiculturalism." In African American studies classes like mine at Brown University, race breaks out in the most uncomfortable but, I think, highly instructive ways. In the conflict between me (and a good deal of my class) and a group of black male students who thought they knew Malcolm and had earned the privilege to define Malcolm for the rest of us and, therefore, cage him up, not only did race break out, but I think Malcolm did too, in all sorts of interesting philosophical and political ways. It reminded me of a statement Malcolm made in his autobiography to the effect that "they won't let me turn the corner," referring to the loyalists and true believers who felt uncomfortable with Malcolm's embrace of whites and his growing tolerance for integration-minded black leadership. They had him hemmed in or, to switch the metaphor to suit my camel example, they had him cooped up.

Race should be at the core of our classrooms, just as it should be at the center of our conversations in every discipline. It does not simply belong in a class on ethnic studies or African American culture. Race belongs in a class on Aristotelian conceptions of inequality, for example, or in a course on Neoplatonic philosophy. It belongs in a discussion of every imaginable subject matter, especially in this country, because race is the veritable suppressed premise of the syllogism of American democracy. It is at the very heart of the American project of national self-discovery. We would be well served to be more explicit about race and therefore take it into account rather than allow it to inform our debates from a distance or by inference. By informing our debates from a distance or by inference, we do not get a chance to theorize race, to fully explore it, and to demythologize racist powers that harm us precisely because they are excluded from our explicit articulations and investigations.

I'd like to pick up on your metaphor of the wild animal in the classroom and ask, Have we made race safe? Have universities done to race what may have been done to some feminisms by saying that we can talk about the discourses in universities so long as this is what we discuss and this isn't? Have multicultural pedagogies taken the thorns out of race matters?

Yes, there is no question about it. But that is the risk we run for the kind of progress we seem to want. The kind of progress we want is that we would rather people talk about race in denuded contexts that deprive race of its real vigor, of its real fierceness, of its rhetorical ferocity, than have fights in the streets. We would rather have rhetoric and discourse than the Los Angeles riots or, as some see it, the rebellion of 1992. We would rather have what you term the safeness of race than situations in which black, white, or other people lose their lives contesting terrain that has become deeply racialized but not theorized as such around race. Yes, there are trade-offs. But with the kind of conscientious objection to the war of multiculturalism that is fought with rubber bullets rather than real ones (excuse this violent metaphor) we certainly want to introduce sharper focus on where the blood is really being spilled on the outside of these debates, in the world of ghetto streets and Korean grocery stores. There is surely an advantage to making safe with race in the classroom, even if one of its apparently unavoidable consequences is the de-fanging of race.

In light of that reality we must work harder to articulate the real divisions that race brings, the real conflicts that it introduces. And they have to be touched on in our debates in ways that make us uncomfortable with our ability to so smoothly dismiss the differences that race introduces without paying the consequences. Despite the real challenges that present themselves, we do not often pay the most horrible consequences of race in our classrooms, in our faculty meetings, in the academy in general. That is why when we have racial representation by proxy, that is one thing. But when flesh-and-blood black folk show up, when real Latinos show up, and they are not as nice and as observant of the traditions of racial etiquette brokered by the white liberal mainstream, real tension is created. I do not think we should gainsay those kinds of tensions. Those kinds of tensions are real, and they are politically instructive about the limits to which we are able to go in dealing with racial discourse—and, more important, racial transformation. So, yes, we have made race safe, but with all of its limitations and frustrations, I'd rather have even that kind of racial discourse and practice against which we must fight—or that we must transform into a discourse of multiculturalism that is more radical, more powerful, more disruptive—than the alternative: the sometimes violent way racial difference and conflict are handled in the world outside the academy.

How do public intellectuals play into that then?

To put it simply, but hopefully not simplistically, we either play the helpful or problematic role. We can play an unintentionally problematic role if we don't challenge the thinking that gives people a false sense of security, even superiority, as they, "Well, I've listened to Michael Eric Dyson or Cornel West or bell hooks, and I feel that I've gotten my multicultural booster, the multicultural vaccination that protects me against any strain of racism." We've got to be careful, as much as these things are in our control, that our work doesn't get used in a way to make people who engage it feel immune to racist ideology. As Martin Luther King Jr. concluded late in his career, such folk can sometimes be more problematic than those who do not give a damn about being vaccinated against racism (to extend the metaphor) who resist it, and who in their brutal honesty present a greater opportunity for true racial conversation, and sometimes even conversion to enlightenment, than those who feel that they have nothing to learn. There are many ways, seen and unseen, that black intellectuals and our work can be used against our will in a negative fashion. But we can do the best we can to disrupt such usage, such distortions. For instance, as public intellectuals we can write op-eds for newspapers, or we can go on radio or television and disagree with the common market version of multiculturalism or diversity discourse. We can insist in such forums that racial progress, and the rhetoric and discourse that support it, is an enterprise that is more complex, much deeper, and much more profound than simply imbibing the words of visible black intellectuals.

What do you do then to keep race from being safe? What kinds of work—both public and academic—do you advocate?

One of the things I do outside the academy is mount the pulpits of churches across the nation and preach. I stay in contact with people whose anger is much less muted and rawer than in the academy. Or I go to prisons. When I visit prison—I have a brother, Everett, who is serving life in prison for second-degree murder and who's converted from Christianity to a Muslim body of believers known as the Moorish Science Temple of America—we talk about race. Everett gives me a hell of an interesting perspective on contemporary affairs of race and culture. Both of us came out of the ghetto of Detroit and are now living what is becoming far too frequently a trope in black life as we experience the sharp divisions between upward mobility and downward plunge—the proverbial difference of the professor and the prisoner. That reality of feeling the sharp edges of his own critique of people like me, even me specifically, delivers me from an anesthetized, romanticized sphere where I'm exempt from the very passions that I claim I want to represent in my work. Or as he tells me, sometimes jokingly, he's helping to keep me "grounded and woke."

Also, I try to get involved with local and national politics, civil rights groups and grassroots movements, and socially active black churches. I also attempt as much as possible to engage everyday black folk struggling on the streets. I understand and feel what drives them. It reminds me of where I was as a poor black kid in Detroit, a teen father who was hustling, who was thought of as a pathologized, nihilistic youth. I try to bring that disruptive, dangerous memory, deeply inscribed in my mind, body, and soul, into the classroom through my style of teaching and lecturing—very animated, emotionally present, deeply in tune with the currents of social misery—and by means of some of the subjects that I try to confront.

There is an interesting division that gets played out in discussions of race and discussions of postcolonial theories. Jenny Sharpe, in "Is the United States Postcolonial? Transnationalism, Immigration, and Race," argues that "when used as a descriptive term for the United States, postcolonial does not name its past as a white settler colony or its emergence as a neocolonial power; rather, it designates the presence of racial minorities and Third World immigrants." She goes on to argue that "an understanding of 'the postcolonial condition' as racial exclusion offers an explanation for the past history of 'internal colonies' but not the present status of the United States as a neocolonial power." With the noted exception of bell hooks, who looks at African American writers, Gloria Anzaldaú, who works with Latina/Chicana literature and cultural experience, and a few scholars of indigenous North American populations, there are very few who address the fact that much of the scholarly work regarding issues particular to the United States are in fact issues of postcolonialism. At the same time, the kinds of academic attention that U.S. scholars give to postcolonial theory is being given to the writers and the cultures of, for instance, India, Sri Lanka, Pakistan, and so on, not to issues of the United States. What significance, if any, do you see in the academy's refusal to validate the postcolonial nature of both the writers and the writing that has been and continues to be produced in the United States by peoples of color?

This is a problem of avoidance—of linguistic and rhetorical and ideological avoidance—of not acknowledging the degree to which this society's racist policies and practices are part of a deeper project of colonial and imperial expansion that happened on the backs of black peoples, red peoples, and other native, indigenous, first-nation peoples. But as scholars of color interrogate colonialism's practices, this discourse is usually put into a narrowly racialized framework that pays attention to black-white differences, without linking such differences to an international context of colonialism, something that was routinely done by Du Bois, Robeson, Ella Baker, Malcolm X, and Martin Luther King Jr. When the colonial context is evoked in regard to such scholarly work, it's usually only in connection to providing a metaphor for the presence of minorities in this country, as opposed to colonialism being viewed as a prism through which we interrogate American political practices. Partly what we're dealing with here is the studious avoidance, in America's collective self-identity and self-understanding, of viewing itself as a colonial practitioner and an imperial power. What that signifies is the ability of America to absorb and redistribute dissent, and to manipulate the banner under which that dissent would fly in ways that are less harmful to the nation's image. So colonial practices are transmuted into the most simplistic of racial terms without sufficient attention paid to the interconnections between domestic and international forms of American dominance. For America to conceive of itself as a colonial power—not simply *vis-à-vis* racial minorities, but as the expansion of its imperialist presence and practice throughout the world—has become so contradictory to its self-identity that people, including many scholars, are discouraged from even thinking or talking about it in those terms.

It's important to note along these lines how, during the '60s and '70s, scholars like Bob Blauner at Berkeley, who generated internal colony theories of racial oppression—which articulated the relationship between blacks and whites, especially relationships of caste, class, and social hierarchy, through colonial discourse—were charged with being narrow and essentialist in their views of how race operates in this country. In short, the closest that we got to any sense of America as a neocolonial power was theorizing the ghetto as an internal colonized space, drawing on the work of Fanon and other Third World theorists to explain our indigenous practices. For the most part, we lacked an indigenous body of social theory about American colonialism within the America academy for the reasons I've cited above.

To many liberal critics of the past, black and white alike, speaking about America as a colonial empire meant diverting attention from the domestic projects of civil rights, which have depended on the ethical largesse and noblesse oblige of white liberals. This is why even Martin Luther King Jr., when he began to talk about America as a colonial power in relation to Vietnam, was criticized not simply by white conservatives, but by black so-called progressives and liberals who were upset that he was pilfering from the resources of the domestic fight for the civil rights movement, which was being heavily funded by Lyndon Johnson's Great Society. But King's worldview was of a piece, and he couldn't separate questions of international aggression, neocolonial expansion, and imperialist domination from such features on the domestic front. The genius of Martin Luther King Jr. and Malcolm X is that they saw the international perspective and linked black freedom struggles to neocolonial expansion and imperialist discourse in the '60s. They courageously dissented from segregating their moral and political rhetoric within the narrow boundaries of the nation-state and figured the global consequences of racial domination. Ironically enough, our nation's liberal political forces have ingeniously provided ready access to a discourse of racial rebellion in purely domestic terms as a way of purchasing scholars of colors' silence about America's international neocolonial romps and imperialist expansion. In other words, the shifting of resources within domestic space—especially from whites to blacks, particularly intellectual and political elites—around the issue of racial justice, through the rhetoric of civil rights, has at times obscured the international character of American oppression, and the degree to which black oppression was an extension of America's project of global supremacy.

The scholars who have insisted on the link between domestic and global oppression have for the most part existed on the periphery of mainstream black intellectual life, especially in grassroots organizations and among nationalist networks in the black academy. These are intellectuals who address conspiracy theories of racial dominance—seeing widespread, coordinated, systemic attempts by whites and their institutions to oppress blacks—while insisting on the expansionist nature of the American colonial project. So most high-falutin' black public intellectuals really don't want to be associated with black scholars on the margins who are willing to indict America for its imperialist impulses and its neocolonial behavior. America, in effect, splits the "good" and "bad" black scholars by organizing, even rearranging, the topography of academic space within the United States—especially through reward and punishment, accolade and stigma, valorization and demonization—to discourage recognition of the nation's neocolonial practice outside its borders. A few bones for the elite translate into lost opportunities to help the masses of blacks. The crushing paradox is that we, as ostensibly free and decolonized intellectuals, exist in an academic and intellectual space colonized by dominant interests while denying or underplaying the existence of a link between neocolonialism and the domestic project of black freedom. I think that the explosion of the postcolonial theory of Edward Said, Homi Bhabha, Gayatri Spivak, and numerous other scholars, along with the resurgence of interest in Fanon, may yet force black intellectuals to adopt a rigorously international perspective on racial oppression, and hence, force America to come to grips with the fact that its oppressive practices here are linked to oppressive ventures abroad. To their credit, marginalized black intellectuals have invited us to see this point for quite a while.

You write in "Benediction: Letter to My Wife Marcia" that "many black men and women believe that placing questions of gender at the heart of black culture is an act of racial betrayal, a destructive diversion of attention away from race as the defining issue of black life." You continue, "I don't think race is the complete story. There's too much evidence that being gay, or lesbian, or female, or working poor makes a big difference in shaping the role race plays in black people's lives." In Reflecting Black *you write that "sex, race, and class have also caused considerable conflicts and tensions between groups who compete for limited forms of cultural legitimacy, visibility, and support." And you write that you want to "help us to begin the process of open, honest communication about the differences within our race." I wonder about the critique that when race, class, gender, and culture get discussed in the same breath, that focus is denied to individual issues. You argue that race can't be looked at as displaced from class, gender, or culture—that it doesn't exist in a vacuum. Is this the same for gender? How would you respond to feminist theorists or class theorists who don't want gender or class swallowed up in discussions of race?*

There are two things going on here simultaneously to which we have to pay strict attention. First, if we say that gender and race and class have their own intellectual integrity, that they have their own intellectual space from which they should be theorized, then I say "amen." As Michael Omi and Howard Winant argue, these are irreducible categories, not only for social theorizing but, I would argue, also for personal identity and for collective, communal mobilization. There's no question about that. But if one argues that these elements are somehow divisible from each other, that questions of gender don't have any relationship to class or to sexuality and so on, I'd say that that is not the way it happens. People experience personal identity and social reality in simultaneous, not successive, fashion. We have to say that questions of gender are implicated in questions of class and race, and vice versa, and all around. We should definitely have specificity of analysis. The particularity with which these problems, or categories of analysis or modes of identity, manifest themselves has to be recognized and taken seriously. I would be the first to suggest that we can't subsume one of these under the other. For instance, the subsumption of race under class is careless and wrongheaded. We saw this in the Communist Party in the '30s and '40s in this country, and more recently in certain orthodox Marxist traditions where theorists seek to absorb racial conflict into class conflict and economic inequality. Race, class, gender, sexual orientation, and the like have their own intellectual integrity, scholarly vitality, and ideological portfolio, so to speak, that encourages us to track their political and cultural significance with attention to the kinds of effects and traces they leave in the world.

On the other hand, I think that these categories bleed into one another in ways to which we don't always pay attention. I don't think we can divide them in as neat a way, practically speaking, as we can do intellectually or theoretically. For instance, what do we do with a person who happens to be gay and poor and black, or a woman who's lesbian and poor and black and a single mother? And I'm not aiming here for the additive view of identity against which feminists such as Diana Fuss and Elizabeth Spelman warn us. Still, it helps to think of the complex convergence of forces of identity and social reality in one person's body. They don't have the luxury of a pretheoretical interrogation of their identity so that they can assign the most merit based on what part of their identity has more consequence. There's a whole range of identities that are competing for expression, that are being constituted, in this one body. What I have to say to fellow feminist theorists who would say, "I don't want gender to be subsumed by race," is fine, but I want gender to be thought of in relationship to race. Otherwise, we might end up with white feminists who ignore or downplay the effect of race in gender matters, so that when they interrogate the O.J. Simpson case, for example, they see Nicole Simpon's body as, generically speaking, a woman's body, and not a *white* woman's body. That means that some white feminists may be in peril of overlooking how the bodies of black women, and other minority females, have been unequally valued in our culture.

Thus we've got to consider black feminists who see race and gender operating simultaneously. Such critics may say to many black men, "Listen, you're not paying attention to the ways that black women's bodies have occupied a segregated rhetorical space within African American popular and intellectual culture." They may want to say to many white women, even feminists, "You don't understand the ways that race has privileged white women's bodies over black women's bodies, and how the discursive terrain that white feminism operates on has all but excluded the geography of black identity for African American women." I think that there's a way of paying attention to ideological specificity and political particularity while understanding, existentially and phenomenologically, that the bleeding of these multiple identities into each other has to be acknowledged as well.

You make clear your conviction that conversations on race frequently silence the voices of black women. You write, "I agree with critics who argue that the rhetoric of black male suffering is often cobbled together from a distortion of black female troubles. Thus, the very language of black male crisis erases black women's faces and bodies from the canvas of social suffering. It is simply not true that black men's hurts are more important than the social horrors black women face." Would you talk about the apparent rift between black women and black men in contemporary discussions of race and how we might productively proceed as academics concerned with both race and gender?

I think the rift between black men and women is the long elaboration of a complex host of factors that have dogged black life from the beginning of our pilgrimage on American soil. The male-female rift reflects the gendering of differential treatment in black life within the political economy of slavery, which has had a particularly lethal effect on the subsequent history and development of black communities. It manifests itself in material and psychological fashion, especially as the economic conditions and self-understandings of black men and women unfold in the long-lasting shadow of slavery's influence. The black male-female rift is, in some measure, a remaking of the divide-and-conquer strategy that was ingeniously deployed on the plantation to undermine any sense of consensus or solidarity that might have provided black people a way to effectively, collectively resist white supremacy. We gloss over this too easily, too effortlessly in our postmodernist black cultural space where tropes of unity and solidarity are highly questioned, and often for good reasons. The rhetoric of racial unity has often been mobilized to silence the voices and erase the visions that challenge hegemonic positions within black culture. That's all for the good. But one of the negative moral and political consequences of the failure to build consensus or to assert provisional solidarity is the inability of black men and women to embrace each other across the chasm of genders. That is in part an outgrowth of political machinations to destroy any sense of common struggle among black people. As a result, black men and women are often in the same bed but at each other's throats.

But it must be admitted that a large part of the reason that black men and women are in gender turmoil is due to black men uncritically incorporating a masculinist psychology as a fundamental structure of our consciousness in combating white racism. As a result, the most powerful rhetorical device that black men have deployed against white supremacy is to see it as an attack on our manhood. By definition, the masculinist chokehold on black male ideology strangles a consideration of the role of racism and sexism in undermining the lives of black women. Still worse, many black men think that black women possess an exemption, perhaps immunity, to the most vicious aspects of white supremacy. As the story goes—told time and again among many black men, and a fair number of black women—black women have it better in white America than black men because they are not as threatening as black men. I think there's a way of stating that in a patriarchal culture in which the codes of masculinity operate to legitimate certain forms of power, black men pose a particular kind of threat, given that we are the *men* who can displace white patriarchs. On such a view, we are undoubtedly their most likely competition.

But the glib, effortless exercise of both white and male power in black women's lives is often undervalued through a black male prism, colored as it is by patriarchal values and male supremacist tendencies. As a result, black masculine suffering is elevated over black women's suffering in a hierarchy of black oppression, driven in part by a male resentment of perceived black female immunity to white supremacy, and the belief that women are favored over men by the white males who dominate corporate, business, governmental, and educational life. These elements constitute the collective imaginary of black masculine identities as seen through the prism of patriarchy and male supremacy at the end of the twentieth century. That's why I understand black feminist objections to the Million Man March. It looked to many feminists that black men were claiming in the march to feed their women and families the new meal of a reconstructed black male identity, when in truth they were warming up and serving the same old patriarchal leftovers from the male supremacist banquet.

Black intellectuals and academics can help remedy the situation. First, we can continue to interrogate how masculinity, like race, is a social construction. We can articulate the belief, and insist on its wide publication in black culture, that there's no such thing as a necessarily black masculine experience that has to be felt or interpreted in a certain way. The spread of such a belief, for example, might help keep young black men from killing each other through the appeal to discourses of authenticity wed to violence and self-destruction. We can begin to interrogate masculine identity as a gender. There are some truths in relation to race and gender that we've got to confront, summed up in what might pass for cultural common sense in the Gramscian definition: white people don't have a race, and men don't have a gender. Now that we've "discovered" that men have a gender, we must investigate the complex gender meanings of black masculinity.

To a significant degree, the obsession with black masculinity in our culture can be usefully exploited to probe the hidden, obscured, and avoided meanings of gender in black life. Black intellectuals and academics can help us understand the social production of gender and how its cultural constructions shape varying perceptions of remedies to racial suffering and oppression. Black intellectuals and academics might also continue to help sketch a cartography of masculinity and female identity that maps the effects of patriarchy, male supremacy, and feminist resistance, even if it's not called that, in the geography of black freedom struggles. We must clarify and reproduce enabling conceptions of gender that aid black folk in thinking about the men and women in our lives and in our communities. Finally, black male intellectuals in particular must not leave it to feminist critics to theorize the negative impact of stereotypical, rigid, and essentialist gender beliefs in black communities. Male critics and academics have to think much more self-critically about the function of gender in American society and about the relationships between gender, race, class, and sexual orientation. Perhaps if we begin to deconstruct and demythologize patriarchal conceptions of gender and masculine identity, we might help our communities move toward understanding and embracing the widest possible view of black identity.

As a public intellectual, you invite criticism and seem to favor keeping your work and the work of other public intellectuals meaningful and effective through criticisms. In Race Rules *you write, "We all slip. And our critics should be there to catch us." Are there any criticisms of your work that you'd like to address?*

There have been insightful criticisms of my work. For instance, some critics and intellectuals were quite interested in my first book, *Reflecting Black*. This book of cultural criticism was one of the first among black scholars to treat its subject matter, particularly popular culture, with theoretical acuity and political engagement, at least in the same text. To be sure, there's a risk involved in trying to join, perhaps even fuse, genres, a point not lost on some reviewers, especially newspaper critics who were used to nonacademic prose or resisted my engagements with poststructuralist theory, and the complicated syntax of expression and grammar of ideas that are often its adjunct, as I addressed modernist and postmodernist black cultural articulations. I wanted to take that risk because I didn't then, and still don't, want to have a limited audience. I want to speak to the academy in very powerful, intelligent, compelling, and interesting ways, but I don't want to be limited to the academy. I know scholars and intellectuals who limit themselves to the academy, and the academy's importance is undoubtedly exaggerated in their lives. As a Christian who was taught to be suspicious of any form of idolatry, I don't want to make a fetish of intellectual inquiry or academic engagement. Although I have great respect, even admiration, for the academy, and for intellectual inquiry, as I hope is apparent in how I think and how I say what I say, I don't want to erect a shrine to the life of the mind and the academy and worship there, as I think is the case with many intellectuals and academics.

Having said that, I want to make the life of the mind sexy for young people in the academy and beyond its reach. I want to have a mode of criticism that allows me to be mobile, to move from the academy to the streets to the world. Hence I want a language that is rigorous, precise, and analytically keen in engaging intellectual and academic interests. And I want to be able to speak to the streets and the world in language that is clear—with all the problematic implications of clarity kept clearly in mind. Let me phrase what I am attempting differently. On the one hand, I defend, perhaps even practice, what might be viewed as unnecessarily difficult, twisted, contorted, jargon-bloated theoretical work that has as its premise the following dictum: anything worth knowing is worth knowing in the very difficult and complicated ways that it comes to us, already shaped by specific intellectual and ideological interests, all of which must be refashioned in the crucible of our own biases, priorities, and interests. On the other hand, I think it is valuable political work to, as the black church admonishes, "make it plain." And to do that, one must speak truth to the powerful and the powerless in words they understand, translating complex ideas into simple sentences. Both goals are laudable. So these two desires—to speak the languages of theoretical sophistication and public engagement with their respective limitations and priorities—shape my intellectual portfolio, so to speak, and may help explain what might look like schizophrenia or perhaps conflicted intellectual goals to my critics.

I have enjoyed wide critical acclaim for much of my work, and I have been subject to enlivened, rigorous criticism as well, which, while not always heartening to the author under scrutiny, may nonetheless be informative and helpful. But then there is another species of critique that is almost altogether intentionally destructive. In my case, I see it in the harsh, ad hominem criticism of figures like Adolph Reed and Eric Lott. Reed practices a variety of critique that can only be called gangsterish in its intellectually caustic pretensions to rigorous, robust, in-your-face engagement. It is both vitriolic and vituperative, apparently driven by personal animus even though I've never met him. I think Reed feels resentment toward younger scholars he feels have reaped recognition for their work while he, in his mind, is unjustly overlooked for his scholarship, such as it is. All I can say to Reed is, in the words of the rappers he often despises, "stop hatin'."

It is interesting that Lott presents himself as a progressive white scholar, in tune with the intellectual and social currents of the black culture about which he writes yet feels free as a white scholar to deploy racially loaded terms like *troglodyte* and *caveman* and *middlebrow imbecilism* in regard to my work. I suppose he's trying to buck—and of course, the double entendre is intended with all of its punning possibilities—what he may see as the trend of white scholars who are sympathetic to black life as being perceived as unduly "soft" on black thinkers. But I hardly think such racially harsh—and personally demeaning—discourse is appropriate in the work of a scholar interrogating another scholar's work. I think he's a very smart, sophisticated guy who knows the historic contingencies of racial rhetoric; he knows the traditional, signifying, white racist content of racial rhetoric deployed through the tropes and metaphors of dominant society intellectuals to "analyze" and assault black people. I would have thought he would have been a bit more careful about associating with such a vindictive and vicious tradition. I would have thought that he would have been more cautious in the enterprise of social critique. Both Reed and Lott practice a lefter-than-thou criticism, which comes as no surprise to the various victims of their tirades, taunts, and tantrums. Of course, I'm not suggesting that many of the issues that Reed and Lott take up are not important—such as how one is held politically accountable for one's intellectual work or how black intellectuals must be careful of the perks and diversions of celebrity. I've addressed those issues myself. But one doesn't have to be mean, nasty, and brutish, to paraphrase Thomas Hobbes, to accomplish one's goals.

A huge criticism made of me and other so-called black public intellectuals concerns our attempts to retain academic standing and intellectual integrity while also appealing to a broad public. Perhaps my own mediating position between the academy and the public sphere may never diminish the tension I feel in traversing those terrains and going back and forth from one to the other. I hope I won't lose that tension because I think it informs my work and gives it whatever moral authority and intellectual integrity it may possess. I can only answer my critics through more work that better achieves my goals: to bridge gulfs, swerve between genres, move beyond narrow disciplinary boundaries, and overcome artificial divisions between the academy and the "real" world in articulating social visions and political possibilities that can be morally defended and are culturally useful.

Interview by Sidney Dobrin
Durham, North Carolina, 1997

6

Giving Whiteness a Black Eye

Excavating White Identities, Ideologies, and Institutions

Let me start by just talking a little bit about what other authors have done. Generally, they have tried to describe what they understand whiteness to be or what the content of whiteness is, identified some of the forms that whiteness takes in the multiple locations in which it manifests itself, and attempted either to redefine what whiteness should be or to spell out ways to combat the oppressiveness that is a part of whiteness, thus trying to rescue the productive content of whiteness. Based on that synopsis of the work of the others, why don't we start, if it's okay with you, with what you perceive whiteness to be or what you understand whiteness to mean.

I think when we talk about whiteness in the context of race in America, we have to talk about whiteness as *identity*, whiteness as *ideology*, and whiteness as *institution*. These three elements are complex and impure; they bleed into one another. Still, as categories of analysis they can help us get a handle on the intensely variegated manifestations of whiteness.

In speaking of whiteness as identity, I am referring to the self-understanding, social practices, and group beliefs that articulate whiteness in relationship to American race, especially in this case, to blackness. I think whiteness bears a particularly symbiotic relationship to redness and blackness; in one sense, whiteness is called into existence as a response to the presence of redness and blackness. Only when red and black bodies—from colonial conquest and slavery on to the present—have existed on American terrain has whiteness been constituted as an idea and an identity-based reality. White people's sense of themselves as being white is contingent on a negation of a corollary redness and blackness, and, for my present purposes, the assertion of that blackness as the basis of a competing racial identity.

White people who understand themselves through narratives of race often do so in response to the presence of African "others" on American terrain. As a result, I think that white identities have been developed unconsciously and hence, for the most part, invisibly, within the structures of domination in American society. For the most part, whiteness has been an invisible identity within American society, and only recently—with the deconstruction and demythologization of race in attacks on biologistic conceptions of racial identity—has whiteness been constituted as a trisected terrain of contestation: over ethnicity, over ethnocentrism, and over the way groups manufacture and reproduce racial identity through individual self-understanding. I think whiteness in that sense has only recently been called into existence as a result of questions about the social construction of race, the social reconstruction of biology, and, in general, how we have come to talk about race in more complex terms.

When I talk about whiteness as ideology, I'm referring to the systematic reproduction of conceptions of whiteness as domination. Whiteness as domination has been the most powerful, sustaining myth of American culture since its inception. In other words, the ideological contamination of American democracy by structures of white domination is indivisible from the invention of America. Another way of saying this is that the invention of America and the invention of whiteness are ideologically intertwined because the construction of narratives of domination are indissolubly linked to the expansion of the colonial empire: America as the new colony. America found its roots in response to an *intraracial* struggle with Europe over the power of representation (i.e., how citizens should be granted official voice and vote in the polis) and the representation of power (i.e., how cultural institutions like churches and schools should no longer be exclusively regulated by the state). The United States was brought into existence as a result of an intraethnic war between white, Anglo-Saxon Protestants and American colonists who rejected their political deference to Europe and defended their burgeoning sense of nationhood and personal identity.

In that sense, there is a fissure in whiteness that is not articulated as such because it happens within the borders of ethnic similarity. This civil war of white ethnicity generated the fissuring of the state at the behest of procreative energies of emancipation. But that emancipation, at least in terms of its leaders' self-understanding, was not ethnically or racially constituted; it was viewed as the ineluctable conclusion to a fatal disagreement over issues of primary political importance, like freedom, justice, and equality.

At the same time, ironically enough, the expansion of American culture, especially the American state, was fostered primarily through the labor of black slaves and, to a lesser degree, the exploitation of white indentured servants and the oppression of white females. From the very beginning of our nation's existence, the discursive defense and political logic of American democracy has spawned white dominance as the foundational myth of American society—a myth whose ideological strength was made all the more powerful because it was rendered invisible. After all, its defenders didn't have to be conscious of how white dominance and later white supremacy shaped their worldviews, since there was little to challenge their beliefs. Their ideas defined the intellectual and cultural status quo. In that sense, the white race—its cultural habits, political practices, religious beliefs, and intellectual affinities—was socially constructed as the foundation of American democracy.

In terms of the genealogy of American nationality, whiteness and democracy were coextensive because they were mutually reinforcing ideologies that undergirded the state. When we look at the Constitution and the Declaration of Independence, the implicit meanings of white domination were encoded in state discourse. State discourse was articulated in the intellectual architecture of the Constitution and the Declaration of Independence; it was also written into the laws of the land that eroded the social stability of African American people, first as slaves and then as subjugated victims of the state through debt peonage, sharecropping, Jim Crow law, the assault on of the welfare state, and so on.

Also written into the laws of the land was the explicit articulation of black racial inferiority and the implicit assumption of white racial superiority. These two poles were reproduced ideologically to justify white supremacy; the mutually reinforcing structures of state-sponsored racial domination and the ideological expression of white racial superiority solidified the power of white people, white perspectives, and white practices. As a result, whiteness in its various expressions was made to appear normative and natural, while other racial identities and ideologies were viewed as deviant and unnatural.

The final component of my triad is the institutional expression of whiteness. The institutions I have in mind—from the home to the school, from the government to the church—compose the intellectual and ideological tablet on which has been inscribed the meanings of American destiny. Let's focus on one example of how whiteness has been institutionally expressed: the church. First, "manifest destiny" found an institutional articulation in the church, even though our country's founders ingeniously disestablished state-sponsored religion and thereby encouraged radical heterogeneity within American religion. While ostensibly free from state rule, religious communities were not impervious to secular beliefs; the theological discourse of many faiths actively enunciated the ideology of white domination.

Not only did manifest destiny bleed through the theological articulations of the churches, but the belief in blackness as an innately inferior identity galvanized the missionary activities of most religious communities as they sought to contain and redeem the black slave's transgressive body; many believed blacks didn't have a soul. With the overlay of theological verity added to embellish the ideology of white supremacy, black identity became the ontological template for the reproduction of discourses of racial primitivism and savagery. The black body became a contested landscape on which the torturous intersections of theology and ideology were traced: it was at once the salvific focus of the white missionizing project and the foremost example of what unchecked transgression could lead to.

These elements of whiteness—identity, ideology, and institution—are articulated and reinforced over space and time. They substantiate the argument that whites don't understand themselves in abstraction from the cultural institutions and the critical mythologies that accrete around whiteness. What we've witnessed over the last decade is a crisis in the myth of whiteness; that is, it has been exposed as a visible and specific identity, not something that is invisible and universal. Whiteness has been "outed," and as a consequence of its outing, it has to contend with its own genealogy as one race among other races. We are now seeing a proliferation of ideas, articles, books, plays, and conferences that question the meanings and significations of whiteness. As part of that process, we've got to understand what whiteness has meant and specify what it can or should mean in the coming century.

Given this "outing" of whiteness, would it be your opinion that the concept of whiteness will continue to be studied, that it won't be just a fleeting academic interest?

That's right. I think we can rest assured that the extraordinary interest in whiteness won't taper off too much. First, there are masses of whites who are absorbed by the subject, a sure index of its staying power. There are also a great number of African Americans, Native Americans, Latinos, and Asians—as well as other subaltern, aboriginal, and colonized peoples—who are deeply invested in reversing the terror of ethnography: of being the disciplined subject of an often intellectually poisonous white anthropological scrutiny. Many minorities yearn to return the favor of interrogation, if you will, though not in nearly as punishing a manner as they've received. Many members of these groups simply seek to unveil the myths of universality and invisibility that have formed the ideological strata of white supremacy.

They also seek to reveal a fundamental strategy of white supremacy: forging belief in the omnipotence of whiteness. This belief maintains that whiteness secretes a racial epistemology whose function is akin to omnipotent narration in fiction: it unifies the sprawling plot of white civilization; it articulates the hidden logic of mysterious white behavior; it codifies the linguistic currency through which the dramatis personae of white cultures detail their intellectual idiosyncrasies and emotional yearnings; and it projects an edifying white racial denouement to the apocalyptic conflict between whiteness and nonwhiteness. One consequence of an investment in the omnipotence of whiteness, and in the unitary racial sentiment that it enforces, is that many minorities have been ontologically estranged from what might be termed the *Dasein* of American race—the racial order of being that defines national and, more fundamentally, human identity.

The great irony of American race—within the discursive frame of whiteness as an invisible entity—is that the condition for racial survival is racial concealment, a state of affairs that produces a surreal racelessness that stigmatizes all nonwhite identities. Thus racial and ethnic minorities face a triple challenge: they must overcome the history and ongoing forces of oppression;

they must eradicate the demonization of racial identity-qua-identity that whiteness generates; and they must help excavate the historical and ideological character of whiteness in the sedimenting fields of cultural and social practice.

Another reason I think that the examination of whiteness will not diminish quickly is the sheer variety of white identities, behaviors, texts, and practices that the current phase of whiteness studies has uncovered. Such variety gives the lie to whiteness as a singular and fixed phenomenon. Whiteness must be viewed as destabilized loci of contested meanings that depend on different articulatory possibilities to establish their identities and functions. Whiteness is now up for grabs; it is being deeply retheorized and profoundly rearticulated. Whiteness is no longer simply good or bad: either formulation is a reductio ad absurdum that underwrites a rigid, essentialist view of race.

Contemporary studies of whiteness explore the complex character of white racial identity and practice. Such studies examine whiteness in multifarious modes: as domination *and* cooperation, as stability *and* instability, as hegemony *and* subordination, and as appropriation *and* cooptation. By no means am I suggesting that a narrow ideological binarism lies at the heart of whiteness; I simply mean to accent the interactive, intersectional, and *multilectical* features of whiteness with other racial and ethnic identities as they are elaborated in intellectual inquiry. Even if such studies are viewed as faddish, we must remember that many substantive intellectual engagements began as trends.

One of the advantages of the *subject(ed)s* of whiteness now *objecting* it (constituting it as a legitimate object of discursive interrogation and thereby objecting to the power of whiteness to iterate domination by remaining amorphous and invisible) is that we demystify the mechanisms by which whiteness has reproduced its foundational myths. We also get a better sense of how whiteness has helped construct blackness, and how whiteness has helped to construct Latino/a, Native American, and Asian identities as well.

We must recognize that current studies of whiteness—especially the groundbreaking writings of white scholars such as David Roediger, Theodore Allen, Noel Ignatiev, and others—are building on the often unacknowledged tradition of black critical reflection on the ways and means of whiteness. To be sure, whiteness studies in its present modes—in terms of the scopes of interrogation, disciplinary methodologies, paradigms of knowledge, theoretical tools of analysis, historical conjunctions, and material supports that make this an ideal intellectual climate for scrutinizing white identities—unquestionably marks a significant scholarly, perhaps even disciplinary, departure in cultural studies of race and ethnicity. But such studies would be impossible, or at least highly unlikely, without the pioneering work of figures like W.E.B. Du Bois, Langston Hughes, Zora Neale Hurston, Fannie Lou Hamer, and on and on.

To be fair, a number of the "new abolitionist" writers have scrupulously acknowledged their debt to this hidden black intellectual tradition. For instance, David Roediger acknowledges that Du Bois was the first to write, in his magisterial tome *Black Reconstruction*, about the "psychic wages of whiteness," arguing that even poor workers derived a psychological benefit from their whiteness. Current whiteness studies will only be strengthened as they refer to those texts and figures in black life, and in other minority communities, which have aided in the demythologization of a homogeneous, uniform whiteness.

I think that the study of whiteness will be around for some time because it can give us crucial historical insight into current cultural debates. For example, contentious discussions about the labor movement and its relationship to identity politics would be greatly benefited from a vigorous examination of the role white racial identity played in the formation of the American working class. Despite their economic disadvantage, poor white workers appealed to the surplus value that their whiteness allowed them to accumulate in the political economy of race. Many poor workers invested their surplus-valued whiteness into a fund of psychic protection against the perverse, impure meanings of blackness. They drew from their value-added whiteness to not only boost their self-esteem but to assert their relative racial superiority by means of what may be termed a *negative inculpability:* poor whites derived pleasure and some cultural benefit by *not being the nigger*.

Their negative inculpability prevented poor whites from being viewed as the ultimate cause of harm to white civilization—despite the social problems to which their poverty and class oppression gave rise. Their negative inculpability redeemed poor whites, at least partially, by granting them powers to deflect their degraded status through a *comparative racial taxonomy:* poor whites could articulate the reasons for their superiority by naming all the ways they remained white despite their economic hardship. Negative inculpability and comparative racial taxonomy were racial strategies by which poor whites appropriated the dominant meanings of whiteness, and the ideology of white domination, while obscuring the intellectual and material roots of their own suffering. Of course, in objective, empirically verifiable ways, poor whites had much more in common with poor blacks: degraded social status, depressed wages, and stigmatization through social narratives of "the deserving poor" that blamed the poor for their plight. Such studies are of utmost importance in explicating the complex intersections of race, gender, and class in the labor movement, as well as in contemporary cultural politics.

In order to solidify the intellectual foundation of whiteness studies, we should distinguish among at least three economies within whiteness: an *economy of invention*, an *economy of representation*, and an *economy of articulation*. Economies of invention explore how and when the multiple meanings of whiteness are fashioned. Economies of invention permit us to excavate, for instance, the construction of Irish as a white ethnicity, as Noel Ignatiev has done; the making of the white working class, as David Roediger has done; and the invention of the white race, about which Theodore Allen has written. Economies of invention address the foundational myths of white ethnicity as they are articulated through metaphysical claims of white superiority. Economies of invention help us narrate the means by which culture has colluded with ideology to reproduce whiteness. They help us understand how cultural privilege is assigned to an accidental racial feature like whiteness, and how such privilege gives credence to philosophical arguments about the inherent goodness and supremacy of white identity.

Economies of invention encourage critics to stress how the project of whiteness was constructed on a labor base of exploited indigenous Americans and enslaved blacks. The irony is that enslaved blacks supplied material support and social leisure to white elites as they constructed mythologies of black racial inferiority. Economies of invention also accent a factor I discussed earlier: the symbiotic relationship between white and black identities, practices, and cultures in the construction of the material and cultural means to express whiteness.

In this matter, Orlando Patterson's important book *Freedom* is crucial in pinpointing the intellectual function of an economy of invention in interrogating the historically and socially constituted meanings of whiteness. Patterson argues that Western conceptions of freedom—as well as the epistemic crucible of Western culture and identity—are contingent on, indeed articulated against, the backdrop of slavery. In other words, there's no such thing as Western freedom without a corresponding articulation of slave identities; there's no ideal of freedom within American culture in particular, and Western cultures in general, without the presence of the corollary slave subject that was being constructed and contained within the narrative of freedom to begin with. Economies of invention help us comprehend the extraordinarily intricate construction of white identities in the interstices of hybrid cultural contacts.

Economies of representation examine how whiteness has been manifest, how it has been symbolized, how it has been made visible. Economies of representation highlight how whiteness has been embodied in films, visual art, and branches of culture where public myths of white beauty and intelligence have gained representative authority to rearticulate the superiority and especially the desirability of whiteness. Economies of representation pay attention to the erotic visibility of white identities and images—how whiteness has been fetishized as the ideal expression of human identity.

Economies of representation also underscore the cultural deference paid to white identities, images, styles, and behaviors even as they cast light on the scorn heaped on nonwhite identities in a key strategy of defensive whiteness: demonizing the racialized other as a means of sanctifying the white self; devaluing nonwhite racial identities through stereotypical representations as a means of idealizing white identities; and bestializing the expression of eroticism in nonwhite cultures while eroticizing racial others for white pleasure and consumption.

Finally, economies of articulation name the specific sites of intellectual justification for white superiority and supremacy. From selected writings of Thomas Jefferson, David Hume, Immanuel Kant, Abraham Lincoln, and Woodrow Wilson to the writings of Dinesh D'Souza (a white superiorist in brown skin), Charles Murray, Arthur Jensen, William Shockley, and Richard Herrnstein, beliefs in the pathologies and corruptions of black culture, and by extension in the inherent rightness of whiteness, have deluged our intellectual landscape.

Economies of articulation specify how, from the Enlightenment to *The Bell Curve*, ideas of black inferiority have been expressed with vicious consistency. Indeed, *The Bell Curve* argues black intellectual inferiority through a tangle of pseudo-scientifically manipulated data, leading to what Raymond Franklin has termed "statistical myopia." Economies of articulation isolate the philosophical architecture and rhetorical scaffolding that joins white superiorist and supremacist thinking to social and cultural practices. Economies of articulation show how myths of value neutrality, ideals of Archimedean-like objectivity, conceptions of theory-free social science, notions of bias-free scholarship, and beliefs in heroically blind moral explanations are deployed to defend (and to coerce others outside of its ideological trajectory to defer to) white civilization. These three economies help us determine, define, and demystify the meanings of whiteness and make sure that the study of white identities, images, and ideologies rests on a critical intellectual foundation.

What about whiteness being discussed outside the confines of academia, or what about the influence of these scholarly discussions on others not in the academy? How can that happen or how is that happening?

I think it certainly is happening. One flagrant example is in the cultural discourse about "white male anger," which, according to its apologists, is the legitimate bitterness of white men who have been unfairly denied employment because of affirmative action. Debates about white male anger take place in employment arenas, especially fire and police stations, where white men, we are told, have had enough. White male anger has focused on black bodies as its *objet de terror*, its target of rage. In the minds of such men (and their wives and daughters), blacks occupy wrongful places of privilege in the job sector because of their color. Black progress symbolized in affirmative action policies constitutes reverse racism for many whites. This is an extremely volatile occasion outside of the academy where the meanings of whiteness are being fiercely debated.

There were also discussions—sometimes explicit, more often veiled and coded—about whiteness in the recent ordeal of the bombing of the Murray federal building in Oklahoma City, and in its aftermath, the trial of Timothy McVeigh. McVeigh became a flashpoint in the resurfacing of a virulent, violent whiteness that had to be contained for at least three reasons. First, the racial violence that McVeigh symbolized transgressed its historic ethnic limits by, in significant measure, being directed toward other whites. Second, by intentionally targeting the American government, McVeigh's white racial violence shattered an implicit social contract where the nation absorbed (i.e., excused, overlooked, downplayed, underestimated, etc.) extralegal racial violence more readily if it was aimed at black or other minority bodies. This was an ideological relic from earlier generations when extralegal white racial violence actually served the interests of the state, or at least multitudes of its officials, by discouraging black insurrection, protest, or rebellion against the legal strictures of white supremacy. Finally, McVeigh's violence had to be contained, even eradicated, because his poor white rebellion against state authority threatened to symbolically contaminate "purer," more elite expressions of white ethnicity.

One really gets a sense, from many of the white cultural discussions of McVeigh, of the ethnic betrayal many whites feel in the Oklahoma City bombing. Judging by what I've read, McVeigh viewed himself as part of a tiny outpost of pure patriotic rebels whose patriotism was expressed in the logic of radical *antipatriotism*: one must blow up the state as it is to get to the state as it should be. I think that McVeigh believed he was reviving a heroic vision of whiteness that he thought was being suppressed within the institutional matrices of American democracy and "legitimate" government. Apparently in McVeigh's thinking, the only legitimate government was to be found in the guerrilla gangsterism of his supremacist, antistatist comrades. They are the real Americans, not the namby-pamby politicians and state officials who cater to racial minorities, who endanger the freedom of religious minorities like the followers of the late cult leader David Koresh.

What's fascinating about McVeigh is that his actions articulate in the extreme the logic of repressive, hegemonic whiteness that hibernates within the structures of legitimate government: vicious attacks on welfare and its recipients; brutal attacks on black progress and its advocates; heartless attacks on the crime-ridden black ghetto; and exploitative attacks on the alleged pathologies of black culture. All of these claims and more have been launched by governmental officials. The cumulative effect of such attacks is the implementation of policies that punish the black poor and stigmatize the black middle class as well as the legitimation of crude cultural biases toward black citizens.

Figures like Timothy McVeigh become hugely discomfiting manifestations of the hidden animus toward blackness and civility that such discourses of attack encourage. McVeigh is the rabid reification of the not too abstract narratives of hatred that flood segments of white talk radio. Bob Grant, Rush Limbaugh, and many other lesser lights discover a living embodiment of their vitriolic, vituperative verbiage in McVeigh. McVeigh is the monster created by the Frankensteins of white hatred. And there's a great deal of shame in him because he's out of control and destroying his creators. In this regard, it's crucial to remember a salient fact: Frankenstein is not the name of the monster but the name of the monster's creator. The real terror, then, is the mechanisms of reproduction that sustain and rearticulate ideologies of white supremacy, and that sanction the violent attack on black and other minority identities.

Finally, debates on whiteness beyond the academy occur in the construction of cultural conversations about "poor white trash." Interestingly enough, Bill Clinton figures as a key subject and subtext of such conversations. For many, Clinton is our nation's *First Bubba*, our country's *Trailer Trash Executive*, our nation's *Poor White President*. It tells on our bigoted cultural beliefs and social prejudices that Clinton—a Georgetown University alumnus, a Rhodes Scholar, an Oxford University and Yale University Law School graduate, and a president of the United States—could be construed in many quarters as a poor white trash, cracker citizen. The study of whiteness prods us to examine the means by which a highly intelligent man and gifted politician is transmuted into "Bubba" for the purposes of intraethnic demonization.

Clinton, or at least his legal representatives, relied on the same prejudice that befell the president in their legal battles over sexual harassment with a very different victim in the poor white trash wars: Paula Jones. The intriguing subtext in Clinton's fight against Jones's suit was not simply about the hierarchy of gender, where a male's prerogative in defining a sexual relationship is under attack through the discourse of sexual harassment. An even more powerful subtext is that Jones was a "po'white trash'ho." By being so designated, Jones's claim to sexual ownership of her body was much less prized in the popular mind-set than Clinton's ownership of his sexual self. As a result, Jones's believability was unfairly compromised by her degraded social and gender status. Beyond considerations of her relationship to political forces that oppose Clinton, Jones's status reinforced the perception that gender and class cause one to be assigned a lower niche on the totem pole of poor white identity. And there are many, many more places where whiteness is being discussed far beyond the boundaries of the academy in ways that scholarly studies of whiteness are barely beginning to catch up to.

What do you think about President Clinton's addresses on this issue of race? Did they serve in your mind as useful or productive means of expanding the public discourse on whiteness and race?

I think it's important that the president of the United States help set the tone for how discourse about race will proceed. If we have any chance of rescuing the productive means by which race is articulated, we certainly have to have the "First Pedagogue" in place. And Clinton in that sense became a figure of estimable symbolic and even moral worth in setting a healthy tone for the debate about race. The means that he ingeniously seized on (which has been discussed in not altogether dissimilar ways in philosophical circles by Michael Oakeshott, Richard Rorty, and others) is that of conversation. The will to converse about race is motivated by an overriding concern: How can we adjudicate competing claims about race without tearing the essential fabric of American democracy that is embodied in the slogan, *E Pluribus Unum*, "Out of many, one"? If we're already fractured at the level of identity, and this fractured identity is reproduced through mythologies of racial superiority and inferiority (or through narratives of whites being victimized by blacks in identity politics, affirmative action, multiculturalism, or political correctness), how can we justly resolve disputes about relative victimization within the larger framework of American democracy? It's a very messy business, and one that certainly calls for the president to become a leader in these matters. But his shouldn't be the only or even the dominant voice. Still, Clinton created space for the conversation to take place.

It was important that Clinton open up the space of conversation about race, talking is infinitely better than shooting or stabbing or killing one another. It's better than black men killing each other in the streets of Detroit or

Chicago. It's better than black people being beaten and killed by white policemen in New York or Los Angeles. It's better than Latinas being victimized by the ideology and institutional expressions of anti-immigrant sentiment. Conversation certainly is superior to destroying one another and our nation.

Still, we mustn't be naive. One of the supreme difficulties of discussing race in America is our belief in the possibility of morally equivalent views being reasonably articulated and justly examined. The implicit assumption of Clinton's ideology of race conversation is debates among equals, or at least among people who have been equally victimized in American culture. But this is a torturous belief that obscures history and memory. We've got to unclog the arteries of collective American political memory.

In regard to race, we are living in the United States of Amnesia. We've got to revoke our citizenship in what Joseph Lowery terms "the 51st state, the state of denial." That's an extraordinarily disconcerting process, partly because what is demanded is the rejection of a key premise of liberal racial discourse: whites, blacks, and others share a common moral conception of racial justice, an ideal that regulates social practice and promotes the resolution of racial disputes. The politics and history of race have not supported this belief. To shift metaphors, what we've got to do is graft the skin of racial memory to the body of American democracy. That demands skillful rhetorical surgery and the operation of an intellectual commitment to truth over habit. In the conversation of race, we really must be willing to discover new ideas and explore ancient emotions. We can't simply shout our prejudices louder than someone else's defense of their bigotry.

If we're going to have real progress in thinking and talking about race, we must not reduce racial issues to black and white. Race in American culture is so much more profound and complex than black and white, even though we know that conflict has been a major artery through which has flowed the poisonous blood of white supremacy and black subordination. There are other arteries of race and ethnicity that trace through the body politic. The tricky part is acknowledging the significant Latino, Asian, and Native American battles with whiteness that have taken place in our nation while admitting that the major race war has involved blacks and whites.

The political centrality and historical legitimacy of dealing with the mutual and dominant relations of whiteness to blackness in the development of what Michael Omi and Howard Winant call "racial formation" is simply undeniable. But such a view must be balanced by paying attention to other racial and ethnic conflicts, as well as the intraracial, interethnic differences that reconstitute racial and ethnic identity and practice. It's extremely important to get such a complex, heated, and potentially useful dialogue started.

A nagging question, however, remains: Who gets a chance to come to the race table to converse? Will poor people's voices be heard? What about young people's voice? In the conversation on race, there is the danger that we merely reproduce a liberal ideology of racial containment and mute the radical elements of race that might really transform our conversation and practice. Such a prospect appears inevitable if we refuse to shatter our ideological and intellectual grids in order to hear the other. What we don't need is the crass and deceitful politics of toleration that masks the sources of real power, that conceals the roots of real inequality, that ignores the voices of the most hurt, and that is indifferent to the faces of the most fractured. What we need is *real* conversation, the sort where hidden ambitions are brought to light, where masked motives are clarified to the point of social discomfort.

Such an aim of honest, hard conversation is what the so-called opponents of political correctness should have in mind when they launch their sometimes pedantic, always pejorative broadsides against the assertion of racial, ethnic, gender, class, and sexual difference. Instead, their ostensible desire to push beyond received racial truths ends up being an operation of rhetorical sleight-of-hand: they end up reasserting in new terms much older, biased beliefs. That's why I'm so skeptical about many of the critics of so-called political correctness—they simply dress up bigotry in socially acceptable form by calling it "anti-PC," when indeed it's the same old political correctness: the Poppycock of socially sanctioned racial disgust.

What we have to do, then, is to aim at a raucous debate where the impoliteness of certain people must be permitted because their pain is deep and unheeded. We must surely shatter the rituals of correctness and civility in order to hear from those whose voices have been shut out, where the ability to even articulate pain and rage has been delegitimized through social stigma. That's the only way we have a chance of striking a just racial contract with our citizens. Taking all of what I've discussed into consideration, I think the conversation on race is a step in the right direction.

That gets us away from what Toni Morrison refers to as the "graceful" liberal practice—in the past, at least—of talking about people as if they were raceless, which we at one time thought was the best way. But what you're suggesting is that that doesn't work.

That's right, such a move simply doesn't work. As Du Bois said, there's no way to deal with race without going through race; there's no way of overcoming race without taking race into account. What we've had in our nation for too long is a willed ignorance about race; on one reading, it's a perverse application of philosopher John Rawls's notion of the "original position" in the social contract where we are placed behind a veil of ignorance in order to execute justice in the social realm. When we've misapplied this model to race, it has been quite disastrous. It's failed primarily because we can't justly assume a statutory ignorance about race and because the means to apply racial justice fall disproportionately into the hands of those against whom claims of injustice have been convincingly levied.

Further, the assumption of racelessness fails to account for the contents and identities of race that have always played a role in fashioning American views of justice. This is why I think identity politics must be given a historicist, materialist, and genealogical reading. Identity politics has been going on from the get-go in American culture, indeed, in cultures the world over. Aristotle and Plato and their followers were ensconced in identity politics; Descartes and Kant and their followers were negotiating identity politics; Foucault and Derrida and their followers are embroiled in identity politics; and Julia Kristeva and Luce Irigaray and their followers are unquestionably involved in identity politics, though they, as I suspect the others I've named, would vehemently deny it.

That's because many of them are or were transfixed by the dream of transcendental truth, Enlightenment rationality, deconstructive practice, or semiotic analysis that, for the most part, severs questions of identity from questions of racial politics. What we must come to see is that even when we deal with intellectual or theoretical issues, they refer to—although by no means are they reduced to or equated with—considerations of identity, even if such considerations are not explicitly articulated. The disingenuous character of too many debates about identity in America is that they deny this process.

After generating a genealogy of identity—that places our own accounts of universalism versus difference into historical context, and that acknowledges that identity politics occur in a variety of intellectual and social settings—we can press forward to an adequate and fair criticism of identity politics. As things stand, too many critics wrongly argue that we must move beyond narrow frameworks of identity to get to this universal identity. I have in mind the most recent writings of Todd Gitlin and Michael Tomasky. I share some of Gitlin's and Tomasky's concerns about the cultural dead ends of vicious identity politics that enshrine tribal preferences over the common good. But right away, I disagree with them about what constitutes tribal preferences, how they can be justly eradicated, and what constitutes successful expressions of universal identities in the social and cultural realm.

In regard to whiteness, Gitlin and Tomasky fail to acknowledge that the particular identities of white people were rendered universal by a cultural and political process that punished blacks and other minorities for seeking to come into their own: their own identities, their own cultural repertoires, their own linguistic and rhetorical facilities, their own styles of survival, and so on. Until we are able to concede this point, we won't get far in this debate about identity, about racelessness, and about the proper role that race should play, both in the American public sphere and in private institutions.

Do you see any contradiction between Clinton's inviting everyone to the table to talk about race and yet not listening to all those voices in making policy—welfare reform, for instance—and excluding the very voices that we need to be hearing from?

There's no question that there's a deep contradiction in Clinton's methodology. Further, there's no question that in the past Clinton has not been above race baiting through very subtle semantic distortions and ideological gyrations. This surfaced in Clinton's first run for the presidency, when his crass opportunism got the best of him as he attacked Sister Souljah for her violent racism without providing a thicker account of the conditions that shaped her comments, something Clinton was clearly capable of effectively pulling off. It surfaced when Clinton, during his first campaign, sent coded signals to alleviate white fears by suggesting that he and Gore would focus their policies on rescuing suburbia and middle America. It surfaced as well when Clinton failed to justly read the complex writings of his close friend, Lani Guinier, thereby encouraging her unjust demonization as a "quota queen." It surfaced with Clinton's support for a heinous crime bill that, like the welfare reform he supported, targeted black men and women with vicious specificity. And on and on.

More important, Clinton failed to understand that if we as a nation are to have a successful conversation about race, it must be seconded at the level of public policy and political implementation. The conversation about race must perform a crucial educational function as well. I think that too often Clinton caved in to the American tendency to demonize what Malcolm X termed the "victims of democracy." Clinton heartily advocated a neoliberal rearticulation of the ideology of racial tolerance that has largely served to hurt the black and Latino poor. One of the great problems with neoliberal race theory is that it writes the check of its loyalty to the black and Latino poor against the funds of conservative rhetoric and social policy. Bill Clinton certainly has a troubled history when it comes to race, a matter about which we must be forthright.

Clinton symbolizes, ironically enough, many white Americans who are well intentioned about race but constantly make faux pas in their quest to do the right thing. Of course, in Clinton's case, his mistakes have cost millions of blacks, Latinas, Native Americans, and other minorities dearly. Clinton's political position, his peripatetic bully pulpit, has given him the authority to amplify his intentions as well as the contradictions of his racial beliefs. But he is as representative of the misguided rhetoric of neoliberal race thinking as we're likely to get. The mixed blessing of such representation is that we get a clear glimpse of just how difficult it will be for the average white American to adequately confront the history and continued function of white supremacy, especially as it is manifested in neoliberal intolerance of radical black insurgence against racism. The bitter irony is that in Clinton black folk are being hurt by friendly fire. The bitter reality is that we have no choice but to find ways to work with him, as limiting as that may be, in the hope of reconstructing racial destiny in American culture.

In addition to what you've already mentioned, how do you in specific ways talk about whiteness, such as in your writing, your public lectures, and your classroom?

As I've lectured across the country, I've witnessed the resistance by many whites to identify and name whiteness in its supremacist ideological mode. Many whites believe that white supremacy is old news, which it is, but they fail to see how it's also today's news. Many believe that pointing to it is divisive and adds to the racial and cultural Balkanization that we're told we're living through. It's extremely difficult to break the hold such a perception has on many whites. So, one of the strategies I try to adopt—in lectures, sermons, speeches, op-eds, articles, book reviews, and books—is the imaginative redescription of white supremacy in its cultural and ideological manifestations.

I also think it's important to emphasize the heterogeneity of whiteness, to stress how the meanings of whiteness are not exhausted by discussions of domination or supremacy. One of the good results of constructivist views of race—and in American culture, "race" has usually signified "black"—is that whiteness is increasingly viewed as a source and site of racial identities and practices. As much as I admire and appreciate the important work of David Roediger, Noel Ignatiev, Mab Segrest, and other new abolitionist thinkers, I think we have to proceed cautiously with the project of reconstituting white identities through their abolition. We have to pose a multipronged question: Do we want to abolish whiteness, or do we want to destroy the negative meanings associated with white identities? I think the latter is what we should aim for.

Of course, Roediger, Ignatiev, Segrest, Allen, and other new abolitionist writers would concede that the whiteness they have in mind to abolish is precisely the socially constructed, culturally sanctioned, ideologically legitimated value of white supremacy that has been a scourge to our nation. In that sense, perhaps they'd agree that we don't want to destroy white identity—because then we'd have to destroy those meanings of whiteness that have been mobilized to resist supremacist thought, or, for that matter, to abolish whiteness. Rather, we want to abolish the lethal manifestations of white identity. The salient issue is whether we can completely and exclusively identify whiteness with destruction, negativity, and corruption. In any case, I applaud their desire to reject white skin privilege and to historicize social and racial identities.

Moreover, Roediger, Allen, Ignatiev, and the new abolitionists have got an extremely useful point: whiteness has been manifest in our nation in hegemonic, destructive, and at times evil ways. Although many whites are loath to admit it, whiteness in its supremacist mode, which has been its dominant mode, has polluted our moral ecology through slavery, colonialism, imperialism, and genocide. Still, I'm uncomfortable with the notion of destroying white folks and cultures, which, by the way, isn't what Ignatiev and the folks around the journal *Race Traitor* have argued. I do think we have a moral obligation to destroy white supremacy. We must speak and think about the rearticulation, reconstitution, and recasting of whiteness to expand, enhance, and embrace its more redemptive, productive features.

This is why cultural studies and theoretical interrogations of whiteness are crucial. Besides the work of the new abolitionists—including Roediger, Allen, Ignatiev, Segrest, John Garvey, Alexander Saxton, and many others—we should remember the important work of W.E.B. Du Bois, C. L. R. James, Thomas Kochman, Eric Foner, Lerone Bennett Jr., bell hooks, Toni Morrison, George Lipsitz, Marilyn Frye, Vron Ware, Ruth Frankenberg, Adrienne Rich, and Peggy McIntosh. And much of the recent work on whiteness is indispensable in coming to terms with its complex cultural manifestations: the brilliant books of Henry Giroux and Tukufu Zuberi, and the important work of Fred Pfeil, Linda Powell, Becky Thompson, Michelle Fine, John Dovidio, Lois Weis, John Hartigan Jr., Robin D.G. Kelly, Annalee Newitz, Ron Sakolsky, James Koehnline, Jesse Daniels, Melvin L. Oliver, Thomas M. Shapiro, Eric Lott, Michael Rogin, Upski Wimsatt, Barbara Ching, Mike Hill, Paul Kivel, Patricia Hill Collins, Sean Wilentz, Jennifer Hochschild, Nancy Hartsook, Michele Wallace, Jose Saldivar, Matt Wray, Laura Kipnis, and on and on.

We should also scrutinize, for instance, white studies of the underclass, which address, reflect, or extend the pathologization of the black poor; many also reveal how white critics make use of blackness—which is an intellectual strategy worthy of examination—and how they construct the ghetto and articulate black identity and moral norms against a rhetorical backdrop of implicit whiteness.

Or think of a brilliant text like Ann Douglas's *Terrible Honesty: Mongrel Manhattan in the 1920s*. Douglas shows in her book how black and white figures were working, playing, loving, and thinking together, how they were engaging across the white-black divide in ways that have been relatively hidden. Douglas's book is crucial to excavating a cultural tradition of interaction, exchange, appropriation, and influence between various forms of whiteness and blackness. Such works help us accent the stratified and complex character of whiteness while paying attention to the history of how whiteness became a socially useful, racially valued, and culturally hybrid identity.

I'm glad you brought that up because I did want to talk about rescuing that productive content because that's an important dimension, so that we get away from some of the accusations of talking about whiteness in terms of an essentialized notion, or of oversimplifying what whiteness is, or of only allying it with domination.

That's right. The importance of the studies of whiteness I've discussed above is that they uncover—indeed, recover—the contradictory, contested meanings of whiteness from hidden histories of racial practice. If we don't speak about the productive, transgressive, subversive, edifying meanings of whiteness, we're being intellectually dishonest. If we don't narrate those stories, we're doing a great disservice to the moral trajectory that our work of historical reclamation often follows. One of the most powerful ways of challenging and ultimately destroying the ideology of white supremacy, the myth of white superiority, and the narrative of white domination is to unearth sites of resistive memory, history, and practice. One way to rescue the productive meanings of whiteness is to accent transgressive whiteness: how whites cooperated with racial "others" in the unmasking of white skin privilege, the subversion of forms of white power, and the destabilization of forces of white oppression.

I think that people tend to essentialize white identities because whiteness has been a consistently malevolent force in a great number of cultures over a long period of time. It is also true that white allies to racial emancipation have often sacrificed blood and body in expressing a redemptive disloyalty to oppressive meanings of whiteness. Hopefully, in a future that still appears too far away, white disloyalty to unjust privilege and power will fuse with the liberation struggles of oppressed people around the globe as we create a world where we can lay down the burden of race.

I want to return to something you mentioned earlier: that is, some other ways of discussing intragroup differences within whiteness, other than focusing on ethnic variation, like, "I'm Irish and you're Italian," but focusing on gender difference and class difference.

One of the benefits of, for instance, ethnographies of white cultures, practices, and identities is that we begin to get a fuller picture of differentiated whiteness. The fissuring and fracturing of whiteness, especially along axes of class and gender, gives us greater insight into how white cultures have adapted, survived, and struggled in conditions where their dominance was modified or muted.

It's also important to explore histories of white difference to highlight how whiteness has not been made by whites alone. Part of what it means to be white in America is to be black. To paraphrase Ralph Ellison: "I don't want to know how 'white' black folk are, I want to know how 'black' white folk are." If we completely, indiscriminately destroy whiteness, we're also destroying what blacks and other racial minorities contributed—sometimes covertly, sometimes symbiotically, often in hybrid interactions, and occasionally in extravagant fashion—to white behaviors, identities, styles, and intellectual traditions. One of the great paradoxes of race is that whiteness is not exclusively owned or produced by whites. White is also black. As we discover how black whiteness is, we discover how interesting and intricate whiteness is. We discover how whites and blacks have cooperated in very shrewd ways to produce alternative structures, rituals, and cultures to dominant whiteness.

Interrogating whiteness in the manner I've just outlined opens discursive space for a post-appropriationist paradigm of cultural and racial exchange. Such a paradigm accents the unbalanced power relations, racial inequality, and economic injustice that often mediates, say, black-white artistic exchanges, where black ideas, products, styles, and practices are stolen, borrowed, or appropriated without attribution or reward. But it also accents the revisioning of whiteness through the prism of black cultural practices, especially as white subjectivities are reconceived and recast in the hues of transgressive blackness.

That's why it's important to explore racialized *communitas* and *habitas*—where whites live and commune—to understand the productive meanings of whiteness through the reproduction and rearticulation of the productive meanings of blackness. In this connection, it makes sense to examine the phenomenon of the substitute nigger or the "wigger"—the white nigger—whites who have been viewed, or view themselves, as black. What uses have they made of blackness? How has blackness allowed them to alter dominant modes of whiteness? How have their knowledges and cultural practices pitted ontological contents of racial identity against strictly biological or phenotypical ones? All of these lines of inquiry are opened up by fracturing and fissuring, by differentiating, whiteness.

In what ways has whiteness in the American context spread its tentacles globally or had some effect at the international level, in productive or in oppressive ways?

Let me answer your question in two ways. First, I'll briefly address how the oppressive meanings of whiteness in the American context have global implications. Then I will address black skepticism about the uses of even productive whiteness to unmask and unmake itself.

There's no question that one of the most powerful claims—though it is often dressed in racially essentialist terms—that certain postcolonialist, black separatists make is that whiteness has screwed things up the world over. It's relatively easy to supply historical verification for such a claim; after all, the oppressive meanings of whiteness have destroyed minority hearth and home, and kith and kin, around the globe. Wherever it has taken root, oppressive, colonizing, imperialistic whiteness has subjugated or tyrannized native peoples, indigenous populations, and aboriginal tribes. Along these lines, American visions of white supremacy have exported well, inspiring, for instance, South African apartheid and modern varieties of European neocolonialism.

The problem with certain criticisms of oppressive whiteness is that they are grounded in discourses of biological determinism and genetic inheritance, turning out to be *The Bell Curve* in reverse: whites are genetically incapable of humane behavior and sane social interaction. Other varieties of racial geneticism and biological determinism—such as that found in Frances Cress Welsing's *The Isis Papers*, a perennial best-seller in black communities—maintain that white supremacy grows from whites' fear of genetic annihilation because they lack melanin, while blacks, who possess it in abundance, are guaranteed survival. In such versions of reductive pseudoscience, white supremacy is genetically encoded and biologically reproduced. In light of such theories, it's understandable that antiracist critics of new abolitionism shudder when they hear of the need to abolish the white race, even if it is conceded that it's a social construction the abolitionists aim to destroy.

One of the most ingenious, deceitful strategies deployed by white supremacists is to insulate themselves from knowledge of white supremacy's evil, of its thoroughgoing funkiness. In this mode, a crucial function of whiteness is to blind itself to its worst tendencies, its most lethal consequences. And one of the ways that dominant whiteness does this is by adopting a facade of ignorance, innocence, or naïveté in the face of claims of its destructiveness. Whether such a facade covers the deep knowledge its advocates possess of white supremacy's ill effects is, and is not, relevant to how racial or ethnic minorities interact with whites in general. On one reading, such knowledge is irrelevant because even if the intent to harm does not exist, the malevolent consequences of white supremacy are just as real.

On the other hand, such knowledge is relevant when racial or ethnic minorities seek to forge coalitions with whites who reject the perspectives, practices, and privileges of white supremacy. How can blacks or Latinas be sure that such a rejection is abiding? The immediate response, of course, is that one must judge white allies, as one judges all people, by their actions. But this is precisely where matters get tricky: it is sometimes the actions of even the most devoted white allies that surprise, stun, shock, hurt, and disappoint blacks, Latinos, or Asians. The claim to ignorance, innocence, or naïveté by white allies in the face of offensive action is the cause of no small degree of discomfort in the relations between whites and racial minorities.

What is even more uncomfortable is when white allies make a merit badge of their resistance to what is increasingly thought of as the hypersensitivity of racial minorities. As a result, alleged white allies of blacks—for instance Bill Clinton—parade their racial accomplishments as a gateway to legitimacy in black communities and as a passport to do harm. The new white abolitionists and other progressive white allies are the first to decry this variety of neoliberal racial manipulation. A more difficult suspicion to overcome in many black communities is the historic pressure of whiteness to make virtues of its vices—and vice versa—even as it creates discursive space to deconstruct and demythologize its own socially constructed meanings.

That may explain why some blacks are skeptical of even progressive versions of white studies: it may be a sophisticated narcissism at work, another white hoax to displace studies of, but especially by, The Others at the height of their popularity and power with an encroaching obsession with the meanings, identities, practices, anxieties, and subjectivities—and hence the agendas, priorities, and preferences—of The Whites. On such a view, whiteness once again becomes supreme by trumpeting its need for demystification, dismantling, or abolition. Thus the cultural capital of otherness is bleached; to thoroughly mix metaphors, the gaze of race is returned to sender.

We've got to keep such skepticism in mind as we attempt to unmake and remake whiteness. As we scan the globe where whiteness has left its mark, the most remarkable fact is not the willingness of whites to become disloyal to their whiteness, but the courageous rebellion of native, colonized, or enslaved folk who fought and, as best they could, remade the meanings of the whiteness they inherited or confronted. Their stories are worthy of serious study.

Related to that, let's talk about in particular a place you just came from—Cuba—and how you see that disguising of the "funkiness" of whiteness functioning in U.S. relations with Cuba and the role that whiteness might play in our relationship with that country.

I'll answer that in a couple of ways. First, the political measures that America has employed against Cuba are simply obscene. It is indefensible for America to treat a neighboring nation of beautiful people ninety miles away with such contempt while it grants China most favored nation status. Our relations with Cuba are hostile for one overriding reason: America has been unable to kill Castro. Like that little Energizer bunny, he just keeps on going. Our foreign policy with the Soviet Union is far better, a fact that is more than a little ironic. We have thawed the thick ice that once froze Soviet-U.S. relations, and in our post–Cold War generosity, we've embraced the big bear we used to fear and hate, but we still can't embrace her cubs in Cuba.

The Helms-Burton Act extends unjust American policies to their logical, imperialist conclusion. The embargo we have against Cuba not only punishes that nation but punishes other nations that might cooperate with Cuba. Our bullying has cost the people of Cuba dearly: extreme poverty, severely curtailed luxuries, evaporation of resources, shrinking of capital, and the deprivation of essential goods and services. In the guise of ostensibly just foreign policy, our relation with Cuba, especially as driven by Helms, is white supremacy in its reckless, destructive mode. America is not killing Castro; he's living well. We're hurting decent, beautiful everyday folk who love their country and are proudly trying to extend the most democratic features of the Revolution: universal literacy, political representation of the poor, and government rooted in historical memory and national pride.

Finally, I think what's interesting is that most Cubans have a very different understanding of race than we have in the United States. Many white Cubans, and black ones as well, denied that they had a race problem. To our American eyes and ears, to mix metaphors, that was a hard claim to swallow. The Cubans *had* undeniably worked to remove vestiges of discrimination from their official quarters; still, many of the members of our delegation of black Americans understood that the rhetorical and representational battles that bewitch racial equity were still being fought. It is equally undeniable that white and black Cubans have been able to forge a Cuban national identity that overcomes in important ways the schisms of ethnic tribalism.

Even if it is not what we black Americans, imbued with the rhetoric of our own racial difficulties, think is altogether just, black and white Cubans at least have the real possibility of negotiating a livable racial situation. It may be what Ernest Becker termed a "vital lie": a necessary deception that preserves the social fabric and keeps at bay the forces that destroy identity and community. The embargo has led to what the Cubans term a "special period," the time of austerity that has thrown their culture into sustained crisis. In such a period, it is perfectly reasonable that Cubans understand race in the fashion they do to preserve the very survival of their nation. In many ways, they've done a much better job with race than we have under conditions of relative material prosperity.

Any closing comments on the past, present, or future of the study of whiteness?

I have just one observation. As we look to the next century of whiteness studies, the field will mature and reconstruct its genealogy by pointing b(l)ack—to those great figures from W.E.B. Du Bois to Zora Neale Hurston, from Langston Hughes to Ralph Ellison, and from Nella Larsen to James

Baldwin. Such a genealogy for white studies brings to mind something Fannie Lou Hamer said. She argued that the mistake white folk made with black folk is that they put us behind them, not in front of them. Had they placed us in front of them, they could have observed and contained us.

Instead, white folk placed us behind them in what they deemed an inferior position. As a result, we were able to learn white folk—their beliefs, sentiments, contradictions, cultures, styles, behaviors, virtues, and vices. Black survival depended on black folk knowing the ways and souls of white folk. It's only fitting now that we turn to African American, Latino, Asian, and Native American scholars, workers, intellectuals, artists, and everyday folk to understand whiteness.

Interview by Ronald E. Chennault
New York, New York, 1998

7

"Is It Something I Said?"

Dissident Speech, Plantation Negro Syndrome, and the Politics of Self-Respect

There are four things I want to talk about, then we can freestyle and flow. First, I want to talk about your personal experiences in Chapel Hill, and about your expectations and your life "here." Second, I want to address your experiences and perceptions of blacks in the Triangle (Durham, Chapel Hill, and Raleigh, North Carolina). Third, I want to address the issue of blacks in the "New South." And finally, I want to discuss your impact on the culture. Do you know how bad you are?

You're very kind. Well, to begin, the University of North Carolina at Chapel Hill is a very fascinating place. It provides a world-class fellowship of scholars where people who are doing some of the most cutting-edge work in numerous disciplines are gathered. That, of course, is very exciting, even though one doesn't always have direct access to them because of busy schedules. In my case, I travel so much that it has prevented me from connecting with people like Joel Williamson, a renowned historian of the South. It has prevented me from spending as much time as I would have liked with say, Catherine Lutz, who is a well-regarded professor in anthropology, or with Reginald Hildebrand, a respected scholar of African American religious history. At the same time, being at Chapel Hill has afforded me the opportunity to meet people like Gerald Horne, a historian who is director of the Black Cultural Center, and D. Soyini Madison, who is a renowned scholar in performance studies and my best friend. In that sense, it's given me a tremendous opportunity to be able to meet some of the most interesting, intelligent, and beautiful people I've met anywhere.

In terms of the larger academic culture, it's also afforded me the opportunity to test ideas that I've had in an academic community among a forceful group of scholars. I've had the chance to ask questions like: What is multiculturalism? How do we think about racial tolerance? What about the complexity of racial identity? How does race intersect with class? How does the classroom provide one an opportunity to test out, pedagogically, one's theories about how race should operate in the world? Chapel Hill has provided an expert laboratory for me to test out the limits of my own understandings of race, gender, sexuality, and class and provided me a space where I can dramatize the extraordinary complexity of identities. One of the things I'm obsessed with in my own work is how people come to a sense of who and what they are. Howard Thurman, the great African American mystic, preacher, and theologian, said there are three basic questions in life: (1) who am I? (2) what do I want? and (3) how do I propose to get it?

One of the most intellectually fascinating and pleasurable things I have the chance to do here is connect philosophical and religious debates about identity to questions of culture, especially black popular culture, extending the work I'd already begun before landing at Chapel Hill. I'd already written a book about black cultural criticism. It's one of the books that helped integrate cultural studies with racial studies, and that tried to forge connections between disparate academic and disciplinary boundaries. Coming here allowed me to forge those connections even more aggressively. I wrote a book on Malcolm X and a book of journalistic essays about black identity and culture, *Between God and Gangsta Rap*. And my latest book, *Race Rules*, is a public intellectual perspective on a range of issues relating to race, especially within African American culture. And I'm working on a new book about the generational divide between older and younger blacks. Chapel Hill has given me an incredible and inestimable intellectual framework and environment within which to explore these questions. And then the best colleagues I've ever had in the world are here, in the Department of Communication Studies. That department, from the very beginning, made it known that they are proud to have me here, that I'm a worthwhile member of the department, that they see me as a crucial element in the larger puzzle of our discipline's identity, and that they want me to be a central player in the role of redefining communication studies for the next century. So I've had nothing but great times and great experiences.

What got you here, Michael? What do you think they really saw—obviously you'd established a reputation—but what do you think they saw, or thought they saw, that made them go after you?

I think they thought my intellectual energy was great, and that I was in pursuit of the kinds of questions and the sorts of themes that they had been preoccupied with, such as: What is the relationship between culture and commodification? What is the relationship between African American identity and mainstream American culture? How do we interpret cultural studies through the lens of black cultural priorities? How do we understand the universal themes of African American culture that are evoked by artists, filmmakers, and intellectuals in relationship to American identity? How do we bring a religious perspective from an African American culture to bear on crucial themes of American democracy? And so on. Those sort of issues that I was interested in really made them believe that here's a guy who's been, hopefully, on the cutting-edge, who's trying to redefine a number of disciplinary pursuits.

Okay, we understand, those are the issues—the correlation between "you're doing it, they want it," but did they understand the impact, the dynamics of the "man" and your method of bringing that to the front?

Well, yeah, they certainly brought me in to give a lecture beforehand, and to take stock and measure of what I could do in a classroom situation. Then the chairman of the department came to Brown University to recruit me personally. They were sufficiently interested in bringing me to Chapel Hill that when the chairman was on some business in Providence, he took my wife and me to dinner and made a strong pitch. He talked about what they could offer, talked about what he envisioned for me. So from the very beginning, they were strategic in their assessment of my capacity to bring a certain kind of visibility, a certain kind of prominence, but also a real cutting-edge intellectual fervor to the process of investigating questions they were concerned about. So they understood the intellectual wherewithal I could bring, but they also understood my personal energy, and what they hoped would be a contagious element in my own pedagogical style that would seduce my students into exploring some of the same kinds of questions I do. I hope some of that happened.

I was going to ask that . . . did it?

I hope so. I guess I'm a decent teacher . . .

Oh, come on, Michael . . .

Well, [laughing] I've had some strong supporters and, as we well know, some naysayers.

Yes, I want to talk about that.

We'll definitely get to that! [Laughs] There's no question that my coming here broadened my perspective, gave me a base from which to think about a certain set of issues and themes that I've been concerned about from a different disciplinary base. When I was at Brown, I was in African American studies and American studies, so I was linked to a different disciplinary foundation than communication studies. I don't have a degree in communication studies—I don't have a bachelor's, master's, or doctorate—but I had some overlapping interests, and some of the theoretical questions I was pursuing were deeply connected to the fabric of communication studies' self-identity. Because of the elective affinities, if you will, that my work and the communication studies department's work had, I was able to fuse with their interests and meld with their ambitions. I do cultural studies and, along with another hire of a very prominent academician, Lawrence Grossberg, I think overnight, UNC began to compete on a national level for some of the best and brightest students within cultural studies, and we began to forge a reputation for having some of the most powerful, insightful, cutting-edge intellectual work.

With people like Grossberg and Soyini Madison, who does incredible work with performance studies, especially around the performance of black women's literature, and in theorizing the intersections of gender, race, class, and notions of the body within both African American culture and in mainstream society, we had a powerful contingent of scholars. And we had the gifted Della Pollack, who does some of the same thing as Madison, only in terms of women's narratives, and in probing the relationship between cultural studies and notions of birth, for instance. And we had the legendary Beverly Long, who's done tremendous work in the performance of literature. There's a wide range of scholars who are now collected at UNC that have really redefined their own bailiwick in regard to cultural studies. So there's no question that they felt that I would bring energy, that I would bring enthusiasm, that I would bring national visibility . . .

And flavor!

Yeah, I hope so. Drop a little science, add a little flavor, and kick a little something from the homeboys. I don't think they were disappointed in that. I try to be conscientious. My father told me if you're going to do a job, do it right or don't do it at all. So I brought enthusiasm, energy, hopefully intelligence, and I hope I had some impact upon my students and colleagues. My students seem to have felt that I did. My colleagues were extraordinarily supportive. Let me say this: Not only were they supportive in terms of my intellectual work here at the university, but they also gave me the kind of release from the immediate responsibilities of the academic environment to provide me greater latitude in going out into the world. Most departments don't do that. When they have so-called superstars, a lot of people get resentful, mad, envious, jealous, or just outright ornery. This department has been nothing but exemplary. They have supported my work, and these are mostly white scholars. They have seen the vision, and they have seen that it's necessary for me to be out there.

So they recognized and felt your impact?

I think some of them have. I think many of them say, "You've brought a different perspective here, you forced us to contend with some issues or invited us to explore more deeply, issues that we'd already been concerned about." But we have vigorous debates in faculty meetings around issues of difference, around issues of marginality, around issues of race, and around issues of gender. We have tremendous debates within our department about the crucial questions of redefining American culture, multiculturalism, racial diversity, racial tolerance, gender difference, sexuality, gay and lesbian identity, and so on. Those debates are part and parcel of what we do as a community of scholars interested in not only bringing enlightenment intellectually but in forging solidarity with other figures who've been marginalized in the world. That's what I like about this department. There's a very passionate commitment to social justice while maintaining the highest levels of intellectual investigation. Head and heart are joined in an extraordinary balance. It doesn't mean it's a perfect place, or that we can't stand room for improvement because we certainly can.

I think many of our students are well served by that process, and by scholars who are not only interested in pursuing questions of the head but are deeply interested and invested in trying to figure out what human beings do in the real world. How do we translate interesting discourses about difference, about marginality, about "otherness," or theories about, as Foucault says, "the insurrection of subjugated knowledges," into concrete action? How do you bring that to bear on what folk who are gay and lesbian do when they need to be supported by their partners who are being denied their claims for insurance? How do we deal with the fact that African American people don't necessarily have to fit into a narrow vision of blackness? What does that mean in the face of the necessity for some form of social solidarity when white hostility is visited upon black communities? These are very difficult questions, and I think we've made a good attempt at answering them.

And that leads to me talking about my role as a *public* intellectual at Chapel Hill, which has been the basis for my further emergence as a public figure able to appear on *Oprah, Charlie Rose, Nightline, Good Morning America, Today,* to write for the *Washington Post,* the *New York Times,* to be quoted in *USA Today,* and to appear on National Public Radio. This has been a secure basis for me to expand my own repertoire of public interventions on behalf of the most sacred principles of, and the highest devotion to, intellectual life. Chapel Hill has afforded me an extraordinary opportunity to be able to live a life that many scholars only dream about and don't have the luxury or leisure to pursue. So I know I'm a very fortunate person, to be able to make an impact, hopefully not simply on one's own immediate environment but on the larger national environment. That takes a group of scholars who understand that certain people are assigned certain roles. I have enormous respect for my colleagues who take care of the business of the university's department. That's no less important, no less meaningful, no less significant, than the kind of work I do. It's different, but it's no less important. I'm appreciative of their ability to see that I can do both. I can pay attention to scrutinizing theoretical concepts with rigorous language and ideas, and on the other hand, I can translate some of that stuff about critical race theory, for instance, on *Charlie Rose*, where Jeffrey Rosen from the *New Republic* is making provocative statements about subjects about which I'm concerned. It has, however, created some controversy outside of my department. There are some other scholars at Chapel Hill who think I'm overpaid, overtalking, and overheated. I think they're welcome to their opinion, but I think the role of an intellectual, especially a public intellectual, is to bring the most serious, rigorous talents one has to bear on issues of importance to people beyond the academy. We shouldn't just be an ostrich sticking our head into the collective sand of our academic enterprise without paying attention to what the rest of the world is doing, and without reflecting on how what we do *affects* the larger world. I'm very appreciative of that role, and I'll try to exercise it with some consciousness and some sense of responsibility, not only to my immediate community but also to the larger community that I feel myself to be a vital part of.

Let's move into some of that "there's a fly in the ointment" . . . last December. You gave a commencement address at the University of North Carolina's fall graduation, and you were criticized harshly in the local media and throughout the community for what some felt was your inappropriate language and your criticism of Michael Jordan. How do you view that speech now?

That speech . . . let me tell you the truth. There's no way in the world I anticipated that there would be that much of a firestorm of controversy. I'm not stupid. I knew as I was writing that speech that there would be some eyebrows raised, but quite frankly, I thought most of the eyebrows would be raised over my comment about Michael Jordan. The thing is, I did quote the "f-word" in the speech and, on second thought, I might not have done that because my point was not to offend people's sensibilities around proprietary language, the most effective language one can deploy to make one's point. I'm a communicator and hopefully, somewhere, I've been called an effective communicator. So I knew what to say and what not to say. I don't mind being provocative, but I don't want to shut people's minds down to the point that they don't hear what I'm saying. But, on the other hand, I have to be honest: I only said one word, the f-word, it's not a word people haven't heard before and the response to it was way out of proportion to the offense that it imposed. So I want to take responsibility by saying, yes if I had it to do over again, knowing that this is not only the Bible belt, but the very buckle of the Bible belt, and I'm a Baptist preacher, I understand it's a difficult sell. On the other hand, these are the same people that go to see a Bruce Willis movie with the word being tossed around five and six times. Of course, I know there's a difference between a film and a commencement service, so let me not be disingenuous.

At the same time, I didn't think my speech merited the kind of vicious, vehement calumny that was heaped on me, from both the press and people who were pissed off and just mad. I think the real insult to many people, the real offense, was not the one f-word, which they might have forgiven. It was the fact that I was criticizing one of their demigods, Michael Jordan, an athletic genius on the court, an anesthetized, narcotized safe Negro off the court. Jordan is a black man who has incredible worth, value, and merit as long as he's a highly paid Negro who keeps his mouth shut, his tongue wagging, and his mouth open only when he's moving toward a basketball goal. Not when he's moving toward the goal of racial reflection. Not when he's pressing toward the goal of making sure that the races confront one another across the chasm of color. Not when he's pressing toward the goal of forging black solidarity among despised black peoples. He is of little support to the political goals of African American people, and I think that's a tragedy. Italian Americans support one another, many Polish Americans support one another, and many Jewish brothers and sisters support one another, so why can't African American people support one another? There's an enormous stigma attached to black solidarity. And I think that's one of the most vicious effects of white supremacy, discouraging black people from openly, unapologetically embracing one another.

Let me ask about that. Do you think the reaction you got was because it was said here in North Carolina on, as you said, the buckle of the Bible belt? Or could you have made that comment and gotten the same reaction in and among many black neighborhoods? As a culture, are we able to critically think about somebody like Michael Jordan?

No. There's no question about it, that's a very good point. First, the black folk who are here are part of the South, so we can't forget they are part of the buckle too. Most belts I know are black, so we got a black Bible belt going on here: the black folk have deeply conservative religious and moral values. And this is what a lot of people miss on the outside of our culture, that black folk are deeply conservative themselves. So when the Newt Gingrichs and Bill Bennetts are jumping on black folk for the loss of morals and values, they don't know the black folk we know. Blacks have profoundly conservative cultural values, even if we are politically progressive. That's one of the interesting paradoxes of black culture. We possess a Ten Commandments religion wedded to sometimes progressive, prophetic, even rebellious inclinations, politically speaking. There's little question that the speech could have been given in several other places, among certain African American communities, and they would have been equally opposed to my ideas, or offended by them, because we don't often have the ability to be critical of black figures who have "made it." We think somehow we have to make them immune to criticism, and we end up being allergic to criticizing them or holding them responsible for their behavior.

I got many letters and calls after my speech from blacks who thought that I'd set the race back. But then I got a lot of supportive calls from black people who said, "Right on, it's about time somebody called this man into question and was public about it." So I think that even though there would have been similarities of response in many conservative African American communities, there wouldn't have been the kind of vehement outrage, and unvarnished bigotry, that I glimpsed in the many calls and letters from whites, and, quite frankly, from the response of the predominantly white press. For instance, there was a cartoon that appeared in the *Durham Herald*, where they caricatured me in a bathroom pulling toilet paper down with expletives deleted scratched on the wall, and beneath are inscribed the words, "Professor Dyson is preparing his next commencement speech." I have a sense of humor that is more ribald and probably more rowdy than most people's. But we have to interpret these things in terms of their symbolic effect in the public space, and the symbolic effect of that cartoon was a rather crude, and I believe, a racist one. If they were trying to point to some problem they had with my speech, there were many ways to do that, as opposed to, I think, a quite coded attack upon me as a highly intelligent, articulate black man who's very offense was the ability to speak the king's English to the queen's taste better than they were—at least, many who were gathered in the audience—and then *defend* black English practices among African American people, including some of the linguistic practices among the so-called lowest blacks who populate hip-hop culture, and then rise back to quoting respected figures from their own culture.

Yes, you did!

Part of that has to do with the ability to be a linguistic acrobat, to move among many communities of language, speech, discourse, and orality, and to bring all of that stuff together in a package that says, "I am an unadulterated black man, ain't got no shame about it, I'm gon' represent the African American interests *while being critical of them*. I'm going to speak to the larger, universal themes of black American culture while being critical of the ways that we fail to live up to our obligation to defend our own people—AND—I'm going to hit themes that the larger American culture can resonate with, because black folk are not orangutans living outside the arch of human experience. We are at the center of defining America." My point is, I refuse to give up on America precisely because I'm able to be critical of the nation. I think what was missed by many is that I spent most of that commencement speech talking about white youth culture when I talked about popular culture. I talked about Alanis Morissette. I talked about Kurt Cobain. I talked about Jenny McCarthy, because I knew my audience. At the same time, I wanted to talk about how black popular culture had redefined American pop culture, and as a result of that, many white kids see their lives through the lens of

Snoop Doggy Dogg or Biggie Smalls or Tupac Shakur. Their crossover effect is not gained by them surrendering the integrity of their African American identities, but by pressing them even more sharply in the faces of the mainstream American culture and press.

The real offense of my speech may be that a lot of the mostly white folk who gathered didn't understand what I was saying. Some of the words were foreign to them. They saw that I was highly articulate and intelligent and, yes, willing to assail the fabled pieties of white bigotry, and to name it for what it is. But I also challenged them to listen to their own children. I defended *so-called* poor white trash. I defended *so-called* underclass niggas. I defended *so-called* Generation X. I defended the *so-called* lost generation. And I challenged all of those people who were graduating from college with degrees—whose mothers and fathers, black, white, or other, were thought by some of them to be of no account because they didn't have college degrees—with a simple message: Don't forget your parents, remember them. And I gently criticized an apolitical figure like Michael Jordan, who makes millions of dollars reproducing and commodifying black juvenile interest in sport, television, and clothing apparel (the same youth, by the way, spend enormous sums of capital on him and thus help support his lifestyle), and yet he doesn't have the inclination to defend them by at least giving money to make sure that future scholars, future ballplayers, future athletes, future businesspeople, will be able to be supported through his own endeavors. And I think I would make that speech even *more sharply* today than I made it in December. Had I foreseen the firestorm of controversy that came, I wouldn't have been as meek and mild in my criticism. I would have been even sharper.

You would have turned up the volume?

I would have turned that volume way up to ten and said: Let's go for what we know.

I know this is far-fetched, but any response from him or anyone in his camp?

No direct response from Mr. Jordan. I think the huge controversy was enough of a chastisement of me in that sense. Here's my point: I don't have a problem with Michael Jordan giving money to the School of Social Work, but the implication was that if he had given the money to the Black Cultural Center, it would have been for only one group. But since he gave money to the School of Social Work, it's for everybody. Last time I checked, the School of Social Work ain't the School of Education, or the Law School, or the School of Arts and Sciences, or the division of Social Sciences, and on and on. Why is it that we believe if we give money to what we consider to be a white institution, or an academic discipline, that it's for everyone, it's universal, and when we give it to African American people it's limited? That is an insult to African American people who have been some of the most broad-minded, universally committed people in this country. We have been among the most patriotic, the most deeply dedicated citizens of this country, and yet there remains a stigma to giving to, supporting, and loving black folk. And some of those who spread the stigma most painfully are other blacks. I don't think Michael Jordan bears responsibility himself; we blacks bear responsibility for believing and allowing the notion to go forth that black interests are narrow and ghettoized, while other people's ethnic and racial interests are automatically invisible, and therefore, universal.

I wonder if, speaking of the donation from Jordan, this was even from him. Everything he does is weighed, talked about, and strategized. I wonder if he was involved in the decision making?

Yeah, I hear you. But you must remember this: Michael Jordan's mother was on the Black Cultural Center's board, raising money for the completion of the center's new building. So the fact that the money did not go to the Black Cultural Center cannot really be charged to anybody but Mr. Jordan or his mother. At that level, I'd have to say he knew what time it was. Not only that, we must recall Jordan's response when he was asked, during the first Harvey Gantt campaign for the U.S. Senate, to contribute money to Mr. Gantt, a former Charlotte mayor, respected architect, and highly regarded member of the black community. Not wanting to offend the Republican candidate, the widely acknowledged racist Jesse Helms, or his supporters, Jordan retorted with the most offensive, self-serving, community-disregarding, and repulsive political insularity, "Well, Republicans buy gym shoes, too." So I think we have to hold Mr. Jordan accountable for the vicious repercussions of not only his apolitical vision but also his deeply dehistoricized understanding of American culture that plays to the worst instincts of white bigotry and white supremacy. I don't think we can let Mr. Jordan off the hook there. Here's a man who's too shrewd, too informed, too determined to control where his money goes, to be let off the hook when it comes to where that money went. He made the statement himself that it would be for everybody if it went to the School of Social Work and *not*, by implication, if it went to the Black Cultural Center. No, no, I can't let Mr. Jordan off the hook on that. Besides, you are responsible for the people you have around you. When we look at Mr. Jordan's enterprise, we notice that most of his business partners are white, the people who take care of his finances are white, the people who do major business with Mr. Jordan are white. To be sure, we should all be democratic and multicultural in our business dealings, which means we should interact with as many different races and genders as possible in our affairs. But, again, there is a huge stigma on hiring talented black folk, especially among well-placed, well-heeled black folk. So, for Mr. Jordan, I think it's legitimate to ask: where are the black people? Show me the Negroes. Show me the black folk!

The Jerry McGuire thing, huh?

Yes. *Show me the brothers*! We don't have to ask Joe Montana: Please do some business with some white folks. We don't have to tell Brett Favre: Please do some business with some white folks. We don't have to tell Larry Bird, please at least have some white folks involved in your enterprises. These folk, without punitive consequence, without compunction, mostly transact business with folk who look like them. It's not beyond the pale of reason to expect that highly visible figures like me, public intellectuals like me or bell hooks or Skip Gates or whoever, or public figures who are athletes like Mr. Jordan, who is the most famous black person presently on the globe, to love your own people, to support them. I don't think they should by any means adopt an uncritical allegiance to all things black. I don't mean signing off with a blank check on everything that African American people do. I'm talking about having selective solidarity with black folk to give the impression, and more than the impression, to give rise to the truth, that black people are equally worthy as others of investment, equally worthy as others of entrepreneurial exploration, and equally worthy as others of being the bearers of the economic future and destiny of this country. We must trust black money to black people by circulating black dollars in black communities. I'm not a narrow, rigid nationalist when it comes to economics or culture.

To the contrary, I believe in a multicultural, deeply complex racial reality, but I don't believe in that at the expense of black folk. I believe Martin Luther King Jr. in 1968, ten days before he died, said that if black people are not careful, we're going to integrate ourselves out of power. He said, therefore, we should practice "temporary segregation." He suggested that we should keep some institutions black in order to maintain enough power to generate the requisite capital to support and fund our own institutions and community interests. I think Michael Jordan has lost a sense of what Muhammad Ali had, a sense of what Jim Brown, at his best had, a sense of what Hank Aaron had, a sense of what Wilma Rudolph had, a sense of what Althea Gibson had: a strong, unashamed commitment to black people. These figures believed that what you did as an individual athlete had racial ramifications. They showed a commitment to uplifting African American interests while fusing these interests to American goals. They believed that their performance as athletes could somehow broker acceptance for a wide range of black people outside of your particular sport. When Joe Louis was beating up on Max Schmeling, he was not only striking a blow for democracy and freedom from Nazism, but he was making a substitute argument for the game of American democracy to be played by one set of rules for all races.

Mr. Jordan lacks any sense of historical perspective about the struggles that made it possible for him to enjoy his incredible wealth and enormous opportunities. I don't think, collectively speaking, we can afford to overlook his shortcomings, since they have such far reach in that they discourage others—even whites who might be influenced by his example—to speak up or reach out. I don't think we should give up; we should love him, we should celebrate his genius, and we should hold him accountable for what he fails to grasp, because what he possesses by way of cultural and racial opportunity is not something he generated by himself. A whole lot of black folk paid the price, gave up their lives, shed blood, even sacrificed personal advancement and education, so that people like him—and me—could rise to the top. What he has to remember is that as he rose to the top, he stepped on some black folks' backs. Don't now step on their interests and in their faces or on their necks to maintain your connection to white folk. *Stop* loving white folk more than you love your own people. I'm not saying hate white folk, I'm saying love black folk as much as you love white folk and *show* the love you got for us by doing what you do to white folk: investing in their community and playing the tune to what they call. *That's* what I'm saying . . . Umm-hmmm!

All right, so that's all part of what came out of that speech. Now, your reaction to the criticism of that speech was, I believe, "I did what I did and I'm not responding to it, I'm not apologizing for it. I did what I did." But in the meantime, the chancellor or some others tried to make excuses. Your position was "no, don't apologize for me. I said what I said!"

Yes! That's exactly right.

So how did that whole thing resolve itself? Did it die a natural death?

Yes, though I still have gotten calls recently from folk who must have been out of the country and who are having delayed responses. I think the chancellor was an extraordinary coward. I think he's a reprehensible representative of the university. He subverts the highest principles of academic integrity by abdicating his role as an objective exponent of the freedom of thought that should characterize any university.

His name?

Michael Hooker. Chancellor Hooker has failed to live up to his responsibility to defend the principles of free speech in an academic environment where the pursuit, by the best and the brightest, of the ideas that have animated our culture, that have challenged our culture, should be protected. I think all this debate about political correctness usually is merely a code word for attacking black folk or Latinos or Native Americans or Asian Americans or women. But we see the fundamental funkiness of political correctness when so-called dominant American society fails to criticize its own practices. Dominant society fails to defend the principles of free speech by preventing dissident, politically incorrect black speech from being equally protected. Not only procedurally, that is by the logic of democracy, but substantively, that is by saying, "listen, I may disagree with this brother, but I defend his right to say it." And I think the chancellor, both procedurally and substantively, failed to live up to his obligation to protect free speech as a hallmark of the modern university.

On a personal level, here's a guy who got a lot of press when he came to Chapel Hill for being an exponent of black interests. Like very many white liberals, he's unable to come to grips with the limitations of what is in truth a neoliberal ideology, which, as Martin Luther King Jr., used to say, is more problematic to black interests than outright Ku Kluxism. At least with the KKK you know where you stand. Many white liberals shift ground so quickly, and they redefine their interests so immediately, that one is never sure where, ultimately, they come down. What's the bottom line for them? I'm not gainsaying the effectiveness of white liberalism. I'm saying that some white liberals surrender their moral responsibility in deference to political opportunism. Because they are in a halfway house of racial liberation, they're neither committed to the most powerful project of black liberation, which demands at times that they commit racial suicide, nor inclined to cast their fate with the outright bigots. So they end up in a mediating position preventing the flourishing of African American interests precisely because they're on the inside bringing the house down like Samson on the heads of African American people.

So now we're saying "bye-bye"?

I'm taking a year's leave of absence. I was invited to go to Columbia University way before this happened, I'm proud to say, because of the character and nature of my work. It wasn't anything political, insofar as my viewpoints or ideology are concerned. It was based on my work and the impact my work had on a national community of scholars and others outside the academy who are concerned about issues of African American culture, especially those involving race, gender, sexuality, and class. As a result of that, I was invited to spend a year at Columbia University to help strengthen the Institute of African American Research. I will be joining scholars like Manning Marable, Mary Patillo, Gina Dent, Lee Baker, and other supremely gifted scholars. Marable will be leading the charge for a model of black studies that, in one sense, takes the best of the Harvard model—where you gather strong, intelligent people together to think about critical issues—joined to the best of the Temple model—where you take seriously the interests of everyday people and join them to the scholarly pursuits of the best and the brightest. We want to embrace the best of those traditions while avoiding their worst elements, and come up with something that's equally powerful and yet, we want to navigate a different path.

Let's talk about blacks in North Carolina. As I mentioned, I'm writing about blacks in Chapel Hill. As I speak with people, a couple of themes keep cropping up. The whole issue of integration, that it was bad for us, as well as the notion of blacks still having a plantation mentality, that it's very much a part of our present culture. That we haven't learned how to get on with the business of being black in America. I found the notion of us having those perspectives very interesting.

That's very powerful and self-critical, which is wonderful because the best of these black southern traditions have always negotiated between explicit articulation of rage against the system, and white supremacy, and a more moderating political influence geared to black survival. The logic of black moderation is that you've got to survive long enough to rebel; if you're dead, you can't rebel. Still, I think there's a resistance to the more disabling features of moderate belief that show up in the disdain among many blacks for plantation Negro syndrome, PNS if you will, a peculiar affliction among black folk who are unduly enamored of white culture. They are deferential to white culture and afraid to speak up for African American interests in fear of offending their patrons. Such behavior suggests that these blacks will always be on a plantation, whether a literal or a metaphoric one. It's a kind of psychic plantation from which they can never quite evict themselves, and to which they can never stop paying rent or homage. We are constantly paying the wages of a psychic captivity to white culture, and that's a situation perpetuated by plantation Negro syndrome. Malcolm X used to say there were house niggers and field niggers, even though I think he was sometimes rather narrow and rigid in his interpretation. But I think we understand that he was fundamentally getting at a power point: the house niggers were those who were invested in oppressive white culture, helping the house of white exploitation remain stable and secure and beyond social challenge, especially from black quarters. When a fire came along, so to speak, they said, "Oh, let's help massa put the fire out with water." Whereas Malcolm said, the field niggers were the ones who, when the fire came along, were trying to blow with the wind to make sure that house burned down. Blow that damn thing down! Burn it down. You know the chant: "The roof, the roof, the roof is on fire/ We don't need no water, let the *!*! burn."

We can't be rigid in the interpretation of black culture through such symbolism because some house Negroes were informing field Negroes about what the master was doing, telling the field niggers what time it was and when they should strike and when they should move. At the same time, there's little doubt there's some wisdom contained in these typologies, in these blunt archetypes of black behavior. I think plantation Negro syndrome symbolizes the truth that some black folk are still afraid of white folk, still afraid of offending white folk by telling the truth about race, about identity, about culture, about politics, and about history. There are many white folk who just want black folk to tell them the truth, but then there are many more who don't want to hear the truth. Many blacks know this and are afraid to speak out. They figure the best way to forge relations with white brothers and sisters is to resort to clichés such as "go along to get along," and "fit in where you get in." Many blacks believe that from such a vantage point, inside the graces and gazes of white culture, they will be able to rework the structure of society, or at least bend it to their advantage. There's some wisdom to preserving your survival long enough to subvert negative influences from the inside, to get educated enough, to look respectable enough, to be able to change things from within the dominant culture. But the problem is that many African Americans who end up getting inside resort to bleaching themselves in an ocean of white oblivion to black culture. They induct themselves into the United States of Amnesia and they *forget* black interests; they divert the psychic and social funds that should be underwriting black liberation to a more palatable, ameliorative relationship with oppressive, hegemonic culture. I think that's deeply destructive. I'm not speaking here of genuinely embracing whites and others as friends, allies, colleagues, and costrugglers with blacks around issues of racial justice and radical democracy. I'm speaking of an unprincipled capitulation to oppressive white culture that ends up destroying the psychic and moral drive among blacks for genuine freedom and true equality.

On the other hand, I think there's some legitimacy to the criticism that aspects and modes of integration have been bad for blacks. Think about our schools. If legally mandated integrated schools are not being sufficiently supported, many well-to-do whites (and some blacks) can bail out of the public schools into which blacks have been integrated to protect their own educational and economic interests. Such public institutions are left to fight on their own, with critically overstrapped budgets. As a result, black interests suffer because many white Americans have the leisure to take their money elsewhere and to support their own schools or institutions where very few minorities, especially African Americans and Latinos, are able to secure entree. I'm sympathetic to some arguments against integration which hold that efforts to desegregate our society have failed to deliver the promise of African American liberation. The only problem is there are even greater failures of certain black nationalist ideas and institutions that do not deliver on their word and promise. Ethnitopia, or the utopic vision of black ethnicity, has been equally problematic in delivering on the goods. So we've got to find a way to circulate and pool resources among African American people that embraces the important dimensions of integration while also taking a measured account of the need for black institutions to regulate and govern themselves.

As I listen to you, Michael, much of what you're saying is applicable nationally. So, while I've been thinking of "PNS" as a southern thing, it's very broad.

Oh, the plantation ain't got no geographical location. The plantation is a state of mind. You ain't living on Georgia soil, the Georgia soil is living in your mind. The plantation is a traveling archetype of black deference to white supremacy, of the deference of black rationality to white irrationality. A major problem with this plantation Negro syndrome is that it makes black folk, whether they are dealing with overt or subtle forms of racial domination in the North or South, East or West, ignore the virtue and vitality of black life while uncritically embracing the ideal—and the ideals of—white life. And those black folk who bitterly oppose any acknowledgment of the historic legacy of white supremacy, or the need of blacks to actively confront white hostility or indifference to black self-determination, are, I believe, deeply ensconced in plantation Negro syndrome. I think we've got to be quite explicitly critical of such mind-sets and behaviors. It's not located simply in the South, but all over this country.

Okay, but is there something that you've become aware of, or more in tune with, that is more particularly southern with black folks?

Well, yes. Speaking in the most general terms, and there is always a risk in doing so, there is a powerful moral bearing of black southerners that is quite remarkable. There's a sense of dealing with the civil rituals of southern culture among black southerners that their northern counterparts are hostile to, indifferent to, or rather impatient to master or learn. Many of the rites of civility in the South are transracial: black and white southerners both respect and revere them, while many other southerners of both races rebel against them. But there is little question that, in many respects, black and white southern culture has been taken from the same fabric. To shift metaphors, they've been created out of the same cauldron, formed in the same crucible, even though it often brimmed with racial conflict. That explains how black and white southerners can have similar points of cultural reference—they both eat black-eyed peas and collard greens, and cornbread, too—but at times hold radically different viewpoints about what it will take to improve race relations. That's also why Martin Luther King Jr. was able to appeal to a common moral worldview in the South. King effectively appealed to the southern "white conscience" because he had been reared in the same psychic space, with its attendant social rituals, where the mores and folkways of southern culture were faithfully observed. In other words, besides the obvious conflicts, there'd always been a fusion of certain elements of black and white southern cultures that gave real heft and resonance to the ethical claims of the civil rights movement in white southern society.

At some level, the civil rights movement appealed to many enlightened whites—or enlightened them in the first place—convincing them that they could overcome their negative debts to a racist world of white supremacy and become more deeply attuned to the common humanity of the black people with whom they shared culture. In some instances, they shared kith and kin, and even when it wasn't a matter of formal kinship, they shared moral and psychological ties. Ironically enough, the world that made even provisional transracial solidarity possible was also the source of its undoing. I think pockets of black southern culture breed an unprincipled deference to white belief and culture. That's why many black folk were enormously defensive of the southern way of doing things, which often meant resisting outright black freedom struggles. Many blacks felt a bond to white southerners that transcended race, sharing in the circumstance of their birth an almost genetic predisposition to defend their mythologized terrain from ideological interlopers—including liberal white students and black militants from the North—or political traitors, such as King and a host of other black southern dissidents. They were almost like the Mob, these white and black southerners, who, despite internal fissures and fights, plaintively proclaimed the virtues of "this thing of ours."

Many southern black folk opposed Martin Luther King Jr. and the civil rights movement because *they* got along with *their* white folk: "We are getting along here," they seemed to say, "so don't come messing things up." That explains the incredible gentility and civility that prevails here, and it may shed light on the speed and style of black response to white supremacy and hence the suspicious function of black dissidents within a southern worldview. Southern black resistance is often masked, ritualized, and performed at a different pace than varieties of northern black rebellion. My commencement speech was probably an offense to many southerners, black and white, because I didn't observe the requisite form of civilized behavior and language that signified, that inferred, that implied. The long implication is the strong suit of southern rhetoric. In my commencement address, I didn't kowtow to ritualized speech and signifying rhetorical practice. I've been preaching in southern culture for nearly twenty years, and I've pastored three churches in the South, so perhaps I should have known better.

A sidebar to that is the recent tour of the Henrietta Marie, *the slave ship that was recovered and restored by black divers. There was an outcry by blacks who said, "this is part of the past, leave it there," and there were those who broke out in tears, terribly moved, feeling compelled to deal with it, saying "it's part of my history." Any words on that?*

Well, I think denying the *Henrietta Marie*'s importance in black life is a powerful metaphor for the tragic amnesia that clogs the arteries of blacks in

American culture. It's lamentable that black people don't realize that the past is so crucial to our present and our future. We need to know everything about the past that we can learn. The *Henrietta Marie* is one of the crucial artifacts of our black past that we need to investigate in order to understand the magnitude of the tragedy we confronted in slavery. Many black folk believe that because they're black, they will know as a measure of their birthright black history, life, and culture. But that belief is simply not true and symbolizes, in many ways, an internalized form of white supremacy that discourages blacks from believing their history is worthy of study, or that its rigors are sufficiently established as to demand critical scrutiny. One cannot by means of osmosis absorb from black environments the collective memory of the race, since it is not passed on through the membranes, or through the nucleus or mitochondria of cells of racial experience. One must critically interrogate the contexts and substance of black history through serious study.

And even as we acknowledge the need for deliberate, dangerous memory—the sort of racial knowledge that contradicts the distorting fantasies and twisted memories of dominant society—such memory should rest on a sustained engagement with the facts at hand, even if one bitterly debates "the facts" and whose interpretation of those facts is most persuasive. The *Henrietta Marie* is potentially a very fertile occasion in the interpretation of black cultural memory and history. We should greet the opportunity to excavate our past with great enthusiasm. Our Jewish brothers and sisters won't be caught saying, "The Holocaust is part of the past; we've got to forget it." No, they say, "Never again! We will never forget." They link memory to survival—as do Mary Frances Berry and John Blassingame in the title of their wonderful survey of African American history, *Long Memory*. We must insist that historical investigation and cultural remembrance are critical agents of witness against the oppressive amnesia of dominant society, which would just as easily forget the painful passages of black struggle and the thrilling triumphs of black history.

But collective memory is also a weapon against self-hatred, a bitter fruit that grows on the vine of racial ignorance and amnesia. We must acknowledge, and fight against, the stigma associated with collective black memory, since black folk are creatively punished in dominant culture for recalling the past as a predicate for contemporary resistance. One of the reasons that quarters of dominant society disparage black collective memory is the fight over apologies and material resources. Thus many whites resent the demand for an apology, tendered, symbolically speaking, by American society for the pain of the black past and present. But the demand for white apology without a radical adjustment in the distribution of social goods like education, employment and economic support for our neediest members is rather hollow. Of course, someone who is severely harmed would like to hear an apology from the perpetrator, accompanied by efforts to reconstitute relations and redress the wrong inflicted. That's a crucial plank in any conception of restorative justice. But if that's a sticking point, I say skip the apologies and get down to justice.

Of course, there have been apologies, such as the one offered by the Southern Baptist Convention for its role in theologically and morally defending slavery. At this rate, we'll get an apology for segregation well into the next century, an apology for Jim Crow a century after that, and maybe by A.D. 4000, we'll get an apology for racist practices of our own day! I say address the material misery that resulted from slavery by restructuring social relations and redistributing financial assets. Still, black collective memory is crucial to this process. Without vigilance on the part of the black elite and grassroots, including intellectuals, politicians, lawyers, community activists, artists, and ordinary citizens, the dangerous memories of black struggle will be lost. If black folk are reluctant to wage this battle, shame on us. The stigma attached to what may be termed memory warfare must be lessened by our relentless pursuit of truth, justice, and honest history. Because so many blacks are concerned with how our efforts appear to the mainstream, we fail to devote the energy and attention we should to our own freedom. We are often fearful of engaging in memory warfare because we know it outrages the white society to which too many of us pay unwarranted homage and unearned deference. When black folk stop obsessing about what our white brothers and sisters think—and start concentrating on what is just and righteous—we will not only love ourselves better, but we may discover that we've got far more allies among other races than we ever imagined.

Interview by Lana Williams
Durham, North Carolina, 1997

part two

Cultural Studies

8

Is Postmodernism Just Modernism in Drag?

Black Identities in Flux

The first thing I'd like to ask is: Who is Michael Eric Dyson? And I want you to take the liberty of answering this in a manner that is not strictly autobiographical. One reason I ask this is because your book jacket begins describing you as "welfare father, ordained Baptist minister, Princeton Ph.D." Then in your chapter on the black public intellectual, you give yourself the shameless self-promotion award.

One of the reasons I take postmodernism so seriously, even as I refuse to make a fetish of its insights, is a notion that has been championed by its theorists, especially in cultural and literary studies: an evolving, fluid identity. What I take from the postmodern conception of identity is captured in the terms beautifully phrased in black Christian circles, namely, "I don't have to be what I once was." That Christian conception of the evolution of character highlights the variability and flexibility of human identity, even if such a view clashes profoundly with postmodern arguments against a fixed human nature on which many Christian conceptions of identity rest. But for black Christians—who are arguably situated deep inside modernism with its impulse to dynamism and disruption, as well as its unyielding quest for the new—and secular postmodernists alike, identity is a process, a continual play of existential choices over a field of unfolding possibility. The self today can be radically different from the self of yesterday.

Taking that seriously, Mike Dyson is an experiment in identity, a testament to a process of evolving self-awareness; some of the elements of my self are surely in conflict, while other fragments of my self are made coherent because they've been sewn together by the threads of history, culture, race, and memory. Who I was, say, ten years ago, was a scholar in the making, and eight or ten years before that, I was a welfare father, a hustler on Detroit's streets, a divorcing husband, a young man who was trying to figure out what to do with his life. I was twenty-one, and I hadn't gone to college or prepared myself academically to take up my vocation. So, who I am is constantly implicated in the themes I take up in my work. What does it mean to be young, black, and male in this country? What are the racial and economic forces that shape black life? How can we achieve racial justice and equality? What does it mean to be an intellectual in a world that prizes image more than substance? How should we treat the vulnerable and the destitute? How can we bridge the psychic and social gulfs between the generations? How can we speak about God in a world where religion has been hijacked by fundamentalists and fascists? How do we untangle the vicious knots of patriarchy, sexism, and misogyny in our nation? How do we affirm and protect gay, lesbian, bisexual, and transgendered people in our communities? All these questions, and many more, play out in my intellectual and political pursuits.

Who I am, then, in many senses, is a bridge builder, a bridge figure. I want to span the streets and the academy, and the sacred and the secular. I also want to bridge traditions and the transformations of those traditions, including religious belief, intellectual engagement, scholarly investigation, racial solidarity, class struggle, resistance to economic oppression, and feminist insurgence. Of course, the parts of my identity that might obviously be in tension, say the academic and the activist, suffer pressure in both directions: the academy is suspicious of the streets, and vice versa. The tension is one of proximity and distance. To the academy, there is the threat of proximity to the chaotic, propulsive, unregulated, sometimes uncivil passions of the world beyond the university. To the denizens of the streets—including its natural constituency of grassroots activists, conspiracy managers, and on-the-ground, indigenous, concrete intellectuals—there is the fear that academics will remain aloof, indifferent to their suffering, and intellectually unavailable to supply strategies to resist their oppression. I want to do the best I can to answer the threat of proximity, not by less but by more interaction between academics and activists, hoping to prove that the interactions benefit the university. And I want to help heal fears of distance by bringing the resources of intelligence and compassion to bear on the hurts of the socially vulnerable. It is that desire to bridge gulfs that unifies my disparate selves, making me much more sympathetic to the prophetic mystic Howard Thurman, who once prayed to God, "make me unanimous in myself."

I'll ask you then this question. Baldwin in Giovanni's Room *says: "Perhaps home is not a place but an irrevocable condition." In* South to a Very Old Place, *Albert Murray begins with this thought: "But then, going back home has probably always had as much if not more to do with people as with landmarks and place names and locations on maps and mileage charts anyway. Not that home is not a place, for even in its most abstract implications it is precisely the very oldest place in the world. But even so, it is somewhere you are likely to find yourself remembering your way back to far more often than it is ever possible to go by conventional transportation." Given that, in that context, where do you feel most at home?*

Yes. Yes. Good question, man. Well, as both of these writers make clear, home is about the geography of imagination. For me, it's also about the architecture of identity through aspiration and yearning, since home is carved from hope and memory. It is both forward-looking and backward leaning. And that means that home is not simply a place forever anchored by concrete foundations. It is not simply a fixed point with tangible coordinates in space and time. Home is a metaphysical possibility that seeds the ground of experience and infuses our finite encounters in local spaces with meaning. That's why Burt Bacharach's writing partner, Hal David, could pen a lyric that makes the philosophical argument that "a house is not a home," distinguishing the two by the quality of relations that turn the former into the latter. Like identity, home, to a large degree, is composed of an evolving awareness about how you can decrease the discomfort you have in the world as a result of your roots. That's why our foreparents spoke of "a house not made with hands," as it says in 1 Corinthians, casting biblical language in their own religious accents. And they suggested that this world "ain't no friend to grace," since it was alienated from God's purpose. For a people who were often homeless—rootless and adrift in a sea of chattel slavery, and later, exploitative sharecropping—home assumed a high priority. That's why many of our foreparents hoped for a day when they could, in the words of one slave, "read my title clear." Home had intense metaphoric value for our foreparents in another way: as the imagined space of unlimited access to God in heaven, a place they hoped to go after they died, signified in songwriter Charles Tindley's familiar refrain in black Christian circles, "I'll make it home, someday."

Of course, there are dangers to the notion of home in black life as well, especially when it comes to elevating one's imagined geography of spirit, one's own sense of home, as the sole source of authentic blackness. After all, roots are meant to nourish, not strangle, us. I'm thinking in particular of the vicious debates raging in many black communities about what is really black, how we define it, and how the spaces of black identity are linked increasingly to a narrow slice of black turf—the ghetto. Our kids are literally dying over a profound misunderstanding about our culture that links authenticity to geography, that makes one believe that if she is black, she must pledge ultimate allegiance to the ghetto as the sole black home of the black subject. The exclusive identification of the ghetto as the authentic black home is wholly destructive.

Out of this grows the "keep it real" trope that punishes any departure from a lethally limited vision of black life, one that trades on stereotype and separation anxiety, since there is a great fear of being severed from the fertile ground of the true black self. But to subscribe to these beliefs is to be woefully misled. Sure, the beauty of the impulse to authenticity is altogether understandable: to protect a black identity that has been assaulted by white supremacy through the assertion of a uniquely guarded and qualified black self, rooted in a similarly protected view of the authentic black home. Plus, too many blacks who "made it" have surely forgotten "where they came from." But the legitimate critique of blacks besieged by what may be termed *Aframnesia*—the almost systematic obliteration of the dangerous memory of black suffering and racial solidarity, a gesture that is usually rewarded by white elites—is different from imposing rigid views on black life of how and where blackness erupts or emerges. Thus we end up with vicious mythologies and punishing pieties: for instance, one cannot be gay and be authentically black in some circles, which means there's no home, no place of grace in many black communities for black homosexuals. Or the black male assault on black female interests is justified as the necessary subordination of gender to race in the quest for liberation. Or the only real black is in the ghetto, a ghetto that in the social imagination of its romantic advocates rarely looks like the complex, complicated, contradictory place it is.

As a former resident of the ghetto, I wholeheartedly concur with the notion that we can neither forget its people nor neglect its social redemption through strategic action. Further, I think it's beautiful for folk who have survived the ghetto, who've gotten out, to carry the blessed image of its edifying dimensions in their hearts and imaginations, and to pledge to never leave the ghetto even as they travel millions of miles beyond its geographical boundaries. That means that they'll never betray the wisdom, genius, and hope that floods the ghetto in ways that those outside its bounds rarely understand. It is, after all, a portable proposition, a mobile metaphor. But we must not seize on the most limited view possible of ghetto life and sanctify it as the be-all and end-all of black existence. That leads to kids killing each other in the name of an authentic ghetto masculinity that is little more than pathological self-hatred. The black ghetto working class, the working poor, and the permanently poor have always been more complex, and more resilient, than they have ever been given credit for. We've got to avoid the trap of existential puniness and racial infantilism and see our way to a robustly mature vision that shatters the paradigm of the authentic black self and, by extension, the acceptable black home.

Given that analysis, I feel most at home in the intersection of all the energies provoked by my different roles, as preacher, teacher, public intellectual, political activist, agent provocateur, and paid pest. In one sense, I couldn't rest all of my energy in one place doing one thing; the ability to do them all gives me the vocational patience to do any of them. And I feel a sense of transgression, a sense of irreverence (and to my mind, those are good qualities) in fulfilling all these roles that gives me, oddly enough, a feeling of being at home, because I feel I'm being truest to my self when I vigorously, and critically, engage my various communities of interest or, as the anthropologists say, my multiple kinship groups. For instance, I love to preach, and whenever I get the chance, I'm in a pulpit on Sunday morning "telling the story," as black ministers elegantly phrase preaching the gospel. For all of its problems and limitations, the black pulpit, at its best, is still the freest, most powerful, most radically autonomous place on earth for black people to encourage each other in the job of critical self-reflection and the collective struggle for liberation. I think theologian Robert McAfee Brown put it best when he said the church is like Noah's ark: if it wasn't for the storm on the outside, we couldn't stand the stink on the inside.

But the stink in the black church is surely foul. There are still a lot of negative beliefs about gender and sexual orientation, and even class, that need to be addressed. There are big pockets of staunchly conservative sentiment that, I think, have to be opposed. I try not to avoid these subjects as I preach, and sometimes what I say goes over like a brick cloud! Still, I try to seduce people into seeing things differently, as I make arguments about why the opposition to gay and lesbian folk, for instance, reeks of the same biblical literalism that smashed the hopes of black slaves when white slave masters deployed it. But I try to win the folk over first, by preaching "in the tradition," so to speak, warming them up first before I lower the boom. When I was a young preacher and pastor, one of my members told me you "gain more by honey than vinegar." So I give honey before I give vinegar. I invite the folk to the progressive theological, ideological, and spiritual terrain I want them to occupy, but I try to issue that invitation in ways that won't immediately alienate them. And once they're there, they're a captive audience.

One gains his bona fides by preaching well, evoking "amens" by articulately referencing the black religious tradition, and this can be done with little fear of surrendering the politics I favor. The rhetorical forms are themselves neutral, so to speak, and thus the political uses to which they're put is something that's strictly TBD: to be determined by the rhetor, the prophet, the priest, the speaker, or the pastor. Then when I've got them where I want them, rhetorically speaking, in a velvet verbal vice, I squeeze hard, using the good feeling and theological credit I've gained from preaching well to assault the beliefs that are problematic, from homophobia, sexism, patriarchy, ageism, racism, and classism to environmental inequities. And sometimes, they're giving assent against their wills, shouting amen to ideas that they may not have otherwise supported without being pushed or prodded—or seduced. They might even muse to themselves, "Well, he's got a point," or "I disagree, but I'll at least think about it." But as much as I love the black church, and see it as my home, it's too narrow to be my only home. That's why I claim the classroom, the lectern, and the academy as my home as well, a place I love immensely, but the inbred snobbishness and well-worn elitism of elements of this home mean that I can't rest my entire self there either. I'm involved in both mainstream and radical politics, but elements of the latter are hostile to the spiritual traditions I cherish, which means my home in such circles is not one that accommodates my entire being. So I float among all of these stations of identification, so to speak. My home, while certainly not carved from a process of elimination—cutting away features I find unattractive, offensive, or burdensome in each "home"—is certainly the product of a stance of critical appreciation that allows me to derive benefit, pleasure, and sustenance from each space.

So I conceive of home as a moveable feast of identity that I'm constantly feeding on. Because of the many communities in which I'm involved, I'm constantly rethinking who I am. In a way, I'm also constantly trying to get back home to Detroit, perhaps in a more spiritual than physical manner, since I go back fairly frequently to preach and visit my mother and brothers. There's an elusive state of contentment that you nostalgically associate with home even when it was a turbulent and trying place. Detroit was, in many ways, such a place for me, but it also provided so much joy and fulfillment, and it gave me a sense of the appropriate things to grasp hold of in life, beyond the material blessings one might seek. It was a great beginning, and as I heard Toni Morrison once say, beginnings are important because they must do so much more than start. While starting is crucial, beginnings also propel us along paths of influence whose real impact we may not be able to detect for years and years to come. That's certainly the case with me.

Detroit has become for me a metaphor of the complex convergence of fate and human volition. It's a symbol for me of how destiny is at best partly determined by living one's life in a meaningful, coherent fashion. That's most acutely obvious to me in grappling with my brother's imprisonment and my quest for improvement in every sphere of my life, including my professional life, my spiritual infrastructure, and my moral landscape. Home is a complicated place for me now, which is why nostalgia is inevitable, pleasurable, even desirable—and quite problematic, perhaps dangerous at points. Nostalgia, of course, is crucial to the project of black identity, largely as a defensive move against the brutal memories of suffering we endured at the hands of those outside our communities, and from within. Nostalgia, at least in that light, is an attempt to exercise sovereignty over memory, to force it into redemptive channels away from the tributaries of trauma that flood the collective black psyche. It is the attempt to rescue ethical agency—and hence manage and control the perception of suffering—from the fateful forces of racial terror. One of the most bruising racial terrors is to have the dominant culture determine what memories are most important to the dominated minority.

In that case, nostalgia is an attempt to take back the political utility of memory. After all, if you remember a horrible experience as something from which you can squeeze some good, then you've refused the hegemonic power the prerogative to define your fate. By remembering the same event with different accents, with different social purposes, through different eyes, one gives memory a racial and moral usefulness that can challenge dominant culture. I suspect that's at stake when black folk wax nostalgic about segregation and the sort of relatively self-determining culture we were able to carve out of Jim Crow apartheid. You hear it as black folk say, "When we were forced to live together under segregation, we had more unity, we lived in the same neighborhoods, we helped each other more, economically and spiritually, and we did not depend on white patronage but promoted black self-reliance. Now under desegregation we've lost the power we had. Our colleges have suffered a brain drain to elite white schools. Our black businesses that catered to black needs suffered when we were able to buy white. And our neighborhoods were turned over to the poor and destitute when 'white flight' was mimicked by 'black track' to the suburbs."

The downside of such nostalgia is that it fails to explicitly engage the radical inequality of such segregated arrangements. It also tends to exaggerate the moral differences between generations, especially as the rose-colored tint of the black past is not used to cast an eye on the present or the future, for that matter. The net result is that one's own generation is made golden, while those following are seen as tarnished by the surrender to urges, forces, and seductions that were heroically resisted in the past. Hence jazz was great and hip-hop is awful. People believe that even though earlier black generations thought jazz was terrible and preferred religious music. But there were problems there too, since many blacks felt that religious music too easily compromised its purity by integrating elements from secular blues. And it goes on and on. Then too, we've got to be careful not to ultimately justify or legitimate the oppression by nostalgically recalling its good effects. Nostalgic blacks end up reinforcing what may be termed *subversive empathy* from the dominant culture, which, after all, provided the conditions under which our race and culture could thrive under segregation, even if those conditions were harmful and oppressive.

Subversive empathy is similar, I suppose, to anthropologist Renato Rosaldo's notion of imperialist nostalgia, where hegemonic culture destroys an indigenous minority tradition and then has the gall to weep with those folk over the destruction of their culture. In subversive empathy, the dominant culture empathizes with our need to restore the conditions of our relative prospering under Jim Crow. While not explicitly invoking a return to the racist past, it nevertheless puts forth arguments and supports practices that have the same effect. That's why black folk have to be especially cautious about supporting Bill Bennett's partnership with C. Delores Tucker in combating hardcore hip-hop. They appeal to a golden age, nostalgic belief about the black family that is turned viciously against us in Bennett's conservative cosmology. For that matter, we ought to be careful about uncritically celebrating Bill Clinton's nostalgic appeal to black America to return to a bygone moral era. In a speech before a black religious audience in Memphis, Tennessee, Clinton invoked Martin Luther King Jr.'s memory to chide black America about pockets of immorality in our communities and pathological family structure, ignoring the harmful social impact of many of his policies on the black family. He sounds like a friend, and in many ways he is, but he is also a foe to our best political interests. His political beliefs, in many ways, are emblematic of subversive empathy.

If the impulse to nostalgia is not disciplined, it can be used to fashion moral judgments out of fantasies of the past that downplay our failures and project them more vehemently on someone, or something, else. A huge example is how older blacks nostalgically recall their idyllic lives in comparison to the ills of modern youth, assaulting their relative moral failures while extolling their own virtues.

But to sum it all up, I suppose home conjures for me that Frankie Beverly anthem, "Joy and Pain." But it remains the quintessential space of possibility, of hope, of unending yearning and unfulfilled expectation.

I guess I'd like to hear you talk about that notion in relation to this generation you belong to, "the betweeners"—very late baby boomers and very early generation x or hip-hop. This also, in the academy, seems to stand right at that modern-postmodern divide. When I hear you talk about your relationship to home, I hear an important question about history and home, time and home. I'm the minister of music at my church, so you know that when I show up with the dread thing going on and I play for the senior choir, there is this odd sense of dissonance and I feel completely at home there even though there are some looking at me as if to say "What's wrong with that brother?" But there's this odd sort of thing that goes on because where you are is always where you feel most at home. I imagine that that's what happens to you when you're in the pulpit: that it's the most natural home, but when you walk out into the classroom there is no rupture. But given our notions of race and culture and some of our stereotypes, it seems as if people would expect there to be a rupture, but there isn't.

No, no. In that sense it's seamless for me, moving from one rhetorical situation to another, from the pulpit as the axis of convergence of history, spirituality, and morality, to the classroom, where there are other axes of convergence, including inquiry, skepticism, and excavation. The orbits of these rhetorical universes might be seen to be in collision with one another. But skillful black rhetoricians, speakers, teachers, intellectuals, and orators can, by virtue of an enchanted imagination, speak worlds of discourse into existence that cross disciplinary fault lines, that move among genres, and that navigate through discursive minefields, such as the question of what constitutes "real knowledge." At its base, black culture has always been about migration and mobility. Its members, in one way or another, have been about the business of adapting ourselves to foreign spaces and creating home in the midst of them. We've constantly raised the question of Psalm 147, "How can we sing Zion's songs in a strange land?" To borrow more biblical imagery, the book of Acts contains that famous passage about Paul and his mates being shipwrecked and making it to shore "on broken pieces." Black people have always been able to take the fragments and shards of our lives, the pieces of our existence broken by oppression, and rework them into a pattern of purposeful existence. That's not simply about fragmentation as a trope of black existence in the postmodern moment. It's also about the black modernist quest for a stable identity in the midst of flux and upheaval, often articulated, ironically enough, through a premodern religious worldview.

Thus the premodern black biblical universe accommodates black modernist pursuits in postmodern conditions. "Making it in on broken pieces" has long been a rhetorical staple in the grassroots theodicies—in both the Weberian, sociological sense and in theological terms—that shape the preaching of figures from C. L. Franklin, Aretha Franklin's father, to Jesse Jackson. Add to that the fragments of European cultural influences and African cultural retentions that shape black life, and the unavoidability of black folk negotiating between disparate vocabularies, indeed, different worlds, should be dramatically apparent. I think that Levis-Strauss's notion of bricolage, of taking what's at hand, what's left over, so to speak, in the construction of culture to shape one's survival and identity, is a crucial concept as well in coming to terms with this black gift to move in and through a variety of rhetorics and discourses. In that sense, then, our identities have always been fabricated out of the content of our surroundings. Forced migration and permanent exile will make one into a sophisticated cultural polyglot and sometimes into a cosmopolitan citizen. Home was often a compromise of contexts: wherever we found ourselves, we made that home or at least we transported our home there. Home was not something we could leave and come to again, so home often had to travel with us, across turbulent waters, into hostile countries, and within resistive communities.

That's not to deny the reality of fixed points of domestic reference in time and space, and in body and memory. But the reality is that black people had to have multiple notions of home, and often multiple homes, which is why there's a thin line between coerced migration and homelessness. You've got to remember that home is a noun, verb, adjective, and adverb, and it is both a means and an end. So the lack of a sense of rupture grows from the seamless interweaving of multiple meanings articulated through a variety of rhetorical situations, whether it's preaching, teaching, writing, and so on. In my case, I can't deny that at some points all the communities I'm involved in may experience tension and conflict because I don't feel a radical rupture in moving from one vocabulary to another. But as Gerald Graff argues, we've got to teach the conflicts, and by extension we've got to illustrate the tensions. For me, that means we've got to mix rhetorical styles in edifying fashion. So when I get up in the classroom, for instance, and I really get going, talking about Foucault and Derrida, perhaps, and about Judith Butler, and about Stuart Hall and his distinction between preferred meanings versus negotiated meanings and oppositional meanings, my intellectual excitement translates to my verbal style and energizes my peculiar semantic trace.

And my Baptist roots begin to nourish my oratorical engagement, and before I know it, I'm *preaching* postmodernism.

So here you have a professor with a staccato rhythm and a tuneful cadence who's invested in the articulation of postmodern conceptualizations of identity and power. I'm baptizing my lecture in the rhetorical waters of my religious tradition. There is no rupture, no discontinuity, nothing but seamless negotiations between diverse styles of intellectual and rhetorical engagement. There may be problems for interlocutors who believe that an etiquette of articulation should prevail, one that polices style and dictates proprietary usage. But I ain't with that, so there's no problem for me. The irony is that even in this so-called postmodernist moment, which ostensibly celebrates pastiche, fragmentation, collage, difference, irreverent fusions, and the like, black style remains problematic. When black identity marks postmodernity with its embodied articulation, there's a rupture going on in the midst of the rupturing context itself. It involves the problem that has confronted us in premodernity, modernity, and postmodernity: race, and more specifically, the issue of blackness and its unwieldy complement of transgressing expressions.

Yes. There seems always to be this move to delegitmitize, to make it illegal.

Literally illegal.

I remember my first semester as an undergraduate at Princeton. So, to my mind, this white guy says to me, How are you ever going to go home again? Aren't you afraid that these people won't understand?

Yes, would have to unbirth you . . .

There's some rupture. I've thought about this black Ivy League tradition that we seem to silence. Although we celebrate these people, we silence the fact that they were educated in and present at these institutions at the same time as the Eliots, Stevens, Santayanas, and James. Inhabiting the same physical space.

That's exactly right. And that's why postmodernity is so crucial, at least in theory: it helps us uncover and claim the useful legacies of modernism that were submerged in its racial silences. Of course, it could be that postmodernism is really modernism in drag. As you said, when you think of modernism, you think of Eliot and Stevens. And as you noted, you think of Santayana and James too, and we could add Royce, just to keep the Harvard modernists in line. And we could add Joyce, Pound, Frost, Crane, and a host of others. Gender got a strong foothold in the modernist canon in a way that race was never quite able to do, with figures like Marianne Moore, Virginia Woolf, Rebecca West, and Djuna Barnes. But at the same time, W.E.B. Du Bois is right in the middle of modernism, along with Countee Cullen, Langston Hughes, Zora Neale Hurston, Dorothy West, Richward Wright, Chester Himes, Ralph Ellison, James Baldwin, and many, many more. They were all thinking, writing, imagining, and populating black universes, even as many of them insisted that it was impossible to limn the American experience without viewing the nation through the eyes of blacks who were more American than African, as Ellison contended, or as they emphasized the universal moral impulse that echoes through black demands for dignity and humanity, as Baldwin argued.

The black modernists were attempting to breathe freely beyond the claustrophobic boundaries of race, trying to refigure black identity and, by extension, American identity. Yet they're always seen in these boxed, fixed, localized categories, when indeed they're trying to help us reimagine the project of America: "I, too, sing America," as Hughes sang, ringing a change, varying a theme, signifying upon and harkening metaphorically back to Walt Whitman's "I sing the body electric." Hughes and the great black modernists inserted black America into the mainstream flow and thereby proved that America must bend itself to our tune, song, riff, beat, meter, prose, rhythm, and the like in order to be truly, fully, wholly itself. For instance, Duke Ellington and Louis Armstrong swung in the mainstream and then swung the mainstream to a black rhythm, and through their music, helped America grasp the self-enlarging principle of subordinating color to culture and craft. Hughes was aggressively insinuating himself, and black folk, into the American stream of consciousness, into the American song—much like King would later do with the American dream—and thus proving that our meters hypnotically swayed the nation to our virtuosic, vernacular voices. Hughes locates the context of the development of his identity in those physical spaces in his American "home" where he is expelled to feed his growing self-awareness on the leftovers of racial exclusion.

But he flips the script. He grows strong on the negative diet of marginality that he turns into a wholesome meal of aesthetic and moral combat against white supremacy, especially its failure to recognize black beauty of every sort. So Hughes in his poem talks about being sent to the kitchen to eat, "When company comes." But he eats well, grows strong, and pledges that when company comes again, he'll be at the table and that no one will dare scold him for his presence and send him to the kitchen, because, "They'll see how beautiful I am/And be ashamed —." And then he ends by declaring, "I, too, am America." So there's a significant shift from singing America to being America, from performance to enactment. And the company, to extend my reading of modernism through Hughes's poem, is Wallace Stevens, T.S. Eliot, Hart Crane, James Joyce, Marianne Moore, and so on, grand figures whose large egos dominate the psychic rooms and intellectual tables of American modernism. At the same time, the black subject, the black ego, the black self, is shunted to the kitchen.

So what Langston Hughes does is articulate the fixed space of his own modernist identity—the kitchen, metaphorically speaking—as the locus classicus of American identity, because when you're in the kitchen, the smell of the food wafts beyond its borders. When you're in the kitchen cooking—and Hughes was cooking, really he was smoking, burning, or whatever term one might conjure form the culinary arts as a symbol of black vernacular for achieving broad excellence—the smells will pull people in to ask, "Hmm, where's that smell coming from? What's cooking in the kitchen?" If you had to be somewhere away from the dining room or living room, it was crucial to be exiled to the kitchen. This is what black folk knew, especially as they served as domestics, butlers, and cooks. Black moderns turned their limited, localized spaces into rhetorical, musical, aesthetic, political, or spiritual kitchens that emitted pleasing smells and seductive scents, so that people who picked up on them were immediately, irresistibly drawn to them. That's the language . . .

To pick up on that, even if they don't come to the kitchen, the kitchen has to come to them. They are sitting at the table waiting for the kitchen to come to them. The kitchen produces that which they consume for nourishment.

There you go, man. Metaphor is power.

I'd like to push a little away from that now and turn to something that seemed to resonate in an earlier comment you made about black rhetoricians and the pre-modernist Christian tradition as it relates to black resistance. The notion of speaking things that are not as though they were . . . this is not a space of acquiescence, but of resistance.

Oh, exactly right. That's very important and I'll just say something briefly about it. Too often, we read the history of black resistance, and the speech or action that supported it, through a distorted lens. Either black folk were for or against oppression, either they cooperated or resisted, and we can tell all of this in dramatically demonstrable fashion. Well, it's not quite that simple. Life has put black folk in complex, often compromising positions, especially during slavery, post-Reconstruction, and Jim Crow. Many folk were not able to outwardly resist, not simply for fear of reprisal but because to do so would have undermined their long-term plans of survival and liberation. Black folk en masse had to survive, even under conditions of harsh oppression, so that they could produce black folk who could liberate us. Their survival tactics had to be hidden, concealed to the larger white world, masked to the oppressor. These networks of hidden meanings and concealed articulations were the predicate of black survival through a signifying, symbolic culture. For instance, many of the sorrow songs of the slaves contained dual meanings. While the white masses found the songs entertaining, the slaves simultaneously signaled each other about plans for emancipation. In effect, they were, as the title of the book aptly summarizes it, "Puttin' on ol Massa." The patterned quilts that slaves made contained crucial directions to black slaves seeking to ride the Underground Railroad to freedom. In a sense, they evoked the principle that later underlay Edgar Allen Poe's famous short story, "Purloined Letter," since the stolen missive was hidden in plain sight.

The very act of imagination was critical to strategies of resistance and proved dangerous to the hegemonic white world order. That's why the white world was so intent on controlling the black imagination, as far as such a thing was possible, by restricting its enabling mechanisms, particularly those rooted in literacy. Reading and writing were outlawed, and even earlier in slavery, blacks were divided from other blacks from the same tribe during the "seasoning" process so they couldn't effectively communicate. If blacks learned to read and write, they might grow restless with their degraded status, gaining a false and subversive sense of equality with whites. Of course, Frederick Douglass perhaps confirmed the worst fears of the white overclass when he reported in his autobiography that knowledge "unfits a man" for slavery. And if slaves spoke to each other without strict supervision, they might hatch plans to escape, so their speech and social organization were regularly policed.

But black slaves were able to carve out free spaces of intimate contact and communication that promoted racial solidarity and forms of resistance that eluded the master's ear and eye. Still, dominant whites rightly viewed the black imagination as a wedge between slaves and their oppression. The act of imagining a world of liberty was threatening. I think in this regard of a humorous statement that Muhammad Ali made about an opponent when he said, "If Sonny Liston dreams he can beat me, he better wake up and apologize." That's a brilliant gloss on the function of imagination and dreaming in black combat, and in the struggle for self-assertion and mastery of one's opponent. The attempt to regulate the black imagination is the attempt to restrict acts of black self-reinvention through dreaming of a different world where justice and freedom prevailed. That's why black folk were full of dangerous dreaming, insurrectionist imagining, and resistive revisions. The act of conceiving of an alternative world, a racial utopia, was a gesture of radical resistance that interrupted the totalizing force of white supremacy.

And a question of values, which we'll return to later. I want to push you in the direction here of talking about black bodies. Black male bodies, black women's bodies. One of the things that enters my mind here is the notion of the black masculine journey. To my mind, Morrison's Song of Solomon *ranks right up there with Ellison's* Invisible Man *as a benchmark text for black masculinity. It's the condition our condition is in . . .*

Right, it's rough all over.

To me, this statement has to do with black male bodies in everything from the Million Man March to Dennis Rodman.

Oh, no question. It's almost a cliché to say by now, but black masculinity is one of the most insightful and complex texts of American identity. For instance, millions want to, as the commercial slogan says, "Be like Mike." They're in awe of Michael Jordan, asking themselves what it is like to inhabit that pigment, that physiology, that 6'6" body whose ligaments, whose alignment of muscles determine the semblance of flight that folk around the globe vicariously identity with. Michael Jordan's head, clean shaven with those two ears poking out, at once conjures E.T.—the extraterrestrial—a sports spectacle, an incredible genius that we can scarcely imagine, while also signifying the globe—round and smooth. And what can be written on its surfaces is always something that can be erased and rewritten. At the same time, that black masculine head is a signifier of the power of the black phallus. In an interesting, perhaps even subversive fashion Michael Jordan's physical and aesthetic genius can be symbolized as a massive phallus whose seminal meanings explode on American culture, fertilizing a range of barren cultural landscapes with creative expression.

His body is a contradictory text of black masculinity. Jordan is at once embraced and fed upon as a Michael Jordan burger at McDonald's. He's being eaten by the masses, consumed, symbolically speaking. So the closest they may be able to get to Mike, besides watching him and emulating his moves on the court in their neighborhood playgrounds, sports gyms, or health clubs, is to purchase a symbolic portion of his body and consume it in market culture. It's a kind of secular Eucharist, where, at least in Protestant theology, the sacramental elements of Christ's body and blood are substituted by wafer and wine, or in Catholic theology, these elements are transubstantiated into the actual body and blood of Christ. Jordan's body is symbolically transmuted, through the material conditions of the political economy of consumption, into an edible commodity.

Or think of the symbolic and contested body of another prominent and complicated black man, the late rapper Tupac Shakur. Tupac's dead but still signifying body has the potential to become one of the first black candidates for cultural survival. I don't mean survival in the sense that he remains a vital cultural influence, like Martin Luther King Jr. I mean cultural presence beyond death through the articulation of a mythological body that defies mortality through urban legend, such as what has happened with James Dean, John F. Kennedy, Marilyn Monroe, and Elvis Presley. Particularly in the case of Elvis, there's a literal quality to his mythological persistence, since tabloid magazines claim to spot him, or JFK, on an island somewhere avoiding their fans, the media, and especially their "past" lives. I've often wondered why no one ever saw Sam Cooke, for instance, or Otis Redding, Dinah Washington, or Donny Hathaway. Tupac may be the first black figure to ascend to such heights—or depending on how one views this cultural phenomenon, to the depths—of pop memorialization.

I must confess I'm an addict, although I hope a critical one, of tabloids like the *National Enquirer* and *Star Magazine,* although since the same company that owns the *Enquirer* purchased *Star,* they often recycle the same information. Without overinterpreting or rationalizing their appeal, I think, at their best—and I place best in square quotes—these tabloids offer counter-hegemonic narratives to prevailing cultural truths. Besides that, they allow ordinary people to sound as if they're speaking the king's English to the queen's taste. Instead of presenting an "informant" as saying, "I got afraid when I thought about that stuff later on," they sound more formal, more literate, and might be quoted as saying, *"It startled me as I pondered it later."*

But in the tabloids, Elvis is spotted in California somewhere, Elvis is in some secluded villa in Italy, Marilyn has joined JFK in what only appears to be a posthumous romp in the Riviera, while black icons remain sequestered in their unsexy, earthbound mortality. I think that Tupac may be the first black icon to join the pantheon of the posthumously alive, people who symbolically defeat their own death through episodic appearances in the mythological landscape. Folk are now saying that Tupac is not dead, but alive somewhere in Cuba, perhaps enjoying a stogie with Fidel. There are Web sites and chat rooms all over the Internet dedicated to debating whether Tupac is dead or is hanging out on some Caribbean retreat to escape the cruel demands of fame. His cultural survival says a great deal about how black masculinity can come to signify contested social and political meanings that erupt in popular culture.

When I think about contemporary black masculinity, I can't help reflecting on another intriguing, contradictory, infuriatingly complex figure: Dennis Rodman. In fact, he's helping redraw the boundaries of black masculinity in the most archetypically black masculine sport there is, basketball. Basketball has arguably replaced baseball as the paradigmatic expression of the highly mythologized American identity, since sport is a crucial means by which America regenerates its collective soul and reconceives its democratic ideals, to borrow Emersonian language. Basketball also has elements of spontaneity; individual genius articulated against the background of group success; and the coalescence of independent creative gestures in a collective expression of athletic aspiration. In a sense, basketball provides a canvas on which American identity can be constantly redrawn. The cultural frameworks of American identity, especially American masculinity, are being symbolically renegotiated in black masculine achievement in basketball.

Dennis Rodman has the sublime audacity to challenge the codes of masculinity at the heart of black masculine culture in the most visible art form, besides hip-hop culture, available to black men. He transgresses against heterosexist versions of machismo that dominate black sport. For instance, he wears fingernail polish and he occasionally cross dresses in advertisements and public relations stunts, wearing a wedding gown in its white purity against that 6′9″ brown body that "the Worm," as he's nicknamed, inhabits. Even his nickname signifies; it suggests the burrowing of an earth-bound insect into the hidden spaces of the soil, deep beneath the surface of things. And it's not as if Rodman were a marginal figure. He's acknowledged as the most gifted rebounder in the NBA today, and one of the greatest of all time. His specialty is unavoidably representative. He's constantly grabbing the ball off the backboard, taking shots that are left over from the failed attempt to score, enhancing the ability of the team to win. His genius on the court is, in précis, a symbolic articulation of black masculine identity; it is a major trope of black masculinity, since black men are constantly "on the rebound," and "rebounding" from some devastating ordeal. Black men are continually taking missed shots off the glass, off the backboard, and feeding them in outlet or bounce passes to some high-flying teammate who is able to score on the opposition. Ordinary and iconic black men are constantly helping American society to rebound from one catastrophe or another and to successfully overcome the opposition in scoring serious points, serious arguments, serious goals.

This is precisely why you are reviled in some circles. This reading of Dennis Rodman, with which I agree wholeheartedly. Consider me now as the organist who plays those chords behind the sermon. Dennis Rodman is terribly fascinating. I laughed uproariously to see him show up with arched eyebrows and fingernail polish in the championship series on the day after wearing a boa to his book signing. And here he is performing the dirtiest, roughest, most "masculine" aspects of the game for his team.

He's inscribing those aspects in the text of black masculinity—because 80 percent of the players in the NBA now are black, so we have to talk about it as a black man's game. Dennis Rodman's relationship to basketball is similar to disco's relationship to American music, and especially black pop music. The black gay aesthetic informed the construction of the post–R&B era before the rise of hip-hop culture. It was widely reviled, although it is now being re-excavated in popular culture for archetypal images of American identity. Disco focused on the rhythm as opposed to the substance of the words; it highlighted the rhythmic capacity of the voice over against the lyrical content of what was being articulated. Disco culture was about a kind of rapturous and transgressive move against the sexual segregation of gay and lesbian bodies in social space. It was about the freedom and ecstasy of dance where clubs became sanctuaries for the secular worship of the deities of disco: rhythm, carnival, play, movement, and sexualized funk, elements that helped its adherents choreograph an aural *erotopia*. Those streaming, swirling globe lights that fixed on the dance floor assured that artifice was taken as the ultimate reality. I guess you could say in a sense that Sylvester got a hold of Baudrillard. The way that disco prefigures and precipitates a postmodern American sensibility often gets erased. Disco was dissed because its black gay aesthetic vogued against what was in vogue, and therefore its sexual transgression was the subtext, or what they call in philosophy the suppressed premise, of the logic of an ostensibly "straight" black pop musical culture.

Dennis Rodman's effect is comparable. He's the suppressed premise of the logic of black masculinity's prominence in basketball. So he helps to construct the public face of black masculinity along with Connie Hawkins, George Gervin, Earl "the Pearl" Monroe, Walt "Clyde" Frazier, Julius "Dr. J" Erving, Earvin "Magic" Johnson, Charles Barkley, and Michael Jordan. Through Dennis Rodman's body of work, the homoerotic moment within sport, and especially within black masculine athleticism, surfaces: Patting one another on the behind to say "good game" or "good play," hugging and kissing one another, falling into each other's sweating arms to boost camaraderie, and so on. This is a sexualized choreography of suppressed black desire and the way it is portrayed from the gridiron to the *hard*wood floor, pun intended! Dennis Rodman's figure invites us to see that homoeroticism has a lot to do, ironically enough, with the seminal production of black masculine athletic identities. The homoerotic and gay sensibility, contrary to popular perception, doesn't stop—and certainly in his case may even fuel—great athletic and masculine achievement. My God! The brother is an outlaw in what was formerly an outlaw and, racially speaking at least, outlawed sport.

There was a time, remember, when blacks weren't allowed to play professional basketball. When they were relatively early in their tenure in the NBA, in the early 1970s, *Ebony* magazine did an annual article that featured every black player on every team, something unimaginable today. And don't forget that the New York Knickerbockers during this time were called by racist fans the New York "Niggerbockers" because of the presence of Frazier, Monroe, Willis Reed, Dick "Fall Back Baby" Barnett, and Henry Bibby. Rodman's homoeroticized black athletic body is "outlaw(ed)" in several simultaneously signifying fashions, so to speak. The outlaw and the rebel, with apologies to Eric Hobsbawm, are countercultural figures whose lives embody the hidden and contradictory ethical aspirations of the masses, or at least some of them, even if the masses are not altogether aware of, or don't consciously identify with, the ideals the outlaw or rebel embodies. So Dennis Rodman is performing a kind of above ground "dream work" for the collective sexual unconscious of black masculinity. What Dennis Rodman's example shows is that even as black masculine culture overtly represses sexual difference and attempts to conceal or mystify homoerotic elements and behavior, it often depends on that very homoerotic dimension for athletic entertainment.

This homophobic dimension would seem to explain why most groups distance themselves from Rodman. Black people explain his absurdities by pointing to his time in Oklahoma. White people can point to his black urban ghetto origins. He thus seems to be an unusual signifier who can be whatever you need him to be. In other words, there are no false statements you can make about Dennis Rodman.

He's a successor text to Michael Jackson, in that sense. Not only is what you say about Dennis Rodman true, but what you say about Dennis Rodman is what you say about yourself. Even as you try to read Dennis Rodman, you're reading yourself. There's a relationship between ethnography and epiphany, between self-revelation and the excavation of the other.

To talk for a moment of this modern-postmodern divide about which you spoke earlier, could you talk for a moment of how your intellectual development has been affected by television and cyberspace. When I look back over Walter Benjamin's "Art in the Age of Mechanical Reproduction," I think to myself how differently he might have perceived things in the face of television.

I think immediately of what legendary singer and spoken word artist Gil Scott-Heron famously said, "The Revolution Will Not Be Televised." Well, in many ways, it has been televised, except the revolution about which he spoke has been replaced by the revolution of the medium itself. It's like Marshall McLuhan meets Barney Fife. I'm a child of television, even though my mother tells me that early on when I was mad at my family because I wanted to read a lot, I'd say, "Y'all don't read enough, you watch too much TV." I think it's God's joke on me that part of my life as a cultural critic is to be an analyst of television. Television has very deeply influenced my understanding of pop culture and my intellectual development in the sense that I take it as another very powerful text that we have to read, that we have to interpret, that we have to consume. I think that my self-understanding certainly has been to a degree both shaped by and articulated against the images, ideas, and ideologies on television, as they enable an on sight—and that's deliberately ambiguous for me, both s-i-g-h-t and s-i-t-e—negotiation of black identity. The evolution of television, along with the evolution and influence of film, sport, and music, has coincided with the evolution of the popular conception of black people in this country.

Besides its effect on my intellectual development and the professional pleasure it has provided me in reading its various texts, television has also extended an outlet to me to advocate social change, analyze culture, and argue about ideas. I know that's not the sense you meant by your question, but it leads me to reflect on another reason I'm drawn to TV. I think it's a legitimate medium through which to educate the public and to disrupt, subvert, and transgress against hegemonic forces. First of all, I talk so fast, which is both a good and bad thing for television. I can get a great deal in during a five-minute span on a news or talk show, and even more when I've got more time. On the other hand, I know I should slow down sometimes, but sometimes I'm really suspicious of slowing down. I sometimes prefer the machine-gun approach, given the often coarse and certainly fast-paced nature of television time and rhetoric. So, on occasion, the staccato, rapid-fire rhetorical style I have is usefully unfettered on television. I want my style to shatter that airtight medium. I want it to put a dent in television because it's an incredibly pedagogical medium.

As intellectuals, we ought to get used to the fact that television is a medium that affects people's identities and perceptions of reality, sometimes for the good. There have been studies carried out that show that people trust their local newspeople more than they trust their clergy people. People still look to conventional news broadcasts on TV to get their information, even more than from written journalism or from the alternative press. So I want to bring my alternative, nontraditional, perhaps even subversive viewpoint to bear on and within this most hegemonic of mediums. In some ways, television has proved to have ideological flexibility, especially when radicals pop up on rare occasions. At least there's the potential to shatter dominant ideological modes, if even for a brief moment. We should definitely take advantage of television's episodic fluidity. I don't see television in a snobbish way. I've been on *Oprah* to talk about black oppression, black masculinity, and female identity. I've gone on CNN to talk about race, white supremacy, and electoral politics. I want to seize television as a pedagogical tool to help liberate or transform folk, or at least contest what Stuart Hall calls the preferred meanings of the dominant culture, juxtaposing them to what he terms the negotiated meanings, as I acknowledge the prevailing ideological framework while arguing for alternative structures of thought and oppositional practices. I want to use television to challenge our culture's common sense, in the way Gramsci meant it, and to help educate and occasionally uplift those who pay attention.

That does fit within the ways that I wanted to hear you talk about the medium. This also points me back to your notion of this betweener generation—people in their late 30s and very early 40s. People just a few years older than the betweeners remember television in its early, formative stages, when televisions weren't ubiquitous. They remember Uncle Milty, and TV was still a novelty. But, for me, when I wake up to memory it's there and it's unremarkable. It's on and it's unremarkable. One of my earliest TV memories, at three, almost four years old, is seeing Jack Ruby shoot Lee Harvey Oswald. That's a vivid scene I remember seeing—sitting on my mother's bed—that scene. That's one of those moments I've somehow written into my mind as an early moment. That and also realizing, somewhere around my thirtieth birthday, that from as far back as I could remember until my thirteenth birthday that the news started every day with the body count from Vietnam. That's pretty deep—to realize that there is a generation of us, eight years old in 1968, old enough to be aware of the assassinations, of the riot in Chicago, of moon landings, of Detroit and Newark, of all the stuff happening around you, seeing it come at you and nobody talks to you about it. So, in 1987 and 1988 I carried around a grudge because People, Time, *and* Newsweek *did "summer of love" and "summer of discontent" retrospectives. So, they talked to (all) the people who were adult participants in '67 and '68. Then they talked to people who were twenty years old in '87 and '88. And I thought: "you did it again!" In 1968 no one said anything about this to me. Here, again, in 1988 you ask everybody but me.*

You're so right. You've brought up here what is not my first memory of television, but it is my most important one. That is when I saw the newscaster interrupt the regular program to announce that *MARTIN LUTHER KING Jr.* had been shot in Memphis, Tennessee. That is the most powerful moment of the television bonding with me, and of me bonding with the TV. I identified, almost beyond volition or consciousness, with the television as a medium, as an apparatus, that brought me an ideologically contested moment in black rhetoric. That is, *MARTIN LUTHER KING Jr.* speaking his last speech. They flashed an image of him as he said what would immediately become some of his most famous words, "I may not get there with you, but I want you to know tonight that we as a people will get to the Promised Land." That was a very profound and electrifying episode that shaped my life forever. I asked my mother, "Which one is he? Which one is he?" I remember distinctly, and I don't know why they showed it, Dr. King at some point reeling back on his foot. I immediately felt his power; his words were like containers brimming with the pathos of black life. Later, the newsman broke faith again with the printed program by saying, "*MARTIN LUTHER KING Jr.* has just died at thirty-nine in Memphis, Tennessee."

And, now, here I am thirty-eight, and you're thirty-seven, so we're basically the same age and almost the age at which King died. King's death was stunning to me. I had never heard of *MARTIN LUTHER KING Jr.* before that point, and when he died in 1968—I was nine years old—it changed my life. Television literally changed my life because, after his death, I began to watch all the programs about Dr. King. I began to go to the library to read all the books I could about him that were available. I then ordered, through a telephone number I got off of the television, speeches that were available on records. I had my little record player back then, when vinyl was the medium of choice and analog was the order of the day. Then, through television, I ordered the commemorative book on Martin Luther King Jr. So, television was a very powerful medium that fused with my evolving self-consciousness as a young black person. The 1967 riots in Detroit also made me pay attention to television. It brought me scenes of social ignominy and racial deterioration right before my eyes, and made me realize that what I could see from my front porch in the streets—as people scurried up and down the pavement with money stashed in their big fros, televisions on their backs, and carrying all kinds of ill-gotten gains and goods—was refracted through the prism of a medium that made it larger than life.

Thinking back on the brothers and sisters in the streets, I'm reminded of the old joke Dick Gregory told about black people being stopped in the riots. These people were carrying a couch when the police stopped them. Dick Gregory said that when these people were stopped, they said, "Goddamn! A black psychiatrist can't even make house calls anymore!" And what else is it that they say? In a riot black people destroy everything but libraries and bookstores. Lord have mercy! Anyway, the reality is that the riots and the death of Martin Luther King Jr. point to how social catastrophe and transformation is either covered or concealed on television. These events spring from deeply embedded social processes of resolving or reinforcing conflict that are not usually explored in great depth on television, save in the rare in-depth documentary.

The contested and conflicted meanings of race in the 1960s were frequently papered over and smoothed out, resulting in the McDonaldization of Martin Luther King Jr. in a McLuhan universe where the medium was the message. It's important to me that the medium through which Dr. King was articulated for me was a televisual apparatus—since I never met him in the flesh. And the message I got from him was about social change. My early identification with TV grew from the fact that it had the radical potential to transform, not merely to anesthetize, to open up and not merely to constrain, to shatter and not merely to constitute, social reality. I saw it as an imaginative apparatus through which, ideologically, we could resist and challenge dominant racial and cultural narratives. Now, I didn't know all of this back then, but I felt a connection to King that transcended time and place and allowed me to identify with this figure whose life just revolutionized my consciousness. So, there's no question that television changed my life.

The next week in Sunday school I remember that our teacher asked us about that. That, I'm sure, was one of the very few times an adult asked about our response to current events. If I remember correctly, it was a Wednesday or Thursday evening when King was assassinated. That was when Batman *came on. That was probably why I was hanging out in front of the tube—waiting for* Batman.

Aww, man! Batman and Robin, brother! My boys Adam West and Burt Ward! And there was Bruce Lee as Cato on the *Green Hornet,* and I don't remember the cat who played the Green Hornet that Cato drove around in the Hornet's Lincoln Continental.

I remember that on the Sunday following my Sunday school teacher asking us how the assassination made us feel—probably the only time anyone asked us. One girl in the class said she was glad King died because some show she wanted to watch had been interrupted. There was some TV show she wanted to see, but the news preempted all that. That seems, again, to be one of the interesting ways television plays out in our culture. And occasionally I'm one of those people—I'd rather watch some sitcom than the Republican convention. I can catch what I need to later on CNN or C-SPAN. I don't have to sit there and watch it all unfold live.

These news programs are part of the option glut that television now presents. Our nation, indeed our world, has been deeply affected by the CNN-ing of American discourse where all information, or at least the information that is deemed worth knowing, is immediately available. Therefore, there's little psychic space for reflection, little intellectual or emotional space in which to recover what we learn or reconstitute the ideas we absorb. We have little time to figure out the meaning of what we learn. As Derrida taught us, understanding is not simply about what something means but how it signifies. However, you can't even figure that out unless you have some space, some remove, from hugely influential events. I'm not embracing the myth of news objectivity, since I think the best we can hope for is fairness, which includes placing our biases right out in the open. I'm thinking here of the need to recover the fragments of events, and to experience them as fully as possible through interpreting and articulating them.

What the immediacy of communications technology has done is to make us believe that because we've perceived something, that because we've got the raw data through our senses, we've thoroughly experienced it. But we don't know what we know until we begin to think critically about what it means, and until we intervene with a conscious, deliberate intent to classify, to categorize, and to filter our experiences. It takes much more than empirical access to information to create understanding. Without interpretation and analysis, experience remains mute and inarticulate beneath the sheer fact of its existence. The phenomenological weight of immediacy results in a distorted capacity for interpretation and analysis.

As you mention the idea of space, there is a glut of options and information such that if you know that you need space to reflect, interpret, and reinterpret, you don't have time before the next fragment hits you. This is a totally unplanned but nice little segue. There was a Jay Wright symposium here at which Harold Bloom was a speaker. Jay Wright said this in a 1983 interview: "These last two terms, explication and interpretation, should call attention to one of my basic assumptions: that naked perception (just seeing something), is misprision in the highest degree. Every perception requires explication and interpretation. Exploration means just that. A simple report of experience, if you could make such a thing, isn't good enough." Although he's talking about the art of poetry, this seems to apply to this sort of experience of information. One of the things that Harold Bloom lamented at this conference was the absence of learnedness, although he put Jay Wright on this wonderful pedestal as a learned poet in the tradition of Dante and Milton. Somehow, it occurred to me that there's something about this peculiar postmodern information glut that makes "learnedness" impossible. Bloom mentioned that earlier in his career, although it wasn't often, he would hear people referred to as a "learned" scholar.

In the light of our postmodern option glut, erudition becomes nearly obsolete and impossible to attain, at least according to a specific understanding of the concept. You can't master the discursive tongues that have proliferated via the media in our own time. In some senses, I lament the loss of such erudition because I'm a nontraditional traditionalist at that level, reared on the Harvard Classics, TV, and Motown. I saw no disjuncture between *Two Years Before the Mast* by Richard Dana, and William "Smokey" Robinson's "My Girl" sung by the Temptations. Although I understand and even empathize with elements of Bloom's lament, I've got disagreements with him and other critics over canon formation and related literary issues, because I think there are multiple canons and multiple forms of literacy that we ought to respect. The intellectual and rhetorical integrity of these traditions ought to be acknowledged, and not in a condescending, compensatory fashion designed to make sure that "the other" is represented, except such inclusion is usually a procedural and not a substantive engagement with a given work. We've got to take the revelations about America that "minority" authors offer as seriously as we do conventional heroes of literature. We have much to learn from black writers' engagement, for instance, with what Baraka termed "vicious modernism."

On the other hand, I think that there's a need to historicize our conceptions of erudition, too. We should constantly be reevaluating what we mean by learnedness and erudition, since those qualities were never absolutely divorced from the priorities and prisms of the dominant culture. The learned and erudite were not simply revered for their knowledge, but they reflected a hierarchy of privilege that provided some the opportunity to acquire such a status while foreclosing the possibility to others in an a priori fashion. Ironically enough, even though the possibility of a particular kind of erudition may be quickly vanishing with the proliferation of information systems, it may offer a relatively more democratic conception of literacy that invites us to acknowledge a wider range of people as legitimate bearers of "learning."

In the past, the erudite person could only be a white male whose prodigious learning was acknowledged by his peers and intellectual progeny. Now, at least, we've widened the view of what counts as erudite and learned, and in many ways that's a very good thing.

Interview by Jonathan Smith

St. Louis, Missouri, 1996

9

The Great Next

Jazz Origins and the Anatomy of Improvisation

How did the music achieve and get assigned such lofty goals?

When you think about 1920s jazz music, you think about what led up to it. The formative period of jazz is from around 1895 till about 1905, 1910. Ragtime was big then. The music was so named because of the ragged time, the syncopated rhythmic structures, that African-inspired musicians were playing against more nonsyncopated, linear, tonal-based, harmonic European music. Musically speaking, jazz evolved out of ragtime with the assertion of the sensibilities of African communal spirits and syncopated rhythmic orders against the more regimented order of Western music. Aesthetically speaking, high society music, the music of civil and polite society performed in the chambers of the elite, was the established canon, the established norm against which all other music was judged and compared.

When ragtime came along with its raggedy, nonconventional, syncopated rhythms against the nonsyncopated, linear conceptions of music in the Western canon, it created a real rub. But I think part of the controversy erupted in response to the function of the music itself. Musicians handed out cards in New Orleans, especially in the 1920s, which had printed on them "music for all occasions." So the social contexts and geographical spaces to which the music was consigned determined its function. If you're playing in parades and picnics and funerals and Mardi Gras, the music is much more lively and syncopated and fit for those situations. But if the music is played in a limited, intimate space, the music has a different sensibility. Even the popular dances of the 1920s reflected the influence of space on aesthetics. For instance, in polite society they danced the quadrille, the mazurka, the waltz, and the polka in association with chamber music. But when there were open spaces and markedly vibrant dance halls, all characteristic of the sites of "the folk," the dances were the slow drag, the eagle rock, and the buzzard lope. All in all, the music and dance outside "official" society—and music and dance were intimately connected—reflected the infusion of African aesthetic values by means of New Orleans Creoles.

A quote: "Beware of a change to a strange form of music, taking it to be a danger to the whole, but never have the ways of music moved without the greatest political laws being moved." That's Plato, The Republic.

Well, there's no question that the high purpose of music was captured in William Congreve's phrase: "Music hath charms to sooth a savage breast." It has been widely, and wrongly, quoted as saying "the savage beast," which appears on the surface at least to be redundant. In any case, music from either perspective is a modifying element with a modulating effect: It brings sensibility and order to chaos. Those musical forms that reflect chaos are seen to be, from a hegemonic, elite perspective, unworthy of recognition or respect. In fact, they don't count as music at all. The aesthetic value of these nonmusical, chaotic forms—the frenzy of ragtime, the frenzy of jazz—reflected in part the chaos of the social circumstances faced by its artists, including Creole musicians losing their jobs downtown, where they were playing European-inspired music in New Orleans, to go uptown, where they had interactions with these more indigenous Negro populations. That meant that there was some kind of fusion going on, and therefore the musical and aesthetic values of the musicians were being "corrupted," so that the "high" and redemptive purposes of the music—to regulate the savage—was compromised by the influence of the very forms of chaos that the music sought to relieve.

The perception of music's purpose is always indivisible, I think, from the political and social contexts through which folk, including critics, interpret the music. Remember in, I think, 1918, the *Times-Picayune*, the newspaper in the birthplace of jazz, New Orleans, the Crescent City, argued against the uncivil-like behaviors of musicians, as well as the uncivil character of the music. "This is not music that is fit for polite society," they opined, and I'm paraphrasing here. "As a result, we should suppress it." So musically speaking, the aesthetic representation of the Western conception of music, with melody and harmony and thematic resolution and tonal structure and so on, was juxtaposed in the minds of the cultural elite to musical forms that fell outside of the realm of music's purpose, or, in keeping with the Greek philosophy of your quote, its telos. The rhythmic intensity of African music, emerging from racially subordinated communities, subverted the telos, the goal of music as determined by dominant society, resulting in a huge bifurcation of musical priorities and aesthetic choices. For the dominant, elite society, music facilitated the rituals of intimate social interaction in close quarters. For the masses, music accompanied big social events that facilitated a sense of social cohesion and personal agency in chaotic and conflicted social circumstances. Now that bifurcation, like all dualities, isn't pure, since social phenomena are fluid and complex, but I think it's a functional definition of the social and aesthetic tensions that prevailed.

From a social place, what is being said?

Well, in a sense, I think we can look at what was happening in New Orleans at the time, from the late 1890s to about 1915 or 1920, as a precursor to the culture wars that are now going on as we debate the differences between Eurocentrism, Afrocentrism, multicentrism, multiculturalism, and the like. There were racial forces behind distinctions between European music and so-called non-European, or African-inspired, music. Those distinctions were really about racial caste, about keeping Negroes in their place, and about assigning less merit to African cultural products and forms of music than to European ones. The irony, of course, is that white musicians later appropriated African forms of music. The first jazz recording, which appeared in 1917 from the Original Dixieland Band, was a whitened and diluted and domesticated version of African-inspired black music. If it wasn't quite rhythmically challenged, it was certainly a watered down version of black music rendered palatable to a wider, whiter American audience.

The racial distinction between European and African music was sometimes coded as the differentiation between what's good and bad music, what's productive and nonproductive music, and what's edifying and what's debased music. Folks were trying to figure out the place of African people in American culture, and the arguments over music were key to the process. So the aesthetics were politicized. The question of what to do with ragtime, and then blues, jazz, and gospel, was never simply a matter of taste, or should I say, that taste was never merely a matter of musical preference extracted from the prevailing racial context. Syncopation indexed race as surely as black skin. Plus, the caste question was never far away, since these ragtime musicians were not often educated musicians who had absorbed the finer points of European music. Their musical trace had to be washed away from the palette of American music, which was little more than an imitation of the so-called classical forms flowing in from Europe. The kick is that across the waters, European classical musicians and composers are digging this indigenous American music being created by mostly black musicians of an ostensibly degraded and inferior pedigree. Figures like Debussy and Stravinsky, and even Charles Ives, are being influenced by ragtime, even as the aesthetic guardians of Western culture are dissing ragtime.

Struggles over music were about social regulation because music was the front line of breaking down racial barriers. Later in the twentieth century, black musicians would play a crucial role in brokering an acceptance of African Americans, limited though it was, within the regime of American apartheid in the South, where segregation ruled. It sounds trite to say, but black music, to a degree, united peoples of different races and genders and cultures in this kind of polyphonic expression of African sensibility. But they had to fight through the social stigma attached to blackness, even though, interestingly enough, in New Orleans, jazz music is also being created by Creoles. I think James Lincoln Collier, the jazz critic, has read this entirely wrong. He says because those musicians were Creoles, they weren't black, and therefore we can't claim that jazz music has black origins. But as Mike Tyson might say, that's ludicrous. Such an argument as Collier advances denies the complexity of race, how it is not simply a biological fact but a socially determined identity. The notion that jazz is not a "black" music because it was created by Creoles not only is a reflection of phenotypical literalism but ignores the politics and history of racial identity in America. A crucial feature of the American racial contract has involved the thorny question of interracial or mixed race identity, or what is anthropologically and sociologically termed miscegenation.

That debate has been renewed recently with the rise of Tiger Woods to prominence in golf. Is he black or Thai, or both, and how do we talk about being both and hence not exclusively either, and how does that nuance our comprehension of racial identity? Contemporary debates about miscegenation were precipitated by the sorts of arguments around race and music that occurred in the Creole–influenced Crescent City of New Orleans back in the late 1800s and early 1900s. There was an Americanization of New Orleans after the Louisiana Purchase in the early 1800s. New Orleans, racially and ethnically speaking, was a mixture of French and Spanish and indigenous American elements. The Creole, or the light-skinned Negro, the French-inflected mulatto, was the product of a fusion of black and white. Creoles began to create ragtime and jazz music only after they had interactions with indigenous Negro or African-inflected musicians in New Orleans, a fact that causes me to be skeptical about Collier's argument that jazz is not identifiable as black music. One can hear in such denials reverberations of the stigma of blackness—of black skin and skill, of black blood, metaphorically speaking, of black styles—that was rife in American culture at the turn of the twentieth century. It's a stigma that persists to this day, even if, ironically enough, black popular culture is the idiom, is the grammar, through which America is globally articulated.

Finally, I think piano-based ragtime accentuated percussive features of black music that were later expanded in ensembles, which highlighted the shift to the multi-instrumentality of jazz music, including, say, a saxophone, a trumpet, and a drum, which facilitated the process of improvisation that was strictly forbidden in classical music, which had to be read note for note off a sheet. It was eye music versus ear music, music that had to be read versus music that had to be heard and learned by ear, the visual versus the aural, so to speak. Since there was initially little sheet music in jazz, at least not to the degree or in the manner of classical music, musicians were free to improvise, to remake the song as they played it each time. There was a structural freshness to the music's improvisational quality, allowing the musicians to enlarge or diminish themes, to rearrange musical elements, to alter tempos and tones, as the occasion or mood dictated. There's still a corpus there, a body of ideas and themes and techniques, but they are the raw material of the riffs that constitute and extend the impulse to improvisation. A huge feature of the debates over African versus European music was over what sorts of music contained our cultural and, really, our political values. If democracy is what jazz is about, glimpsed in the equal participation of varying elements in the construction of a whole, European classical music is about a kind of oligarchy of aesthetic taste; that is, there is tight control over what can be played, what can be said, what can be articulated, and who gets a chance to play it.

Talk about the imagery.

An interesting feature of African music is how it incorporates the communal basis of racial and cultural survival into its aesthetic vocabulary. That's number one. Number two, African-inflected music, at least in the case of black music in America, existed and eventually flourished in a foreign land, in a context where black folk had to struggle to create a culture of signification among each other as a survival strategy in an oppressive culture. So the double entendre, from the spirituals, blues, and so on, allowed blacks to communicate with one another in liberating fashion. When slaves sang "Green trees are bending/My soul stands a'trembling/Ain't got long to stay here," white plantation owners were being entertained while black slaves were being emancipated, since they were signaling each other about when Harriet Tubman was coming through to liberate slaves and lead them along the Underground Railroad to freedom. So the double entendre fused emancipation and entertainment in many African and African American musical forms. But black emancipation and white entertainment weren't the only functions of the double entendre.

In jazz music, the double entendre went secular as it funneled sexual play into the aesthetic creations of black folk culture. Or should I say, the aesthetic creation funnels the sexual play of certain subcultures in black life, especially among working-class black folk. But the sexual did not exhaust the double entendre in the cultural realm, since black folk through our music signified on what we understood ourselves to be and played with those images, whether of the barbarian, the savage, and so on, even as we enlarged on the narratives of complex humanity that all great art promotes. We could parody the stereotypes of black identity even as we extended our creative freedom to engage our libidos, to revel in sexual mischief, to take utter joy in what Richard Wright called the "erotic exultation" of some forms of music. He was referring primarily to gospel, but I think it can be applied equally to early ragtime and jazz as well.

Another level of double entendre reflected the utter playfulness of linguisticality and orality at the heart of black culture. Long before poststructuralists who were hooked on European traveling theories of postmodernism talked about the playfulness of culture and language, black folk comprehended jouissance, the sheer hedonistic pleasure and delight of experimenting and playing with black cultural forms, including music. A crucial feature of double entendres was the articulation of culturally coded messages and styles that signified on white dominant cultural structures while promoting black self-definition. Even though the dominant culture may have viewed blacks as barbarians and savages, as dumb animals incapable of abstract reasoning or "high" culture, they nevertheless reveled in the robustly playful elements of black cultural creativity. At their best, black folk refused to get stuck in narrow Victorian modes of identity where they repressed consciousness of their sexual selves while exclusively engaging their spiritual nature. They didn't buy into that bifurcation between mind and body. As critic Michael Ventura argued, African cultures often overcame the Cartesian dualism of the West because they contended that there was no such thing as being mental and spiritual over here and being physically embodied over there.

The double entendre was about black folk having their cake and eating it too, so to speak; it was about healing the rift between body and soul; it was about playfulness while contesting white power in signifying fashion; and it was about enjoying and celebrating their culture even as vicious stereotypes abounded. That was terribly liberating to black folk who had been indoctrinated with the belief that they were inferior, that they were, in the words of Margaret Walker, "black and poor and small." You must remember that at the turn of the century, black popular culture was broadly assailed in magazines and journals. A title from one magazine asked, "Did jazz put the sin in syncopation?" The *Ladies Home Journal* argued that young people listening to jazz music would produce a holocaust of teen births. Now where have we heard that recently? There was an enormous groundswell against black and white Americans who embraced jazz music, especially as cultural guardians were attempting to control the sexual chaos and erotic frenzy of this rhythmic, syncopated music.

That's because ragtime was associated with the brothel, and jazz music in the 1920s was associated with the speakeasy. Given my earlier analysis about how the physical and social contexts in which the music was played shaped its use, the brothel and speakeasy provided a space for blacks to exult in their own bodies. The speakeasy, the brothel, and other dens of ill repute are where ragtime and jazz were regularly played. So there was an association in the public mind of morally suspicious behavior and black music. This was not strictly a contention between blacks and whites, since during the Harlem Renaissance, upper-class Negroes were inveighing against the vagaries of ghetto gutter music. When you went to the cribs of the leading lights of the Harlem Renaissance, they were playing Beethoven, Bach, and Brahms. They were not engaging the debased folk culture of the masses. Even politically progressive figures such as W.E.B. Du Bois, the young A. Phillip Randolph, and Chandler Owens spurned jazz music. At some level, there's an internalized self-abnegation, a disparagement of quotidian blackness displayed by the Negro upper crust who spurn black folk culture while uncritically deferring to European canons, codes, and norms. Thus the black cultural double entendre was directed against not only white supremacist culture but also the Negro bourgeoisie, which lacked serious appreciation for its indigenous art forms.

Was it starting to creep a little too close to home? In modern times, we see as many white as blacks kids buying rap music. Is that maybe an issue?

Absolutely! The degree to which ragtime and later jazz—especially through figures like Baby Dodds, Buddy Bolden, Jelly Roll Morton, and later Louis Armstrong—reached out beyond the confines of black culture certainly sparked wide cultural controversy. There's no question that when jazz penetrated the husk of white cultural circles, there was a great deal of consternation among the white artistic and political elite. Just as with hip-hop culture today, there was an enormous degree of anxiety about black art forms like jazz darkening white artistic enclaves and social settings. As a result, white elites stepped up the policing of boundaries between black and white cultures, even as jazz inspired interracial cultural exchange. The music facilitated what Jim Crow with its segregated social practices failed to prevent: different cultures connecting and interacting. Jazz helped promote the syncretic moment, the fused moment, the moment of cultural contact and cooperation between races that existed beyond the restrictions of custom, code, and law.

That's why Jelly Roll Morton, Sidney Bechet, and Louis Armstrong, who was the young cornet player in King Oliver's group, and others like them were dangerous to the white musical establishment, especially when jazz and its musicians flowed down the Mississippi, fanning out from the Crescent City to Chicago, New York, St. Louis, Kansas City, and Los Angeles. The music and its musicians were now mobile, and many critics deemed them even more harmful because they could reach a much larger audience, especially white youth. Jazz culture was seductive to white kids, and they turned from the quadrille, the mazurka, the waltz, and the polka of their parents to the slow drag and the hoochie-coochie, while reveling in the blues of the Delta filtering into New Orleans from Mississippi. This explosion of African creativity constituted a veritable Negropolis, a black cosmopolitanism whose influence sprawled beyond its original indigenous borders to capture large segments of American society.

Hence the development of the Jazz Age, which in its mainstream cultural embodiment was qualitatively different from the ragtime and jazz juke joints. But it retained enough aesthetic ferocity, in both music and fiction, to scare some and shake up many others. F. Scott Fitzgerald reflected some of the ferocious and fertile impulses of the juke joint in the linguistic creativity of his novels, where slang leapt to the foreground, and his characters were not trying to close out the body. In certain European canonical works, the body becomes irrelevant or merely instrumental, an appendage to the mind's operations, merely instrumental. For instance, the body was good for producing wind for the brass instruments or for the muscle to stroke the string instruments in the classical orchestra. But the body itself was never as *present* in European classical music as it was in Negro hot spots, the indigenous dives of brown divas and majordomos—at least not when it was primarily interpreted by Europeans. I'm speaking here of musicians, with the singers who rose to prominence later, including folk like Caruso and Callas, being obvious exceptions. Basically, in European music, you saw the segregation of the body into measured utilities, where the hands were good but not the feet, where the lips were fine but not the eyes, and so on.

In jazz, the body was aesthetically desegregated, freed from the artificial constraints of taste, custom, and tradition. In jazz, the entire body was implicated and was truly integrated. The values of jazz include a profound vocal tonality, since the musical instruments were manipulated in varying degrees to sound like the voice. That's why we love Lester Young's and, later, John Coltrane's sound, because the very textures they evoke on the saxophone remind us of the human voice crying, sighing, laughing, speaking and shrieking, complaining, and expressing joy. Let's move from the reeds to the brass. In a sense, the blues shouts and the field hollers get reexpressed, reemphasized, rearticulated in the longing, yearning, feral tones of the trumpet and the cornet. When you hear Louis Armstrong wailing on his trumpet and cornet, when you hear him cutting through the aesthetics of polite society with its measured, rigid, precise tonalities, lashing, as only Armstrong could, in a viciously insistent tone that suggested he was indeed "stomping the blues," you hear the quality I'm talking about. It's anger and joy, anxiety and peace in shuffling cadences that trade hope for despair as he's trading fives in King Oliver's group and later his own.

And beyond jazz, in gospel music, for instance, when you hear the transcendent aesthetic possibilities that transmute suffering into ethical vision and religious passion, you're hearing the full-bodied character of black music. Black music, and the contexts of black experience it introduced, were just too much for an often repressed mainstream society. And you don't have to buy into stereotypes of the oppositional figures of the white savant and black savage, with the former a glutton for reason and the intellect, and the latter addicted to primal urges and nature, to get my point. The aesthetic priorities and intellectual musings of black artists (and for me, the two go hand in hand, especially when we're talking about jazz) provided white youth a different and daring prism through which to view themselves. Remember, Du Bois had written in 1903, at least that's when the essays in *Souls of Black Folk* were gathered, that it is a strange thing to see oneself, that is, the black self, through the lens of another world, a world that was in many ways a foreign, judging, hostile world. But what happens with jazz music and culture is that the prism is inverted, metaphorically speaking, so that now, in the 1920s, black culture provides the lens through which many whites begin to view and understand themselves. That was a monumental philosophical reversal achieved largely by aesthetic means.

What was it that was bringing black folks from the rural South to urban centers in the North?

Economic opportunity was one thing that drew black people from rural agrarian culture, where they were brutally segregated on post-Emancipation plantations in sharecropping arrangements. Sharecropping was little more than the evolved form of slavery. You see, after Emancipation, 90 percent of black Americans lived in the South until the early 1900s and the great black migration North, to Chicago and Detroit and other big cities, in search of greater economic opportunity. Even before the great black migration, blacks had been drawn to urban centers like New Orleans, which was steeped in racial history. Congo Square was there; it was the place where black slaves had been sold on the auction block. Congo Square prefigured the urban cultures that coalesced around New Orleans in the late 1800s and early 1900s because it was where all these Africans from every part of the world were brought, or literally *bought,* together. There's nothing like the oppressive commercialization and commodification of black culture to forge the solidarity of blackness, even if it was a defensive, protective, reflexive move, and to create modern blackness in ways it didn't exist in Africa before the coerced diaspora, the forced migration.

But this new thing, this *tertium quid,* this not-European, not-African-but-somehow-American racial reality that formed in Congo Square, was the forging of the black Atlantic, as Robert Farris Thompson, Peter Linebaugh, and much later Paul Gilroy, have described it in their work. In Congo Square, music was played outside the control of the dominant white society. Blacks reappropriated the space of domination as a source of liberating aesthetic self-expression. The drum was crucial to this process. It was the dominant symbol, the dominant metaphor, of the convergence of political meanings and aesthetic articulation. In the Congo Square, the rhythm of black life, with its percussive tonalities, was literally drummed into existence. That's why the drums were outlawed: they were the language of black emancipation. The drums allowed blacks to facilitate community, to communicate valuable political messages in a percussive tongue. It was a testament to the fertility and generativity of blackness, even for those Creoles who were *passer blanc*, passing for white, although it was routinely the case that they were marked in their bodies with the outlaw(ed) meanings of blackness by the dominant society.

Still, there was something crucial about Congo Square to black identity. New Orleans provided a gumbo ya-ya of disparate black identities of African origins. People think when you say black, these identities are self-evident, but they're not. They think the same for Africa, but when you say African, what are you really saying? Are you talking about East, West, North, or South African? Are you talking about Yoruba or Hausa? And in the African diaspora, things are no different. When you speak of African religion, for instance, are you talking about Candomble from an Afro-Brazilian experience, or are you speaking of Afro-Cuban Santeria, or perhaps a Haitian expression of Vodoun? The gumbo ya-ya of black identity evokes the African appreciation for the integrity of multiplicity, which is essentially what black urbanity is all about. The black urban experiment of the early part of the twentieth century, in its edifying moments, was about mass black exodus to cities that were ports of call for the migrations, mixtures and mergers of all kinds of black identities, both within indigenous U.S. populations and from all over the Americas, from Caribbean cultures, and later from British cultures as well. The expansion of economic opportunity that drew blacks to big northern cities from all parts of the country, indeed the world, had a concomitant virtue: it not only eroded the vicious de jure segregation to which they had been subject in southern apartheid, but it multiplied the rambunctious collocation of ethnic, regional, religious, sexual, gendered, and class diversities within black identity.

Talk about the atmosphere of Chicago in 1919.

Chicago during that time was home to upwardly mobile blacks, relatively speaking, who had limited success in challenging the norms, the ethos, the very superior self-understanding that even average whites possessed. As a result, blacks suffered violence as reprisal for their "uppity behavior." So the de jure segregation of the South was replaced by the de facto segregation of the North. A lot of the violence blacks suffered was not simply of the top-down sort—violence regulated and mediated through political structures in an ostensibly democratic society. The violence had largely to do with the politics of resentment from white working-class folk who frowned on the even limited success of this burgeoning black working class. Tensions between the races were exacerbated when black scab workers were brought in to bust the unions, most of which barred black workers. In effect, the white power structure was playing musical chairs with nonunionized black workers and exploited white unionized workers, pitting the latter against the former. All this means that around 1919, the second great fire razed Chicago. The first fire happened in 1871, when Mrs. O'Leary's legendary cow kicked the lantern that started the fire that nearly burned down Chicago.

The second fire was more redemptive, ignited when some blacks joined the working and middle classes, turning Chicago into one of the great centers of black culture in the modern West, similar to what would happen later in Los Angeles when the booming war industry drew blacks in record numbers during World War II. In Chicago, circa 1919, the stockyards were the huge attraction that helped spark Chicago's great black migration. The stockyards and the sometimes apocryphal stories that transplanted black southerners in Chicago sent back home that exaggerated their standard of living in the big city, as if they were, in the parlance of hip-hop, "living large." Maybe in comparison to their old southern haunts they were living large, but they were hardly living in the lap of luxury up North; and there were virtues to the old southern geographies that formerly dominated black life. In the South, even if they were poor, they had open spaces in fields, but in the North, their enhanced economic status confined them in tenements that stretched upward several stories and choked the landscapes and skylines of ghettoes and slums.

The North had its own variety of Jim Crow, except that it was Jim Crow, Esquire, or James Crow III. Northern racism was more subtle but no less vicious. Twenty years after 1919, during the 1940s, Chicago exploded with black aesthetic creativity, with jazz, blues, gospel, and later its own variety of soul music, making it very difficult for white Americans—especially the recently arrived white ethnic immigrants, including Poles, Italians, Lithuanians, and Irish, who populated Chicago's burgeoning lumpen proletariat—to accept even marginal black mainstream success. The battle was classic: recently migrated southern blacks and recently immigrated white European ethnics—in Michael Novak's famous book title (at least during his radical phase) *The Unmeltable Ethnics*, something I'm sure he'd disavow now as a leading conservative and advocate of the melting pot. In short order, tensions mounted and eventually led to race rioting in Chicago.

Were the objections concentrated on the influx of people or was it reaction to what the people brought with them, the culture?

It was both. They were indivisible because the greatest thing the people brought was themselves and their itinerant, mobile cultural meanings. According to many conservative social scientists, the urban situation was messed up because black people reshaped industrial urbanity in the first half of the twentieth century in Chicago, Detroit, Philadelphia, New York, Los Angeles, and so on. Blacks brought their culture with them, a culture pervaded by blues and jazz and gospel music and spiritual sensibilities. They brought a particular understanding of what their place was, both geographically and racially, but they had to adjust as well, because transitioning from agrarian, rural life to urbanity's more regimented, geometric living (R. Buckminster Fuller gone ghetto, so to speak, in cloistered, crabbed cubicles, geodesic domes writ small) was very difficult. The geopolitics of industrial urban space didn't necessarily bode well for some blacks who brought cultural habits and lifestyles more suited to the South. Many blacks brought the cultural norms of creative collectivity and communal sharing with them, which were healthy and productive; black southerners helped each other out of the meager resources they had. They also brought the habit of having a lot of family members, relatives, and friends live in one room, in the shotgun shacks that were common in parts of the South, a habit that proved to be counterproductive in some instances. Thus cultural adaptability worked for and against blacks. You usually only hear the negative side in books that detail the effect of the black migration on family structure, cultural thriving, and social cohesion and stability. But you rarely hear of the vital social and cultural habits (such as adaptable familial structures and flexible gender roles, since black women have always worked outside the home) that allowed black urbanity to flourish.

At the same time, though, the aesthetic cultures that black southerners brought—and the joy, the frivolity, the edifying frenzy, the passionate investment in bodily expressions and syncopated rhythms and cultural significations that were important to sustaining their lives and nurturing their strong sense of self—was crucial to black survival. It also clashed with certain elements of the white mainstream, not the least of which was the perception by older whites that this black culture was ruining their children. When Louis Armstrong left New Orleans and headed to Chicago, one of his great fans was a high school-aged cat named Bix Beiderbecke. As a result, the great black migration, with its southern roots, influences the northern white populace, especially youth who are fumbling toward maturity while experiencing alienation from their parents' world. A major way many white youth articulated their alienation, and affirmed their sanity, authenticity, and legitimacy, was by latching hold of the mores mediated through the artistic values of black culture as expressed in the imaginations and visions of its great artists. What happens is predictable: Bix becomes better known than his mentor in many artistic circles and gets the opportunity to make more money than Armstrong. Or think about Benny Goodman, who reaped huge aesthetic and financial benefit from his association with (read: appropriation and downright ripping off of) black musicians. But at least Goodman had enough sense to bring Fletcher Henderson along as his musical director, even though Goodman became famous in the first place because he had purchased twenty-four of Fletcher Henderson's songs to make him the "King of Swing." Damned, Duke, my sincere apologies!

So urban migration meant much more than black bodies occupying the menial workforce. It also meant the widening influence of black cultural sensibilities, even if, as was the case with Bix and Benny, they were appropriated and diluted. Black cultural influence caused great tension in the industrialized North because it meant that blackness was just so *present*. Its proximity was a problem. It was one thing for whites to minstrel blackness, to appropriate it for pecuniary and performative gain. Hence you had the Cotton Club in Harlem controlled by white mobsters, catering to a white clientele in the fabled bosom of blackness with a public face that was colored by its black entertainers. But it was another thing for Negroes to show up in the North looking to benefit from their own culture. Thus the aesthetic demands of Negro art caused a quake in racial and economic relations, shifting the plates along the fault lines of race that underlay the social geography.

But what was really trying for even white liberals was the actual, embodied presence of the blacks they had spoken for by proxy. When those black folk took the boat up the Mississippi to speak for themselves, it was mutiny on the white bounty! When other folk speak for you, no matter how informed or impassioned, it's just not the same as you speaking for yourself. And part of the problem with black migration was the aesthetic encounters it forged in the public square, in the clubs and joints, and the churches and houses of worship that dotted the black urban landscape. The emotional sweep of black experience, which was largely abstract even for white sympathizers, became flesh and dwelt among the white world up North. That experience included the pain and pathos of black life; the utter despair and the defiant hopefulness of black existence; the anguished love that strode through the rhythms of black music; the sweat and strain and aspiration of black bodies in worship or erotic wooing or work or play; the murmurs, the shrieks, the barely suppressed guffaws, the edifying laughter, the comic sensibility that confronted the doom or tragedy or evil that blacks fought, elements that they refused to make their ultimate home, their ultimate reality. All of these moods and modes of blackness were indivisible from the great black migration. While the cultural rituals that mediated the normative beliefs of the black cosmos were appealing to some whites, they were to many more a source of horror, of pity, of condescending tolerance, or of grave misunderstanding, more often outright hostility, but rarely fair engagement. Often black culture alienated whites who sought to keep blacks at arm's length. White liberals didn't mind fighting for black freedom, but they didn't want blacks living next door. T.S. Eliot, the great modernist poet, said, "Between the ideal and the reality falls the shadow." This is what Chicago was grappling with, the shadow, the dark rim of black urban existence as black bodies and beliefs challenged American notions of democracy, cityhood, and industrial civilization.

Speak to the black embrace, or not, of the migration.

Black people were greatly affected by the mainstream culture's perceptions of their bodies, beliefs, value systems, and social visions: the baggage, metaphorically speaking, of migrating from South to North, as well as the virtues and vices that characterize black culture. Many black people accepted what white Americans believed about black culture: that it was barbaric and savage when it centered in jazz and blues, which meant that black culture at its best must move to embrace the transcendental traditions of spirituality that coursed through gospel music and evangelical, revivalist preaching. A huge problem occurred when Chicago-based musician Thomas Dorsey, the father of contemporary gospel music, introduced jazz and blues riffs in his music. Beyond the aesthetic dimensions of racial propriety, there were the social divisions of black society that were magnified in the great black migration. So the internal contradictions of black culture proved transportable as well. For instance, up North, blacks updated a habit they had practiced in places like New Orleans, known as the "paper bag" test—blacks who were darker than a plain paper bag were prevented by lighter blacks from participating in social clubs, civic organizations, or, informally, from marrying above their color-driven caste.

A hierarchy of sorts was generated among blacks when relocated southerners who had been in place for even a year looked down on and teased their more recently arrived compatriots. It was pretty hilarious for barely seasoned former southerners to view their kindred as hicks or "Bamas"—the sometimes affectionate catchall term for a country bumpkin or hayseed that derives from a shortened form of Alabama. Like some second-generation Mexican immigrants who were among the most visible and articulate opponents of further immigration because it challenged their own space and security, as well as their ability to smoothly assimilate, many black migrants expressed the most vocal outrage at newly arrived hicks, when they were barely "unhicked" themselves. Chicago was little more than a suburb of Mississippi, and you can trace that genealogy all the way from blues icon Howling Wolf to the stable of stars on Chess Records and the blues lounges along 43rd Street, most famously, perhaps, the Checkerboard Lounge. So these racial contretemps within black culture were part of the black modernist experience as blacks negotiated between the margins and the mainstream.

Talk about the musical establishment and their criticism of this new music, jazz.

As already noted, the first jazz record was made in 1917 by an all-white group, the Original Dixieland Jazz Band, led by Paul Whiteman. How suggestive can that be, if you break down and parse Paul and white man, which is both Freudian and Jungian, since the symbol and the archetype converge? Paul, we remember, was the first great missionary of Christianity into the gentile world, and so Paul Whiteman as a missionary of sorts, acclaimed by whites as the first great king of jazz, is just too much of a signification to overlook. And "white man" as the acceptable ambassador of this music to the white world was surely glimpsed in Paul Whiteman's Aeolian Hall concert, which marked the aesthetic mediation and economic commercialization of a black music harshly demonized by dominant society. The first jazz record and Whiteman's Aeolian Hall concert tell us that part of the music establishment wanted to commodify and control this music—to package, market, and distribute jazz to consumers in the marketplace, benefiting its white distributors, appropriators, and dilutors. Even as the music was being dissed in elite white circles, the white musical establishment still wanted to make a buck off of jazz. The artists weren't making the biggest money; it was the producers who were cleaning up. If you were a songwriter, you might sell your music, but you weren't going to accumulate enough capital to really make a living from that. So the white record producers, executives, and owners who were interested in jazz reaped enormous financial remuneration from black creativity and genius, a pattern, by the way, that continues to this day in some artistic circles.

Still, there were huge debates about whether this was real music, in the European sense. Moreover, conservative elements of the musical establishment railed against jazz because they couldn't control the music. Jazz just wasn't the conservative music establishment's ideal of good music. It was similar to what happened later on when ASCAP got caught with its pants down, so to speak, and was unable to control rock 'n' roll music because it was exclusively promoting the music of Tin Pan Alley, with artists like Cole Porter and later Frank Sinatra. As a result, ASCAP missed a huge cultural moment and overwhelming financial opportunity. Since the conservative elements of the music industry hadn't anticipated the degree to which jazz would invade white youth subcultures and become influential in significant white circles, it settled on curtailing the music's circulation. Louis Armstrong made a very good living because he appealed to blacks and whites. The same was true for Duke Ellington and Count Basie and the swing movement. In one sense, mainstream white swing music was the attempt to domesticate the hot beats of ragtime in early jazz into lightly syncopated orchestral riffing. But again, it wasn't Jimmy Lunceford or Count Basie or Duke Ellington who got the biggest advantage from the swing they helped invent. Rather, it was Paul Whiteman, Guy Lombardo, Woody Herman, the Dorsey Brothers, and Gene

Krupa. Harry James, who was Benny Goodman's trumpet player, was routinely favored over Louis Armstrong in jazz polls. What's up with that?

How do you reconcile a lot of the musicians feeling honored with appropriation?

I think it's the contradiction between individual artistic expression and the burden of representation. You're an individual but as a well-regarded musician, you're inevitably a race man; you're representing more than yourself.

On the individual level, I'm sure that black artists were honored that white musicians who greatly admired their music imitated what they heard and duplicated it as nearly as possible in circles that black musicians might never be allowed to darken. Some black artists took great satisfaction in the belief that America was indebted to them, even without name or attribution, for having created an art form so powerful that white musicians paid it the compliment of emulation. But we can't deny that the failure to reap recognition and reward for their achievements greatly disturbed many a black artist.

As a member of the race, as a representative of a larger agglomerative interest, there's no doubt that such appropriation was damaging. Not only were these black musicians being exploited, but there was a feeling that they should actually be grateful that white musicians were taking their music into arenas they could not enter. The coercion to black gratitude is a staple of dominant white culture in most areas of endeavor. Black students, it is felt, should be grateful for getting into good schools, despite their excellent qualifications. Black voters should be grateful for the attention from politicians that other voters take for granted. And black citizens should be grateful to live in America and hence should not criticize the nation's inequalities and injustices, especially when the nation is at war. Black jazz musicians, like any other artists, were certainly grateful in the strictly generic sense of that word, to be able to exercise their gifts. But why should they have been grateful to be exploited? Only the logic of white supremacy, with its punishing mission to make blacks actually desire their domination, could explain this phenomenon. Many of the musicians were not overtly political, even if they quietly resented the restrictions on their livelihood. Many black artists simply took things on face value, knowing what they could and could not expect. They knew they would never make it into prime time, into mainstream venues, where manifestly inferior white musicians were Pat Booneing jazz, if you will.

White appropriation of black jazz has to be placed in a social context that explains the efforts of individual white artists. What was it like to be Bix Beiderbecke, a blessed borrower, and to know that the acclaim you receive for originality of expression in fact derives from the appropriation of the artistic heritage of unheralded black artists, including a palette of aural shadings, a grammar of timber, and a tonal structure that supports their artistic endeavors. On the other hand, as a working white musician, you realize that the fate of any musician, regardless of color, is to experiment with borrowed sounds until you find your own voice. Although it was never simply a one-to-one correspondence between white appropriation and black exploitation, the larger social structure within which such dynamics take place underscores how crucial a factor race is.

Without being essentialist or romantic about these black musicians' humanity, many black artists recognized they would never get the fame or make the money they deserved, but they took solace in the fact that the aesthetic values they cherished would in some form make a contribution to the national and global cultural good. These black musicians were being called every name in the book except child of God, as they were pelted with epithets like savage and barbarian while displaying the most ennobling version of individualism, the highest vision of American idealism, and the most democratic conception of artistic creation imaginable. What purer artists can we imagine? So my hat's off to them.

What was the relationship of the mainstream white community to jazz?

From the beginning, jazz was caught in the technological forms that drove the music industry. As already noted, the first recording of black music involved its packaging, dilution, and distribution by white cultural forces. The mechanics of industrialization are coterminous with finding an available market for black music, a market that was created by the urges and desires of the masses and was shaped by the desire of white producers and record companies to make money from an art form that the doyens of American taste found morally reprehensible. On the other hand, there was the sense that the moral overtones of jazz were quite hostile to white aesthetic sensibilities and cultural authority, since blackness was perceived as polluting and contaminating white purity. To paraphrase anthropologist Mary Douglass in her classic book *Purity and Danger*, there was a sense of taboo associated with black bodies, beliefs, and behaviors.

At the same time, many whites were drawn to this allegedly polluted culture and were, in the view of their critics, fatefully sucked into the vortex of the black libido. The unlicensed and unchecked expression of sexuality, sensuality, and eroticism in jazz culture was antithetical to the repressions and virtues of Victorian culture that were selectively observed by the white elite. Unsurprisingly, the black aesthetic carried political meanings. Powerful whites sought to control the transgressive expressions of black music by suppressing its public exposure. They kept it off the radio waves, and they restricted race records for the most part to their intended black audience. When whites began to buy these records, influential whites in the recording industry began to market black music to other whites. If they couldn't whip black music into shape, they figured they'd at least benefit from the sale of this sonic pathology.

The first positive mention of jazz music in official, public white circles didn't occur until around 1933; between 1895 and 1933, jazz was evolving and undergoing tremendous transformation even as it was being demonized. In the end, to pinch the title of Robert Pattison's wonderful book, jazz proved the "triumph of vulgarity." That's not only because the music ultimately proved to be compelling to the masses and superior to its critics' aesthetic objections, but because the music, through the humanity of its greatest creators, helped America concede the vulgarity of its racism and antiblack hatred. That's not to suggest that pockets of black America weren't upset with the music as well. The vicious stereotypes of black hypersexuality made many blacks uncomfortable with openly embracing a music shot through with double entendres, sexual innuendo, erotic play, and sensual evocations. Already saddled with notions of savagery and beast-like behavior, many blacks spurned jazz as the devil's music. Many black people resented elements of jazz because they believed it compromised the complexity of black art by capitulating to white people's notion of the savage. These blacks believed that jazz culture played up the image of blacks as sensate animals and sexual predators to the exclusion of the image of the morally circumspect black. That's an argument, of course, that we hear repeated now by the black opponents of the worst elements of hardcore rap, who claim that it plays up black savagery to the pleasure and benefit of largely white producers. The only difference now, they say—a difference, by the way, that sickens the opponents of hardcore rap—is that contrary to musicians in the jazz age, black artists today are being paid for piping black pathology to the white world.

Then too there was a big dispute about whether black music could be said to exist at all. One of the most famous debates about this issue took place between Langston Hughes and George Schuyler. George Schuyler wrote a piece for *The Nation* called "The Negro Art Hokum," arguing that there's no such thing as black art; according to Schuyler, it's American art. Schuyler contended that there was caste art because lower-class black people produce a certain kind of cultural expression, but it's not the result of an indigenous or unique black artistic gift. Of course, other critics argued the opposite. Anthropologist Melville Herskovits in his book *The Myth of the Negro Past* writes about the deification of accidence that *is* a defining feature of black identity. For Herskovits, black culture deifies accidental, contingent occurrences by integrating them into the vocabulary of black purposefulness.

To borrow a nonblack example (although, arguably, he embodies profound black properties and identity traits, perhaps a black aesthetic in a postmodern white face), when Pee Wee Herman falls off of his bike in his important film, *Pee Wee's Big Adventure,* he says, "I meant to do that," which captures part of what is meant in the deification of accidence. I suppose another way of speaking about this is to call it an *improvisational intentionality,* that even when one did not intend a particular action or behavior, one incorporates it into one's grammar of activity as a willed event. It's a way, I think, of attempting to exercise control over one's environment. Herskovits's conception of deification of accidence is an example of a historically constructed element of black consciousness and culture. In direct response to Schuyler, Langston Hughes argues that there is such a thing as black art in his influential essay, "The Negro Artist and the Racial Mountain." The racial mountain refers to the inability of black folk to affirm a splendid folk culture about which they should have no shame. Hughes argued that one day black folk would wake up and love and embrace black art and take pride in the achievements of the so-called lower castes and classes. With the worldwide veneration of jazz, Hughes has proved prophetic.

Talk about how jazz, once on the outside, is now being celebrated.

It's at once ironic and instructive. I think that jazz has traced the nearly inevitable path traveled by all sorts of music that has been stigmatized and morally outlawed. It finds its way into the vocabulary of American artistic acceptance, even veneration, and lands at the heart of American identity. What we now mean when we say American, we mean when we say jazz. It is now recognized as *the* singularly original American aesthetic achievement in music, which is why, I think, we've got white critics arguing that it's not really a black musical expression. You didn't get those arguments when the music was associated with the brothels and the brothers in the streets. In light of its history, I happen to believe that jazz musicians should lead the defense of contemporary black music that is demonized. I'm not suggesting that they have to like it, or even regularly listen to it, but that they should, on principle, articulate an informed aesthetic defense of the right of stigmatized black music to exist. I think that's a reasonable expectation, but one that neotraditionalists in jazz constantly forget.

I often think they need a refresher course in the history of aesthetic contusion on jazz's developing body of work in the 1920s. For all intents and purposes, be-bop was hip-hop—if you don't believe me, just check out even Louis Armstrong's negative reaction to Dizzy, Bird, and company. What we have turned into nostalgia was once notorious. Bluesmen, in effect, were B-boys. Let's face it, jazz was the rap of its time. Now that jazz has been severed from its association with stigmatized blackness in the public mind, it has been elevated to an aesthetic perch from which it is favorably compared to the ostensible pathology of some contemporary black music. Of course, there are differences between jazz and, for example, elements of hip-hop, which arose under different historical and racial circumstances, but which nonetheless share a history of assault upon their early incarnations as the devil's workshop, as examples of barbarism and savagery. Of course, that's a lesson that hip-hoppers could absorb as well, a lesson, interestingly enough, which might supply rappers help in their defense of their artistic and cultural endeavors. Theirs is not the first black music to be dissed.

Speak to the irony or appropriateness of dealing with art in a congressional forum, and more specifically, jazz and hip-hop.

One can imagine a world guided by Plato's *Republic*, envisioning the philosopher king as the arbiter of truth. Still, we don't want to concede such authority to American politicians, most of whom are neither philosophers nor kings. We don't want politicians determining and regulating "good" art or becoming arbiters of aesthetic taste. Do we really want Bob Dole telling us what films to see, or Tipper Gore, Bill Bennett, and C. Dolores Tucker telling us what music we can listen to? What these figures miss is that true art opposes such artificial restrictions and embraces individual self-expression, or collective articulation, as its raison d'etre. What's intriguing, and truly sad, is that black activists from the sixties who fought the racist and fascist restriction of free speech and black cultural expression have now joined forces with white politicians and moralists, whose views on other subjects put them at tremendous odds with the liberation agenda of these activists. Plus, some of these politicians opposed the very freedom struggles black folk waged in earlier decades of the century.

Now I certainly understand, even empathize with, figures who speak against the misogyny and sexism of hip-hop culture. But it cannot be fought by legislation against the music; it's got to be fought in the trenches, in the cultural and aesthetic cul de sacs where music makes its mark. We've got to take the message of sexual equality and gender justice to the streets, clubs—and yes, to the schools and religious institutions—where sexism, patriarchy, and misogyny thrive and are planted deep inside the minds of our youth. That's not as sexy as sounding off before a Senate hearing, which I've certainly done, or trumpeting our views before an eager audience of journalists, something to which I'm not immune. But it's harder work, and it demands a long-term commitment to addressing the underlying causes of social injustice. But I think it's ultimately more rewarding than the simplistic pleasures of assaulting politically unprotected young blacks.

We've got to remember that all black art at one time or another has been similarly attacked, and that the effort to legislate against black music's alleged moral perversities is nothing new. Not only jazz in the early teens and 1920s, but rock-and-roll music in the 1950s—of course, it's hard to imagine that "Work with me Annie," a hit for Hank Ballard and the Midnighters, caused consternation, but "work" was euphemistic for a sexually suggestive motion of the pelvis—and rhythm and blues in the 1970s were lambasted. The attempt to censor black music was the attempt to censor black bodies, black voices and black identities unleashed in the naked public square. For blacks to join Senate hearings aimed at suppressing speech, policing art, and reinforcing our second-class citizenship as producers and even consumers of music, is, I think, tragically mistaken.

We need Senate hearings, instead, into the causes and conditions of economic and racial desperation that drive some of our youth to express themselves with profanity and vulgarity. Until we do that, the real vulgarity is not the curse words that pepper hip-hop lyrics, but the stigmatization and criminalization of our youth that leads to a precipitous hike in incarceration rates. The raison dêtre of hip-hop's vocation of angry articulation may lie in the lyrics of one of its greatest poets, Notorious B.I.G., or Biggie Smalls, when he declares on his song "Things Done Changed": "Back in the days our parents used to take care of us, Look at them now, they're even fuckin' scared of us/Calling the city for help because they can't maintain, Damn, things done changed." That entire song to me is a translation of Weber's conception of theodicy, which, as ethicist Jon Gunneman argued, expresses the disjunction between destiny and merit, between what you get and what you think you deserve.

I think in its clever rhymes is contained a sophisticated social analysis of the conditions under which young blacks and Latinos mature in post-industrial urban spaces, especially those enclaves of civic terror called ghettos and slums. Plus, Biggie noted the shift in power from older to younger people in what I have elsewhere termed a juvenocracy, or the rule, and in some cases, tyranny of younger people over social and economic resources in domestic and public space. Many black critics in particular have wrongly concluded that black youth are in such terrible shape because they are somehow morally alienated or ethically estranged from the legacies that produced them. While there's no denying the huge generational gulf between older and younger blacks, we must, in searching for an explanation of what's gone wrong, think about the ready availability of guns, the ever growing economic and social inequality in black communities, and the political economies of drugs that prevail when aboveground economies fail. In the final analysis, we've got to help connect our youth to meaningful cultural traditions while respecting—and hence, engaging and critiquing—their own newly developing aesthetic aspirations and cultural articulations.

Comment on the likening of jazz to a boxing match.

The first thing that comes to mind is that, like a boxer, jazz music, as well as most black music at one time, has been counted down and out. For instance, some people say that the blues is down and out, complaining, "Blues culture is mostly listened to and appreciated by white Americans." Well, B.B. King thanks you, white America, and so does Bobby Blue Bland, and Denise La Salle and Koko Taylor, because they're trying to get paid and stay on the road, and they don't care who supports them, because black music fundamentally embraces whoever will listen. But that's not to deny that blacks have not appreciated crucial elements of our culture, including urban blues, or for that matter, some agrarian forms of the blues that have more in common with what we call country music than some music executives of Nashville might want to acknowledge. So I think black music is always down and out, always against the rope. But like Muhammad Ali, black music does the rope-a-dope: It just keeps on taking the punches, and when it looks as if you're about to destroy it, it takes your worst—appropriation, commodification, ghettoization in narrow categories on the radio—and wears you out. It turns the energy of your opposition against you, like some aesthetic jujitsu, and strikes the fatal blow, like Ali striking George Foreman down in that invigorating, mythological contest between black masculinities—the "appropriate" and American flag-bearing one (remember Foreman at the 1968 Olympics?), and the outlandish, outlawed Muslim-imformed one.

Of course, in a sense, Ali was a great jazz performer, because his movements were like extended riffs on the great themes of grace, power, and precision. But he was also symbolically precious, and the metaphoric value of his craft was hardly lost on his legions of followers, as he "floated like a butterfly," like a solo jazz melody arching effortlessly above the backdrop of supporting instruments keeping time and pace. Except, of course, Ali was a one-man combo, varying his pitch, and punch, and the velocity and force of his delivery, "stinging like a bee," to razzle his opponents and dazzle his fans, much like Miles Davis as he switched from *Kind of Blue* to *Bitches Brew.* And in his flight, in his mobility, Ali also struck symbolic blows against the demobilization of black culture and the restriction of our unique voices, as did so many great jazz instrumentalists and vocalists, from Satchmo to Prez, from the Duke to Bird, form Lady Day to Sassy. And this is where, perhaps, we can see the relation between jazz and hip-hop, too, at least in Ali's artistry, because when Ali came out with his doggerel disguised as edifying ring rhetoric—"rumble, young man, rumble" and "I'm pretty" and "I shook up the world. . . I'm a bad man"—his braggadocios behavior prefigured rap rhetoric.

But when you think about the metaphor of boxing and fighting as jazz, and jazz as fighting and boxing, we've also got to focus on the serious sense of contest at the heart of both. Not only two pugilists testing their ring generalship, but two or three or four or more instrumentalists in the "cutting sessions" where they lift their level of play and vision by virtue of engaging their fellow artists in friendly competition—and maybe here is where, like all analogies, the one between boxing and jazz breaks down, 'cause there ain't nothing friendly in boxing until the match is over, and sometimes not even then. But if we compare jazz and boxing, we might also compare jazz and running, since black music is truly engaged in a race. But it's a marathon, not a sprint, since jazz and black cultural products are about the long haul.

One of the advantages of the long view in black culture is that it allows us to comprehend the durability and resilience of black music. Despite its appropriations, imitations, dilutions, and domestications, black musical creators are perennially preoccupied with the next thing. You can trace the anatomy of innovation within given genres, and in looking at how one form gives way to another. For instance, as proof of the former, think of the varieties of what we know today as jazz. To name a few changes within jazz, termed America's classical music. Look at the progression. First there's blues; after blues, there's ragtime; after ragtime, there's Dixieland; after Dixieland, there's swing; after swing, there's be-bop; after be-bop, there's hard-bop; after hard-bop, there's post-bop; after post-bop, there's avant-garde; after avant-garde, there's fusion; after fusion, there's smooth jazz. Of course, each of these musical expressions survives, in varying degrees of intensity, but they symbolize the restless evolution of black musical forms.

And when we examine the historical development of genres of black music, we observe a constant engagement with innovation, progression, and expansion, from the spirituals, blues, ragtime, jazz, gospel, rhythm & blues, rock & roll, soul, funk, disco, hip-hop, house, go-go, new jack swing, techno-soul, acid jazz, bass and drum, and on and on. And when these forms are occasionally, almost unavoidably, appropriated, imitated, diluted and domesticated in mainstream culture, black folk are on to something else. With black creative cultures, it's always about the great next. Indeed, the great next is the secular telos that pulls black America forward, even as we reappropriate what has been appropriated and generate the next form of creativity. The great next stands as the sign of an inexhaustible black possibility and fecundity that spawns newer forms of cultural expression.

"Next" is surely one of the keywords in the vocabulary of black improvisation, related to and driven by what the French anthropologist Levi-Strauss calls bricolage, making do with what is at hand. For black culture, the great next and bricolage is about the possibilities inherent in taking the fragments, the leftovers that are both literally and symbolically at hand, and doing something imaginative and substantive with them. In one sense, black cultural creativity, the great next, is driven by what may be termed the political economy of chitlins: taking the most unsavory element of an already undesirable entity and making a living from commodifying, marketing, and consuming it. A leftover becomes a lifesaver, in the case of many blacks who had little to nurture their hunger beyond pork bellies, which later became an item sold on Wall Street. Black artistic expression often involves taking the sonic fragments and cultural leftovers of dominant culture and making a black cultural product that is desirable, even irresistible, to the margins and the mainstream. The beauty of black culture is its ability to recreate and reinvent itself as the great next thing in the long evolution of creative possibilities, at precisely the moment it's being written off.

Interview by Maria Agui Carter and Calvin A. Lindsay Jr.
New York, New York, 1999

10

Black Fists and Sole Brothers

The 1968 Olympics

Okay, this time period that we're talking about, the late '60s, is a time period in America that somebody classified as the athletic revolution. In regards to the black athlete, why did things have to change during that time period?

During the middle to late 1960s, the events of American society impinged on the consciousness of many black athletes in a way that had not happened before. One thinks of an earlier epoch, for instance, in 1936, when Jesse Owens made his famous run in the Olympics with Hitler in the stands. The opposing elements were clear: white supremacy on the one hand, black athletic genius in the service of democratic ideals on the other. But racial events didn't come to a head the same way they did in the 1960s, including the ongoing civil rights movement, the enormous upheaval of the antiwar movement, the peace movement, the social presence of the so-called hippies and yippies, and the death of Martin Luther King Jr. in 1968. Many black athletes became more aware of their roles and responsibilities, not only as athletes but also as *African American* athletes.

Moreover, the rise to prominence of figures like Jim Brown and Muhammad Ali conscientized the white athlete as never before. So these forces together conspired to make black athletes much more on point, much more socially and politically conscious, and much more conscientious about being representatives of something deeper and larger than just sports. They became awakened to issues beyond hitting a ball, running a pigskin, or racing in a track and field event. They realized that they were carrying symbolic weight beyond their own athletic contests, and that they were carrying the interests of the entire race. Many of them for the first time understood that they bore what James Baldwin termed the burden of representation.

So there was a representation where their responsibility came with a high profile?

Yes. The more high profile these athletes were, the more responsibility people attached to them. Any black athlete who gains a certain level of prominence in America has attached to him, whether fair or not, the desires of his people. Folks emulate these athletes just because they're athletes. They want to make the basket catch like Willie Mays or, more recently, they want to "be like Mike." In the 1960s, such identification with black athletes was even more intense and important because they were ambassadors for black culture. Like entertainers Duke Ellington and Louis Armstrong from an earlier era, these athletes carried the burden and responsibility of a message to white America: "We are intelligent, we are athletic, we are capable, we are not here to burn your town down or to be offensive, but we are here to exercise our craft. Furthermore, we're bearing the responsibility for all of those millions of other black people who will never get a chance to come to your television or be seen on your large screen, or on your local gridiron." The more high profile they were, the more demands they faced.

I'm sorry to use the race issue in and of itself, but it was also the first time where sports had really come under the microscope. There was a new surge in black awareness that took in black athletes as well, right?

In the 1960s there was a convergence of rising racial awareness and cultural reflection on the role that sport plays in our society. Well before the 1960s, sports had a prominent function in the culture, especially baseball, which was crowned "America's favorite pastime" and enjoyed unparalleled supremacy in capturing the national imagination. The boys of summer ruled from the '20s through the early '60s. But in the late '60s, baseball got a serious challenge from within and outside its borders. If baseball was seen as the quintessential American sport, the unique articulation of American identity, its face changed as integration and immigration brought black and brown ballplayers into the fold. Then too, football began to give baseball a run for its money, and much later basketball supplanted baseball as the nation's most popular sport. And with the heightened visibility of the female athlete, spurred in part by the feminist movement, things were in upheaval in the sports arena and beyond.

If sport was not immune to social change, neither was it immune to the fetish of commodity, as baseball, football, and later basketball became big business. Sport was now a vigorously contested terrain where the meanings of national identity competed alongside athletes for recognition and reward. There was a transition from the realm of "pure" sports (although sport had always been infected by commercial interests, just not to the degree it suffered after the '60s) to the notion that sport was now fatally intertwined with the bottom line. Sport lost its virginity in the '60s, so to speak, as critics and others began to debate what sport meant, how athletes should be responsible, how they should behaves and the like.

And the project of human rights. What ultimately was the message? What did people mean here?

Well, I think that the project of human rights spearheaded by people like professor Harry Edwards had a simple message: We are human beings who deserve to be treated with dignity and respect. It was the message of blacks in America who sought to be treated with justice and equality, a message these athletes now adopted for the sports arena. They simply wanted to be fairly treated and to not be exploited. I think Tommy Smith and John Carlos said in essence, "We're not animals, we're human beings. We can be celebrated on the gridiron, we can be celebrated on the track and field, we can be celebrated when we're carrying a football or shooting a ball through a pair of nets, but we can't be treated as equal human beings when we are away from the field of play." Smith, Carlos, and the others understood the need to demand equality of opportunity in the sports arena and beyond.

I guess in its simplest form there was a clear difference, an awareness in these athletes that, hey, we may be good and we are all the best players here in the world, but we still can't get an apartment. It came down to those simple things.

Absolutely. These athletes realized that despite their extraordinary achievements on the field, off the field they were just another black person. It brings to mind that famous query from Malcolm X, in his autobiography, when he asks, "What do you call a black person with a PhD? Nigger." So what do you call an athlete who is able to win the 100-yard dash, or the 200, or the 440, or the 110 hurdles? You call him a nigger when he's not running, a realization that was painful to these athletes. And it gnawed at their conscience. In a real sense, the human rights project the athletes undertook made them the kind of critical social actors and agents they hadn't been before. Some of them had a fragmented awareness of what was wrong, but I think this particular issue called together a group of men who were outraged by the limits that were artificially imposed on them. As a result, they grew in their understanding of what it meant to be a representative of one's group, to not just run for the sake of running. That was the extra burden that black athletes bore.

Harry Edwards, at the very least, seemed difficult to miss. I mean, he was an imposing guy . . .

Yes.

. . . a brilliant, likable guy. He had a lot of interesting attributes that clearly made him rise above others. He also agitated a lot of people, didn't he?

Sure. Harry Edwards is an extraordinary figure in the history of black athletics over the last thirty years. He was at the time a smart sociologist well versed in the field's theories and jargon about race who also understood the internal dynamics of sport. So he was a perfect bridge figure between those athletes and the wider society. He was a young man himself, not even twenty-five years old, and served as an instructor in sociology at San Jose State with these barely eighteen- and nineteen-year-old kids. So he was able to get closer to them than other older, more estimable figures in the black community. He understood their worldviews. And yet at the same time he had his own charisma, his own authority that derived from his considerable knowledge and education. As a result, he was able to spur their consciousness, and of course he agitated people as well. But remember, Martin Luther King Jr. was also viewed as an agitator by many whites and a fair number of blacks. So in the late '60s, Harry Edwards was an extraordinary, difficult, and flamboyant figure. Now he's on the sidelines of the San Francisco 49ers and working with other mainstream groups helping them manage their athletes. So times change and so does our understanding of the figures that helped to change them.

How much of this, though, in the way Harry projected himself publicly was shtick, and how much of that shtick was really necessary?

All great orators and educators, especially those in minority American traditions, learn sooner or later that you better put some entertainment in your education. I suppose it's what the legendary hip-hop artist KRS-One calls "edutainment." There's no question that Harry Edwards was a severe taskmaster who capably deployed shtick and performance. After all, he's dealing with performers. He's got to perform himself. What's his niche? It's partly that "I can talk that talk." Harry Edwards had to publicize the athletes' case; he had to dramatize their beliefs. Again, if we look at the civil rights movement, Martin Luther King Jr. knew that an old bigot like Bull Connors was tempted to beat up on black people and wash them against the walls with firefighting water hoses. But King wanted that; he wanted to dramatize the unjust, assaulted condition of African American people. Harry Edwards wanted to similarly dramatize the condition of African American athletes. He knew how to shake the rafters and rouse the rabble. He knew how to exaggerate for ethical ends, how to deploy hyperbole for an ultimately good purpose, which was to show that African American athletes were first-class athletes but second-class citizens. He wanted the nation to get that point, and he made it with gusto and verve.

Harry could do things, but he had a difficult task at hand. He was dealing with a group of athletes who were on the same path as he was. And yet he was having to deal with a certainly far from monolithic group of athletes, all teenagers, all from across the country . . . so he did exercise control. The main thing is how do you make these athletes believe in that?

Edwards did indeed face an enormously difficult task, namely, how do you bring together and solidify young black men from different parts of the country with different views about how best to attack the problem. Some wanted to be explicit in their resistance to what they considered unfair tactics. They wanted to raise their fists, to wear certain clothing, to stylize and literally fashion their resistance. Others wanted to be subtler, more implicit, and more covert. Of course, these are alternatives that black people have always faced, going all the way back to slavery. Some slaves were quite explicit about their rebellion, including figures like Nat Turner and Gabriel Prosser. They ended up getting hounded, harassed, and sometimes hanged, but they spurred the action of their fellow slaves. Other slaves were subtler. They sang songs that signaled knowing blacks about the route to freedom. They hid their liberating intent behind haunting harmonies.

So black people have always understood that you can't always come out and say what you mean, since it might undercut your purposes. There's been an enormous dispute around this issue within black culture that continues to this day. Do you expose your hand and therefore make it more likely that you will be put down before you're able to be successful? Or do you somehow signify your intent to rebel by doing it very, very smoothly? Many blacks said, "We've got to take it to the mat, we just have to come out and say that we will take it no longer." There's a constant tension in African American culture about what's the best route to racial uplift, and those things were present in Harry Edwards's group of athletes.

I clearly think it would be foolish to think that all those guys would have thought the same way. And you have guys going through what would have been their last Olympics.

Right.

Charlie Scott, from the University of North Carolina, the first black basketball player to play at a major school, was sort of the Jackie Robinson of college basketball. And you had Larry James who was going to a conservative white institution like Villanova. All these guys were now listening to Harry Edwards, and they probably perceived him in the way some white American might have viewed him.

in many ways fighting the same battle as athletes. It was John Carlos, I think, who said, "When we race, we're considered Americans, but if something bad happens to us, we are those Negro athletes." These black athletes understood those contradictions and they were trying to deal with them the best they could.

So is "angry black athlete" a fair term, or is that a mischaracterization?

Well, it's an ambiguous, multievidential term. On the one hand, these black athletes are absolutely angry. But when such a term tumbles out of the mouths of many white Americans, it means something altogether different. It's often an attempt to demonize black people, to label them as somehow peculiarly possessed of an unwarranted ungratefulness for what our country offers. Thus it is in some ways a species of un-Americanness. The subtext is that such angry people are not accepting of the American way, that they're not going to stand up as George Foreman did at the 1968 Olympics and hold a flag and wave it and be proud. Angry black man, angry black athlete: Those terms work in the most precise, objective sense of the phrase, shorn of its ideological overtones. These athletes are angry about racism, they're angry about the unfair treatment they are receiving, they are angry about the poverty that their black brothers and sisters confront. That's why they pulled heir shoes off with their white soles to show their black socks. And they aised their black fists into the air as a profound gesture of solidarity with ıose black folk who will never get to where they are. So they are unapolo- ·tic about their anger, and they are convinced that their anger is quite legit- ıate, in the same way that disgruntled citizens were legitimately angry ıen they were subject by their government to taxation without representa- n. Is it fair to call Thomas Jefferson an angry white man? Yes, it is. But ob- us differences in stature and function aside, Jefferson doesn't receive the ative label that is attached to Tommy Smith or to John Carlos.

'he summer of '68 was extremely volatile, hot, and disruptive. The time od between April and June, between King's murder and Bobby ıedy's death, was harrowing. Talk about that time period with regards to aps the crystallization of the ideas and beliefs of some of these athletes may not have at first quite understood what was at stake. You might de- some of them as initially sitting on the fence.

Sure. Harry Edwards probably came off like Malcolm X to many of these black athletes who were not used to black people being that flamboyant, that articulate, that explicit. We can think about it now in terms of, say, the first time you heard Snoop Doggy Dogg or Ice Cube or some gangsta rapper who was cussing, and you repeated his words and said, "Oh, my God, my mama can't hear me saying those words in public." Well, we can liken the effect of hearing Harry Edwards to Malcolm X or gangsta rap. He was bold and defiant, making these rhetorical gestures of resistance, telling those athletes that they had to rebel, that they had to be principled. And many other blacks who were part of the group, whether it was Charlie Scott, or whether it was Ralph Boston, or whether it was Brother James at Villanova, were used to a much more sophisticated variety of resistance, perhaps even going along to get along. We must not forget, after all, that O.J. Simpson was just emerging as a national figure in 1968. He was one of the figures to whom Tommy Smith and John Carlos were compared. O.J. Simpson was an exemplary figure to the white world who would go on to win the Heisman Trophy. He was the kind of black man whom whites like and desire to promote, a depoliticized icon of racial amnesia. Of course, in the aftermath of his radical fall from grace, we might question what model of black manhood was ultimately redemptive for the black male athlete.

It's difficult to put a title on any of this, but it is apparent to those in the mass media or the general populace that there was a rumble in the order of things, and there was the passing of a "good" generation of black athletes. They weren't dealing with Rafer Johnson or Willie Mays when they confronted the athletes of the 1968 Olympics. They are usually categorized as the "angry black athlete."

There's no question that in the 1968 Olympics, this was a different athlete. One of the most remarkable exchanges that marked the difference occurred when Jesse Owens, on behalf of the USOC, went to meet with the black athletes, some twenty-five in all. It was enormously tense because Jesse Owens, of course, represented a different aesthetic, a different approach, a different racial weltanschauung. He represented an era when athletic prowess alone was a symbolic gesture and a political act. When he performed with Hitler in the stands and he ran for America, he was racing for democracy against the scourge of Nazism, for America against Germany. But now Owens is the odd man out, and a new generation has risen up to say, "we want to tell our story differently." And Jesse Owens is there trying to convince them to do something much more restrained. A white athlete, I think it was Hal Connelly, said, "Look, why doesn't the ISOC get mad when America refuses to dip its flag in acknowledgment of this country [Rome]." America's refusal to dip its flag in respectful acknowledgment of the host country for the Olympics, Connelly argued, dated back to 1908 when America didn't want to dip its flag to the king of England.

So Jesse Owens says to Connelly, "Shut up, I'm not even interested in what you are saying anyway. Plus, who invited you here? I'm just talking to my brothers." Here is the great irony. Jesse Owens is trying to get these black men to acknowledge their Americanness, and yet they've already done that by inviting a white athlete in their midst. When they tried to include him as part of their group, Jesse Owens, the great inclusionist, all of a sudden becomes a separatist and says, "I just want to talk to black people." That's a remarkable moment, and then what do these black athletes do? They say, "We invited this man here to be part of our process, and what he's saying, Jesse, what you don't understand, is that not dipping your flag as an American is a political act. Why then jump on us blacks who hold our fists high or engage in some other form of political activity? That's political too." That's an extraordinary moment in the history of the 1968 Olympics and the protest by the black athletes that is not often told. But I think it is representative of the contentious times in which they lived, and the different quality of rebellion that those black athletes were willing to engage in.

For the most part they felt like he was there to kind of tame them at that point.

Right. Jesse Owens was the Tom for them. He was the handkerchief-head Negro, to put it in the blunt terms that were then popular. Jesse Owens represented to these black athletes the attempt of the USOC to contain them by sending the black emissary to represent it and to knock the African American interests that Jesse Owens should have been concerned about. So there's no question that there was an enormous generational tension between Jesse Owens and Tommy Smith and John Carlos and Larry James and Lee Evans and so on. These people were more than willing to put it on the line, to use their own position as athletes to advance a political cause, whereas Jesse

Owens was from a generation when the sheer fact of your black athletic superstardom was virtually enough to guarantee political implications.

How was that and why and when did that change? Was it a natural result of some of the violence and some of the failures that some people might have looked upon in some of the civil rights legislation? When did all that kind of happen?

There was an enormous shift in sensibilities from older athletes like Jesse Owens (or for that matter, Jackie Robinson) to newer, younger athletes like many of these 1968 track and field Olympic team members. Part of the shift can be explained by the tensions and ideological conflicts in black communi
ties themselves. What's the best route to racial redemption? Should we follo
Martin or Malcolm, nonviolence or armed self-defense? Malcolm was roo
in the noble articulation of how black people were suffering; he was ab
specifying the nature of the hell blacks endured. His method would s
have rocked Jesse Owens and company. Martin Luther King Jr. would
been upsetting to the USOC and Olympic community because he belie
civil disobedience, and what these black athletes were engaging in, if y
is a form of athletic civil disobedience. The racial conflicts in black co
ties encouraged these black athletes to speak out and to make poli
tures. It would not have been conceivable thirty years earlier.

But the racial hostilities that ordinary blacks confronted gave
letes the courage to speak up. After all, what Tommy Smith and J
and Larry James and others confronted in the Olympic Village
of black affliction; it was a microcosm of the forces the larger bl
nity confronted. They dealt with the same questions that all
with: How do we get along with white Americans? How do we
How do we express our rage and our anger about the limits in
lives, and at the same time try to further progress by integra
munities? How can we deal with people who fundamental
be with us and at the same time explore our own abiliti
Think, for instance, of those returning black soldiers fr
They had guarded German soldiers in our own prisoner
had fought for American democracy, but they came hor
into the same bars that white Germans could frequent.
contradiction to the freedom for which they fought. W

There's little doubt that ten months prior to the 1968 Olympics, many black athletes had not yet signed on or agreed to a boycott. They were, if not fence sitting, at least on the net of the volleyball court, but they were energized and galvanized by the seismic shifts in race relations in 1968. The events of that smoldering, sweltering summer propelled them into a political consciousness that they had not previously enjoyed. The death of Martin Luther King Jr. was extraordinarily catalytic. It really made the athletes think hard and sharp about the consequences of race in American society. And the death of Bobby Kennedy later on only sealed their conviction that something was wrong here. If these men could die for the principles of American democracy, and in the case of King, for the ability of black people to enjoy the fruits of an American democracy for which we fought, then they could at least, through their own small gesture as an athlete, make their contribution to this cause. There were a number of athletes who were fence sitters unsure about what route they should take. They were convinced that the best thing they could do was to compete valiantly on the field of contest and therefore represent the highest, noblest ideals of American sportsmanship.

But they began to understand that although those ideals were constantly appealed to, nothing changed. Therefore, many athletes believed that they had to invest their sportsmanship with an added element, and that added element was a realization that they had the world's attention, if only for a few minutes, in a way that many black people would never have it. So they seized the opportunity to become part of this global connection of black people, forging solidarity with other people who struggled against oppression. The Cubans, for instance, sent all their medals to Harry Edwards, so there was a kind of solidarity, a kind of simpatico, that was generated as a result of their gesture. These athletes understood that they had the world's attention. The question was, How should they best use it for the advancement of African American people, and how could they move beyond being self-centered, selfish athletes, and for once in their lives be part of the larger movement for the reconciliation of the races and the struggle for radical racial justice?

What was that three- or four-month period in the summer like that it fatefully shaped the lives of these young men and even made it possible for someone like myself to totally be aware of the impact of losing those two leaders? And how do we think about whatever hope there might have been for social change and for these particular athletes as well?

For millions of Americans, the death of Martin Luther King Jr. and Bobby Kennedy was the death of hope. There was also the death of social imagination about what we could do to make sure that America wouldn't explode. In the immediate aftermath of King's death, many cities were consumed by riots. They burned night in and night out with the smoldering fires of racial discontent. Martin Luther King Jr. had already warned America that a riot is the language of those who are unheard, those who are socially neglected. And now with his death, black people felt that if this is what they do to Martin Luther King Jr., who never harmed anybody, who never hurt anyone, who never intended anything but good will toward Americans of every caste and color, what are they trying to tell *us*? Many black athletes were both angrier and more willing to use their athletic glory to make a humanitarian gesture. After Martin Luther King Jr. and Bobby Kennedy died, they were willing to make a sacrifice themselves. I'm not arguing that they were somehow deluded in the belief that they were acting with the same level of sacrifice as either King or Kennedy. But at least they *would* do what they *could* do to make sure that the ideals for which these men nobly died would not go into the ground with them. And so you can imagine what those few months were like. Burning fires, the death of inspiration for black people, and the feeling that with the death of the best spokesman for our issues came the death of our unquestioned investment in nonviolence. As a result, a more militant and aggressive racial politics gained prominence in black circles, and a more "in your face" ethic prevailed. As a result, perhaps, many black athletes who had ignored Harry Edwards just seven or eight months earlier were now willing to listen to him.

The fact that the athletes spent all summer together really meant a great deal to their boycott efforts.

Absolutely. Many of these athletes didn't know each other well. They only knew each other through their rhetoric, through their respective stances. When they went to retreat for the three or four months that they trained together, they formed a much stronger, more purposeful bond that gave the

Olympic games in Mexico City that much more meaning. The best statement they could make was to show up in Mexico City in force, en masse, and make a unified gesture of political resistance, even if they didn't quite know what form it would take. So it was important for them to spend time together and to talk to each other. It was crucial that Ralph Boston speak to Larry James, that James speak to Tommy Smith, that Smith speak with Bubba Hines, and so on, even though they knew that they believed different things about race. But by training together, they at least began to understand more where each was coming from, and for those who were marginal, or those who were, if you will, fence sitting, they began to be persuaded by the logic of Tommy Smith. They saw that he wasn't a fire-breathing radical. He wasn't some behemoth of ideology ranting against white people. He was simply saying, "Look, I want to be treated like a man; I want to be treated like a human being."

In one sense they were the athletic counterparts to the men who protested in Memphis, Tennessee, right before Martin Luther King Jr. was killed. Those black garbage men were holding signs that read, "I am a man." They didn't only ask for better wages, they also demanded to be treated like human beings, like men. These athletes were better able to understand one another by talking in an environment free of the enormous tensions that would come later in the Olympic Village. Although they didn't decide until they got to the Olympic Village on what course of action to follow, the time they spent together in retreat, in training, was critical to the process of knowing and learning to trust each other.

Do you think that some of the smaller, let's say more militant communities of San Jose, or other parts of California, and perhaps in some pockets in the East Coast, that there was a degree of expectation within the black community that when these athletes went to Mexico City, people were waiting for something to happen other than pure athletics?

With these athletes going to Mexico City in 1968, the time was certainly pregnant for just the sort of symbolic gesture that they ended up making. And it's reasonable to believe that there was enormous pressure on them from segments of the black community to represent their racial aspirations to some degree, particularly in light of the social upheaval of the previous months. And it didn't necessarily have to be direct. Just "the temper of the times," as Eric Hoffer put it, was enough to suggest such a line of response. Of course, it's almost unfair for eighteen- and nineteen-year-olds who were vastly inexperienced in politics to represent the interests of African Americans, but such a burden was part of the unavoidable representation that athletes began to feel. Coming from San Jose, from where some of the athletes hailed, and from pockets in Oakland and along the West Coast, and from some East Coast addresses, many of which were hotbeds of radical insurgence, made it likely that these athletes felt the pressure in the most generic sense of the term.

And remember, Oakland was the base of the Black Panthers, so there's no question that their proximity influenced the athlete's paraphernalia of resistance—the black gloves, the black beads, the black socks—so that their aesthetic reflected black political insurgence and black power. All of this undoubtedly affected Tommy Smith and John Carlos and Lee Evans and Larry James and many others. Harry Edwards, of course, was a major catalyst who conjured the spirit of both racial romance and resistance, factors that made the athletes likely to want to respond to what was going on in the world around them, to introduce it into the athletic arena.

How much of what had happened athletically was overshadowed by the protest? This is an extraordinary team, mainly made up of African Americans that just put on an unbelievable show.

The extraordinary athletic achievements of these young men and women at the 1968 Olympics have been dwarfed by a focus on fists over cleats. Some of the records they amassed didn't fall for another fifteen to twenty years. Obviously, their achievements were overlooked because of the bold actions of Smith and Carlos. I don't think they quite calculated it that way. They knew that this gesture would be powerful, but I don't think they anticipated that it would overwhelm the news to such a degree that their achievements would be dwarfed. And I think this is one of the real tensions in athletics, as athletes calculate just how harmful their political actions will be on their future, on their careers. Did Muhammad Ali, for instance, a few years later know that by refusing to enter the draft, he would have his title snatched away from him for three years and would never fight again as the same man, having arguably sacrificed his greatest athletic achievements in the ring to politics? Did Paul Robeson, one of the nation's first professional football players and later a lawyer, linguist, and world-class performer, know that being involved in politics would cost him millions of dollars and his career?

I don't think Smith and Carlos and others fully understood (and who could have, at that time?) that their symbolic political gesture would not only dwarf their athletic achievement and the supreme confidence that they displayed on the field, but that it would also cost them their careers? Tommy Smith, and I believe John Carlos as well, also played college football, and their prospects for pro ball immediately fell flat. In fact, Jim Brown, who would soon gain a reputation himself for political defiance, sought the immediate repayment of a loan of $2,000 to Smith because he felt the track star was not likely to play professional ball and be able to pay him back. Carlos went back to school and was kicked out of the ROTC. So they paid an enormous cost, one they shouldn't have had to pay and one they couldn't possibly imagine would be so damaging. They lost their athletic reputations and their prospects of a profitable livelihood from their sport. If we think about it in today's terms, the shoe companies didn't want to associate with them. Some of the athletes lost other contracts and endorsements. And some even paid with disturbed marriages and otherwise interrupted domestic lives. It was a price they didn't and couldn't anticipate. Sure, they might have believed that people would be upset, but I don't know if they really understood that the world would shudder in disbelief and turn their backs on them, as un-American, as unpatriotic, as unforgivable. Such a vicious, vengeful response would cause many of them for years afterward to wonder if they had done the right thing and to be more self-critical and conscious about what they did.

From Jesse Owens through Jackie Robinson to Rafer Johnson, black individual athletes had distinguished themselves tremendously. The year 1968, though, was the first time that the team was highlighted. I mean, it was almost like a coming-out party that seemed to be connected at the hip, in a lot of ways, to James Brown's, "Say It Loud, I'm Black and I'm Proud," and the "black is beautiful" and black power movements. There seemed to be sort of a convergence there where they got the stage and athletically they performed on it. I mean, is it fair to say that it was sort of a coming out party in some respects?

I suppose you could say that the 1968 Olympics was a coming-out party of sorts for these black athletes. After all, the sentiments of the "new breed" Negro as they were being called—and later they demanded to be called "black"—were very much in the air. James Brown's new-breed aesthetic was crucial to the invention of soul and later funk music. The Temptations at Motown were becoming more politicized. I can still remember the lyrics to one of their songs: "No matter how hard you try/You can't stop me now, Say it loud, I'm black and I'm proud," reflecting not only the James Brown sentiment but the racial pride that was then blossoming. Black pop music was beginning to catch on and to sum up the African American desire for social and political freedom.

In a sense, the black athletes of 1968 in Mexico City were critical actors in the coming-out party of black pride and solidarity among sports figures. As you noted, individual heroism was well established, from Joe Louis to Jackie Robinson. And the achievements of individual champions like Jesse Owens and Rafer Johnson were well known. But with the 1968 Olympics figures, it was more of a group effort, and the group identity was key. That was a new phenomenon, ushered in by the times and by the self-conscious efforts of the athletes themselves to present a united front. Their solidarity, although not perfect or untroubled, sent a powerful message that these athletes could not be easily dismissed. If it had been just one athlete's political resistance at stake, he or she might have been viewed as the "exceptional," lone, angry athlete. But their unity deflected such claims. The goal to which they aspired—and when we look back on it, we can note how modest yet basic it was: to be treated fairly as a human being—was viewed as something that not just one of them desired, but that all of them wanted.

They were truly concerned with how they could best represent their community, a laudable, even noble goal, given the self-centered, self-regarding, utterly narcissistic character of even most black athletes now. That's why their sense of style was so dramatic. The flair and flamboyance they exhibited were not simply ostentatious but were subordinated to substantive political ends. When they took their shoes off to show black socks to represent their solidarity with poor people, or when they wore black beads or raised their black-gloved fists, one on the left hand, one on the right hand of Smith and Carlos to symbolize their unity, it was simple but profound. They stylized black rage, resistance, response, and rebellion, and they fully engaged the politics of representation. Black style was enlivened at the intersection of the personal and the political, while the particular meanings of the black aesthetic in sport found universal application, not only for other blacks but also for all oppressed people who identified with these athletes.

From a sheerly athletic point of view, the image of Evans, James, and Freeman, one, two, and three in the 400 yards, and I just remember the image of them walking, three black Americans, and this was America. I mean, whether people liked it or not. I mean, all our great athletes now winning all these great medals were African American runners.

When Evans, James, and Freeman finished one, two, and three, it was an enormously important moment in the history of American sport. The myth of black singularity was overcome by the substitute image of black solidarity. Isolated blackness was displaced by cumulative blackness. The lone black athlete striving against the odds—whether Jackie Robinson in baseball, Jesse Owens in track and field, Bill Russell in basketball, Joe Louis in boxing, and so on—was offset by the image of blacks collectively running the field and representing not just themselves or their political interests but America! Of course, running the field here signifies in a number of directions, not all of which are consoling to white America, since it implies that they are *running* things, they are now taking over, so there's fear attached to the idea of black men running things. We know that had nothing to do with the business end of things, where the real power lies, but it had to do with the representational warfare over image, which is still a big deal.

Plus, that image froze in the collective national imagination the belief that *all* the athletes are black, and that all the Americans are black, since national identity on that stage was constituted and articulated through athletic achievement. That was both heartening and jarring, I'm sure. What's also important about this moment is that the artificial opposition, the suspect binarism with which black folk are constantly faced—namely, are you black first or an American?—was resolved on the track and field. These black men displayed black pride, athletic achievement, and American identity in one fell swoop. So they addressed issues of racial, vocational, and national importance in one monumentally signifying event. Truth for these black warriors was not serial or successive, as if they could be first black, then American, and then athletes, at that moment. They were all three at the same time. Truth was simultaneous for them, just as it is for any group that maintains multiple identities, loyalties, allegiances, and kinship groups. The real problem for many onlookers may have been the fact that these athletes were helping to redefine American identity, to shift our perception of national interest, and to repoliticize our comprehension of athletic contest.

It must have caused cognitive dissonance in some observers to know that even though these black men and women were disappointed with their second-class treatment and disgruntled with American apartheid, they nevertheless competed excellently and represented America at its best. Their best was America's best. They were the best America could produce, a disturbing thought that was turned on its head by disgruntled critics who lamented, "is this the best that we can do?" Furthermore, the athletic field was the one domain where sheer ability could win the day. There was no segregation or Jim Crow. When blacks were finally able to compete against the field, the only question for a contestant was, what can you do? Can you go out there and run the race? Can you best the person next to you? And so athletics expressed the desire of blacks to be judged on their own merit.

What was equally incredible about the 1968 Olympics, besides the political significations, is the notion that when you allow black folk to compete openly in a fair contest, they have the potential to do well, really, to dominate. That was an omen-filled observation, especially to biased critics interested in keeping sports segregated, and hence artificially dominated, by whites. The real threat was the recognition that black dominance needed nothing more than opportunity to assert itself, where white dominance had to be arranged and scripted through the unnatural restriction of competition.

And I think that another important aspect is, at least the feeling that I got from a lot of these guys, is that it was less about intimidation and "I told you so" than it was joyous for them.

Oh sure. Many people have a misconception about the purposes of rebellion and resistance. Most of the folk who engage in acts of civil disobedience and the like don't do it out of hatred for America and its principles. On the contrary, it is to invite the nation to live up to its vaunted ideals, to close the gap between what it preaches and what it practices. In the end, they do it because they love America in the strongest possible sense of that word, a demanding, engaging, critical love that issues forth as cooperation with the nation's best impulses by critiquing its worst. They just want the country to act right, to behave humanely, or, as Martin Luther King Jr. said the night before he died, they want the country's leaders to "be true to what you said on paper."

And so the black athletes performed with real zest because they were excited about their own potential. They were excited about testing themselves against the best athletes in the world. They didn't lay that aside. That was enormously important to them because without the raison d'être of sports, they wouldn't even have the opportunity to display their pride and outrage. So the first order of business was to win. That's why, when Tommy Smith and John Carlos, even after they were kicked out of the Olympic Village, went to Lee Evans and said, look, you win first, and then you do the protest, because if you don't win, no press follows. So the reality is, you've got to compete, you've got to succeed, to make anything else possible. They were still Americans and athletes. They still sought to represent the best of their people and national tradition.

It's not about hatred; it's about joy, it's about celebration, and in this case about protest as well. But a protest for more, not less, celebration of all peoples, races, and nations. The best traditions of black protest are about making America understand that we are part and parcel of this nation. We engage in resistance in America so that the best of America can flourish. We don't do it strictly out of resentment or rage, but also out of the zeal to be the best we can. All these athletes were asking, in the place of millions of black Americans, is for the artificial barriers of race to be taken down. They seemed to be saying that "if we can do our part to destroy these boundaries and eradicate these impediments," our people, and the nation, will be the better for it. They were unquestionably happy to win, but to their credit, they weren't so shortsighted that their personal victories would in any way substitute for demanding the justice and equality that they and their brothers and sisters were denied.

Still, they had a joie de vivre, an unspeakable feeling of elation and satisfaction that few others beyond world-class athletes probably ever experience. It is the kind of feeling that comes to those who are capable of doing something great that few others can ever achieve, a fact that doesn't keep billions around the globe from fantasizing that they also can achieve. That's why sports are so charged and permanently appealing. They and the athletes who engage them are unavoidably representative: we dream we can be like them or we live vicariously through them. In the case of the 1968 Olympics black athletes, the hopes and moral aspirations of millions of oppressed people, in America and around the globe, found fit expression in the raised fists of world champions who refused to lower them for convention, tradition, or fear. Because they raised their fists, a lot of us back home raised our heads in pride and fought even more aggressively and passionately for the things we believed in. That's not simply the sign of a champion, that's the mark of a hero.

Interview by George Roy
New York, New York, 1999

11

Adjusting the Color

Television, Race, and Culture

We've been talking to a lot of kids and some of the kids say one of the reasons why they choose to watch a show with a cast with a similar ethnic background as themselves is identity. I just wanted to talk about this issue of identity and how important it is for young people to relate to the people they see in a sitcom.

I think it is enormously important. For so long in America, minorities like Latinos, Native Americans, Asian Americans, and African Americans have been virtually invisible on television. Otherwise, they enjoyed negative visibility, appearing in the role of the maid, the immigrant, or the white person's foil. When people look at television, they are looking for a reinforcement of who and what they are. They are looking for some sense of possibility represented on the small screen. I don't think that we can deny the importance of young people identifying with a character who is literally a role model, who through his or her portrayal opens up the imagination, or closes it down, of the people who watch. Believe it or not, a television character grappling with thorny issues can help young viewers think about similar problems they may confront. So I think it's a matter of identifying with the character and then working through identity issues that may be evoked, however clumsily, on television. I think it's very important for young people to identify with a cast of characters who are friendly, insightful, acerbic, humorous, thoughtful, and serious, and to see in their characterizations ways to think about the world.

But isn't it possible for there to be exceptions to this, that if you are black and, you know, you could relate to characters on a show, like Seinfeld *or* Friends, *that just because the skin color is different you are going to automatically say, "Well I can't relate," and vice versa?*

Right.

You know, do you think that just by trying to identify who you are through the color of your skin, isn't that dangerous?

It's dangerous and limiting in some ways, perhaps, but that's American culture. First, there's not a functional equivalency between whites and minorities, since many minority viewers look beyond race and identify with white characters. But white viewers do not identify with minority characters nearly as frequently. There are exceptions—Bill Cosby, Oprah Winfrey, and to a lesser degree, Arsenio Hall—but they are the exceptions that prove the rule. Blacks, Latinos, Asians, and other minorities have no choice (given the racial situation in America and the powers that fund the images on the small screen) but to see through pigment and identify with the universal features the white characters embody. The more difficult trick is for whites to see themselves implicated in the goings on, the moral dilemmas, and the quotidian aspirations of black characters. To examine the silver screen for a moment, it would be interesting to witness whites going to see *The Preacher's Wife*, the black remake of the *The Bishop's Wife*, which featured Cary Grant and Loretta Young. *The Preacher's Wife* stars Denzel Washington, Whitney Houston, and Courtney Vance. Can whites go see that film, not because they see Denzel and Whitney as black icons, but because they spot in the film universal romantic frustrations and marital problems that befall every group, all human beings?

Going back to the small screen, I think that the best black sitcoms and situational dramas offer a keen peek into the themes that occupy all human beings, and yet such shows are for the most part rigidly segregated in both the viewing audience and the ways they are marketed to racially targeted groups. *The Cosby Show* phenomenon in the 1980s proved that the concerns of black folk are the concerns of the nation: work, home, children, play, school, love, and so on. *The Cosby Show* was a huge hit across all demographics. Unfortunately, that's a rare occurrence. Many black shows may not have the same quality as *Cosby*, but then it's also true that many of the white shows that are popular across race don't come anywhere near *Cosby*'s quality either. So the pattern is set: minorities identify across barriers of race, ethnicity, or region with at least some white characters on the small screen, but that's not the case with large numbers of white viewers. As a result, we are not often the person or character being admired or identified with on television, which has a significant impact on how minorities are perceived in the real world.

Well, what's interesting about Cosby is that one of the kids we interviewed said that at first The Cosby Show *wasn't "real" and that he felt that Cosby was a white man in a black man's body.*

The raison d'être of *The Cosby Show*, to a large degree, was to break down some of the stereotypical images of blacks on the small screen. Bill Cosby was waging war against a bitter history of stereotypical representation of black people, so he self-consciously attempted to explode these recalcitrant attitudes toward blacks, some of which, unsurprisingly, were held by other blacks! As studies suggest, if black folk watch more television than most other populations, it stands to reason that we'd imbibe and internalize some of the imagistic detritus and backward assumptions that gorge ethnic niche television programming and marketing. So it's not hard to believe that some blacks thought Cosby was a white man trapped in a black body, that he was "faking the funk," that he wasn't really dealing with the nitty-gritty realities of black culture.

What Bill Cosby brought to America in an ingenious fashion is the notion that black people are a diverse community. We can't talk about the black community in the singular; we've got to speak about black communities in the plural. Black communities are united around and divided by class, gender, sexual orientation, and regional differences. Some black communities are constituted around the vicious persistence of colorism, where the shade of your skin determines your social standing and racial appeal. The gay/lesbian/bisexual nexus is quite controversial in black communities, as it is in the nation at large, which is why it receives such patently stereotypical and crude treatment in many black sitcoms. *The Cosby Show* showed us by its sheer existence that there is a black universe that is largely ignored, one that is complex, heterogeneous, and robustly diverse. Cosby sought to challenge rigid beliefs about black folk in an implicit, indirect manner, allowing the show's richly drawn characters to refute the half-baked ideas of blackness that pass for common sense in the public domain.

The unfortunate aspect of the Cosbyization of American television is that it didn't show—and until the end of its hugely successful run, wasn't necessarily interested in showing—the class diversity in black America. Of course, no one show can be expected to carry the water for the whole of black culture, which is one of the unfair expectations attached to any black cultural product, whether a book or a film, that gains visibility and acceptance in our nation. That demand exists in large part because of the dearth of decent representations of black folk in so many fields of intellectual and cultural interest. Having said that, I think *The Cosby Show* might have tried a bit harder to deconstruct some of the uninformed perceptions about working-class people with little threat to its successful formula. Too often on the small screen, it's an either/or world: Either one gets ridiculous stereotypes through comedic shenanigans or, less likely, one gets a view of the upper echelon of black life devoid of consciousness or concern for the average Tameka or Tyrone. That was part of the trade-off we got with *The Cosby* Show, which nonetheless managed to be quite a refreshing break from the buffoonery and minstrelsy that often won out.

At the same time, I don't think Mr. Cosby identifies with his "children" on television, including the best of what UPN or the WB networks have to offer. A lot of people are out of sorts because they think that black folk have hijacked these networks, that our presence betokens the blackening of American television. Well, that's a stretch, to be sure, but it is an interesting development, made possible in part by Cosby's success, even if these shows don't necessarily look like their parent. We don't talk about the whitening of American television when most sitcoms represent white America. Instead, we talk about universality, or at the least, racial neutrality, a code word for the wan, pallid, almost lifeless, certainly lowbrow, lowest common denominator that rules television.

What's interesting about TV is that it reinforces an idea in the culture that we haven't adequately grappled with: whiteness is invisible because it is seen as a sign of universality. Blackness, browness, and yellowness are almost always seen as particular, as part of a niche market, and therefore limited in their appeal. That doesn't mean we shouldn't challenge the narrow visions of blackness that are portrayed on UPN or WB. But I don't think that we should be narrowly obsessed, as some blacks are, with representing *the* authentic black experience because there's no such animal. Blacks are a diverse group of people. Some people speak the so-called king's English to the queen's taste, while others are hooked on Ebonics, while still others are past masters at both, happily code switching their way from the margins to the mainstream. I think the ebonicist and the so-called standard English–speaking people should be represented because that's what the diversity and complexity of black culture is about.

Do you think that UPN and the WB network show that, or do they really just kind of cash in on that one stereotype that seems to get over?

They have a huge affinity for comedy and stereotypes. It's also true that WB and UPN are opening up a range of opportunities for young black comics. Now they need to explode the narrow boundaries that keep black people and other minorities ghettoized in a specific kind of racial and ethnic humor. I suppose, in a limited, narrow sense, these networks represent racial progress of a sort. For instance, most black characters on television used to be locked into what we might term emotional instrumentalism: they were catalysts for a white character's dramatic or comedic resolution of their problems. Hence they were largely disposable in terms of story lines and character development.

On that level, WB and UPN represent a measured progress, since black characters are central to many of its shows, even though they are virtually Johnny-one-noting blackness, viewing black culture through a small prism of comedy and rehashed, if updated, stereotypes. The expansiveness of black culture is not seen. Television has not evolved to capture black complexity. Cosby valiantly fought stereotype but slighted the full range of black reality in the effort to combat negative representations of black culture. So we're caught between stereotypes and archetypes of blackness that necessarily block the difficult-to-portray breadth of black identity and culture.

What do you make of the Wayans Brothers Show?

I think the Wayans are unquestionably America's first family of black comedy. They have tremendous talent, skill, and comedic ability. Of course, like any of us, they don't always measure up to their ideals or gifts. As for Marlon and Shawn, the youngest members of the family, and their series, the *Wayans Brothers Show*, some of it is inane, some of it is silly, and some of it is funny. While it's probably unfair to make such a comparison, I don't think that the two younger Wayans brothers have yet measured up to either their comedic talent or that of their brothers Keenan or Damon. They certainly have the potential to do so, but I think they are hampered by the sorts of scripts they routinely receive, and by their limited notion of what black comedy at its best is all about. I think once they begin to deal with a more complex understanding of comedy and of black life, then their own show will either be overhauled, but more likely canceled, or they'll move on to new projects. Among their peers, their comedy is not as engaging as, say, the *Steve Harvey Show* or the *Jamie Foxx Show*. Although they are extremely talented, they've got their work cut out for them.

What do you make of the fact that they [the Wayans brothers] were under fire by the local Hollywood chapter of the NAACP for the type of comedy that they do? I talked to them about it and they said, "Look, we're just employing our brothers." Otherwise they would be out on the street committing crimes.

Right, right.

You know, I am kind of like, well, I don't know if that really works in this world today. What do you make of that kind of . . .

I think both sides are missing the point. On one hand, the local branch of the NAACP has a right, perhaps even an obligation, to say stereotypes are offensive and need to be addressed. But we don't want to practice or support censorship. That sort of thing is already happening with regard to rap music, where sometimes well-meaning black adults attempt to police the boundaries of cultural expression for our youth. Such adults think that they are going to tell these youth what's right and what's really black. But you can't do that anymore (if you ever could) because these youth have an understanding of what they think is black, even if we severely disagree with much of what they believe and feel obligated to argue with them, which I think is just fine. But we can't determine proprietary blackness for them through dictatorial or censorial methods; we've got to make our case and win the day with persuasive arguments. On the other hand, I think that Shawn and Marlon should certainly be made aware of critics' perception of their aesthetic drawbacks, weaknesses, flaws, and failures.

True enough, we want to employ brothers who otherwise might be out robbing us, as many a rapper has reminded us, from the late great Tupac Shakur to Treach from the group Naughty by Nature, who, on the documentary *Rhyme & Reason*, I believe, says that if he wasn't rapping, he'd be in our houses pilfering our earthly goods. We're thankful at a base level, I suppose, that many of these youth are rapping and not ripping us off, but that's surely no reason to give them a pass on social, aesthetic, and moral judgment. We can't willy-nilly dismiss our critical instincts because of our gratitude for their deferred or redirected criminal careers. What balderdash! No artist or intellectual is or should be immune to criticism. We have to be pushed, criticized, judged, and examined, though not from a narrow ledge of reflexive prudishness, moral squeamishness, racial correctness, or proprietary blackness. Art, after all, does not exist simply to calm and soothe us, but to transgress and subvert and challenge our most cherished ideals and beliefs. We can't have a priori cultural determinations of "good" art. Instead, we must have ongoing debates about what constitutes productive, if irreverent, art or in this case television. But it's got to be art and not dreck. Still, we've got to get rid of the racial and aesthetic police and bring in the true critics.

How do you think white America perceives them and their show?

It depends on what part of white America you are talking about. White Americans who are sensitive to the complexity of black identity, which, as you know, may be a relatively small number of folk, would understand that the Wayans brothers are comedians with talent and problems . . .

. . . I'm speaking of our viewers, who are eighteen to twenty-four . . .

In that case, it may be that the *Wayans Brothers Show* provides their primary understanding of black culture, which I'm sure to many blacks is a truly scary thought. But I don't think that's as much a criticism of Marlon and Shawn as it is of a culture that relies on young adults barely past adolescence to educate white folk about black culture on commercial television. How unfair is that? It's not that Marlon and Shawn don't have their responsibilities, as I've outlined above, but it is patently unjust to expect them to bear the burden of giving white youth a complex view of black culture and identity, when they've got teachers and parents with more than enough material available to help do the job. We can't collapse the racial pedagogical obligations of the society at large on the heads of two black sitcom actors. That argument might have made sense forty years ago when there were hardly any blacks or minorities on television. Now we have a range of outlets, although not as wide as it needs to be, to understand and explore and to get a vision of what black life, black love, black hope, black aspiration, black existence is about.

So the burden of representation, as James Baldwin termed it, shouldn't be placed so heavily on the shoulders of young people who are often barely literate about critical historical and racial issues. We tend to forget that Shawn and Marlon are in their early twenties. They are growing up themselves, although with much greater influence, and unavoidably, with greater responsibility than their peers, since they're growing up on camera. That means that their mistakes, growing pains, and foibles make headlines, or are literally caught on camera, and that they have influence beyond their expertise or wisdom.

We sometimes forget that artists change their minds and images as they mature. Think of Eddie Murphy and his earlier comedy routines, say, the one at Constitution Hall in Washington, D.C., that included his infamous routine on the "bush bitch" that stigmatized female African identity. I'm sure he looks back at it now and shudders in disbelief at his unvarnished malevolence toward women. Now he's a changed man, one supposes, and is, as they say, "married with children." I'm sure he doesn't want some cad similarly thinking about his daughter, much less treating her in a fashion that suggests she's a "bush bitch." When you are growing up in public like that, the stupid things you do, the mistakes you make, are captured for posterity and unfortunately may be forever fixed in the collective imagination. I think the younger Wayans brothers are going through their own growing pains.

I'm sure some young whites see them as talented, funny artists, others see them as harmless and silly, others still see them as perhaps detrimental because they traffic in stereotypes, while some may deem them banal where others may believe they're insufferable. I don't think there's a monolithic white response to the Wayans brothers, and besides, what whites think of Shawn and Marlon may say as much about themselves as it does about the two actors. Making them *the* representatives of black youth is wholly misled because there are so many other ways to think about black youth culture, from hip-hop to basketball to cutting-edge academic theory put forth by engaging young black intellectuals, which gets nowhere near the publicity that sports or entertainment receives. Of course, speaking of hoops and rap as a way to understand black youth culture ain't improving things in the minds of many critics. But the Wayans brothers shouldn't take the heat by themselves, even as we push them to critically reflect on their roles and responsibilities, given their influence and privilege.

Well, you know what's interesting, one of the kids said that each race has different things they find funny, that it's a different type of humor, which is why the kid didn't watch the UPN or WB sitcom. I wanted to find out what you think is behind that, with kids thinking there is a different kind of humor that distinguishes the races. Is that possible for a race to have a different type of humor?

That's a loaded question. I think immediately of, say, Jewish comedy in the '30s, '40s, and '50s, which really set an incredibly high standard that continues to define how we understand what's funny in America today. What's remarkable, of course, is that an ethnic group that was being mistreated and oppressed in the larger society seized this medium of cultural expression and expanded the boundaries of Jewish identity even as they translated their experience into universal terms that were appreciated by the masses. Their success is summed up in that old Jewish saying in entertainment, especially in comedy, that goes something like "think Yiddish and write goyim." The insecurities, idiosyncrasies, and ingenuities of Jewish identity were brilliantly compressed into comedic practices built on sharp social observation, edifying self-deprecation, and relentless signifying. From Jack Benny to Milton Berle, from Shecky Greene to Alan King, from Jerry Lewis to Jerry Seinfeld, from Lenny Bruce to Robert Klein, from Gracie Allen to Penny Marshall, from George Burns to Billy Crystal, and from the Borscht Belt to Broadway, Jewish comedians have injected profound moral, aesthetic, and spiritual qualities into American comedy, transforming it with their own views of human identity and existence.

They've given us a vocabulary of witticisms, interpretations, philosophies, and character types—think of Penny Marshall and Cindy Williams hopscotching during the opening credits of *Laverne and Shirley*, chanting in unison, "schlemiel, schlimazel." Or for that matter, think of all the Yiddish terms deployed by acerbic Jewish comedians, from schmuck or schmo, to terms we now take for granted, such as schmaltz, schmear, schmooze, or schlock. And consider all the Yiddish words injected into the American language that derive from that wonderfully hyperactive prefix *schm*, that, when replacing a word's initial consonant or used before the first vowel, gives a sense of gentle, rhyming derision, like fancy, *schmancy*, or dirt, *schmirt*, or money, *schmoney*, and so on, a practice largely popularized by Jewish comedians. So there is some legitimacy to speaking about race, ethnicity, or humor as giving a genealogy of influences, but that's different from saying there's some kind of genetic makeup to racial humor, that there's a comedy gene peculiar to each race. That's an essentialist argument, I believe, that would be hard to sustain. Historical accents that constitute racial or ethnic humor, for sure. But race or ethnicity as the biological template of a comedic sensibility, I don't think so. Having said that, I don't think we can deny that some things may be funny to certain races and ethnicities because of the codes and internal significations that may be evoked through comedic material. For instance, if you go to a film that is geared toward black youth with all of their slang, or a film that treats black '70s themes, say, with references to the styles and aesthetics of the time, there's bound to be a lot of "inside discourse" that will be picked up on by folk inside the culture. That happens with every group, racial or otherwise. For example, it happens among gays, lesbians, the transgendered, and bisexuals too. Inside language, for instance, referring to "gaydar" or the most recent neologisms driven by queer culture or homoerotic life, establishes a common framework of reference. That doesn't mean that folk outside the given culture of signification cannot appreciate a book, film, play, or comedic routine pitched to a particular audience. It simply means that the nuances of a particular art form or practice or aesthetic expression are best appreciated by those who stand within its symbolic and representational universe. There are dialects and vernaculars within comedy, but in the end, humor is a universal language that can be understood by everyone. Black folk can watch and enjoy *Seinfeld* with its inside ethnic humor and its accessible jokes, and whites can watch *The Cosby Show* and appreciate both its racial accents and its universal themes.

That's interesting. Yeah. There is another comment [that we've been hearing] . . . "It's not for me . . . they have a different type of humor, you know. Black shows are for blacks."

That's sad but predictable. Some of us naively expect television to rise above the racial politics of our society, but our television watching habits are of a piece with our nation's prides and prejudices. The critic George Lipsitz has some interesting things to say about the relationship between culture and politics. He says that some of us believe that culture, and hence in this case, television, is a substitute for politics, that instead of engaging racial divisions and social forces in the outside world, we retreat to television and the big screen. Lipsitz also says that culture could be a rehearsal for politics, so that things we can't do in the real world we try to do on television or in film, for example. And to a certain degree that's true. We can imagine, or keeping with televisual and cinematic genres, we can literally *picture* a black president because we know it ain't happening any time soon in the real world. But, as Lipsitz says, it is more likely that television and culture become a form of politics.

As a result, we can't expect television or the big screen or any other cultural product to somehow be immune to the racial politics of the larger world in which they exist. The same world that was divided about O.J. is the same world watching television. The same world that was caught up with believing Rodney King was, or was not, innocent is the same world watching television. The same folk trapped in racial malaise and ethnic conflict are the same ones who turn to television to see their own reflection or to reinforce their beliefs about how the world operates. People are drawn to what they can identify with. Sometimes, if it sharply departs from what they believe, they will turn it off. Because they live in a society that tells them you can't learn anything from a black show because that's for black people, such pernicious beliefs are subconsciously passed on from one generation to another. So I think television often indexes the racial blindness of the broader society.

People every day sit down and watch TV without thinking they are making some big political statement by what they are choosing to watch. They are watching TV.

That's right, yeah.

So people are choosing whatever they choose, Seinfeld *and so forth, because that's what they want to watch. They probably aren't thinking, "Wow, I'm making a real statement about my attitudes towards race."*

Sure, right.

But what are you supposed to say when somebody truly believes that a show that has all black characters is only for black Americans to watch?

Let me try to answer that by addressing the role of television in our culture, thus placing the discussion about the belief you've mentioned in an analytical context that allows us to make sense of it. There are a whole lot of folk who don't have the opportunity to pursue higher learning, who can't extend their formal education beyond high school. They don't have the chance to hash out conflicting social, intellectual, and ideological differences in the context of a university or college classroom where, at least ostensibly, critical debate and scholarly research are encouraged. These folk often turn to television as a source of information about the world in which they live. I'm not suggesting that college-educated folk don't do the same, but they are supposed to have a level of skepticism about what they watch, hear, and read that is a benchmark of critical thinking. Millions without the benefit of college education do that, while many who have been to college blindly follow some ideological or party line with little question. So there's no elitist vision operating here. The bottom line is that there are millions of viewers who buy hook, line, and sinker what they see on the tube. And one of the messages they get is that the world is aesthetically, socially, and racially segregated in niches of color, class, and caste. White folk are dominant and thus dominate the small screen and the silver screen as well. Their opinions and beliefs are often reinforced as normative, even if they express a depressingly narrow range of the complex lives of the majority culture.

Needless to say, minorities are shunted to the periphery of television, existing in an extremely isolated aesthetic and intellectual ghetto. To a degree, that reflects the ways of the world, although other parts of the same world don't operate that way at all, say, in New York or San Francisco, where racial interactions are far more frequent than in Boise, Idaho, or Butte, Montana, or, for that matter, in Chicago, one of the most persistently and rigidly segregated cities in the nation. Television obviously has choices to make in regard to race, and often it is rather lazy, reflecting stereotypical thinking more often than fresh engagement, something it probably does with the dominant culture as well, just not with the same disastrous consequences, since there are far fatter pickings in the majority than among the minority. For every ridiculous, inane, mindless show about whites, there's a thoughtful, innovative one. The same is hardly true for minorities. All of which means that it's no surprise that many, if not most, whites believe that black shows are for black people; that, after all, comports with the world they narrowly observe and see even more narrowly reflected to them on television, the token minority on some shows notwithstanding.

In a sense, television has some obligation to combat the forces of racial and social segregation, which ignores the complexities of minority and poor communities. Part of the problem has to do with the executives in charge of programming, producing, and marketing television. Many of them are young, white, and inexperienced with true diversity. Even when they're older, they may have lived in a world where they had little idea of the existential and moral realities of most minorities. The multicultural makeup of contemporary society has only slightly helped younger white executives get the message of complexity, since they often fall into the extant television mix instead of pushing for change. The aesthetic and racial inertia is simply too overpowering. One answer must include hiring executives from underrepresented minority populations. That's no guarantee of complexity, but you stand a far greater chance of it occurring on their watch than with the status quo. It couldn't get too much worse. In other words, by expanding the range of opportunities for black, Latino, Native American, and Asian directors, producers, marketers, and writers, we might see a big difference in television, a difference that might actually influence the majority culture that turns to television for entertainment to believe that black shows might be for them too.

Existing shows might more successfully incorporate complex, accomplished, or even fully human characters into the mix, as a few have done. For instance, if *Homicide* or *NYPD Blue* deals with issues of racial animosity or true differences in black, Latino, or white views of social inequality, that's a powerful tool to inspire critical self-reflection in viewers without being condescending or didactic. And without making minorities, as television so often does, *necessary saints*, morally unblemished figures who embody virtue without possessing complex character traits that make such virtue believable, perhaps even compelling. If we had an expanded pool of minority talent behind the scene, shaping what we see on television, we'd stand a better chance of entertaining the nation while educating it at the same time. We might also have a clearer shot at getting folk to understand that what they do, the choices they make, what shows they will or will not watch, are not only matters of personal taste but, more broadly, matters of politics as well. We might have more space to make the point that politics is not simply what we do when we elect a congresswoman or president, but when we choose to challenge or reinforce social beliefs through the things we read, write, watch, and transmit to our children.

What turns us on, and what we turn on, is not altogether isolated from what we hold important in both the personal and social realm. Television can, with little effort, allow us to educate society about what scholars term the "social construction of reality and desire." That means, for instance, that one is not born with a desire to have a pair of Air Jordans on one's feet. Such a desire must be deposited into one's consciousness and field of pursuit by marketing and the media, including television and print advertising, creating a culture of consumption and a culture of admiration and glamour around a pair of $125 gym shoes. Television can be a powerful tool for good, despite the fact that many intellectuals and scholars universally pan it without making distinctions among the programs. It has a huge influence on the culture, and it is the media, other than the Constitution and the Declaration of Independence, that supplies the most powerful fiction of citizenship. So it's not simply the boob tube; it's a tube that glares at us, that gloats over us, that gloms onto us, that invites us to confront ourselves; it can either challenge or reinforce our prejudices and perspectives.

What's interesting was we were just doing our own surveys, and on the list of top ten shows, when divided by race, Seinfeld *was number one in America. But it is very low on the list for black households, which we are finding a little odd because in New York, everybody that we interviewed so far who is black watches* Seinfeld *and loves it. Maybe the numbers aren't wrong; maybe it's the region that we are in. But it seems that what you said earlier is true: black Americans can definitely relate to a* Seinfeld *and find that show funny. I wonder if the reverse could happen, that if a cast was all black, similar to* The Cosby Show, *and doing niche humor, as opposed to trying to appeal to everybody, it could be successful.*

I'm quite skeptical about that. Listen, we can't even have a black actor playing Jesus without controversy, and that is a real-life example. Some whites responded by saying, "You can't be God" because they couldn't even conceive of a black Jesus. What's revealing is that the black actor playing Jesus said he got no objections at all when he played the devil or Judas. But when a black person dares to portray what Hegel termed a "world historical" figure, a larger than life character, such a prospect appears, as Mike Tyson might say, ludicrous. Conversely, it might be equally problematic for the mainstream to catch on, at least in television, with the niche humor, the inside jokes, of black culture. Of course, part of the ingenuity of hip-hop is that many of its brightest artists understood that it didn't have to cross over to white folk but could seduce whites to cross over to their perspectives and styles and to literally buy into their idiosyncratic views of life.

But the same success has not for the most part tracked black television or film, for that matter. Black styles, sensibilities, and worldviews have not, with notable exceptions, translated well. That's because many whites conclude in advance of screening a black show that "this isn't for me, there's nothing relevant here, so I'll just keep channel surfing." And yet Robert Townsend and Suzanne Douglas, the black stars of the sitcom *Parenthood,* are dealing with universal issues that everybody in America can understand and identity with: kids, drug usage, peer pressure, coexisting peacefully with your parents, and the like. Those are problems everybody confronts, every family faces, and yet such shows are often overlooked by the mainstream. Subtle niche humor—not the stereotypical sort—and niche drama are even less likely to cross over to the mainstream, even though they sometimes find enough support among blacks to stay on television for a few seasons.

Similar problems prevail on the silver screen. For instance, when Whitney Houston was filming *The Preacher's Wife*, she admitted that she grew tired of people asking her if white Americans would come to see her film. As it turns out, her first two films were far more successful than *The Preacher's Wife*. Of course, the success of her second film, *Waiting to Exhale*, was driven by the enormous interest of black women in the film, which drove its box office take above $75 million through repeated viewings and peripatetic pajama parties, so to speak, to screen and discuss the film. It was truly a niche market that proved to be hugely profitable. Houston's first film, *The Bodyguard*, costarring Kevin Costner, was pitched to the mainstream and made over $300 million domestically. *The Preacher's Wife* was likewise a film that addressed mainstream issues, even though it featured an all-black cast, but was nowhere near as successful as *The Bodyguard* or *Waiting to Exhale*, for that matter. One can only conclude that whether on the small or big screen, it's extremely difficult to get the mainstream to identify with complex black representations of reality, niche or otherwise.

There is no deficit, however, of white attraction to black stereotypes, hence the proliferation of drastically flat character types on black situation comedies. I think we've got to figure out a way to slip in some subversive messages about the diversity and complexity of black life. We should also encourage more thoroughly mixed casts that feature role reversals of the usual fare. Take film again, for example, and think of the movie *Jerry Maguire*, starring Tom Cruise and Cuba Gooding Jr., who won a best supporting Oscar for his role as a football star client to Cruise's sports agent. Gooding was, yes, the athlete, perhaps a stereotypical part, yet his performance was anything but hackneyed. He displayed the almost archetypal bravado and machismo of the black male athlete, but he twisted it into something more substantial. Sure, "show me the money," was one of Gooding's character's lines and bled into the pop cultural consciousness to become, for a time, an unavoidable, ubiquitous phrase.

Even more fascinating was the role reversing that occurred: Gooding's football player, despite his flash, was a profoundly dedicated family man who warned Cruise's single character not to romantically and sexually exploit his girlfriend, played by Renee Zellwegger, or, in Gooding's character's more colorful phrase, he warned his agent not to "hijack the pootie." He urged his agent to be responsible and faithful. Cuba Gooding Jr. got a chance to teach the nation, indeed the world, about a healthy, ethically upright, morally sensitive side of black America that is not often featured in film. We ought to aim for the same goal on television, without being hokey, romantic, or condescending. We want to avoid the necessary saint while highlighting the beauty of black complexity.

Do you think when it comes to sitcoms—because most of the shows that we're talking about are sitcoms—that it's possible in the future to have an All in the Family *type of show where you are honest about people's racial views? Why don't the characters on* Friends *have any black friends?*

Exactly.

Do you think that we can actually have an integrated cast and have it be a top ten sitcom in America?

I think we certainly need such a show. More specifically, I believe we need the kind of humor popularized through Archie Bunker, the irascible but irresistible bigot who was brilliantly played by Carroll O'Connor from the mid '70s to the early '80s. The power of *All in the Family* and O'Connor's portrayal rested in showing just how ignorant and self-defeating was Archie's bunker mentality, to coin a phrase. Still, a lot of people were put off by Bunker's character and missed the point of the show. It wasn't exalting Bunker; it was exposing him. A lot of black people, and a goodly number of whites, thought it was a literal representation, and therefore an endorsement, of white racism. Like some rap music after it, what *All in the Family* and its creator Norman Lear were trying to do through the artistic exploration of politically incorrect territory was to highlight the idiocy and insanity of Bunker's bigotries. Lear used television and a sophisticated comedic forum to probe the ethnic tensions and racial conflicts of a newly emerging post–civil rights society.

All in the Family showed us that Archie Bunker was the real dupe because of his bigotry. Archie's wife, Edith (played by Jean Stapleton), was superficially daffy but evinced humanity and wisdom beneath her character's loopiness. George Jefferson was the equally cantankerous black neighbor with prejudices of his own, played most famously by Sherman Hemsley, who later starred in *The Jeffersons*, a black-themed sitcom that in the '70s spun off from *All in the Family*. To an extent, *The Jeffersons* explored the black side of things in the bigot's universe. George Jefferson was both an upwardly mobile entrepreneur who escaped his old Queens digs to live with his family in a tony apartment on New York's East Side and a honky-baiting character who was often made to face his shortcomings by his wife and his sassy maid. We could certainly use another black sitcom that was updated to honestly confront social issues today.

On the other hand, I think we need an integrated cast where black, white, Latino, Asian, and Native American friends, colleagues, and neighbors interact. Not in a stew of melted ethnicities and races, but a universe where race, class, ethnicity, sexuality, and the like, spice up the world we see on television, as it does in some real quarters in the world. Otherwise we end up believing that we live in these tightly compartmentalized, segregated worlds, and the real world is often more interesting. Or even the way the compartmentalization, segregation, and ghettoization gets represented on television, largely through avoidance, can be more usefully and interestingly explored in sitcoms and dramas, or some hybrid of the two.

Despite the persistence of rigid de facto segregation in our culture, there are enough interactions and intersections of races, genders, and sexes to see that reflected on the small screen. What we usually get are shows with minority tokens, such as the teen sitcom *Saved by the Bell*, which featured in its first incarnation the lovely and talented Lark Vorhees, and in its later installment, with a new cast, a lone black teen male. Integration in such cases usually means assimilation, where the trace of racial or ethnic specificity, however broadly that may be conceived, is washed away. As a result, there's really no genuine exchange or real tension between the races or characters, as there was in *All in the Family* and *The Jeffersons*.

It would be interesting to find some of the tension and conflict that we see in the real world reflected on the screen. That's not to say that it doesn't occasionally happen, but it's rare enough to want a lot more. What we usually end up with is staged conflicts between archetypal representatives of, just to take the black-white divide, The Bewildered And Defensive White Man, The Liberal White Woman, The Angry Black Man, and The Aggressive Black Woman, which do little to enlighten the nuanced interactions between blacks and whites in the real world. Of course, television plays to the least common denominator of human experience, so it's seldom going to deal with the bruising truths of the given world. But there's enough space for us to broach difficult subjects on television with much more subtlety and sophistication than we do now.

When you talk about reality, isn't the reality of our society that we're divided? We stay in the neighborhood that reflects our ethnic background. Outside of the workplace, most Americans choose basically to stay with their own.

What you say is largely true, as I spoke of it earlier. And you've put your finger on the pulse of social contradiction in America. We have the ideal of democracy and citizenship where everybody comes from different races, ethnic origins, genders, religious beliefs, and sexual orientations to form the nation. *E Pluribus Unum*: out of many, one. And in some cases that's true, but only in some. By and large, we certainly endure the persistence of de facto segregation. As you say, we may work together but we don't often play or live together. Many people do choose to stay among their own kind because it's easier, it's more comfortable. Even if you don't like them, it's a familiar dislike, since you know what you don't like about them, and you know how to avoid them. But when you are in a new situation with people you don't know that well or people who are different from you, you can't predict what you don't like. As a result of that unpredictability, folk tend to shy away from such uncomfortable interactions. On the other hand, American culture is just bleeding hybridity as it produces interesting aesthetic, racial, and social fusions.

For instance, a lot of white kids are buying rap music and hip-hop culture, and perhaps vicariously they are consuming black culture. In the fashion industry, there's already a lot of mixing and merging going on in ways to which we don't always pay attention. There's quite a bit of intermarrying going on, but you couldn't tell by television. We don't see many serious interracial relationships on the tube. What would happen if we ever saw a white woman coming home to her black husband, reporting to him the heat she's getting, verbally and through harsh looks, from black women? Wouldn't it be great to see a Latino brother married to a black woman, or an Asian woman married to a black man, and so forth? Or television could produce real drama around a biracial child who's being forced to settle the issue of her identity by being asked to choose one or the other racial identities. But most of the racial dynamics of the real world are being ignored by television.

But to make it a sitcom though?

Of course. For instance, there's all kinds of funny stuff that could happen to biracial children or interracially married couples. Black folk found ways to make the tragic funny and to transform the negative into something productive and healthy. We've got to move beyond the narrowly scoped racial and ethnic humor demanded by the mainstream.

Do you think though that Hollywood is willing to take that risk knowing that such narrow visions of minorities work?

Right.

Separating people and giving them what they can identify with is what works, no?

There's no question that Hollywood's big and small screens are steeped in the copycat phenomenon. If something works, we'll work it to death. We're not daring at all, and when we are, it's usually to tease sexual boundaries. We're not daring in terms of thinking beyond the given racial, gender, and class limits. In one sense, I know I'm hungering for an ideal world. At the same time I don't think it would take much to ease us into an ecumenical worldview. Think about comedienne Ellen Degeneres having her television character coming out, which is a hugely controversial topic. Not too many years ago we couldn't even begin to broach the subject on television.

Now the shows that "go there" like *Ellen* are signing up big stars to make guest appearances at the coming out party, so to speak. That's certainly a move in the right direction. Perhaps that's because there are so many closeted and openly gay people in Hollywood. So the climate is right to explore controversial social issues like sexuality, race, and class. What we need is a critical mass of executives, producers, directors, and actors who are willing to duplicate these efforts on all fronts. To my mind, that's a compelling argument to open the doors of opportunity to as many minorities as possible, both behind the scenes and in front of the camera. Only then will television begin to maximize its potential to make imaginative art and to embody the breadth of identities and social realities in our nation.

Interview by Abby Lynn Kearse
New York, New York, 1994

12

“I Love Black People, But I Hate Niggas”

Intellectuals, Black Comedy, and the Politics of Self-Criticism

As any student of professor Michael Eric Dyson's will tell you, it's not easy taking notes in his class. A Visiting Distinguished Professor at Columbia University's Institute for Research in African American Studies, Dyson talks a mile a minute and drops more pearls of wisdom than a school of oysters racing to get their Ph.D. In the course of an hour-long interview at his Union Square hotel before a recent appearance at Modern Times Bookstore, Dyson discussed themes central to his latest book, *Race Rules: Navigating the Color Line.*

Gently rocking in his chair like a kabbalic mystic, stroking his thick goatee in the professorial tradition, Dyson held forth on the responsibility of African American athletes to be political, comedian Chris Rock's latest challenges to a reluctantly self-critical black community, the commercial viability of intellectual rap, the Million Man March, and his own legacy as a public intellectual. An ordained Baptist minister, theologian, music critic, and *New York Times* opinion page regular, Michael Eric Dyson is an academic who, as fellow scholars have noted, is equally comfortable discussing the theories of Martin Heidegger or trends in hip-hop music.

He peppers his disquisitions with convincing renditions of stand-up routines and gangsta rap samples, and ought to be seen in person to be fully appreciated, but if grad school is not in your cards, this interview will hopefully suffice.

Let's start with your book, Race Rules, *and the chapter that I had the most fun with, on the black public intellectuals. In it you take some risks and air some dirty laundry, though I thought that the fake awards you make up for yourself and other public scholars were pretty funny . . .*

I'm glad you thought they were funny because I meant the awards to be tongue-in-cheek. That chapter is my attempt to come to grips with the burgeoning fame and celebrity of a group of intellectuals that had up until now been largely denied broad public recognition. That's both amazing and lamentable, especially when you consider that in the past the group has included figures like Anna Julia Cooper, W.E.B. Du Bois, Oliver Cox, C. L. R. James, Paul Robeson, Zora Neale Hurston, E. Franklin Frazier, and the like. These intellectuals made their living combating black oppression with wit and word, bringing their academic expertise to bear on social problems to enhance the public good. My essay on black intellectuals was an attempt to say, "Look, we've had enormous progress in terms of public recognition of black intellectuals and scholars, but let's turn the powerful criticism that we train on a range of issues on ourselves. Let's not uncritically celebrate and valorize this process of celebrity-making within the academy; there are some downsides." As one of the fortunate few to be included in the contemporary group, I wanted to highlight its good effects, and to profess and clarify my role while refusing to be silent about its negative consequences.

How have people taken the criticism? Intellectuals are sensitive people too.

We certainly are. We're all for criticism except when it's aimed at us! I was by no means attempting to be mean-spirited. This is not, after all, the Adolph Reed/Eric Lott School of ad hominem critique. Mine is a kind of tongue-in-cheek, sardonic, satirical attempt to poke fun at what some people take so seriously and are so self-righteous about. A lot of people think my essay is funny, but they're not the people who were described in the piece. For starters, I lampoon myself in my essay, so I figured that most folk would understand that I had no harm in mind. I think that some feathers were ruffled. So be it. Some sensibilities were offended and so be it. I think the point of the essay was to say: "We vaunt our credentials as critical and analytical intellectuals; we give criticism on a range of subjects because our job as paid pests is to raise issues that people want to sweep under the carpet. So let's not except ourselves from scrutiny." Others have not appreciated my sense of humor in formulating these awards. Some even believe that I have unwittingly played into negative portrayals of black intellectuals. For that I am truly sorry because that wasn't my intent. But I think we have to run the risk of being perceived that way in order to make a more fundamental point: as intellectuals and critics we have to criticize intellectuals and critics.

You mentioned the lineage of those African Americans who lived by their "wit and word" and it, like your chapter on black intellectuals, reminds me of the thesis put forward by Henry Louis Gates Jr. that slave narratives were an attempt for African Americans to write themselves into existence. Do you—as someone who is frequently asked by people like Charlie Rose, "What do blacks think about this?" and "What do blacks think about that?"—see yourself a connection between that tradition and what you do?

I think what I do is an extension of the African American tradition of writing the self into being, and of articulating the self through narrative means. I think that the lyrical, ethically intentional black narrative highlights some of the most heinous and offensive elements of American culture that black people have had to overcome. In that sense, yes, I certainly agree that the powerful antecedent oral and literary tradition is very much in my mind and on my pad as I scribe and scribble about the nature of contemporary black intellectual life. At the same time I think that it is vital to constantly rethink that tradition, and in so doing, to renew it. Beyond generating new inquiries, paradigms, and interests, the participants in that tradition should also be looking for new outlets to reframe persistent intellectual questions, like, What does it mean to be a marginal person in American life? What does it mean to be a black intellectual in a culture where literacy was literally outlawed and prohibited?

That's why I was so interested in that debate about Ebonics, or Black English, that went on right here in Oakland. The brouhaha occasioned by Ebonics was an index of our black obsession with white America and what it thinks and feels about black folk. Because of that obsession, I think that we failed to critically understand the most edifying features of that debate—the ongoing relevance of black language practices for American society and the denial of their importance among the white elite and bourgeois blacks, even as these practices are exploited for commercial benefit in the billion dollar rap music industry and by network television, where comedies on WB and UPN reap big bucks by featuring Ebonics users.

As we rethink antecedent oral and literary traditions, we must also make space for new issues that ought to be broached. In the main, new issues are brought into existence because of the progress and evolution in black cultures. For instance, as part of that progress we've got to figure out the relationship between the cyberscape and new forms of cultural consciousness. In relationship to black communities, we must ask, Is it true that interactions in cyberspace are more akin to oral traditions than writing? And if so, how does that shape our reflections on the process of constructing narratives to represent and symbolize black identity? One of the jobs of any serious critic is to discern the relationship between settled and evolving intellectual traditions and to identify and address new problems and possibilities in black life.

Another thing that struck me is that in that chapter on black public intellectuals you give yourself the Spike Lee/Terry McMillan Award For Shameless Self-Promotion and it's apt, because you seem to be everywhere. You're on the radio, on TV; every time I turn around you've got another book . . . and yet your more recent writing is frequently infused with topics from your personal life. You seem more comfortable talking about your own sexual temptations in the church, your relationship with your brother who's serving a life sentence for murder—you included a letter to him in Between God and Gangsta Rap*—and I wanted to ask you where the line exists between Michael Eric Dyson the public intellectual and you as a private citizen.*

It's a good question, man. The turn toward the personal in my writing is an attempt to make sense of existential crises that inevitably arise in any person's life, and in my case, as an intellectual, I wrestle with these crises in full public view. I feel a certain obligation to be open and honest about these problems, but with the necessary discretion and respect for others whose lives are unavoidably implicated. So I don't advocate a pornographic domesticity, where one reveals every peccadillo and temptation to which one has been subject. I think we must sharply criticize a species of confessionalism that seeks to commodify and commercialize prurient details in order to sell books and make money. My activity is a more political one. The political utility of confession, and of personal narrative more generally, is to humanize intellectuals who are concerned with momentous public issues. Such a process of humanization suggests that there is a person behind these words that needs to be reckoned with.

Another purpose of the confessional mode is to try to show readers through the example of the writer's life a plausible response to the sorts of crises that they might confront. Often people think that we're abstracted from the material effects of the writings that we commit to paper or the computer screen. What I want to say is, "No, we're caught and implicated in bloody and sensuous ways in the interstices of our sentences, and in our gerunds and pronouns and participles," and that there is in the midst of all that a real person grappling for space to think, write, and reflect. Finally, I think that the turn to the personal in my writing is also about engaging in grassroots ethnography, as I turn the critical gaze away from the external world I am committed to examining onto myself. The author is often both the object and the subject of his or her writing, implicitly if not explicitly, and that's not necessarily narcissistic or vainly self-preoccupied; it's about the inevitability of the "I" showing up in the "they" or the "we."

For me, personal writing, especially about my sexual ethics, my marital life, and coming to grips with my brother's imprisonment for murder, is about charting a course for honest self-reflection in the midst of the celebration of the intellectual life. In a sense, it's a way for me to be honest about my roots, about where I came from, and about the forces that produced me. Although it is by now a cliché, it's still worth noting that I could have ended up in prison just like my brother. In my writing, the turn to the personal is also a way of grappling with the forces that have lifted me above my brother's predicament. It is also about me being as intellectually self-reflective and self-critical as I can be in defining the responsibilities that attend my privilege.

It's Michael Eric Dyson picking up where John Edgar Wideman leaves off . . .

In some sense, it is an extension of the narrative that Wideman and a few others have had to engage in as a result of that cruel bifurcation between professor and prisoner, a narrative that is unfortunately becoming nearly a sub-genre within African American literary tradition.

Let's talk about something you write about at the beginning of Race Rules: *the legacy of O.J. Simpson. You say that for a long time he managed to outrun his race and that he managed to have a successful career because of his "teflon raceless-ness." This morning I heard Chuck D on the radio, and he was talking about the "the deafening silence" of African American athletes, who also seem to forget, or play down, their racial identity—Chuck takes them to task for it. You can criticize O.J. in retrospect, but do you hold people like Jerry Rice or Michael Jordan at fault for not being as political and race conscious as Muhammad Ali?*

We have to be critically conscious of these athletes who are largely O.J. in the making, O.J. before the crime. Deeply depoliticized, racially denuded, conscienceless figures when it comes to race, who for the most part take the money and the acclaim, whose definition of sacrifice is putting up with signing more autographs or being mobbed as they emerge from stadiums. Jerry Rice and Michael Jordan are perhaps the greatest figures to play their sports in the history of the games they so ingeniously embody, but each is more than a little troubling on this score. I gave a graduation speech last December at the University of North Carolina, where I taught for three years and where Jordan attended school. I criticized Jordan very gently, but my speech caused a firestorm of controversy in the news media for more than thirty consecutive days. Alumni demanded my firing and some pledged to withhold money until I was dismissed.

The day after my speech, the chancellor of the university came out in the press against me. A local newspaper printed a critical caricature of me, primarily because I quoted a Notorious B.I.G. lyric that contained the word "fuck," and in the South that didn't go over well at all. But to thousands, the most heinous offense by far was the Michael Jordan criticism. Jordan, you see, had given a million dollars to the University of North Carolina's School of Social Work, which was great. But when he was pressed about why he didn't give the gift to the Sonja Haynes Black Culture Center (where his mother serves on the governing board), he said that he didn't want to give it to one group but to all groups. The problem with that logic, of course, is that the School of Social Work is not the School of Education; it's one group, one school, one institution, just as the Black Culture Center is.

In my speech, I suggested that Jordan was an undeniable genius, that he was wonderful in many ways; but I criticized him for his failure to recognize—a recognition I invited the graduating seniors to claim—that one can love and embrace black people who love and embrace you before you become, like Jordan, a kind of Hegelian, world-historical figure. And it was mayhem; there was hell to pay. I recount this as a way of suggesting that we must honestly engage in dialogue about the moral responsibility of athletes who have enormous influence, visibility, and sums of cash but lack a serious understanding of the political consequences of their public profile. Think about it: Kevin Garnett signed a contract worth $121 million at age twenty-one; Rasheed Wallace signed a contract for something like $80 million. They are young people of enormous talent, sometimes genius, rightly being compensated for their gifts, and both of them, I think, are relatively conscious of the history of sacrifice that produced their economic windfall. But often many black athletes have no appreciation for the struggles and sacrifices that got them where they are today.

For instance, yesterday I ate at Nate "The Great" Thurmond's restaurant. As I ordered my food, I was thinking, "Here is a basketball player selected as one of the fifty greatest NBA players of all time, and were he playing today, he'd be making a ton of money." But athletes during his era had to work in the off-season to support their families, since they didn't make enough money from sports to support themselves. So the pioneer figures in the game have been doubly marginalized: their sacrifices have been largely overlooked by the younger athletes, and the political stands some of them took to elevate the standard of living for other athletes, and to defend black freedom struggles, have been undervalued and certainly not duplicated in this Age of the Amnesiac Black Athlete. I have in mind figures like Muhammad Ali, who was a doubly marginalized person—marginalized in mainstream society because of his African American identity, and within African American society because of his Nation of Islam beliefs; Henry Aaron, who was demonized because he was closing in on Babe Ruth's record all-time home-run record, but also because he took a stand against racism in baseball; and even Jim Brown, that "uppity-in-your-face-buck-nigger" who always insisted on telling the truth about race.

O.J. Simpson, until his murder trial, had no apparent concern for the significant sacrifices made by these pioneering figures. And Jordan surely gives no indication that he has any idea of, or appreciation for, the values these figures stood for, values that made his career possible, both as a basketball superstar and as a spokesman for corporate capitalism. In my mind, we have to be critical of figures like Rice and Jordan, who are socially anesthetized and whose depoliticized, deracialized bearing comports well with the demands of the marketplace in selling goods to white consumers. We have to engage athletes like Rice, Jordan, and many others, helping them understand that black folk—including themselves, even though they have huge buffers—continue to live in a white supremacist context. We've got to get them to see that even athletic superstars bear historic traces and the contemporary residue of race in their bodies. They have big, black, masculine, athleticized, and eroticized bodies. The culture collectively dreams Michael Jordan; millions of its inhabitants want to "be like Mike," as Jordan transforms black cultural aesthetic preoccupations with style, cool, and hipness into a financial juggernaut for corporations like Nike. Nike, of course, commodifies black cultural interests, skills, and identities, and then sells them back to black folk in the guise of a $120 pair of Air Jordan gym shoes. Talk about completing the vicious cycle of the commodification of black youth culture by pillaging and plundering their aesthetic imaginations and stylistic innovations; it's certainly obscene!

For instance, I was once in Portland and white men who work for Nike were going out and scouting black neighborhoods, "the 'hood," engaging in what they termed "bro-ing," as in looking for, interviewing, and investigating "the brothers," or black males. They were transporting to the postindustrial urban landscape the African safari hunt for wild animals, except in this case it was mixed with a damaging ethnographic and economic intent: it pursues the populace for its hides, its skin, while absorbing information about the cultural habits of the targeted group to better exploit its styles and tastes for white commercial interests. They were "bro-ing," hanging out with the brothers, to corral yet another black meaning, to surround yet another black signifier, to colonize yet another black cultural space. Many of these black athletes—including Jordan and Jerry Rice—are the iconic figures who justify such practices by giving them a black face. In other words, these black athletes who are reaping social and economic benefits are said to be on the cutting edge of the capitalist structure that dominates American sports, and yet we know that the owners of corporations like Nike, and of basketball and football teams, continue to be the overwhelming beneficiaries of such unequal distribution of wealth. It's a very ugly and problematic situation.

Chris Rock is caught in the unique position of being a tremendously popular figure who is acknowledging the political dimension to what he does, but I'm not sure it's for the best purposes. He's on the cover of Rolling Stone, *his album is selling like a crazy, but his routines are controversial. One in particular is centered around the refrain "I love black people, but I hate niggers." If it was Rush Limbaugh who was criticizing blacks who were stupid, who were ignorant, who were dependent on government welfare, it would have a different resonance. So how does Chris get away with it?*

Chris Rock is a very complex figure. During a recent *Oprah* appearance he explained to a white member of the audience why the use of the "N" word is problematic to people outside of African American communities, but acceptable within at least certain quarters of black life. The standard argument goes that white America has intended such lethal meanings by deploying the word that it's off-limits to whites, whereas black folk use it among themselves as a term of endearment, often wearing it as a badge of honor. I think there is a historic argument to be made for such usage among blacks. Chris Rock is a brilliant comedian who lampoons and satirizes some of the weaknesses he finds in black communities. Although one may never totally agree with him, I think he has successfully compelled many blacks to come to grips with the necessity of certain forms of internal criticism. He does it in a way that doesn't play into the hands, at least not completely, of those critics of black culture who claim that we are victim mongering, and that we are deploying reverse discrimination to justify our failure to gain access to social goods like education and employment on our own merits.

Chris Rock, in his instant classic HBO comedy special, *Bring the Pain,* and in his comedic audio recordings, is a genius in figuring out a middle ground between the vicious assault on black culture and the self-critical practices that are demanded of any serious social commentator. The comic-as-cultural-critic-and-social-commentator does not merely celebrate or valorize the culture from which he or she emerges. Such comics also enable us to understand our culture as they honestly explore it and thus help explain black culture's internal contradictions, stress its positive features, and acknowledge its detrimental characteristics. That distinction he makes between "blacks" and "niggas" (and by the way, he had in mind a specific conception of "nigga," one that in black communities signifies negatively, where other meanings of "nigga" are decidedly more positive) is one that refers to codes of belief in black life, something you've got to understand for the distinction to make sense. That distinction means something altogether different beyond the boundaries of black life.

What's the difference, though, when he does his routine, on the record, for an audience in D.C. that is predominantly African American, and yet he is on the cover of Rolling Stone*—which caters to a different demographic? Certain things one says inside the house, one would not go around saying outside; the meanings of words shift based on the contexts in which they're spoken . . .*

They do, they do. What we are evoking through our discussion of Chris Rock is a problem within literary and cultural theory about intention and reception, where the following questions emerge: Is an author or a speaker morally responsible for the interpretation of her words? Is one ethically culpable for understanding the context into which one's words will be read? To a certain degree, of course we are. We can't pretend that College Park, Maryland, is the same as Harlem, USA—they're different social and intellectual contexts, whatever similarities they might share. One of the ingenious things that Chris Rock is doing is making white America aware of these contradictions and conflicts within black culture of which they may have been oblivious. The question asked by some whites, Why can black folk call themselves nigger, and we can't? falls into that category. In one sense, Rock is a cultural translator, an arbiter of contested black meanings in a safe public space of comedy where he's able to broach controversial issues. For instance, Rock educated his multiracial television audience beyond the largely black Washington, D.C., setting of *Bring the Pain,* when he referred to black complaints about stereotypical representations of black people in the media as sometimes overblown. "When I go to the money machine tonight, a'ight, I ain't looking over my back for the media," Rock said to uproarious laughter. "I'm looking for niggas. Ted Koppel ain't never took shit from me. Niggas have." I was howling, man, because in some ways, he's absolutely right. But then we must acknowledge that meanings shift according to contexts in which people understand what they hear.

At the same time, I think both blacks and whites and many other groups are being enlightened and prodded to a level of discomfort to interrogate their practices and their cherished beliefs. As black critics, we encourage our people to take it to the next step, the next level—and to have enough maturity as black people to be willing to risk misunderstanding among white Americans about the nature of our self-criticism. Refusing to air dirty laundry has been the reason for not admitting cultural contradictions, which does two things. First, it gives credence to those critics who say, "If you blacks were willing to be a little more self-critical about your shortcomings, then you could have a little more social progress." Even though I know that at some level that argument is legitimate, I also know that it can be a convenient excuse for people who want to continue their old bigotry in new forms by calling it an assault on political correctness. Number two, when we aired our laundry in our own community . . . well, ain't nobody invited me to those meetings. They haven't invited a whole lot of black folk I know to those meetings—and the "they" here is a nonspecific, arbitrary, ambiguous "they," signifying the inability to pin down who is responsible for the meetings and who should take the heat for those who are invited or, as it turns out, uninvited. It's not like there was a notice posted in Harlem on a streetlight pole that read: "There's a closed-door meeting of the black community tonight. Be on the corner of 125th and Lennox Avenue at 7:00 P.M."

Often the presumption of such closed-door meetings is that they would occur among black leaders, however defined. But even that gathering of political, cultural, and intellectual elites, if it occurred, might well be antidemocratic, too. At least when criticism is public, a wider range of black people get a chance to participate in cultural and political debates. Even if we are turned off by what Chris Rock says, it is healthier to have open rather than closed cultural conversations—I suppose it's where Chris Rock meets Karl Popper. In that sense, I celebrate Chris Rock's transgressive notions of blackness. I also applaud the seepage of his discourse beyond the boundaries of ethnic and racial communities. But your point is well taken. We can't pretend that we don't live in a political context in which white Americans say, "See, what we told you about those black folks must be true, since there's a black man on television saying the same thing." I think we have to run that risk to get to the "truth" as we see it, as we're willing to argue for its existence in given cultural and social contexts.

I think it's crucial, even if it is hurtful and controversial, for Chris Rock to go on television—including his appearance on *Oprah*, a show watched by 20 million people, most of whom are white—and talk with devastating accuracy, as well as some measure of pitiless self-examination, of our culture. Talk about how when black folk get out of prison, other black folk give them much "dap," or respect. But if they've just garnered a master's degree, "niggas" look down on them with contempt. Say that brother, and say it again! It's hard to hear; it's painful, but it's often true. Many black people who have been fortunate enough to go to school have paid an extra price, a black tariff on educational success. I got called "braniac" and "professor" in junior high school. To be sure, a lot of black people dug me, who said, "Hey, watch out for the brother, 'cuz he's down, and he's cool." At the same time, a lot of people were angry, even jealous, and tried to be creatively subversive of my success—one that they often failed to achieve, were prevented from achieving, or were discouraged from believing that they could achieve. So I later understood the complexity of their assaults, but at the time, some of their jabs hurt.

What Rock is really speaking to, at least implicitly, is what educational theorists call "rival epistemologies," that is, competing ways of knowing the world or competing schemas of existing in the world, as *either* smart or cool, as if they were mutually exclusive, that to be one rules out being the other. And of course, in many black communities, especially in inner cities, there is a high premium on being "cool," which sometimes means placing a stigma on formal education and erudition. Chris Rock is speaking as well to the problem of literacy in black communities and, by implication, to the multiple forms of literacy that are either privileged or assailed, depending on which segment of black communities we engage. All in all, I think Rock's kind of relentless self-investigation is important for a black comedic social commentator. That's why I think he's one of the most important African American comedians and critics. His *Bring the Pain* ranks right up there with classic black stand-up comedic performances caught on tape, including Richard Pryor's *Richard Pryor: Live and Smokin'* and *Richard Pryor: Live in Concert*, Bill Cosby's *Bill Cosby: Himself*, and Eddie Murphy's *Delirious* and *Raw*. Whether we agree with him at every turn or not, Chris Rock is a crucial cultural presence, a valuable gadfly, and above all, a great comedian, which I'm sure is his ultimate goal. After all, if he weren't funny, we wouldn't be having this conversation.

How do you feel about the fact that it seems like a lot of the intellectual rappers sell less than the so-called gangsta acts? How do you feel about the fact that as intellectual a rapper as Busta Rhymes is, it's his party songs, like "Wu-ha," that are the ones that make money?

Well, to phrase it oxymoronically, it's the almost inevitable result of being involved in the culture industry driven by the machinery of capital in corporate America, where you have to dummy down to a certain degree to get to the lowest common cultural denominator. There's no question that American culture doesn't have space, patience, or time for tasks, products, and processes that demand rigor, that demand a degree of critical intelligence for ideas that can't be understood very quickly. Still, I defend popular culture at a certain level in certain modes for its ability to reproduce images, styles, ideas, visions, and even challenges to stereotypes that make partial use of these stereotypes, that people might not otherwise have any democratic access to. It's a double-edged sword. Take Nas's debut, *Illmatic* (1994), one of the greatest rap albums of all time, which featured many brilliant songs, including "New York State of Mind," which contains a verse that provides a bracing raison d'être of the rap vocation: "It's only right that I was born to use mics, and the stuff that I write, it's even tougher than dice."

On the equally powerful "Life's a Bitch . . ." Nas references Shakespeare when he declares, "I never sleep 'cause sleep's the cousin of death." Now we got the great Bard integrated into the lyrical cosmos of a New York rapper! Given the fact that Nas's father is a respected trumpet player, we have this rich, straight-ahead hard-bop jazz tradition being brought to bear on the soundscape of an extremely gifted lyricist. Still, for all its aesthetic punch, its exceeding high rhetorical and musical values, it took a long time for that album to go gold and sell 500,000 copies. Its eventual success was driven by word of mouth. Some would say that his second album, *It Was Written*, while very, very sharp, isn't up to the standards of that first classic album: it doesn't have that underground aesthetic and lyric-driven genius of *Illmatic*. Then again, Nas's persona went from "Nasty Nas" to "Nas Escobar." So one must account for his aesthetic and lyrical shift by underscoring his transformed artistic identity, from ghetto projects denizen whose hardcore themes were wed to high concept if idiosyncratic articulations of an urban weltanschauung, to a more traditionally identified hustler/gangster whose aspirations to the high life are filtered through conventional if compelling narratives of upward mobility linked to spiritual and moral aims fueled by racial romanticism and altruism. We've got to grant Nas the right to change, even if we prefer one persona to the other.

Few artists and groups can sustain a uniform expression of excellence over several projects, especially with the rush of commercial success. First, although it's surely a cliché, artists are hungrier when they're poorer, when they are undistracted by the demands that celebrity imposes on them. Therefore compromises and concessions—to the marketplace, to hegemonic elements within one's fan base, and to the ubiquitous lure of crossover success—appear nearly unavoidable, especially for ambitious hip-hoppers. Of course, a few groups get wider and deeper and broader as they mature. Think, for example, about Wu-Tang Clan and how they're pushing the borders and expanding the boundaries of rap, so that their alternative, basement, or underground hip-hop has found a commercial niche while remaining intellectually vibrant. Of course, their case is unique because Wu-Tang is composed of individually gifted rappers and producers who disperse to make their own projects—often with other members of their group, say, rapper Raekwan hooking up with fellow member Ghostface Killah, or they pair with other talented rappers outside their fold, say, group member Method Man joining forces with Biggie Smalls—and then come back together for their group efforts.

But Wu-Tang's is an unusual case. It is more likely that the intellectual and aesthetic vitality of hip-hop is compromised and subordinated to the imperatives of commerce, finance, and the market: how many units one can push and sell. Even the more intelligent, self-reflective, self-critical gangsta and hardcore hip-hop is taking a back seat to crassly materialistic and crudely misogynistic rap—and bowing to the *mere* groove, the *mere* rhythm. Hip-hop has always been about the pulsating polyrhythmic structures of African American musical traditions. Remember the words of legendary wordsmith Rakim, who said: "My mind starts to activate, rhymes collaborate 'cause when I heard the beat, I just had to make somethin' from the top of my head. . . ." Of course, within hip-hop culture, an aggressively intellectual vision has to be sustained against the odds. For instance, Chicago-based rapper Common Sense is a self-critical and brilliant lyricist whose craft has been unfairly overlooked, for the most part, except by the genre's cognoscenti, its insightful "heads."

In hip-hop, it used to be that geography drove vocational destiny. Hence the East Coast was cerebral, articulate, and reflective, but after a while, they didn't sell as many records as their West Coast brethren, who didn't have intense intellectual presence—with the exception of figures like Ice Cube and the great Tupac Shakur, who was really a product of both coasts. But they knew how to make you shake your behind, and they had rappers like Snoop who had great flow. So the imperatives of the market were segmented according to regional practices. The West Coast got more deeply mired in the "keep it real" movement in hip-hop. Such posturing makes me think immediately of the 1969 jazz crossover song, "Compared to What?" recorded by gifted jazz veterans Eddie Harris and Les McCann. In applying that song to hip-hop, I suppose the question is, What are rappers claiming to keep real, and what is the unreal or inauthentic experience to which it is compared? Some rappers, especially on the East Coast underground scene, claim they exist in a pure sphere of artistic engagement apart from the crassly commodified marketplace. Well, the moment you put your voice on a tape and sell it out of the trunk of your car—just like Too $hort did when he started right here in Oaktown a decade ago—you're involved in commodity culture. Now that's keeping it real.

Your writing touches on a wide range of topics, yet there are some constant familiars. You write about the plight of black women, and in sermons of yours I've heard you talk frankly about homophobia. But from the opening of Making Malcolm *to the closing of* Race Rules, *your principal audience, or perhaps concern, seems to be the education, fate, and roles of black men. If for some reason you never wrote another essay, would your focus on educating the world about the lives of black men in America, and conversely, speaking to black men about the world they're inhabiting, be a satisfying legacy?*

It would be a satisfying legacy if I could be perceived as a brother who spoke *to* black men in order to speak *against* the pain and bias we both confront and perpetuate. It would be satisfying if I could challenge us from within the temples of our familiar bigotries—to join Alice Walker and Sampson from the Bible—to take down the pillars of machismo that sustain the structures of our masculine identity. Hopefully, unlike Sampson, we won't have to go eyeless in Gaza and bring the house down on ourselves, murdering our hope and possibility in the process. I want to think and write more critically about issues of gender, especially the relationships between men and women. It is true that even as I and others try to create discursive space within black criticism to address homophobia, machismo, and gender discrimination, it would be a fair criticism of my work that the obsession about the lives and limits of black men in my writing is the constant familiar, or as Baraka beautifully phrases it, "the changing same." So I think that if I can invite black men to think more critically about our condition and unmask some of the more detrimental patriarchal moments that not only stigmatize women but also hamper us from realizing our best goals and our most edifying interests, then I could be satisfied. When I went to the Million Man March over the objections of many of my feminist sisters and brothers, I did so because I knew, as I discuss in *Race Rules*, that the desperation in our communities is so profound that abstract theorizing and academic interrogation ain't gonna fix what's broke. In fact, remaining distant from the pain and the pathos of these black men may be part of the problem. I think that progressive intellectuals and activists need more, not less, contact with ordinary black men.

That's why I continue to slug it out with black men, and others, in the trenches of black communities. For instance, one night in Seattle, after spending a great day giving a few lectures and signing quite a few books in local colleges and universities, where the audiences were largely white, I spoke at a black church. I was assailed for nearly three hours by what I term hypersensitive black nationalists who were speaking about Africa in an utterly romantic fashion and referencing the "white man" in a way that was painfully anachronistic, as if the "white man" were actually the "bogeyman." In one sense the mixture of half-truths—the Fanonian self-critical consciousness mixed with crude applications of Malcom X's beliefs about internalized self-hatred and neocolonial occupation of our brains with whitewashed political ideology—was intriguing, even if it was personally painful to endure the brunt of such discourse when it was turned on me. I don't say that for self-pity, because these folk have a right to be critical of me. But the reason I stayed long past my appointed time with them was to have the opportunity to fight some of the sharper bigotries within black masculine communities. Many of these communities don't enjoy the leisure needed to think critically about some of the issues I broach. Many of them are sharp and reflective, very intelligent, but they are also hurt by the traumas of white supremacy, economic inequality, and social injustice. If I become their temporary target as they cathartically express their own rage, then so be it.

I hope I'm not being unfair to such audiences in describing their activity in this way. I'm simply trying to suggest that in an already difficult world for many black people, black nationalist patriarchal insularity—truth be told, it's fascism in a certain way—is counterproductive to our very survival. If I can invite black men to unmask our patriarchy and undo, or at least unlearn, our homophobia and to challenge our detrimental views of masculinity, I believe our communities will be immeasurably strengthened. Women will not be harmed as frequently; children will not be routinely abused and abandoned; and fewer black men will die at the hands of other black men. That's why I think Chris Rock is a very important comedic flash point along the larger trajectory of black self-criticism within masculine community. You know, when Chris Rock says that at the Million Man March, with Washington, D.C., Mayor Marion Barry on hand, it means that at our highest moment, black men have a crack head on stage as one of our symbols, that's part of the tough but necessary exercise of self-critique.

Again, we don't have to agree with the substance of his critique, but I think we have to embrace the substantial contribution of moral and social critique to our communities. True, white America can take Rock's words and run with them in the attempt to prove our self-defeating habits and our visible pathologies. But hopefully black ethical maturity will convince us to look beyond this inevitable consequence of our critical self-examination in a majority white society. We can't let what white folk *might* say or do keep us from what we *should* say and do. In that sense, I would hope that my legacy in examining black masculinity would be one of relentless self-critique, even as I embrace the virtues of black masculine culture while refusing to ignore how black men have been demonized in a still unjust society.

Interview by Marc Vogl and Tonelius Oliver
San Francisco, California, 1997

part three

Religious Beliefs, Theological Arguments

13

"Searching for Black Jesus"

The Nietzschean Quest of a Metaphysical Thug

Michael, we know that Tupac is dead, and therefore we may now speak of him with a finality not possible before his death. Tupac's life was a chaos of possibilities, a huge quest for meanings and relations. And for us, to reveal tendencies in his words is an operation that is permitted today, and it's not always permissible when the subject is still alive. But then, as with every man, the death of Tupac actually achieved a dazzling montage of his life. It certainly highlighted the most significant moments of his life and put them end to end, picking up—actually dealing with—his infinite, uncertain, and unstable past, turning everything into a very solid and clear present. After Tupac's death, it's easier for you to write your book; it's much easier for me to ask questions. But here are two questions that come to mind: How essential is it for us to know that Tupac is dead? And was his life translatable before his death?

Good points. I think that the ambiguity surrounding Tupac's death is indicative of the inexhaustible possibility that characterizes human life. When he was alive, Tupac represented the evolution of human possibility in the ghetto. He was transformation in flux. He was constantly rearranging his identity, constantly changing the pieces of the puzzle of what it meant to be a human being, and constantly searching for the best understanding of how to be humane in the midst of the chaos around him. The ghetto became the source root, the major metaphor, for Tupac's art and life, and the means by which he engaged the transformative possibilities of his existence. Through his fixation on the ghetto, Tupac made sure that there was a black tint on the universal human quest for meaning. I think in this regard about Victor Frankl and logotherapy, or the quest for meaning in the midst of the horror and death of the Nazi concentration camps. Tupac was articulating, in a sense, a kind of ghetto logotherapy, a quest for existential holism in the midst of the horror of poverty, material deprivation, and social dislocation. By remaining true to exploring the specific elements of the ghetto experience, he gave it universal resonance.

People from all over the world were attracted to Tupac's vision because they felt it was authentic and compellingly accurate about the critical limits of reason in addressing absurd social circumstances. Such a recognition of, and identification with, the universal character of social suffering portrayed by hardcore rappers, by the way, led protesters in Poland to blast N.W.A.'s agitprop anthem, "Fuck Tha Police," because there's a globally recognizable language of rebellion against political tyranny and police force. There's also solidarity in fighting the distortion of human identity under oppression, as the poor the world over fight against their bodies being trapped, contained, and demobilized by social structures and governmental practices.

Getting back to your question about Tupac's death, it's important to acknowledge that his death and his constant stream of rhetoric and lyrics about death are part of a culture of death that circulates in the ghetto. The culture of death is manifest in the fascination with the limit, with the end of life, and with the closing of the infinite horizon of possibility through finite acts of murder that are both metaphorically and literally rampant in the culture. It showed, too, in Tupac's elegiac poetry. Tupac seemed to be in love with death in a Freudian sense; but at the same time, there is in him a resistance to death, since the very act of art is a refusal to die. The very assertion of one's authentic identity is a refusal to accept the conditions and limitations and aesthetic death that opponents seek to impose from outside one's spiritual and intellectual arc of expression.

As with any great artist, it is probably doubtful that Tupac's life was fully translatable before his death. We now think about Tupac's career with its beginning and ending in place. We can never determine when our lives begin, and with the exception of suicide, we don't determine when they end. But we can determine what we do with our lives in between our emergence and exit. A large part of what attracted the world to Tupac, and not always in edifying fashion, was his recklessness, the sense that he was flipping back and forth along the tightrope stretched across an abyss as he pursued his dreams and goals. I don't think his life could be translated so easily because it was in many ways a mess, a chaos, a contradictory, paradoxical pursuit of sublime artistic expression on the one hand, and on the other hand, it was a harmful valorization of death-dealing impulses. The desire to "keep it real" was one of these impulses, as Tupac reduced the complexity of black identity to the hood, and a depressingly narrow view of the hood at that. His very existence, the facts of the case, as it were, trumped such a narrow view of the ghetto.

Tupac was a poor black boy from the ghetto, a high school dropout who was extremely well read and well trained in aesthetic expression, from art to acting, from interpreting poetry to reciting Shakespeare. He read Pierre Teilhard de Chardin and George Orwell, Alice Walker and Maya Angelou, Anaïs Nin and Aldous Huxley, J. D. Salinger and E. D. Hirsch, Jonathan Kozol and Jamaica Kincaid, Herman Hesse and Gabriel García Márquez, Friedrich Nietzsche and Sigmund Freud, Sonia Sanchez and Nikki Giovanni, and on and on and on. He was an incredibly eclectic reader and catholic intellectual who tried to address questions of identity and spiritual revolution. He tried to creatively manage competing material and moral aims in his life. But that's apparent now that he's dead; whether it was altogether clear when he lived is doubtful. But Tupac believed in his heart that he had a mission in life, and that mission was to tell the truth about black male suffering as powerfully as his gifts would allow him. Even as he narrated the misery black males confronted, Tupac's frequently self-destructive choices turned his narratives into autobiographical tales of woe. Now that he is dead, that's even clearer.

The Zeitgeist snatched him by the collar and seized him by the throat, vibrating his vocal cords into shrill but poignant expression. He's a kind of black Hegelian figure who articulates and embodies the spirit of his times. He was not the greatest rapper in terms of the natural gifts or skills that mark flow, rhythm, poetic description, breath control, and the like, even though he was by no means a slouch at the mic. What distinguished Tupac from most of his peers was the quality of heart and honesty of expression he brought to his craft. He possessed an emotional immediacy and psychic intimacy that are hard to fake, that are difficult to drum up or duplicate through sheer manipulation of tone, timber, wordplay, and so on. Tupac was a transcendent figure in hip-hop who used every fiber of his being, every muscle in his body, to articulate the rage, wonder, despair, hope, death—but most important, the love—that he had in his heart and by extension that existed in the hearts and souls of the millions who identified with him as the vehicle of their ideals and visions. If that was true when he walked the earth, it's even truer now that he's joined the ancestors.

Michael, let's talk for a second about your book. What distinguishes my attempt today is not an emphasis on those stylistic characteristics which I consider self-evident. You yourself emphasized this in your book, when you titled one of the chapters, "But Do the Lord Care?" I tend to find something else. What is the source of that conflict which clearly comes through in Tupac's musical and literary form? And simultaneously, what accounts for the universalism of Tupac? That is, who today will be interested in this great conflict?

Well, the source of the conflict I think is the perennial question that all human beings face, especially artists: How in the face of death do you embrace life? Toni Morrison addressed this question in her Nobel lecture when she said, "We die. That may be the meaning of life. But we do language. That may be the measure of our lives." So doing language and, as hip-hoppers say, doing the knowledge—which accentuates an active, agency-driven conception of both linguistic and epistemological practices—is a crucial means to fending off death in life. For Tupac, as for the rest of us, that is an insight that came with maturity, a luxury he barely got the chance to enjoy because he was murdered at twenty-five. Tupac was extremely sensitive to the social forces that trumped the quest for humane existence, which is one reason he paid so much attention to the misery and suffering of his peers, especially the black poor. He knew firsthand the underside of American capitalism. Tupac, you'll recall, was desperately poor until he found fame. Although he faced material deprivation, Tuapc, in his own words, was "rich" because of the intellectual and moral values his Black Panther mother instilled in him, especially the commitment to radical social transformation.

Part of Tupac's existential anguish grew from the recognition that although his mother was totally committed to the cause, the party's leaders didn't support her, especially as she faced economic hardship and eventual drug addiction. As he witnessed his mother's ordeal, Tupac got his first taste of the contradiction between ideals and practices that dog any group, institution, or social movement, no matter how righteous its goals. To be sure, that wasn't the only contradiction that Tupac had to confront. As an evolving artist, he had to wrestle with how his art could combat the suffering he endured and witnessed. Death in a variety of forms became a reminder of the ultimate suffering and injustice that the black poor were subject to in the ghetto. Hence, thinking and talking about death, embracing and resisting death, loving and hating death became a way for Tupac to tease out the authentic connections between his aesthetic preoccupations and his ties to an increasingly mythologized ghetto home front. The "hood" was reified as the archetypal ground of legitimate black identity. And since death was, in some quarters of the ghetto, encountered, encouraged, and embraced, Tupac felt an ethical obligation to represent its furious ubiquity.

The ethics of representation that consumed Tupac also pushed him into the arms of fans around the world. Tupac's universalism was sealed in the recognition of fans who saw in his struggle to live by dying—the paradoxical politics of survival practiced by many a self-destructive gangbanger, drug dealer, or hustler—an articulation of the existential absurdities that unite people around the globe. One absurdity that Tupac and his peers in hip-hop confronted was trying to live in a society that wants to wipe you out while exploiting your genius. People throughout the world resonated with Tupac's powerful artistic vision, a vision, I believe, that joined him to artists and intellectuals like Samuel Beckett, Zora Neale Hurston, Eugene Ionesco, Simone de Beauvoir, Langston Hughes, Hannah Arendt, Paul Robeson, Frantz Fanon, and Simone Weil, since they, like Tupac, sought to find a legitimate voice through developing their gifts. People around the globe felt Tupac's spirit, felt his love, his passion, his anger, his rage, his confusion, and the chaos of the conflicting ideals that engulfed him. Above all, Tupac identified with the underdog, and that gave him cachet among the world's downtrodden and those who faced huge odds, from poverty to political oppression. Tupac represented and spoke to that brother, that sister, that human being who in the face of enormous crisis called on God, spirit, transcendent artistic and moral figures, and their own passion as a resource to fight the destruction, suffering, pain, and even death they encountered.

You mentioned in your statement American capitalism, and I personally believe that this country firmly stands on the road of technical opulence. At the same time, when this capitalism, and I will even add, monopolism, is spreading around this world, we see that a huge percentage of people—I would estimate that 70 percent of people around the country, including blacks and whites—affirm the ease and quality of life, which is nothing else but the clear, external manifestation of the profound declaration of conservatism. And there is no escape from that. Now in terms of that, will we be able to ever measure, in all senses, the black problem in this country?

That's very well stated, and I think that's the kernel of the problem. When we look at conservatism versus liberalism in their generic forms—the former concerned with the conservation and perpetuation of political and social tradition, and gradual change, and the latter with the idea of progress, individual liberty, and the preservation of political and civil liberties—the interests of blacks will never be exhausted or comprehended by such an ideological dualism. Why? Because black diasporic cultures have largely fought to recover and reinvent political and cultural traditions from the ash heap of historical oppression and racial amnesia. At the same time, blacks throughout the diaspora have sought to conserve and revise social traditions that have been said by some critics not to exist at all; or when acknowledged as real, they are charged with having been invented whole cloth out of the psychic needs of blacks to prove they are in league with European cultures.

In part, such differences drove the debate between white anthropologist Melville Herskovits and black sociologist E. Franklin Frazier about African retentions, that is, whether there exists continuity in black cultures from their African heritages, which Herskovits affirmed, or whether the traces of such roots have been largely wiped out, which Frazier believed. In many ways, that debate continues to this day, with Afrocentrists arguing the almost genetic inheritance of African identity and Eurocentrists arguing that the black past, at least as presented by Afrocentrists, is a figment of the black romantic imagination. Multiculturalists, of course, split the difference between the two, arguing for a nonessentialist, resilient racial identity that is historically constituted but undergoes profound transformations in varying historical and cultural contexts.

Black culture has an extraordinary romance with aspects of Kemet, the Egyptian name for Africa, and with black kings and queens and the like, because racial romance was denied to blacks as a condition of our oppression. Never mind that such racial romance is rife in mainstream, white American culture. At a certain level, black romance about the African past barely approaches the romantic preoccupations of the American populace in the veneration of its founding fathers, or as Joseph Ellis makes clear, its founding brothers, including figures like Thomas Jefferson and John Adams. There are countless biographies and studies of the historical minutia of white European male achievement on the Continent and in the United States.

And let's not even speak of the strand of regionalism and geographical parochialism that runs through American history with the nostalgic evocations of the South and the defenders of the Confederacy in the Civil War. There has not been anything nearly parallel to that in the fictions, mythologies, and romance of black culture with legendary figures. Nothing in black culture rivals the idealization of the artistic and intellectual achievements of European and white American men. In short, black genius has rarely been recognized, except in its instrumentalist and exploitable varieties, including sports and entertainment. Blacks have got credit for their intellectual achievements during the Harlem Renaissance, but that's about it. And even that pales when it comes to the justifiable recognition accorded jazz or other expressions of pop culture.

All of this is a backdrop to the point that the conservative black cultural tradition, broadly speaking, is concerned with preserving a tradition of racial achievement that the white world has rarely recognized. On the other hand, the liberal impulse—one that rides a wave of progressive politics, autonomous individualism from a suffocating state-sponsored oppression, and demand for social justice—makes clear that the ingenuity of black survival is articulated through the cultural and political forms that happen to lie at hand. So whether blacks are living in Senegal, the Ivory Coast, Brixton, Harlem, or Bahia, the political forms they encounter will never exhaust the meanings of blackness. That's because black culture is always cooperating with and subverting the political forms that shape racial identity. Conservatism and liberalism and, indeed, radicalism are always part of the ideological mix of black political identity.

These peculiar circumstances may help explain why black people always appear to accept the finite social conditions and political limitations imposed on them, while at the same time yearning for freedom, a yearning that is often expressed in our art and that resonates with people all over the world. Our artistic and spiritual traditions have created in us the desire for a future that could never be fully realized in the present (and if the truth be told, in *any* present), but that was no reason to surrender hope in such a pursuit. That desire, that yearning, defined a hope that must always be pursued. The social and political critique we developed rested on measuring the gap between the pursuit and the practice of freedom, between its ideal expression and its concrete embodiment.

At one end of the ideological spectrum, black American political figures, like many conservatives, embraced the status quo as the means of expressing and enhancing black freedom. At the other end, black radicals severely criticized American political culture. Still, it's ironic—an irony that's often lost on black conservatives—that the very existence of black culture is, at the least, an implicit critique of the status quo, since the status quo has often sought to exclude black identity and culture. In its most radical political moment, black culture is critical of the social, political, and moral order. At the heart of progressive black culture is the prophetic mode of social critique that looks skeptically at prevailing cultural and political forms and institutions.

Hip-hop culture is important because hip-hop at its best advocates the belief that we must do away with the inhibiting, even paralyzing, social and political practices that have been passed on to us from outside our culture—and sometimes from within. Hip-hop culture has sparked the latest chapter in an ongoing debate in black culture about the clash between bourgeois values and conservative traditions on the one hand and, on the other hand, the assertion of liberal values and progressive, even radical, political traditions. It has also raised the question of whether political engagement through traditional political actors in conventional costume, so to speak, is the only means to effect social change, or whether cultural forms like hip-hop can have any effect on the political front. For many advocates of hip-hop culture, Tupac, as an artist, raised pressing questions that demanded political redress. For them, his art had, at least tangentially, a political effect. Hip-hop may not by itself fully measure the hurt and trauma to black life, but it is a rather faithful barometer of the hurt and trauma faced by millions of poor young blacks living in postindustrial urban centers throughout the country.

All his life Tupac was searching for a solution. He never found one. But as long as his word remains multivoiced and multileveled, as long as the voice was still arguing, then the despair over the absence of a solution would not set in. Now here comes what I believe is a very important question, What does his death signify? And doesn't his death just signify another fall of a new Tower of Babel?

There's no question that Tupac represented something very suggestive and certainly very articulate within black culture: he embodied the conflict of the language of hope and the rhetoric of hopelessness. And the despair about which you speak—the despair that many human beings confront when the possibility of transforming their situation is foreclosed by economic suffering or material deprivation—inspires artists and others to focus on spiritual resources to catapult the despairing person beyond his or her immediate situation. The great writer Howard Thurman, who was also a preacher and a prophetic mystic, once said that a vital moral trait of black slave forebears was their ability not to reduce their hopes, dreams, or visions to the level of the event that was their immediate experience. One's immediate experience may be nasty, problematic, hurtful, or even evil, but one must foster within one's heart and soul a vision of the future that allows one to escape the immediate consequences of despair. Hopelessness results when one is unable to imagine a different future. Tupac represented both sides of the coin.

On the one hand he was full of extraordinary, if unorthodox, hopefulness. He told young, single welfare mothers to "Keep Ya Head Up." And when writing a paean to his mother, he managed to acknowledge her addiction while underscoring her regal status as he proclaimed, "Even as a crack fiend, Mama/You always was a black Queen, Mama." But Tupac was also "searching for Black Jesus," a cosmic ally to the despised street thug. As Tupac pleaded, "In times of war we need somebody raw, rally the troops/Like a Saint that we can trust to help to carry us through/Black Jesus." It's here that Tupac's request departs from orthodox theology, since he wants, as one of his mates on "Black Jesus" pleads, a God "not too perfect" but someone who "smoke like we smoke," who "Drink like we drink," and before that, someone who, in their Ebonicized grammatical construction, "hurt like we hurt." That last part reminds me of a passage in Hebrews, around the fourth chapter and the fifteenth verse, where it says, "For we have not an high priest which cannot be touched with the feeling of our infirmities; but was in all points tempted like as *we are*, yet without sin." I think the New International Version of that passage goes something like, "For we do not have a high priest who is unable to sympathize with our weaknesses, but we have one who has been tempted in every way, just as we are—yet was without sin."

So in one sense Tupac was the secular articulation of a religious belief in the possibility of identifying with a God who became what we are. A crucial source of hopefulness in black Christian culture has precisely to do with believing that God identifies with our condition as the underdog. That's why the infancy narratives in the Gospels involving the birth of Christ are carefully read and heavily leaned on: they express the fact that God sides with the homeless, the oppressed, those besieged by the state, those who are the victims of political terror. When God was born in a manger as Jesus, it showed just how far God was willing to go to prove to humanity that God loved us.

That message is especially critical to the theological reflections of black Christians looking for a God who looks after us, who appears, in Tupac's terms, as "Black Jesus." Of course, this is also where Tupac and Black Theology meet, since as black theologian James Cone maintains, to argue God's blackness is an ontological assertion of God's radical identification with the oppressed that transcends phenotypic correctness. When the divine intersects human identity, a transformative energy is unleashed that redeems finitude and furnishes the human project with unshakable purpose, or what Paul Tillich called "ultimate concern." That's what Tupac was searching for, I believe, this Tillichian modality of existence, this embrace by ultimate concern, and to stick with Tillich, this "courage to be" in the face of the death and destruction he witnessed in his neighborhood and in his life.

The question of the meaning of Tupac's death is particularly poignant, since it throws light on the existential struggles waged by Tupac and a number of artists and young people in his generation. Your question about Tupac's death being another fall of a new Tower of Babel is highly suggestive, much too deep for me to explore here. I'll just say that the languages of grief and despair, and alternatively, of hopefulness and faith that Tupac's rhetorical acrobatics engaged, do indeed represent a fluidity of tongues, a multiplicity of vernaculars, and a proliferation of sometimes competing grammars, through which he articulated the conflicting ideals of black youth culture.

To be sure, the image of the Tower of Babel falling afresh in Tupac's death possesses a semiotic suggestiveness that Umberto Eco would surely relish, or for that matter, Bakhtin and a bunch of Russian formalists would delight in. I suppose we might throw in a few French structuralists and poststructuralists as well, from Levi-Strauss to Foucault, although Foucault swung among the structuralisms, depending on what stage of his career you caught him at, or what interview he was giving. Suffice it to say that Tupac's death unleashed a contradictory force of linguistic urgency to name the furious griefs that arose in the wake of his demise, confounding observers and critics and confusing those whose minds were made up about his ultimate meaning to our country and the world. So I guess the Tower of Babel fits in just fine in Tupac's linguistic landscape.

Beyond that, and more in line of thinking about the effects and meanings of his premature demise, Tupac, like scores of his anonymous peers, both embraced and resisted death, often in the same breath, in the same gesture, in the same argument, in the same rap. Tupac is so important, so relevant, because his art was at once the solution to suffering and death as well as its insidious embodiment. That's why he continues to resonate not only in this country, but around the world wherever young people are in the throes of death and endure the eclipse of hope, fighting and surrendering to what Tupac confessed in his posthumously released song "Unconditional Love" was "the urge to die." Tupac was both ghetto saint and metaphysical thug, both the transcendence *and* triumph of black urban trauma. He valorized homicide, lyrically speaking, even as he lauded the life force of the "rose that grew from concrete."

I suppose it's the ghetto version of "flower in the crannied wall," where Tupac's celebration of the persistence of life in the most harsh, unlikely circumstances meets the query about the ultimate meaning of life revealed in the simple yet profound miracle of a petaled existence. For that matter, it might as well be the urban exemplar of Gray's "Elegy in a Courtyard," where he reflects that, "Full many a gem of purest ray serene/The dark unfathom'd caves of ocean bear/Full many a flower is born to blush unseen/And waste its sweetness on the desert air." That was true of Tupac. Although he flowered feverishly in his twenty-five years, there was so much more of his bloom that was lost to the arid climes of death, and so many more of his intense gems of hope and inspiration and art are now contained in the caves of infinite silence.

In the end, Tupac's death and the competing forces of redemption and futility unleashed in his furious torrent of words underscore both his genius and his torment. The genius of Tupac is his universality and ethical omnicompetence, so that any human being traveling any path can identify with him and can tie into his work. Tupac's torment is that he glimpsed the beauty of existence beyond the damaging distortions of racism and economic inequality, but he often surrendered to the surrounding gloom from which he at other times extracted an implausible hope in combating these forces. That was his gift and his burden, one that blessed millions even as the contradictions he let fly boomeranged on him in harsh retribution.

As you very well know, I've been interested in black culture for quite some years now, and I have noticed something—and correct me if I am wrong—but I have noticed that there is a huge difference between blacks and whites when it comes to religion. Generally speaking, black religion is epic, mythic, fantastic. The religion of whites has, in my opinion, typical bourgeois characteristics. I believe that the bourgeoisie has not dealt with a transcendental religion. White religion is largely catechistic and therefore agreeable. And whites, for the most part, have replaced the problem of the soul, which is transcendental, with conscience, which is purely a social thing. Tell me something about Tupac's religious contradictions. Tell me about his religious fights. Tell me something about his religion.

Well, I don't think it's so much about how we can speak of black and white folk and their religions as constructed on diametrically opposed philosophical foundations, but rather about how blacks and whites have historically understood the crucial ingredients of faith. I don't think we can be essentialist about European-based religions and African-centered religious traditions, although we might observe differences in how each group has behaved its religious beliefs. For instance, we might observe the similarities and differences between white and black traditions in their approaches, say, to the "soul" as a transcendental force tapped into and accessed by means of rituals and catechisms, and "conscience" as a socially produced consciousness about the moral limits of human existence. Soul and conscience are keywords in both black and white religious traditions, but they have been played out in the social order in radically different ways. For instance, in black Christian traditions, conscience has sometimes been viewed as a critical adjunct to secular law in articulating the social implications of religious belief in a way that white believers might never acknowledge.

Let me give you a perfect example, and then I'll answer your larger question about Tupac's religion. During the civil rights movement, Martin Luther King Jr. and other black leaders faced heated opposition in their quest for racial justice from white religious figures. In mounting opposition to King's religiously inspired revolutionary social agenda, white figures appealed to their religiously informed and socially constituted conscience. King consciously appealed to what he termed "the white conscience" early on to achieve his goals; he completely understood the terms of the game being played, the war being waged. Moreover, Martin Luther King Jr. believed that the state, by sending troops into southern cities to protect black citizens from white citizens, would keep one body of Christians—since many whites, even Ku Klux Klan members, professed to hold Christian beliefs—from hurting, sometimes even killing, another body of Christians, as many of the black protesters were also Bible-quoting believers. For King and other black Christian believers, the state, when it behaved justly, was an extension of God's will, a belief that ran contrary to that held by many sectarian white Christians who defended segregation by interpreting biblical texts through the lens of a racially distorted theology. In the most generic meaning of the phrase, King was a natural law theologian in ways that all black people must be when they believe that the righteous forces of the universe conspire against organized religion when it does injustice to the oppressed in God's name.

In that sense, Tupac was, after a fashion, a natural law theologian, although an admittedly irreverent one, who gave voice to a black quest for meaning in the midst of suffering. I think Tupac believed very strongly in God, but in a very unorthodox manner. Tupac can be usefully viewed as a person who, in John Hick's terminology, played the theodical game, in both the theological and sociological meanings of the concept. Tupac was concerned with the disjunctions between assertions of God's goodness and the prevalence of evil and suffering. He was also concerned with how one might remedy the suffering of the black and poor masses. The kick, so to speak, is that Tupac was on both sides of the evil equation: he was both the term symbolizing the evil to be resisted, and the formula for the relief of evil, at least for those who found inspiration in his career. His religious impulse consisted in bearing witness to the hurt and pain he saw, and sometimes caused, while indicting the social and cultural forces that shaped the psyches of those who wreak the most havoc.

Because Tupac sought to enliven the Weberian take on theodicy by giving meaning in his lyrics to the social suffering of poor blacks and other oppressed people, he was actually in profound conversation with the very religious and spiritual traditions he appeared to spurn. That's why, in a way, the impulse to authenticity, to "keep it real," as the hip-hoppers say, drew from the same moral passion of traditional black religion. "I want to live the life I sing about in my song," was a musical credo and a creed of conduct for gospel legend Mahalia Jackson and blues icon B.B. King. Tupac and other rappers embraced the mantra, if not the spiritual urgings behind it. But they replaced the religious pieties that animated its fulfillment for religious people with a secularized, ghettocentric, thug piety that mandated that the ghetto supply the taproot of true black identity. Tupac was big on niggas and thugs, and he edified and exhorted them with religious passion. He gave them a transcendental force in his worldview because he believed they were cooperating with the best, most enlarging impulses of the universe. Tupac's religious beliefs were quite unorthodox but quite powerful. His beliefs could never fit easily into Christian or Muslim or Jewish faith, even as he self-consciously engaged each of these traditions in crafting his unique views. I suppose one might summarize his beliefs as ghetto spirituality, street religion, urban piety.

Tupac's quest for Black Jesus symbolizes his religious views. Black Jesus was for him that cultic figure who, as I said earlier, identifies with the downtrodden. That view jibes with the prophetic vocation of the Christian witness articulated in progressive black religious circles. Tupac adhered to the prophetic tradition versus the priestly one. The prophetic moment within African American religious traditions is about critiquing and transforming the social order as a result of the revelation of God. The priestly tradition preserves through rites and rituals the personal ethics and edifying ethos of religious community in the extant social order. Tupac wanted to preserve moments and modes of black spiritual warfare gleaned from priestly traditions—although they would be applied in his idiosyncratic vision of black religious community. He also interrupted the orthodox religious ideals of black communities with a prophetic articulation of a thug theology in support of an equally unorthodox Black Jesus.

Tupac raps on the song "Black Jesus," that "I went to church, but they underhanded, I don't understand it." So he's implying that there is a contradiction between the ideal of serving the masses through the enactment of one's religious beliefs and the exploitative practices of certain religious communities and their representative priests, preachers, and prophets. He measured the integrity of black religion by the litmus test of the ontological distance between preaching and practice, between proclamation and performance, and between words and one's spiritual walk. Like many critics, even those within the black religious world, Tupac lamented in some of his later interviews how a gospel of crass materialism had gutted the faith for many who were skeptical of the iron link between wealth and the Way asserted by too many Christians. For Tupac, Black Jesus was the advocate of the marginalized and the ostracized who were, in his terms, the thugs of our culture. He was disheartened by religious traditions that counseled adherents to nurture spirituality through practices—say, taking a sabbatical from work or retreating to quiet places for weeks at a time—that failed to address the social and economic inequalities that prevented the wide distribution of such privileges. The more radically Black Jesus could be identified with society's outlaws, the better he was able, in Tupac's view, to redeem his ghetto adherents.

You mentioned Black Jesus, which I consider to be a very important issue, and here's my last question, which I am even kind of proud of formulating.

You should be proud of all of the questions, brother.

In my opinion, Tupac was never interested in reconsecrating things. He wanted to deconsecrate things, as much as possible. And at the same time, he wanted to demythicize things. When he spoke of Black Jesus, he was not looking at Jesus himself, he was looking at Jesus plus two thousand years of religious translation.

Absolutely.

Because he knew so very well that it is the two thousand years of religious history which have mythicized this biography, which otherwise would have been an almost insignificant biography as such. Now, Black Jesus is someone totally new in my opinion, someone we've never given thought to in the past, because in him you see

Jesus, plus Tupac's understanding of two thousand demythicized years of storytelling about Jesus. Now, if we accept that, doesn't Tupac's Black Jesus kill everything we grew up with and learned from spiritual men? Doesn't Tupac stand next to the most famous killer of God, Nietzsche?

That's a very profound question. And in one sense we have to answer yes. And in one sense we have to say perhaps. And in a third sense we have to say no. Let me answer all of them but not necessarily sequentially. The profundity of what you just talked about (and we might add Feuerbach, with his conception of belief in God as a wish-fulfillment and a projection of human imagination and fantasy, to stand alongside Nietzsche, along with Spinoza for his theodical reflections, and Schopenhauer for his pessimism and for his role, as Heidegger said, as a metaphysician of evil) is that in Tupac's Black Jesus, there is, as you have already acknowledged, an impulse toward radical deconsecration. In other words, there is no attempt to reconsecrate a world that has been left by God, rejected by Jesus, because that world will only serve the purposes of the powers that be. In a sense, it's the flip side of salvation: God through Jesus spurns what orthodox Christians call "the world," what H. Richard Niebuhr might map in his religious sociology of knowledge as an altogether secular weltanschauung, one, at least in Tupac's view, that is impervious to the salvific principles of justice and fairness.

So you are absolutely right in that sense of aligning Tupac with the death of a certain view of God, perhaps Nietzschean in its consequences, or even Spinozian in its more positive dimensions, and certainly Feuerbachian in its attempt to deconstruct and demythologize the projection of religious symbols. And to tell the truth, there's a Marxist moment in Tupac as well, since his will to deconsecrate was an attempt to subvert the political utility of a religious ideal advocated by those in power, those who sought to sanctify the status quo. Tupac would have been down with the notion of religion as the "opiate of the masses," especially the sophisticated interpretation of that statement beyond its pop misinterpretations and misreadings. Nietzsche, Feuerbach, and Marx, among others, certainly gave us a vocabulary to critique "man-made" gods, the sort that Tupac had in mind as he lambasted the authoritarian, hierarchical, and exploitative consequences of orthodox religious praxis.

Such a Nietzschean, Feuerbachian, and Marxist demythologization of religious practices comports well, at least philosophically, with the argument that all worship is "man-made" because none of us has direct access to transcendence. We don't have privileged access to the mind of God—all claims to revelation and a direct connection to providence aside. In fact, the belief in revelation and direct connection to providence is evidence of the difficulty of justly adjudicating competing claims of religious knowledge and truth advanced by a wide variety of believers. If such believers claim to know what God wants, then they foreclose, in their heuristic cosmos, the counterclaims of other bearers of knowledge. Or, to put it another way, rival claims to knowledge are, a priori, viewed as false if they range outside the hermeneutic circle and discursive frame of a given religious community. There's very little humility in such claims and communities, which, I think, riled Tupac and lead him to proclaim a thug theology whose deity was Black Jesus.

Ironically, by asserting a belief in Black Jesus and a thug theology grounded in the relief of personal and social suffering, Tupac might have been closer than he realized to the epistemic warrants of a traditional New Testament theology. In gaining the spiritual maturity to confront the unavoidable miseries of finite existence and to fight more wisely to change the world he inherited, Tupac and his mates joined St. Paul, the first missionary and theologian of Christianity, who said, in 2 Corinthians 4:8–9: "*We are* troubled on every side, yet not distressed; *we are* perplexed, but not in despair; Persecuted, but not forsaken; cast down, but not destroyed." Of course, Paul's words earlier, in 1 Corinthians 13:11, are also apropos, as he says, "When I was a child, I spake as a child, I understood as a child, I thought as a child: but when I became a man, I put away childish things."

And in their insistence that they must not simply focus on God and heaven while neglecting one's neighbor, one's homeboy, Tupac and his comrades found companionship in 1 John 4: 20, when the writer said, and I think the New International Version captures it nicely, "If anyone says, 'I love God,' yet hates his brother, he is a liar. For anyone who does not love his brother, whom he has seen, cannot love God, whom he has not seen." Of course, judging one's authentic religious devotion by how one treats the poorest, most destitute among us—what Tupac termed the thug—is a view shared by Tupac and Jesus. In fact, Jesus, in that wonderful New International Version translation of Matthew 25:40, said that when one feeds the hungry, gives drink to the thirsty, clothes the naked, and visits the sick and imprisoned, one is helping God: "'I tell you the truth, whatever you did for one of the least of these brothers of mine, you did for me.'" And when Tupac's mate Kastro raps on "Black Jesus" that he's "Trapped, black, scarred and barred/Searching for truth, where it's hard to find God," he reflects Paul's admission that knowledge of God is, at best, partial and clouded, when he declared in the powerful King James Version of 1 Corinthians 13:11 that "For now we see through a glass, darkly; but then face to face: now I know in part; but then shall I know even as also I am known."

As Tupac knew, when it comes to fully knowing the ways of God, we ain't there yet. We have not penetrated transcendence and seen the face of God, at least not in its pure, unfettered, unfiltered immediacy, a prospect that the Hebrew Bible warns would surely kill us were we to meet God without protection. God's glory is just too great, so God's presence must be mediated, prismed, filtered, and inevitably interpreted, nuanced, and shaded. None of us who claim to be God's children have had direct access to God. So strictly speaking, we're all working with "man-made" conceptions of God, even if we believe that ours is true. That's part of the Pascalian risk of faith, to know that we could be wrong, distorted, deluded, but that we assert our connection to the ultimate regardless of those inherent risks of belief.

But Tupac, like Feuerbach, Nietzsche, and Marx, was onto something genuine that might ultimately help believers confront the prisms through which we view God and come to an even more powerful and disciplined conception of religious faith. But as with some of these figures, many (black) believers were just too afraid or fearful to hear Tupac out. What Tupac brought out, what he externalized, was the (theo)logical contradictions at the heart of meaning-making in conventional religions. He also suggested that the ultimate test of any religion was its ability to confront suffering. Tupac realized that it was difficult for many religions to do so, since the way many believers practiced their faith was a source of suffering for many others. That's why he embraced Black Jesus: he believed that Black Jesus embraced him. Black Jesus was the name he gave to the implicit acceptance he found in the universe at the intersection of existential vulnerability, spiritual presence, moral guidance, and intellectual integrity. The hurt and suffering he experienced lead him to do a difficult thing: to tell the truth about the pain he confronted and to search for its relief, even as he often contradicted himself in perpetuating the very forces he sought to disperse.

It is interesting to note that, in the way Tupac conceives him, Black Jesus is a new figure in black cultural history. Black theologians of at least a couple generations, and black preachers of several more generations, have asserted the primacy of Jesus' (and God's) identification with oppressed blacks as the predicate of authentic black religious identity. In a sense, Tupac's radical divinization of an imperfect deity in concert with suffering black humanity is much closer to arguments of humanocentric theism put forth by scholars like William R. Jones and Anthony Pinn. Jones and Pinn argue that we've got to get rid of a stultifying religious theism and belief in a transcendent God, and privilege human activity as the locus classicus of our human striving for justice, mercy, and truth. In other words, the human being herself is at once the bearer—and the intellectual basis—of understanding and interpreting the attributes ascribed to God in traditional theology.

In that light, Tupac's Black Jesus resides in the urban thug, in the black citizen of the persistently oppressed black postindustrial cosmos. That's why, at the beginning of "Black Jesus," one of the Outlawz, with whom Tupac recorded the song, says, "You can be Christian, Baptist, Jehovah Witness, Islamic, don't matter. Me, I'm a thug; thugs, we pray to Black Jesus, all day." Two things are crucial. First, one need not surrender one's connection to traditional religion to pray to Black Jesus, to find succor and relief in worshiping him. Second, the thug life is itself a religion. As Young Noble, a member of the Outlawz, raps, "Outlawz, we got our own race, culture, religion, rebellin' against the system, commence to lynchin'. . . ."

Black Jesus stands over against the manipulations and distortions of truth fostered in conventional religious communities and texts. Kadafi, another member of the Outlawz, queries in his rap, "Wonder how shit like the Qu'ran and the Bible was written, what is religion? God's words all cursed like crack, Satan's way of gettin' us back." Tupac clarifies his skepticism about orthodox religion and its negative effect on community; asserts his Moses-like messianic authority derived from intimate engagement with God; and proclaims the power of Black Jesus to judge the exploitation of religion just by showing up, as he raps: "Went to church, but don't understand it, they underhanded, God gave me these commandments, the world is scandalous."

Although Tupac is not attempting to reconsecrate the given world, he wants it to make sense or at least wants to square it with the world he inhabits. Some critics might counter that meaning-making is an attempt to consecrate nonabsurdity. In other words, absurdity is the idol to be resisted, and thus meaning-making is a consecration of the moral logic behind the universe. I've got no problem with that argument, and I don't find it necessary to resist such a distinction, since these are largely philosophical arguments about imagined worlds anyway, joining Benedict Anderson with his "imagined communities," and Nelson Goodman with his "ways of worldmaking." The bottom line for Tupac is the central question faced by all religions, How do you make suffering make sense? Tupac's answer, in part, is Black Jesus.

Upon deeper reflection, Tupac's Black Jesus might have more to do with the actual Jesus, the real Jesus, the Jesus of history, than the one whose crucified body bears the marks of his misappropriations and mischaracterizations, and whose resurrected body suffers under the weight of two millennia of historical accretions and theological distortions. Black Jesus is the Jesus of deep, dark history, the God of the underside. It is the Jesus we rarely seriously take into consideration beyond pat phrases and cursory acknowledgment, the God who literally got beat down and hung up, the God who died a painful, shameful death, subject to capital punishment under political authority and attack, but who came back, and keeps coming back, in the form and flesh we least expect. The Black Jesus about which Tupac speaks is an irreverent creation that most people who talk about and identify with Jesus would never recognize. "We don't want a Jesus who is too perfect," Tupac and the Outlawz are basically saying. "Wait a minute, we thought Jesus was the definition of perfection," Tupac's critics will cry. "No," Tupac and his mates will reply. "We want somebody who smokes like we smoke, drinks like we drink, hurts like we hurt." A God who smokes marijuana? A blunt-smoking Jesus? To most believers, that is not simply the catechism of the irreverent; that is pure blasphemy! So in that sense, you're absolutely right about Tupac joining the "god killers" like Nietzsche.

But that's not the only position one might adopt in examining Tupac's art and beliefs. Here's where I insert the "maybe" in response to your question of his being in league with the Nietzschean impulse to deicide, even though, if we had more time, I'd explore the complex dimensions of Nietzsche's project that might garner more sympathy among believers. In any case, I've already inductively and implicitly explained my "yes" to you. The "maybe" has to do with my contention that Tupac's articulation of Black Jesus may point to his perception of the need for transcendence to create sympathy and social solidarity among the masses, even among the thugs. Thus Black Jesus does not simply possess a political utility for thugs, but there's a spiritual dimension as well. So that's why I say maybe.

Now let me spend a little time on why I think we have to answer your question "no." What's interesting about consecration is that Tupac Shakur is deconsecrating and, more to the point, desacralizing the world of religious belief. To some believers, that is a blasphemy worthy of the auto-da-fé during the Spanish Inquisition. Critics certainly demonized Tupac through the organs of the mainstream media and within pockets of the black press. But what's interesting about Tupac is that the corollary activity of desacralization is the world's resacralization through an alternative discursive framework afforded by investment in Black Jesus. To borrow from literature and child psychology, in deconsecrating the world, Tupac also pointed to what Bettleheim termed "the reenchantment of the world." True enough, Tupac's reenchanted world looked absolutely scary and morally repulsive to those who weren't denizens of the fragmented, fractured postindustrial urban world of the black oppressed. But to many within its moral arc, Tupac's experiments in ontological archaeology looked impressively authentic, as he dug beneath the strata of racial stigma to unearth the precious beings of demonized youth.

The fascination with, and redefinition of, the thug (since for him, the thug was redeemed by the acronym he invented, T.H.U.G.: the hate you gave little infants fucks everyone) was crucial to his religion. The thug was sacralized and, yes, consecrated in Tupac's theological expression. That means that Tupac did not escape the very religious language that he so brilliantly critiqued, even if he sought to evade its dogmas. In pioneering a religious interpretation that challenged orthodox belief, he retained critical elements of conventional faith. In the end, I don't think he could shake the need for transcendence, even if it was paradoxically expressed as an immanent transcendence, immanent in the sense of being right here on the ground. Immanent transcendence for Tupac meant the attempt—and for him the struggle—to transcend hopelessness, to transcend economic misery, and finally to transcend the ghetto's worst effects while simultaneously transcending its vile stigmatization in the world beyond its borders. Tupac's language of transcendence both distinguishes his quest and ties him to a journey embarked on by religious and secular saints. But it also links him to fearless critics who were unafraid to be called godless to get to God, or to truth, which for some of them was one and the same.

Interview by Yanko Damboulev

Los Angeles, California, 2001

14

"Speech Is My Hammer"

Black Preaching, Social Justice, and Rap Rhetoric

Why don't you tell us something about yourself, such as where you presently hold your professorship.

I am presently the Ida B. Wells-Barnett University Professor at De Paul University in Chicago, Illinois. I am the first person to hold that position and it's an honor, especially because it is, I believe, the first university professorship in the nation named after an African American woman. When I went to De Paul, I wanted to make sure that my professorship acknowledged the historical significance of black culture in general and in black Chicago in particular, and even more poignantly, the monumental contributions of black women to black freedom struggles. So we chose to honor the brilliant legacy of the fierce warrior and public intellectual Ida B. Wells-Barnett. Besides teaching, I continue to lecture and preach throughout the country about 150 days a year. I maintain a very active teaching, writing, and preaching itinerary, but above all, I am a preacher who is a practicing intellectual in the academy, the primary site of my vocation.

African American Pulpit is very excited to have you. Let me begin by asking you if there is a new social activism in the African American church in the new millennium, or is it the same struggle but the clock has simply changed?

I think that it's a bit of both. On the one hand, current activism extends the initial moral trajectory of the civil rights movement that so uniquely colored the twentieth century for African American people. Such activity gave voice to a social movement within African American religious culture of which ministers in particular were a significant part. I think that on the one hand, the black church continues to face the monumental eclipse of social hope that spurred its best activists on to brilliant response, from Martin Luther King Jr. to William Gray. These activist ministers were concerned about the social inequities of African American culture and viewed those inequities through the lens of their religious commitments. The church was the most viable and vital center of response to the social oppression that prevailed—not only in the twentieth century, of course, but prior to that as well. In the eighteenth and nineteenth centuries, during slavery, the inchoate black church gave rise to powerful voices of opposition to oppression.

Black people often left white religious bodies to form their own denominations, making sure in most cases to link the gospel to the message of social salvation. That species of social activism continues to live in pockets of the black church in the twenty-first century. The twentieth century saw Dubois's prophetic declaration that the problem of the century would be the problem of the color line lengthening its shadow across the biblical horizon of interpretation for black people. How could the Bible address racial oppression? How could the black church deal with it? And how could black religious culture in general rebel against racism? The difference now I think is that after the civil rights generation, in this so-called post–civil rights era, there's been a kind of paradigm shift in terms of the particular forms of response of black religious culture to the political environment.

First of all, the extraordinary expansion of the black middle class has meant a rise in black church membership after many blacks dropped out of the church for a decade and a half. Hence, the class dynamics of black church membership have been dramatically transformed now that the black middle class has returned to church with a vengeance. By expanding so rapidly, the black church, its coffers swelling with disposable income, has expanded the economic and social opportunities of the black community. It has also helped underscore sharp class conflict in our communities. As a result, economic inequality, especially for the black working class, working poor, and permanently poor, looms large as one of the most devastating forces that curtails black liberation.

Equally poignant is the fact that there is a huge generational divide in black communities. That divide affected how black people fostered social rebellion twenty or thirty years ago and shapes the forms it takes now. The post–civil rights paradigm of social struggle means that young people have seized economic striving and class warfare as the major means to express their commitment to black religious traditions, or their alienation from them. For instance, it would be almost impossible to overlook the rise in black communities of the so-called Word Church, or churches that are primarily concerned with the economic viability of their members. This is not to be confused with the historic concern about economic inequality. There is today a kind of narcissistic preoccupation with the elevation of the individual black church member and not the amelioration of the collective black fate.

In one sense it's an old phenomenon of crass materialism creeping into the new church formation. The advent of the black mega-churches, where you have thousands of members congregating in one particular community, has in some instances embodied what Robert Franklin calls "positive thought materialism." Positive thought materialism is characterized by glib psychological self-affirmation and an inordinate preoccupation with upward mobility as the major thesis of black religious culture. There is no longer in such circles a concern with liberation from oppression. Of course, if we're honest, we'll admit that even though the black church has always been at the heart of social change, most black church members have not routinely or widely embraced a theology of liberation. For example, most churches were not physically involved in the civil rights movement or the struggle for liberation.

The black church has provided the freedom struggle with its major actors as well as tremendous economic and moral support. The black church, collectively speaking, was still the tangible and vital engine that drove black liberation. But now, it seems to me, there has been a turning inward of African American religious traditions, and a preoccupation with materialism has really clogged the arteries of our social conscience. Now it's about *me* getting ahead; *my* individual success becomes the primary index of God's blessings. In earlier times, the most progressive and prophetic black religious leaders articulated their belief that the black church was a collective enterprise geared toward the social transformation of the black community.

Number two, there has been an alienation among many of the younger people from the social vision of the black church. If in the past the black church was deemed by its critics to be politically irrelevant because it failed to translate its religious ethics into social protest, it is now even more the case that a particular segment of young blacks has discovered its authentic voice outside the boundaries of the black church. The increasing secularization of American society has certainly had an impact on black culture—in the sense that large numbers of religiously unaffiliated young people who operate outside the parameters of black religious discourse have expressed their dismay with the black church. They have also explicitly critiqued the religious preoccupation with upward mobility at the expense of social transformation. These youth direct their rhetoric of social conscience in opposition to the dominant social trends of many black churches.

And finally, I'll say this. There is a renewed mode of social activism occurring in the black church in response to these changes. It is a social activism that centers in the delivery of vital social services to the black community. Social service delivery becomes a primary means by which the church intervenes on some of the economic and social crises that devastate black communities. The black church continues to be the most important outlet for the disbursement of crucial social and economic resources, whether pantry programs geared toward relieving the homeless, outreach programs around issues of domestic violence, or attempts by the black church to stem the rising tide of gentrification. At the same time, the black church is trying to offset the effects of a commuter congregation on its social witness, as people who don't live in the immediate communities of the church come in from the suburbs and outlying areas in order to maintain their church membership.

There is a conscientious attempt by many churches to deal with those people who are left behind as a result of gentrification, or who are economically marginalized by the government takeover of urban spaces. Often urban renewal means Negro removal in large postindustrial urban centers where poor and marginally working-class people no longer have access to downtown or inner-city housing. Such housing, or at least the space on which it rests, is now seen to be the preserve of those who want to come back into the city after years of white flight and black track to suburbia. All of this means that the character of social activism, especially in the black church, has dramatically changed. Indeed, we might not easily recognize some of that social activism today. We still have Jesse Jackson and Al Sharpton addressing traditional social problems through organizing people in public protests on the streets. But the new social activism may not include traditional civil rights activities. Instead, it may consist of galvanizing the black church to channel its economic resources to the poor and marginalized.

You paraphrase Tupac Shakur saying that the church needs to rethink its commitment to social progress, a commitment that has been derailed by inordinate materialism. Would you reflect on the fact that while hip-hop culture would accuse the church of crass materialism, many preachers would accuse the hip-hop culture of crass materialism?

Absolutely, and they would be right. There has emerged within hip-hop a subculture obsessed with material goods, the prizes of wealth, and huge disposable income. This subculture is characterized in the vernacular by the term "bling-bling"—referring to the sound of the cash register ringing up expensive consumer goods, including "ice," the revived term for the platinum jewelry hip-hoppers swing around their necks and wrists. Elements of hip-hop are motivated by an ethic of narcissistic materialism that thrives on "getting paid" and rejecting conservative black communal values, thus opening the door to the glorification of violence. So the simultaneity of these effects—the valorization of crass materialism and the glamorization of violence—has had lethal consequences on black youth cultures. Many members of the younger generation have literally cashed in on the moral and spiritual capital that was in some measure available to the civil rights generation. I think that speaks to a bankrupt moral vision that matches the moral bankruptcy of black churches that uninhibitedly pursue material blessing. This suggests a crisis of class and social conscience in both sacred and secular culture.

What's interesting about hip-hop—and this is true as well for quarters of the black church—is that the genre's prophetic dimension is often silenced at the expense of the socially anesthetized music and videos that are played on BET or MTV. The rappers who are highlighted in mainstream culture—

those who get the fattest paychecks and the biggest video budgets that help procure the latest cars and hottest girls to flaunt their ornamental eroticism—are those who brag about their sexual prowess, cultural prominence, and deep pockets. But in the midst of the crass materialism, sexual excess, and glorification of violence is a group of gifted urban scribes and pavement poets who are rarely feted, including figures like Common, Mos Def, The Roots, Talib Kweli, and Lauryn Hill, who has proved to be the exception, since she's been showered with mainstream praise and reward. These artists bring profound social critique and historical awareness to bear in their in brilliant lyrics that address black pain and oppression as well as the need for racial self-critique.

But I don't want to artificially segregate the discursive terrain of hip-hop, since hardcore rappers like Tupac Shakur and Notorious B.I.G., a.k.a. Biggie Smalls, have generated some of the most poignant and prophetic rhetoric in hip-hop. Although widely celebrated as the East Coast's answer to the rhetoricians of glorified violence out West, Biggie Smalls could deliver brilliant social analyses and moving portraits of poverty with metaphoric wittiness and rhythmic flow, as he does on a lyric from his first album, *Ready to Die*, remembering how "the landlord dissed us/I used to wonder why Christmas missed us/Birthdays were the worst days/Now we sip champagne when we thirsty/Damned right I like the life I live/Cause I went from negative to positive." Biggie's lyrics, like those of Tupac, speak directly to the question of black suffering and what's known in theological circles as "the problem of evil." Biggie shares honors with Tupac in the articulation of a grassroots secular urban theodicy.

Of course, that's a perennial theological problem that preachers at their best have always paid attention to. It was evident, too, when Shakur pleaded: "Somebody help me/Tell me where to go from here/Cause even thugs cry/But do the Lord care?" Here's a rapper asking, in effect, "Does God care about the human suffering I see and endure? I want moral leadership. I want ethical guidance. I don't derive that from a connection to a religious community. But I am still obsessed with God language." Tupac's like a Reformation-minded Martin Luther in Fubu! What fascinates me about young rappers who are critical of religious culture is that they are obsessed with many of the same problems and questions that are debated among believers. The farther many rappers claim to be from religious culture, the closer they prove themselves to be to these communities in the moral grammars and even the secular heuristics they deploy. In fact, hardcore hip-hoppers like Tupac Shakur and Snoop Dogg were reared in the church or influenced by its discourse, practice, and witness.

However, it would be disingenuous not to note the civil war going on in hip-hop between so-called conscious rappers and hedonistic gangstas. A prominent rhetorical skirmish occurred when Lauryn Hill, on the Fugees compact disc *The Score*, uttered the now classic words: "And even after all my logic and my theory, I add a muthafucka so you ignorant niggas hear me." She self-consciously deploys the rhetoric of hardcore hip-hop as a means to open up spaces of reflection among the gangstas and macks. Hill and her conscious colleagues admonish hip-hoppers to examine social issues critically and to use art to fuel the psychic and aesthetic liberation of black people. Then there's the inspiring example of the very gifted Mos Def, who claims on his compact disc, *Black on Both Sides*, that, "Speech is my hammer, bang the world into shape, now let it fall." Mos Def understands that the words which come out of one's mouth can be socially redemptive and culturally significant, and have the potential to create or destroy worlds.

Observers and critics outside hip-hop culture often miss the war being waged within its borders because they ignore its different forms, shapes, and textures. That means that in hip-hop, artistic identities and styles can be quite deceptive, and they don't necessarily embody the stigma that dogs them. Along these lines, the group Outkast, from Atlanta, asks a poignant question on its album *Aquemini*: "Now question: Is every nigga wit dreads for the cause? Is every nigga with gold for the fall? Naw, so don't get caught in appearance." Outkast helps us look beyond the emblems of our generational and stylistic differences to understand that there is conscience within hip-hop, just as there is hypocrisy in civil rights and black religious cultures. The arguments made in hip-hop can bear remarkable resemblance to the thematic obsessions of religious culture. That link, perhaps, can be glimpsed when Outkast says: "We missed a lot church, so the music is our confessional."

Is rap, hip-hop culture, therefore, a rhetorical form in the same manner that preaching has been to the black church?

If we take the four crucial ingredients of hip-hop culture—break dancing, deejaying, rapping, and graffiti—then rap certainly is the rhetorical form that is most emblematic of hip-hop culture. I think rap often functions within hip-hop culture the same way that preaching does in black religious cultures. First, rappers deploy rhetoric as a means of self-expression; second, rappers deploy rhetoric as a means of social critique; and third, rappers deploy rhetoric as a means of ethical engagement and moral suasion as they make assertions about the way life is and the way it ought to be. Further, rappers at their best are preoccupied with honing their skills and possessed of a hunger for linguistic excellence. The best rappers are not interested in generating speech for its own sake, but in crafting superior rhetorical vehicles to articulate their distinct worldviews. They deploy a variety of rhetorical strategies and verbal practices—enjambment and clever rhyme schemes, for example—to achieve these ends. As a rhetorical form, hip-hop has a lot in common with a variety of antecedent oral and musical practices, whether it's signifying within street discourse, the articulation of playful hyperbole around sex in blues culture, the poetic musings of Gil Scott-Heron, Bessie Smith rapping to a beat, or Lou Rawls and Isaac Hayes weaving extended monologues into their music. Hip-hop fits right in with the panoply of black musical expressions that feature elements of speech that extend black oral traditions.

Perhaps more specifically, rap functions on the same level as black preaching in this sense—it puts forth social imagination and rhetorical dexterity as the means to racial and cultural expression. Some critics have made a major blunder in assessing both hip-hop and black preaching. For instance, both casual observers and theorists of hermeneutics and homiletics—the so-called science of interpretation and art of preaching, respectively—suggest that black preachers have been obsessed with style more than substance. But the magisterial artists of black sacred rhetoric have always understood that style is a vehicle for substance, a means to realize significant intellectual and spiritual engagement, and not a substitute for meaningful, substantive expression. How we say what we say is crucial, but that's only because what we have to say is extraordinarily important. Black preachers inspired survival by their skillful deployment of rhetorical strategies. The way black preachers spoke about God—the visceral, tangible aesthetics of black hermeneutical and homiletical practice—convinced black folk that God's rule was unbroken by history's tragedies, and that black social and moral striving was a reflection of the divine will. Whether it was the elongated extension of a syllable into a "whoop"; the articulation of a staccato rhetorical practice that employed edifying repetition to drive home the truth; or the skillful deployment of the textures, tones, and timbers intrinsic to black folk rhetoric, the performance of religious rhetoric in a racial vein wasn't just for "form or fashion," as elders in the black church say. Black sacred speech wasn't simply about wedding style to substance; but style itself was an index of the peculiar experience of black people in the modern world as they worshiped God in hostile circumstances. And, in that sense, the rhetorical practices of the best black preachers parallel the rhetorical practices of the best hip-hoppers.

I want to push you with an example out of your new book, I May Not Get There with You: The True Martin Luther King Jr. *I would imagine that one of your favorite speeches is the one Dr. King delivered on April 3, 1968, "I've Been to the Mountaintop." Would you take that vignette and compare it to a hip-hop vignette?*

Of course, King is unparalleled in most fields of endeavor. If we look at what King did in that speech, we must first acknowledge that he was very tired that evening and decided to send his closest friend and second in command, Ralph Abernathy, to speak in his place. But Abernathy phoned King at this hotel and informed him that "this is your crowd." Just think if King had not deferred to Abernathy's judgment that night and remained buried in his gloominess; he would have been murdered before leaving us with what in essence is his last will and testament. Anyway, King unburdened his heavy heart by climbing into a car and transmuting his existential agony into a transcendent moment in American oratory. It is mind-boggling to recall that King's speech was largely improvised, a daunting prospect for those merely mortal rhetoricians who aspire to King's expansive eloquence and oratorical genius.

To be sure, his speech brimmed with premonition, an emotional catharsis that wasn't hard to conjure in light of his relentless pace, his courageous behavior, and his daily existence under the palpable probability of his imminent death. You can hear what Max Weber termed world-weariness in King's statement in Chicago in 1968 that, "I'm tired of the surging murmur of life's restless siege . . . I want to live as long as anybody in this building, and sometimes I wonder whether or not I'm going to make it." So here was a man who inhaled his finitude like a breath of stale air but hurtled toward history and apocalypse with courageous indifference to the movement's cost to his life. So all of these realities ganged up on him that night, and he came through with nothing short of verbal virtuosity.

Furthermore, King takes the occasion of what would be his last speech to give a panoramic overview of his entire career and of the moral import of the civil rights movement within the context of twentieth-century social struggles. Moreover, he toured the intellectual landscape of Western civilization with pithy summations of the epochs and ideas that characterize our hemisphere. His unique ability to condense the social values and moral goals of cultures and civilizations into one speech is enough to speak of his rhetorical genius and of that speech as a landmark in the history of ebony eloquence.

But the particular vignette to which you are referring occurs near the end of King's speech where he speaks about his own death and associates his life, metaphorically and theologically, with the biblical career of the archetypical prophet of racial exodus—Moses. "Well I don't know what will happen now," King says, referring to the rumors of the threats to his life "from some of our sick white brothers." But he forges on, suggesting that "it really doesn't matter with me, because I've been to the mountaintop." Judging from his audience's thunderous response, they immediately caught the Mosaic reference. "And I've looked over, and I've seen the Promised Land," he continued. "I may not get there with you, but I want you to know tonight that we as a people will get to the Promised Land. So I'm not worried about anything, I'm not fearing any man. 'Mine eyes have seen the glory. . . .'" And then he suddenly turned on his feet and fell into the waiting arms of Abernathy and his young aide Jesse Jackson. King had, in one majestic act of rhetorical articulation, brilliantly linked himself to Moses, and then linked the exodus of black people—from the land of oppression into the wilderness and on to the Promised Land—to the children of Israel's exodus experience. I don't think that hip-hop is nearly mature enough to produce a figure who might conjure that sort of rhetorical genius or summon that sort of transcendent humanity in the face of hostility and death to exorcise one's demons and transform the social landscape of one's people, as King did in that speech.

That's not to say that there haven't been moments of sheer brilliance in hip-hop, and occasionally raw genius, because there have been. I think artists like KRS-One, Rakim, Public Enemy, Common, The Roots, Lauryn Hill, Nas, 2Pac, Biggie, and Mos Def, at their best, articulate at moments the fierce rhetorical genius that Martin Luther King Jr. routinely displayed. I think that Talib Kweli offers one instance of such genius on his compact disc, *Reflection Eternal*, recorded with deejay/producer Hi-Tek, where Kweli performs brilliant hermeneutical surgery on Nina Simone's classic "Four Women." I think that Kweli's achievement is a fusion of rhetorical strategies and practices: his remake of "Four Women" (really, it is so far beyond a remake, it is really a deconstruction and a reworking, a brilliant extension of the song's rhetorical thrust, discursive domains, and implicit philosophical arguments about race, gender, and generation) consists in its skillful deployment of radical reinterpretation, incisive interpolation, redaction criticism, and homiletical signification.

To top it all off, it's part of a "hidden track," which means it's not even numbered as a title on the compact disc's menu, and that only the truly curious, the truly desirous, will initially find their way to the song. In Nina Simone's original, the narrator portrays four women who suffer a host of injustices due to the difference in their shades of blackness. Kweli's version takes the form of an anecdote about a chance encounter with a centenarian that becomes the predicate for a powerful survey of black history. I'll drop one verse just to show you its power:

A daughter come up in Georgia, ripe and ready to plant seeds,
Left the plantation when she saw a sign even though she can't read
It came from God and when life get hard she always speak to him,
She'd rather kill her babies than let the master get to 'em,
She on the run up north to get across that Mason-Dixon
In church she learned how to be patient and keep wishin',
The promise of eternal life after death for those that God bless
She swears the next baby she'll have will breathe a free breath
and get milk from a free breast,
And love being alive,
otherwise they'll have to give up being themselves to survive,

Being maids, cleaning ladies, maybe teachers or college graduates, nurses,
housewives, prostitutes, and drug addicts
Some will grow to be old women, some will die before they born,
They'll be mothers, and lovers who inspire and make songs,
But me, my skin is brown and my manner is tough,
Like the love I give my babies when the rainbow's enuff,
I'll kill the first muthafucka that mess with me, I never bluff
I ain't got time to lie, my life has been much too rough,
Still running with barefeet, I ain't got nothin' but my soul,
Freedom is the ultimate goal,
life and death is small on the whole, in many ways
I'm awfully bitter these days
'cuz the only parents God gave me, they were slaves,
And it crippled me, I got the destiny of a casualty,
But I'll live through my babies and I'll change my reality
Maybe one day I'll ride back to Georgia on a train,
Folks 'round there call me Peaches, I guess that's my name.

The entire song is a study in the narrative reconstruction of the fragmented elements of black survival and a cautionary tale against the racial amnesia that destroys the fabric of black collective memory. By appealing to Simone's rhetorical precedent, Kweli situates the song's heuristic logic inside the matrix of racial identity and cultural continuity. By baptizing Simone's sentiments in a hip-hop rhetorical form, Kweli raises new questions about the relation between history and contemporary social practice, and fuses the generational ambitions of two gifted artists—himself and Simone—while depicting the distinct political imperatives that drive his art. Finally, Kweli thrusts a rhetorical saber into the heart of hip-hop's patriarchal obsessions and narrates the black future in a female voice and vision, without which the race will not survive. That's more progressive than a hundred sermons waxing eloquent about a universe made by a God who, according to *his* homiletical representatives, can't shake the masculine pronoun or the masculinist psychology of biblical and theological interpretation. By placing the woman front and center on the song that concludes his compact disc, Kweli offers a stirring theological lesson: That our race's future, like the terms that describe it, is best secured when it has feminine endings.

At its best, hip-hop, like black preaching, is concerned at crucial moments with exploring social issues and using rhetoric as a means to educate its audience. But it's important to remember that both forms—preaching and rap—also take linguistic delight in using words well as a meaningful exercise in its own right. Still, what King did on April 3, 1968, is virtually unachievable anywhere else in any other vocational pursuit because of the unique set of circumstances under which he lived and spoke.

You spent a tremendous amount of time writing and researching your book on Martin Luther King Jr., I May Not Get There with You: The True Martin Luther King Jr. *What do you believe is the true genius of Dr. Martin Luther King Jr.?*

The genius of Martin Luther King Jr. is that he is a vitalizing and energizing force—and I use the present tense here because his words still live in our memories—through which millions of people continue to experience the richness and sublime character of religious commitment. King felt that we can't experience the fullness of our religious passions and gospel beliefs until they are translated into social action. If anything motivated Martin Luther King Jr.'s career, it was this ethic of translation. He translated the work of philosophical theologians who advocated personalism, like Henry Nelson Wieman, into principles that ordinary people could comprehend. Besides his genius for translating ideas and beliefs, King also possessed the gift to translate love into concrete political action. As I've argued in a couple of my books, Martin Luther King Jr. believed that justice is what love sounds like when it speaks in public. In King's mind—and in the critical reflections of Paul Tillich, whose philosophy King examined in his doctoral dissertation—justice, love, and power could hardly be divorced. King believed that power exercised without the mediating forces of love and justice was ruthless; that justice without power and love was weak because it was empty of vision; and that love without power and justice was mere sentimentality.

King's social activism grew from his extensive study of Christian ethics and liberal theology, and his intuitive grasp of the black religious tradition. For King, black religion at its best was concerned with how we speak the truth of the gospel to brothers and sisters who are worried about rent payments, keeping the lights on, getting an equal education, reducing economic suffering, and achieving racial justice. Because he cared about these things, Martin Luther King Jr. spent his life translating the philosophical tenets and ethical demands of the gospel into concrete social resistance to interlocking oppressions.

Finally, what's absolutely critical about King's genius is his ability to change his mind and methodology. Although Malcolm X is credited with transforming his life in the last year of his life, King is rarely given his due in embracing a thoroughgoing radicalism in regard to the aims and means of nonviolent social change. King initially desired to appeal to the white conscience to effect racial progress, but later he contended that social change must be forced in more dramatic fashion. He began to advocate a more aggressive version of nonviolence that focused on blocking the flow of traffic and commerce in local municipalities as a sign of severe displeasure with the status quo. King also began to articulate his belief about the inextricable link between militarism, racism, and materialism.

King's theology near the end of his life was radically incarnational, insofar as he was fairly obsessed with making the gospel of Jesus come alive off the biblical page and thrive in our nation's cities, especially among the broke and the brokenhearted. King was committed to pushing the black church to become much more intentional about directing its social, political, and economic resources to enable social revolution and to ameliorate the plight of the poor. If the gospel of Jesus is concerned with impressing God's identity on the human psyche and with imprinting it in human community, then the church must expand the boundaries of social intervention in seeking to render service and to improve the chances of social redemption. We have by and large failed to embody King's ethic of translation and his theology of radical incarnationalism, and I think American Christianity and the black church are the worse for it.

Finally, please reflect on our theme, "Sometimes It Causes Me to Tremble: Black Social Activism Now."

When we recognize the enormity of the theological, ethical, and political task at hand, we might surely tremble. We tremble because what is at stake is nothing less than the future of our race and the future of human community.

Social activism exists to wage all-out war against the inequities of society, a daunting task and one that might make any reasonable person quake.

But even as we battle the bruising inequalities that bewitch our nation, we must be careful to resist the seduction of singularity, or the Elijah complex, which I've named after the prophet who believed that he was the only righteous person left to spread God's message and to keep God's people from perishing. But God spoke to Elijah in practical terms that had profound results: "Rest your mind and soul, and get something to eat," God said to Elijah, and I'm paraphrasing here, "and then look and see that there are seven thousand others who have not bowed their knees to the false god Baal." The sense that we are alone and bereft of the moral energy of even a single compatriot is the perennial plague of the prophet. But we are often reminded that God has other warriors, messengers, and prophets who speak the truth. Such a recognition should relieve our stress and challenge our often arrogant assumptions that we are the exclusive bearers of God's word.

We ought to tremble because of the social suffering of our black brothers and sisters, ordinary people who often cannot appeal to education, status, or wealth to fend off the vicious consequences of racial and economic inequality. For instance, black youth are being warehoused in substandard schools in poor communities until they are sent to prison in unjustly disproportionate numbers. Prisons, of course, are among the fastest growth industries in America. Many rural white communities literally make a living at the expense of black and brown suffering. Then too, our juvenile justice system is being circumvented in the exercise of its obligation to rehabilitate youth by unfairly targeting, tracking, and trapping minority youth for offenses that earn young white offenders little more than a slap on the wrist. In the midst of this, the church has to speak up and help mobilize social conscience and moral outrage against this brutal treatment of our children.

Finally, we ought to tremble because we recognize that we are the servants of God, which means that we are the servants of humanity. It is awfully presumptuous to suppose we can even speak for God, a presumption to which Paul refers in the Bible when he claims that we who preach are fools for God because preaching is essentially foolish to the unconverted and, at times, to the "saved" as well. Still, we've got to recover that sense of audacious foolishness to take the gospel into the world, not in an imperialistic fashion or in an attempt to colonize the unenlightened "savage," but with a mind to help our brothers and sisters make suffering make sense. And even when we can't make it make sense, we can share the solace of a God who walks with us to the ends of the earth. And while we ought to tremble in the recognition that we are God's cocreators of sane social order, we should also be comforted in the belief that our efforts are not in vain.

Interview by Frank A. Thomas
Memphis, Tennessee, 2001

15

Ecstasy, Excess, and Eschatology

Black Religion in Crisis

Somewhere between this body thing and other cultural issues you've spoken about is Marvin Gaye. He fits somewhere in a discussion of Tupac and black male spirituality, sexuality, culture, and entertainment. In a Lucille Clifton poem titled "Them and Us," she deals with the racial and cultural difference between whites and blacks, in that Elvis is sighted but not Marvin. What is it that's going on in culture now that allows people to envision Tupac alive in Hawaii, yet Marvin, killed by his father on April Fool's Day, has never become that type of urban legend who is a candidate for bodily survival beyond his actual death?

That's right. That's an intriguing question: What is it about this particular era that grants permission to a lost black icon like Tupac to roam freely over the imaginative landscape and to be reembodied, at least symbolically, in tales of existential persistence? One of the reasons is that hip-hop culture has so powerfully confronted the forces of radical evil and what Orlando Patterson has brilliantly termed social death. They are constantly preoccupied with the forces of death and dying. The writer Michel Marriott, in an essay that appeared in the *New York Times*, quotes somebody who terms this genre of rap music, which is obsessed with suffering and evil and death, "requiem rap." I think because such artists as Tupac were so concerned in life with death, it makes sense that we might see life in their death. In a sense, it's bringing into our postmodern world a premodern conception of resurrection, although it is culturally mediated. Even so, hip-hop evinces dissatisfaction with a delayed or postponed resurrection coming at the end of time. Much of the death rhetoric of hardcore hip-hop borrows from the tropes and metaphors that are deeply embedded in black religious culture, specifically black Christian culture.

Ironically enough, much of this hardcore hip-hop rhetoric owes a debt to black sacred musings about the limits of life and the function of death to transform and transcend the limits of our being, at least our physical bodies. It is interesting to relate Tupac to these musings and mythologies because he's constantly asking, "Does the Lord care?" He's asking, in effect, Is God interested in me? You hear it in Snoop Doggy Dogg as well—"Dear Lord, I wonder can you save me?" I think the survival of a figure like Tupac is the result of fans and followers being unwilling to defer his resurrection, hence the stories circulating about his bodily existence, akin to Jesus appearing to his disciples after his crucifixion. Such stories not only combat mortality with cultural mythology and urban legend, but they situate Tupac at the intersection of religious belief and secular faith. After all, Tupac represents to some of his followers a true voice of his people and his God. Tupac is projected as the resistive theological sign of their refusal—and retrospectively through discerning, esoteric interpretations of his cryptic words full of veiled, omen-ridden meaning, *his* refusal—to accept death as the ultimate determiner of their lives. Thus a secular theology of soteriology is joined to postindustrial urban missiology—since salvation is linked to the mission of the "church" of true believers—and Tupac is articulated as the messianic figure at the heart of black urban existence. He is a ghetto saint, an urban messiah.

When you look at Tupac's last video, which he codirected and which was shot a month before he died, it's quite revealing, at least in its portent and religious symbolism. It's essentially a video picturing Tupac after he's been shot five times and murdered, appearing in heaven, being met at the Pearly Gates by a character playing Redd Foxx. It features other actors representing still more black immortals, like Donny Hathaway, Sarah Vaughn, Dorothy Dandridge, Nat King Cole, Billie Holiday, Miles Davis, Louis Armstrong, Marvin Gaye, and several others. It's eerie and haunting, and unavoidably premonitory. What's interesting about Redd Foxx's appearance, of course, is that the comedian was himself believed by many street critics and urban gossipers not to be dead but hiding out in an undisclosed spot because he was trying to avoid paying the huge tax bill he owed. Like Tupac, Foxx is the subject of urban legend, except in this case, it's one urban legend in the making, signifying posthumously on the other, casting even more doubt about whether either is truly dead. Talk about a feast of significations! Tupac is signifying on Foxx's urban legend while at least symbolically keeping his host of black geniuses alive, if only in memory, especially those who met tragic ends such as Dandridge, Hathaway, and Gaye.

Tupac's artistry, and certain elements of his cultural memorialization, is representative of the hip-hop generation's confrontation with social theodicy. It is theodicy in both the theological and sociological senses. In Christian theology, theodicy is, etymologically speaking, about *theos*, God, and *dikes*, justice. In Milton's terms in *Paradise Lost*, it's the question of how one justifies God's existence and ways to human beings, especially those who have done nothing to deserve the evil they endure. In a sense, it's the question of how one justifies the claim that God is good and all-knowing and all-powerful while acknowledging the evil and suffering that exist, and at the same time maintain theological cogency, existential respectability, and rational credence. Can one maintain God's good intent for the world, with the power and knowledge to carry it through in a world of pain, suffering, and evil, without doing damage to one's Christian identity, human solidarity, and ethical obligation of truth-telling to oneself, to one's community, and to the global human family? Max Weber talked about theodicy as the incongruity between destiny and merit. There's a "great gulf fixed"—in those biblical words describing the posthumous relationship between Lazarus, the poor beggar in life, now in heaven, and Dives, the rich man in life, now in hell—between what you get and what you believe you deserve.

So it seems to me that hip-hoppers, and hardcore rappers in particular, are trying to confront the discontinuity between destiny and merit, between social evil and the contention that God is good, a claim they hear from intellectuals and preachers like me. I think these hardcore rappers, and their fans, are attempting to negotiate the dominion of death and the sovereignty of suffering by rejecting its ultimate logic—of the utter finality of existence—and insist on an immortality of expression that is undiminished by physical displacement. The survival of a figure like Tupac through the creation and dissemination of an urban legend is a kind of resistance to the erasure of their lives from the text of temporality. This is why I think Tupac

Shakur is such a powerful figure who bears what literary critics term a literary future, since his seminal symbolic presence continually generates stories, images, citations, and sightings of his productive existence. Not only is his status as "posthumous" brought into serious question, but he is allowed, at minimum, to posthumously contest his erasure through the myriad expressions of work that continue to be issued.

Let me get myself in trouble here as the members of my church read this interview. There seems to be an uncomfortable proximity between the ideology of gangsta rap and the traditional theology of the black church. The gangsta rappers see themselves as being at the end of time and all the things that black Christian eschatology has suggested about the end of time, these brothers (predominantly) who see themselves as out of time . . .

They're feasting on the black eschaton and the black apocalypse . . .

There seems to be an interesting correlation to the Old Testament prophecy in Isaiah about the Messiah being despised and rejected, a man of sorrows and acquainted with grief and we knew him not . . .

"Surely he hath borne our griefs, and carried our sorrows . . . But he was wounded for our transgressions, he was bruised for our iniquities: the chastisement of our peace was upon him; and with his stripes we are healed." I mean, my God, you're absolutely right, there is a transgressive moment there. You read those last interviews with Tupac in *Vibe Magazine*, I believe, and he says, essentially, that if the church ever used half of the money it had to help society, it would be powerful. Or take his new album, *Makaveli: The 7 Day Killuminati Theory*, in which Tupac, or his alter ego Makaveli, hangs on the cross like Jesus, with the religious imagery unmistakably prominent, even though Makaveli disavows any blasphemous intention by stating on the disc's booklet, and I'm paraphrasing here, "In no way is this portrait an expression of disrespect for Jesus Christ." But he's nonetheless challenging the Christian faith in a wonderfully transgressive, disruptive, and subversive fashion that I think we need. He's also signifying on Niccolo Machiavelli's magnum opus, *The Prince*, in the subtitle of his album, and in his appropriation of the Italian political theorist's name, even if it is spelled colloquially.

Tupac/Makaveli is also signifying on the two sides of his nature. On the one hand, as Makaveli, and hence as the postmodern embodiment of *The Prince*, he's suggesting that one hold on to power and execute one's will by faking one's death, at least according to Machiavelli. At the same time, Tupac/Makaveli portrays himself as a victimized figure who's hanging on a cross.

I think that many of the eschatological insights of black religion are secularized in much of hardcore rap culture. They deal with what theologians like C. H. Dodd term realized eschatology. In Christian circles, realized eschatology is the doctrine through which theologians argue that the ultimate matters in life—death, hell, judgment, and the grave among them—have been manifest, have been realized, within time and not in a transcendent space beyond time. In biblical terms, there are two conceptions of time, *chronos* and *kairos*. Chronos is chronological time that extends forward and backward in linear fashion. Kairos is about the fullness of time—the resplendent, resonant sense of time replete with all the significations of eternity. Kairos is about time being pregnant. In that sense, hardcore rappers are invading chronological time with kairotic time. The irony of hardcore rappers' kairotic time, however, is that their sense of fullness and pregnancy has a great deal to do with death and with God's judgment. This is neatly summarized in Tupac's song, "Only God Can Judge Me," found on *All Eyez on Me*, the last album he released before his death. In fact, Tupac was obsessed with God: he constantly referenced the judgment, mercy, and forgiveness of the Creator.

In fact, some of the most hardcore rappers are more God intoxicated than some believers in religious circles, some of whom claim to be obsessed with God but who are in truth consumed with their worldly goods and status. To a remarkable degree, many hardcore rappers, as profane and as vulgar as they can be, are figures who by virtue of their meditations on fate, judgment, death, and God force us to contend with the ultimate truths and proclamations of the gospel. They are, in a sense, secular hermeneuts who through their work invite us to reflect on the kerygmatic content of religious identity, spiritual truth, prophetic articulation, and ecclesiastical assertion. We love to preach on Sunday mornings that if God ever came back, God wouldn't come back in a way that would be acceptable, but in an offensive fashion or persona. Well, what's more offensive than a hardcore rapper dealing with the edge of existence, with the limited experiences of life, who is constantly embodying uncomfortable, uncompromising truths about the damnable, and the damned? These hardcore rappers are relentlessly exposing what Roland Barthes calls the "what goes without saying," and also the things, I suppose, that Gramsci would call "common sense."

This is also where Stuart Hall, it seems to me, is very important. What these hardcore rappers are forcing us to do is to contest what Hall terms the "preferred meanings" and the "preferred readings" of a particular text or experience. The preferred readings of black theological tradition center in waiting until the end time when God will bring ultimate justice to the world, right the wrongs, and balance the books, so to speak. At the end of time, God is going to reveal God's self to God's followers, and true believers will be unified in perfect harmony and agreement with God's will. Well, that's a preferred reading that has invested in it the hopeful yet stoical meanings of black religious traditions that counsel discipline, forbearance, and Spartan relief from the satiety of life. But many hardcore rappers explode such notions by forcing us to deal with the end matters now. Hell and judgment are not realities that will come in the next life; they are present and concrete in this world, in this life, to which their rhetoric bears painful, powerful, sometimes tragic witness. I think they are troubling to many religious believers precisely because they are living at the outer perimeters of the eschaton in more powerful ways—and yes, more destructive ways, too—than the bearers of black religious traditions can even stomach, and, God knows, that's even more so for the wider American religious landscape.

Of course, I'm not trying to romanticize hardcore rappers as the unblemished carriers of the black eschaton in ways that are totally edifying. They certainly are contradictory, even profoundly flawed, but they also transmit vital messages. And that's not a combination, flawed but vital, that Christians are not used to. That's why the Apostle Paul uses an apt analogy to capture how the truths of God are entrusted to imperfect human beings when he says, "We have these treasures in earthen vessels." It seems to me that the black apocalypse and the black eschaton are being joined in a secularized form in black hardcore discourse in ways that are deeply troubling, especially to black Christians because they are ostensibly the ones who embody that tradition in its purity. I think these traditionalists, however, are at points being judged and shown up in relation to some of these rappers who, by comparison, are bringing the noise, so to speak, in more vivid if disturbing fashion. But that, too, is consonant with biblical tradition. "These are they," the book of Acts says, "who have turned the world upside down."

Hearing you talk about this, it occurs to me that gangsta rap, of all hip-hop culture, is most concerned with the confessional mode. My personal experience of the black Baptist church is that the confessional mode is disappearing. I think of all the subterfuge, all the things that go on beneath the surface, that no one talks about. We know who's sleeping with whom, who's doing what, but no one's speaking it or naming it.

That's a brilliant point. We've lost that sense of "I've sinned." We've lost that sense communicated in the book of Romans where it says, "For all have sinned and come short of the glory of God." And there's that Negro spiritual we sang in church that says, "Not my mother, not my father, but it's me, oh Lord, standing in the need of prayer." There was a greater sense, when such scriptures and songs were popular, that believers had done some things wrong and had to seek God's forgiveness. Now things have shifted noticeably. There is a hierarchy of black sacred rhetoric, with preaching at the top, followed by prayer, testimonials, and, only then, confession, that is, beyond formulaic, abstract prayers of confession. And testimonies are far more frequent than confessions. I'm not suggesting this is all bad—after all, confessions were sometimes driven by hegemonic patriarchal power, for instance, where the church forced women to stand up and confess they had sinned and were pregnant, reinforcing male supremacy in black religious face. On the other hand, true confession was driven by a self-critical scrutiny in the light of divine truth mediated by conscious reflection on God's word and ongoing revelation in one's life through events, thoughts, ideas and, yes, the words, especially the testimonies, of other believers.

Unfortunately, in today's black ecclesial order, testimony has been hijacked by commercialist theology. Now it's not simply about testifying about how God has been good to the believer, how God has brought one through trial and tribulation, or how God has allowed one to "get over," and I'm not speaking of the hustling sense. Now testimony in many black churches is occupied by a "name it and claim it" theology—where one affirms one's blessing, usually something material, and proclaims its realization through proleptic discourse—that values earthly goods. Now that's equally true in branches of hip-hop culture where material goods are prized and vigorously pursued. But at its best, hip-hop culture, including elements of hardcore, cultivate confession and testimony as critical narrative means to self-reflection and ethical critique of hip-hop's practices. These are secular confessions and testimonies, to be sure—except, of course, where rappers explicitly reference their religious beliefs, for instance, as a Muslim Five Percenter.

The hardcore rapper's confession and testimony is linked to acknowledging both the moral limits of their lives, since gangsta rappers are the first to confess their own sins, and to testifying about what got them over, often unapologetically evoking and embracing the hustler's rhetoric. What got them over could be a blunt, a woman, sex, a mother's love, a grandmother's remembrance, and so on. And it could be a connection to God. Snoop Doggy Dogg is a deeply religious person, and so was Tupac, but in nontraditional ways, in ways that disturb and transgress against our neatly ordered ecclesiastical lives where the site of religious performance—and for black Christians, it's the church building—is crucial. Since these hardcore rappers often operate outside the physical and philosophical boundaries of the church, maybe even its ontological limits, they are spurned as the "unsaved." But even Jesus said, in response to his disciples' desire to narrowly define the members of the kingdom, "I have sheep ye know not of." At its best, the church has always understood that its true life is beyond brick and mortar. It is constituted as the *ekklesia*, the church assembled, from *ekkalein*, to call forth or summon, which is about the people. Hence the church's identity is truly defined by the people, not the building. At its best, it moves beyond the architecture and geography of identity, since the church is not a noun but a verb. Many of the best, most insightful hardcore rappers comprehend that, and at our best, so does the black church.

You mentioned also the "name it, claim it" theology that seemed most prevalent in the '80s. That neo-charismatic theology seems to have changed the function and relationship of testifying and confessing in many black churches. Testifying seems still to occur, but in this theology it becomes a litany of material things given by God—

houses, cars, jobs, and so on. Perhaps true to prophecy, the church has become quite material and secular. And, as you say, this is not meant to romanticize the gangsta rappers, but they are at least honest about material aspirations.

Exactly, because these artists have their houses, Benz's, Lexus's, and Rolex's, but at least they're honest about it. Even as they're complicit in the capitalism that undermines their lives, they're at least going to tell the truth about such complicity. Elements of the church, however, are less honest about their bald pursuit of materialistic ends. In fact they give such pursuit theological foundations. In that sense, the church has become materialistic in the bad sense. As I argue in *Race Rules*, the Christian theologian and former Archbishop of Canterbury, William Temple, said that Christianity is the most material religion there is because we address the flesh, we deal with the body. We deal with what it means for God to transgress against what Paul Tillich calls the *apos sigeis*—the eternal silence, the barrier—to come down and to become a human being, to become vulnerable to mortality and finitude, to become what Gardner Taylor calls "death eligible" as he references actuarial tables. God in Jesus became subject to death, betokening God's radical identification with the human condition. Of course, Christians believe that God in Jesus conquered death, too. In one sense, it's like believing, for example, that the world is infected with AIDS and God says, "I'll get AIDS in order to die and show you that you can live again, to show you that you can survive and that those stigmas associated with the disease will be burned in the crucible of my suffering, and that your burdens will be transformed, even lifted, by my sacrifice."

In some significant ways, elements of the black church have lost such a line of theological interpretation, or at least it has been subordinated to more material and self-aggrandizing themes. That's especially true of the "name it and claim it" theologies found in one form or another in "Word churches," so named because they place a premium on expositing and strictly adhering to "the Word"—exhibiting a variety of biblical literalism, maybe even bibliolatry. Current varieties of Word theology are in fact the resurfacing of earlier trends in twentieth-century theological materialism, termed the gospel of health and wealth, that emerged during the '20s, '30s, and '40s, and which influenced white and black preachers. There's a recirculation in black religious circles of the Christianization of material wealth. I think one explanation for it is the attempt of new members of the black middle class to negotiate their recent access to the upper echelons of income by lending their upward mobility theological justification. The black nouveau riche has to find a way to legitimate its climb to higher status without feeling guilty, or responsible, for those left behind. As a result, we get a *materialistic*, not a *material* religion. Contrary to the materialistic religion I've just described, a material religion is one that takes seriously notions of the Incarnation, of God becoming flesh, and of black finitude and the black eschaton, including the realities of disease, suffering, pain, death, and so on. But materialistic religion capitulates to gross economistic interpretations of the faith and attempts to baptize financial pursuits as the summum bonum of Christian existence, spurning our obligations to the poor and to analyzing and opposing ideologies and political practices that reproduce economic inequality.

To give it more historical perspective, can you talk more about the relationship this bears to Daddy Grace, and perhaps Father Divine . . .

. . . And even Harry Emerson Fosdick was temporarily ensnared in the trap of the gospel of health and wealth, which suffered, I believe, from a reductive relationship between health, material success, and faith. What you get with such a theological perspective is that ordinary believers, especially those who are poor because of structural inequality and social injustice, think that there's something wrong with them, that the moral defect lies in their failure to believe or behave correctly, and not in flawed public policies or political systems. This gospel of health and wealth is, in one sense, a playing out of one of Elisabeth Kübler-Ross's stages of death and dying, where you bargain with God before you accept death. Materialistic theology is almost like that; it's the attempt to deal with the dark night of the soul that can result from material deprivation and financial misery by trying to negotiate with the economic forces of the universe, which in the view of such a theology are controlled by God. I think the Word churches and the gospel of health and wealth and theological materialism is a way of negotiating with God about the economic and material limits of one's life. What happens is that those who get blessed feel that they've somehow been saved from the economic hell to which others have been consigned. I think we have to acknowledge that Daddy Grace, Father Divine, Harry Emerson Fosdick, and a host of others were caught up in the gospel of health and wealth in the early to middle parts of the twentieth century, and that it was a precursor to the theological materialism we're now witnessing in many religious circles, including significant pockets of black Christianity.

Having grown up deeply immersed, and still so, in the culture of the black Baptist church, I am convinced that there's some interesting racial component to this "name it, claim it" theology. Much of the new approach to black Christian charisma seems to have derived its impulse from the white televangelists who only recently discovered charisma—the Bakkers, Swaggarts, and so on. And all of a sudden, it seems, black Baptist churches rediscovered charisma.

This speaks to the kind of ideological apparatuses through which black culture is filtered and interpreted. This is an extreme example, I think, of appropriation and expropriation of blackness by whites and its reappropriation by blacks. Not only is it an indictment of how black people are taught to be what they used to be by whites who ripped it off or borrowed it from blacks to begin with; but it's a reflection of the severely limited control we exercise over the identities, resources, ideas, and beliefs that we produce within our culture that are stigmatized when identified with us, but sanitized when adapted to the mainstream. When our culture is given a white face, it gains a legitimacy that we seemingly discover for the first time when we see it reflected back to us in new skin and garb. In truth, it's about discerning the anatomy of our own culture baptized and bleached in the "curing" pools of whiteness. The bottom line is it's about *rediscovering* black culture under such circumstances. We're like Columbus—discovering something that's already been discovered. But it's doubly tragic in this case, since we created what's being discovered again. This is a case of what Fred Jameson would probably argue as the underside of the postmodernist moment: historical amnesia joined to narrative corruption, since the story of black origins is manipulated and distorted, underwritten by capitalism and the material subversion of African American cultural forms.

The result, I think, is minstrelsy of, and in, black culture. Minstrelsy is in large part about the commodification of black culture to further the telos of white capital and artistic achievement, literally at the expense of black faces. Of course, such minstrelsy is practiced among blacks as a recirculation of black identity once removed, an adaptation of alienated blackness for survival or career—think of *Amos & Andy* and other blackface black performers. So we end up with a caked black reality: black on white on black. The cake on the black face ultimately points to the masks of black culture, after the fashion noted by Frantz Fanon and Paul Laurence Dunbar, and also by the hip-hop group the *Fugees*, who rap: "M to the A to the S to the K, we all wear the mask." The reality is that we are constantly negotiating between and behind these masks to figure out how we represent ourselves, since the bottom line is surely about the politics of representation, and in the case of white televangelists, about how the televisual apparatus changes the ideological forms and theological messages of black religious identity.

And I think that you're right about the Jimmy Swaggarts of the world who blend black and white southern evangelical rhetorical styles—the fiery preaching and the powerful moments of religious ecstasy—and transmute them in white apostolic settings where they make millions of dollars off of elements that when associated with blacks have been largely demonized. Black folk have been told that our religious rituals have expressed emotional compensation and catharsis because we were symbolically combating oppression. Because we couldn't beat up the white man, we were jumping pews, being ecstatic, speaking in tongues, and evincing an overwrought physicality in our worship. Then we turn the tube on and here are these white folk deploying black styles to make millions of dollars talking about religious renewal and revival. Beyond that, the Kenneth Hagins and Kenneth Copelands and the so-called white Word churches remove attribution for the black religious sensibilities that hug their Pentecostal roots, only to feed them back to black people through the ideological apparatuses of evangelical conservatism, whose political effects are often disastrous for black communities. That's really messed up.

This brings Fred Price to my mind. When I hear him tell his story of how he was a black Baptist minister who was burdened by poverty and sickness until he discovered his current theology. So there's this rupture in how he reads things, so to speak. As black as the community of the Crenshaw Christian Center is, he erases the sense of race and culture in this theology.

The price of admission to the gospel of health and wealth, in this case, is the erasure of the racial marks and the ethnic identities that have nurtured and sustained black people for a long time. As I've said, roots are for nurturing, not for strangling. Still, we must feed from them in healthy ways, in ways that respect the integrity of the people produced by them. And I think one of the great disservices of the Word churches is that they for the most part destroy those racial roots and then extricate those black traditional meanings from their original contexts. The racial rhetoric is neutered, so to speak. Some might argue that, in a sense, these Word church ministers are like DJ's, in that they experiment with and recode the musical forms they inherit on wax. True. But the manner in which such Word church ministers recode black religious forms is deeply problematic because it obscures any continuity between ancient biblical worldviews and black traditions of struggle and faith.

However, it seems to me that where the racial rhetoric isn't neutered has to do with poverty and pathologies. I remember a student saying something to the effect that Michael Jordan wasn't really black because he wasn't giving back to "the community." And, of course, by black community—which everyone speaks of as though there were one monolithic black community—the implication is poverty, drugs, crime, and any number of other pathologies. So, if in the religious rhetoric you lose all the racial rhetoric, except for that connected to black pathology, you leave poor black communities in a position where the black church no longer speaks to them, to the body. In a sense, poverty becomes a pathology and a sin.

Yes, we begin to pathologize ourselves. V. Y. Mudimbe talks more specifically about the pathologization of the urban, and part of pathologizing the urban is inextricably tied up with black bodies, which in turn are pathologized because they are so closely identified with the urban. It's *petitio principii* (taking for granted that which has not been proved) in social theorizing about black folk, where the vicious circularity of the argument catches us in both directions. What happens is that theology begins to justify the pathologization of the urban by talking of the moral quandaries of black people in a vacuum, without paying sufficient attention to the structural features that shape their lives. It has little to say about political practices, public policies, and social mechanisms that harm black life, which is qualitatively different from blaming black urban dwellers, especially the poor, for their own problems. But you're absolutely right: the theological emphasis on a radically atomistic individualism underplays such a liberating theological reading of the condition of the poor. Further, the Word churches discourage the ethical assertiveness of the poor, who might defiantly argue, "We may be poor but we're blessed by God, and we're still human beings." Whereas in so much of the theological materialism that overruns the Word churches, there's the contention that if you're poor, you're damned by God. And that leaves an incredible ideological and rhetorical vacuum for the propagation of all kinds of materialisms, both from the Word church and from the quarters of hip-hop culture.

This seems to be different from Cornel West's conception of black nihilism. It seems to explain how certain behaviors and institutions can come about without finally and completely blaming the very people who are the victims of these behaviors, yet it allows for a sense of the complicitness. This creates a space in which we can understand how a group of people can arrive in a culture and appear to be morally strange. If, for instance, we get completely locked within the black church or the black middle class and the accompanying materialism, and participate in this strange metamorphosis of black theology and social thought, then we become mutually responsible for these people who look so morally strange to us.

This is why I came up with the notion of "juvenocracy," which seeks to explain the shift in the balance of power in postindustrial black communities from the older to the younger generations. But my explanation doesn't rest on maintaining the moral estrangement of our youth from earlier ethical traditions. These youth are not Frankensteins. After all, Frankenstein was the name of the doctor, not the monster. We make these youth appear to be the moral monsters when in reality it's the doctor that needs to be implicated for creating them. We want to monsterize our children, and not the doctors, social engineers, politicians, and even elements of the black bourgeoisie who are complicit in stigmatizing and demonizing our youth.

At this point, things take on a very personal cast for me. I am still deeply committed to and involved in the black church. I do, however, make a point of wearing a certain rhetoric of resistance. Often I will not adhere to the unspoken dress code. I wear my hair in dreads and hope that this resistance effects some change. A few weeks ago a younger brother with dreads also joined.

Creating space already. It reminds me of Marvin Gaye saying "everybody thinks we're wrong, but who are they to judge us, simply because our hair is too long." I had a level of bravery and transgression against the church when I was about fourteen or fifteen years old. I'd go to church in blue jeans and an old sweatshirt without combing my hair. I was mad at the bourgeois captivity of the black Baptist tradition. I was waging an aesthetic fight on a rhetorical battlefield, if you will. The visual aesthetic was in terms of what I wore, but the rhetorical battlefield was composed of my statements and views about the insufficiency of traditional black bourgeois dress, or even working-class and working-poor dress, that *dressed up* the realities of black life as opposed to exposing them. So, being a working-class poor kid anyway, it was about me saying through my dress, "pay attention to this other side that you're keeping out." It was about keeping the authentically liberating character of the church from finding expression, that is, reaching out to the poor and the dispossessed. We talk a good game, but living it is altogether a different thing. As the saying goes, we can talk the talk, but we can't walk the walk.

Your story makes me think of my Baptist parents, whom I love dearly and who raised me right. I was thirty years old when I got my ear pierced, but whenever I would go home and go to my parents' church, my mother would ask me to take the earring out as a sign of respect to my father.

There's an old joke that asks: Why don't Baptists have sex standing up? Because someone might think they're dancing. There's this arbitrary sin system that we've established here that says you can't do this and you can't do that. Yet we're doing all kinds of stuff that we know is out of bounds and unquestionably sinful. And if we would be honest about it, we could talk about how complex our real theologies our. Not our written ones, but our lived ones. That would make a great difference in terms of our deeper understanding of sin. But we're heavy on the symbols of sin—the earring, the dreads, the suit, and the demeanor. We're focused on communicating our respect through a system of symbols, precisely because those symbols have been among the major reasons we have been attacked in dominant white culture. So we express our resistance and signify our respect for one another through that same system of symbols. It is painful and quite understandable at the same time.

Interview by Jonathan Smith
St. Louis, Missouri, 1996

16

The Anatomy of Radical Christianity

Tracing Martin Luther King Jr.'s Dangerous Legacy

In an era in which African American icons like Muhammad Ali are capriciously resurrected and "fashioned to deflect our fears and fulfill our fantasies . . . [to] cheer us up more than they challenge or change us," Michael Eric Dyson's *I May Not Get There with You* offers a candid, refreshing, and stirring portrait of civil rights leader Martin Luther King Jr.

In this "work of biocriticism," Dyson, a professor at DePaul University who has taught at several U.S. campuses, casts a critical eye at King, his legacy, and the often disturbing attempts of liberals and conservatives to pillage and harness the leader's moral capital for various political ends. Dyson sets out to both rescue King's memory from romantic adulation and politically motivated character assassination and to show that the civil rights leader was "a sublime mix of the profound and the profane."

At the heart of Dyson's revisionist view is the argument that King, toward the end of his life, experienced a dramatic transformation and went from "liberal reformer" to "radical revisionist," a "change of heart and mind" often overlooked by liberals and conservatives alike. The "cultural amnesia" that has selectively interpreted and exploited King's legacy, Dyson argues, is a symptom of America's "politics of racial evasion," a tendency to study and explore racial history but "minimize its effects," shifting responsibility from whites to blacks or presenting blacks as equally culpable in racial injustice.

Readers will undoubtedly be taken aback by Dyson's claim that King was deeply influenced by Marxism (Dyson quotes the distinguished Marxist historian, C. L. R. James, who describes King's ideas as "fundamentally Marxist-Leninist"), and that by 1968 he had become disenchanted with liberalism and committed to "democratic socialism." But Dyson fully supports his contention, offering a compelling account of King's exposure to black economic misery in the rural South and in northern ghettoes, his repeated appeals to whites' consciences, and gradual turn toward the belief that "most Americans are unconscious racists."

Dyson describes how King's beliefs about the inherent goodness of whites began to change precisely when the media and the political establishment "suddenly crowned [him] the Negro of choice," a leader whose conciliatory views and philosophy of nonviolence made him a welcome alternative to the firebrand militancy of Malcolm X and Stokeley Carmichael. King, however, shunned mainstream acceptance as he began to identify with the poor black (and even white) masses, and denounced President Lyndon Johnson's Vietnam policy, arguing that war, poverty, and racism ("the triplets of social misery") were inextricably linked.

Distilling evidence from dozens of letters, speeches, and sermons, Dyson vividly illustrates King's newfound radicalism and his belief that the U.S. government owed compensation to African Americans. This was the King who accused northern whites of "psychological and spiritual genocide" and said, "I'm tired of marching for something that should have been mine at birth."

Dyson has been criticized for his frank treatment of King's sexual malfeasance and academic plagiarism ("intellectual thievery," as Dyson puts it) and his complaints that the King estate has commercialized King's memory and attempted to control research and scholarship about the leader's life. But, however controversial his observations, Dyson has produced a nuanced, critical, and provocative book that successfully underscores King's ethic of love and justice, exhorting us to heed the leader's call for moral regeneration and profound social change. As the revolutionary civil rights leader so unforgettably prophesied, "The whirlwinds of revolt will continue to shake the foundations of our nation until the bright day of justice emerges."

The subtitle to your book I May Not Get There with You *is* The True Martin Luther King Jr. *In the introduction you say your goal is to rescue the legacy of Martin Luther King from both liberals and conservatives. You say liberals don't fully appreciate how King's legacy challenges many liberal racial remedies and goals, and conservatives such as Ward Connerly use King to undermine progressive politics and black interests. Could you elaborate on this point?*

King has been used as a convenient political football by conservatives and liberals alike, both of whom attempt to undermine his most radical threat to the status quo. The liberal status quo was threatened by King precisely because he was willing toward the end of his life to embrace a much more aggressive critique of the pathology of liberals' denial of their complicity in white supremacy—and that liberal denial was rooted in a presumption of conscientious one-upmanship over conservatives. It was also rooted in a kind of implicit self-righteousness in regard to race vis-à-vis the conservatives—"We're not the redneck racists, the corn-fed crackers from the South, so therefore we are superior morally to those folks."

King challenged that liberal status quo by forcing it to come to grips with its own inherent racism—inherent in that its own white supremacist legacy was masked as an equally intriguing sort of racial détente. They (the liberals) were believing that they had somehow tackled the issue and had moved forward. Racial remedies for the most part involved correcting the pathologies of white racists, who were the conservatives from the South, but not in confronting their racism, their white-skinned privilege, and their inability to understand how they were, as King said toward the end of his life, "unconscious racists."

The conservatives, on the other hand, have used King's image in ways that are quite destructive. Ward Connerly and his ilk have seized ingeniously on King's interpretive capital, making tremendously fertile use of King's words in distorted contexts. They have ripped his words from their original and, most importantly, their political and social contexts, and applied his words in far different social and political waters. And that means that King's words have been boiled down from their tremendous challenge to conservative ideology and to the sorts of ideas and beliefs and behaviors that conservatives have championed, including self-help strategies that mask an attempt to avoid structural critiques and the like. So King's critique has been ingeniously coopted by Ward Connerly to make King eventually say things he didn't say and to mean things he didn't really mean. And that kind of rhetorical legerdemain has redounded on conservatives. That metaphoric sleight of hand, to switch metaphors, has really ricocheted off of King's original intent, deflected as it has been by conservatives' ingenious manipulation of those words, and has ended up messing up a whole lot of people's understanding of who King really was.

I think liberals and conservatives alike have to confront King's radical legacy, which is about challenging the status quo and forcing all Americans to come to grips with their own racism, their own unconscious and conscious behaviors that contradict an ethic of love and consideration of the "other." And, finally, both liberals and conservatives have sought to avoid the more radical threat that King represented—that is, he was bringin' da noise, so to speak, on the heads of both the people who were the friends of the civil rights movement and those who deemed themselves to be its opponents.

Recently we have seen quite a bit of the resurrection and selective reconstruction of black icons. Arguably the same thing that was done to King was done to Muhammad Ali. Is this what you refer to as "cultural amnesia" in your book?

Muhammad Ali's fisticuffs, his brash discourse, his braggadocio, his rhetorical rebellion have been appropriated by the contemporary generation as a symptom of black style, black machismo, black male rhetorical rebellion, to be sure, but mostly [as] a kind of politics of style that is denuded of and deprived of and shorn of its intense political meanings. So that now we see a figure such as Muhammad Ali reduced virtually to inarticulate groans and moans, although his mind is still sharp. He is seen as the carrier of the Olympic torch, and hence we are easily able, simultaneously, to forget or erase the fierce verbal torch he brought to bear on the premises of white supremacy, and to overlook the aggressive fiery speech and behavior that he used to undermine the presuppositions of white superiority and black bourgeois capitulation to the white status quo. Muhammad Ali has been similarly appropriated, commodified, and emptied of his political meanings in deference to this kind of valorization of the politics of style. And that is deeply problematic and unfortunate.

Martin Luther King has been used in the same way, and Malcolm X, too, for that matter, as signifiers of black rebellion while their complex, contradictory, and conflicting ideas, identities, and images have been watered down or reduced to a simplistic sign—of black men who spoke well, who articulated well, who were either full of rage or compassion or love. In contemporary life, our rush to embrace them is a symptom of our hunger to reproduce these black icons' style without confronting the serious political times they weathered or the political legacies they have left behind. Neither do we want to confront the hard ideas that they put forth, ideas of justice, truth, love, self-sacrifice, and, in Muhammad Ali's case, especially, giving up one's own career for the sake of the movement and of the people. So there's been a rather easy reproduction of these icons for the purposes of commodity fetishism, so to speak, and there has been great fascination with them in the larger culture. We can say the same thing about the reproduction of cultural icons like Shaft, so that Samuel Jackson's and John Singleton's updating of the Shaft icon is an attempt to put a black fingerprint on a '70s black icon for contemporary aesthetic purposes.

You argue that the liberal mainstream's tendency to overly focus on King's "I Have a Dream" speech has obscured the dramatic change of heart that King underwent toward the end of his life, when he became more radical and more anti-imperialist, and demanded reparations for African Americans. King, you contend, spoke out against "the triplets of misery: racism, militarism, and poverty." Black leaders are so often pigeonholed into only talking about race, but King seems to have had a broad and international vision of radicalism and progressivism.

No doubt. Martin Luther King was one of the most progressive figures not only of his time but also in the history of American political activity. He was a figure who did the hard work of translating progressive ideas into social behavior and political practices that really trumped the ability of America to totally control and dominate the lives of poor and marginalized peoples, and that's a whole lot.

He dealt with the racial realpolitik he confronted, and from there extracted his political principles of progressivism by trying to have a good degree of fit between the ideals he nurtured, and that nourished him, and the political situation he confronted. A lot of people have great and progressive and radical ideas that never get translated into political activity. King, then, was one of the most successful progressives in American political history, and even C. L. R. James, as I say in my book, acknowledged that King was as progressive as anybody could be on the left. And all those purists who nurture fantasies of rebellion in orthodox, crude, and pure fashion miss the genius and complexity of Martin Luther King's lived radicalism.

Martin Luther King Jr. had an international vision that linked local forms of suffering with global forms of corruption and oppression, and that allowed him a very powerful critique of American practices when he refused simply to be a nationalist. In an era when King came to maturity—an era of American exceptionalism and American isolationism—King shattered the prism through which America viewed itself as a world power and linked its own global expansion to forces of oppression that made it a bully. He made America confront its own bully status—that's what he did with Vietnam. He said, "We are criminals in that war, and we have committed more war crimes than any other nation, and I will continue to say it."

That kind of radical resistance to the American status quo and to America's self-identity and self-conception was radically threatening, in a way that proved ultimately, I think, harmful to King himself, maybe even leading to his death. His broad, catholic social vision linked issues of economic misery and social suffering of American blacks to blacks in South Africa, to brothers and sisters dying on Asian soil. And he also saw the connection between American domestic practices and American foreign practices and the suffering of poor people globally, people from the so-called Third World. Martin Luther King was insistent on connecting, as Malcolm X and Frantz Fanon brilliantly did, what was going on here to what was going on abroad, and saw the vicious consequences of colonialism and tried to resist them as powerfully as he could.

Ultimately, because black leaders have been pigeonholed and cornered, King's vision was marginalized in deference to his viewpoints on race. Ironically, King was told as a black leader he should only speak about black leadership and the problems of black America, although his white critics felt no similar compunction to restrict their viewpoints, visions, and verbal practices to what they knew best—which was American imperialism and the expansion of global capitalism and the containment of black folk. But they felt quite capable of speaking about what they wanted to talk about. King, despite having a Nobel Prize and a Ph.D. in philosophical theology from Boston University, was deemed incapable of making major moral and foreign policy pronouncements because of his lack of expertise. So this is the dilemma of black leadership: on the one hand, if it speaks out against, or for, American practices that have nothing to do with race, it is often castigated or pushed aside as being incapable of making such pronouncements. On the other hand, if they push the race agenda aggressively, they are viewed as parochial, provincial, and narrow, and incapable of busting out beyond the narrow confines of the racial ghetto. So King faced that dilemma with exemplary bravery and courage, by refusing to be restricted and making his pronouncements as loudly and prophetically as he did.

In your book, you have a very interesting quote from Coretta Scott King, who says Malcolm X came down to Selma, Alabama, in 1965, when King was in prison, and told her, "I want Dr. King to know that I didn't come to Selma to make his job difficult. I really did come thinking that I could make it easier. If the white people realize what the alternative is, perhaps they will be more willing to hear Dr. King." I knew King became more attractive to the establishment when X rose to prominence, but I didn't know the two leaders were consciously playing off each other.

Playing off each other consciously, if not strategically. And even if they weren't in cahoots, so to speak, they understood their own bailiwick and understood how each contributed ultimately to the American equation of racial justice. I think Malcolm X was much more conscious of the need to present an alternative to King on the radical fringe, so that his own activity, although principled and committed to the ideal of black freedom, also was a strategic strike against America's refusal to listen to King. He presented this alternative by saying, "I'm the crazy nigga on the fringe" who, if King was not listened to, would become the acceptable leader of black America. Malcolm attempted to force white America in that light to consider King's relatively moderate appeals and to see how sensible and logical King turned out to be. Malcolm ingeniously and quite correctly diagnosed the problem to be that America could not take King unless there was another threat out there of a more radical black leadership, so to speak, a more visibly militant leadership—because in the end, King was much more militant than Malcolm—that would threaten American race relations in the eyes of the white majority. King then was presented in such a scenario as the acceptable and desirable black alternative within the politics of black leadership.

You also say that Malcolm X was a hypocrite in calling Martin Luther King an "Uncle Tom," a chump, and "Reverend Dr. Chickenwing."

You know, when you're in a position of the minority within a minority, and you don't have the levers of the media working as smoothly as King did, as the civil rights movement did, then you use what's at hand, a kind of ideological bricolage. You seize the political authority or the interpretive authority that you can through the media by turning political spectacle into racial advantage, or at least racial spectacle into political advantage. And Malcolm X did that. So he called names like some black nationalists were wont to do and talked about King mercilessly in many instances, which is why, by the way, with the exception of their meeting at the Capitol for the Senate debate about the civil rights bill, they never met. Malcolm constantly reached out to King, but King was loath to meet one-on-one with Malcolm, and not only because of his ideological disagreements with Malcolm. I think in a one-on-one debate, King would have been witheringly assaulted by Malcolm's rapid-fire rhetoric. King was a much more slow and deliberate speaker, though brilliant, but Malcolm X had mastered the brilliant mechanics of public rhetoric and articulate debate, and he would have assaulted King with a verbal volley that would have made him look foolish. So King avoided him for these reasons.

But Malcolm X was quite hypocritical to stand in the black bosom of Harlem casting aspersions on King's strikes against white supremacy in Birmingham without loading up a bus of three or four hundred Black Muslim Fruit of Islam warriors and going to where the action was. You see, the action was not in Harlem; it was in Birmingham. So if you're going to talk *bad*, deliver the goods at the site of struggle, at the scene of conflict. And whatever one may say about King's strategies and tactics and his commitment to the philosophy of nonviolence, he lived that commitment on the front line and he bore the burdens of his words by allowing his flesh to be assaulted, to be attacked. Young black boys and girls were beat up on, the flesh of black people was attacked by police dogs, they were washed against the wall by vicious fire hoses unleashed on them in a tirade of unmitigated hatred by Bull Connor and his hooligans, who masqueraded as police officers. The reality is that Martin Luther King put his body where his mouth was. Although common wisdom says Malcolm X wanted to do so but was prohibited by Elijah Muhammad, he had disobeyed Mr. Muhammad on many other occasions, why not now when it really counted and the ultimate stakes were hanging in the balance?

So, I think, in that sense he [X] was hypocritical to attack King because King's ability to be brave and courageous in the face of white supremacy by putting his body on the line more than matched the ingenious aggression and edifying rage that Malcolm's words signified to black America. I think Martin Luther King Jr. was a courageous and brave man who in the ultimate sense was more militant because, like Samson, he went into the temple and pulled it down from the inside. And though one might argue that the edifice fell partly on him and destroyed him, the reality is that King was more effective because he got inside the edifice of American democracy, the edifice of white supremacy, inside the edifice of American moral hypocrisy, and revealed to America the basis of its own fundamental contradictions between its speech and its practices. He made it change in a fundamental sense, and I think that more than any other figure, he is responsible for the success that black America enjoys today.

You say King understood black nationalism and eventually embraced "an enlightened black nationalism" after going to Chicago and experiencing the vicious racism of the northern ghetto. It was after experiencing northern racism that he became more radical and said, "Maybe America should move toward a democratic socialism." How and why did northern racism have such an impact on King?

As the cliché and the received wisdom goes, it [racism] was much more open and bold-faced in the South than it was in the North. Southern racism's tyranny was evident. The terror of its racial practices went virtually unmasked, despite the accretion of southern rituals of civility, whereby white southerners maintained civil relations with black people, since public etiquette demanded a certain kind of facade that belied the terror that lay beneath. King, having grown up on that southern terrain, was a master at trying to deconstruct all that madness and getting inside the heart of white supremacy by comprehending its ultimate logic, though it was contradictory. He confronted it by comprehending it. And so King understood that mélange of rituals and practices and behaviors that, to people outside of that terrain, looks like sheer stupidity and outright hypocrisy. King understood the southern soul and understood what it was after, even as it paraded its own weaknesses and its own blindness, if you will, in broad daylight.

The North, on the other hand, was much more subtle. Northern whites thought they were much more progressive and sophisticated than southern whites. Yet at the heart of the urban contract with black people was an enormously problematic presumption: as long as blacks stayed in their place, they would do fine. Once they began to bleed beyond those restrictions, whether it was in real estate or physically in terms of the geography of the city, or whether they were trying to get uppity by getting too many jobs in the wrong arena—the professional arena—and challenging white hegemony there, then they wouldn't be all right. So there was a much more powerful, implicit racism—what Stuart Hall calls "inferential racism"—in the North than there was in the South. The South was ensconced in the *ugly evident*. The ugly evident, or the obvious racism of the South, marched against the inconspicuous evil of the North.

So there were two different terrains, two different battlefields. When King came up north, he not only discovered that the recalcitrance of white folk in Chicago or in Cicero was far greater than what went on in the South, but he also discovered that black people were much less inclined to fight for their rights in a fundamental sense than were their southern counterparts. King understood the psychic bruising and battles in the North that had stymied its progress and even stagnated its own push for real freedom in ways the black South had been forced to do. As a result, the white South had been forced to confront its racism as openly and as directly as the black South had. Ironically, the "behind" and "backward" South proved to be in front of the enlightened North. King understood that when he got to Chicago and Cleveland. He also began to understand how difficult it was to use southern strategies for northern racism. He got beat up on pretty badly by a mayor like Richard Daley who simply outwitted him because he understood the terrain in a more fundamental sense than King did. So I think that the vicious racism of the North, and the people who practiced it, proved to be much more wily, much more tricky, and much more deceptive than the buffoons like Bull Connor whose racism got the best of them.

You say that black youth a few years ago "embraced Malcolm X as a griot, but King, with his successes and failures, may be the spiritual father of the hip-hop generation." You say King has as much in common with Tupac Shakur as he does with Reverend Ralph Abernathy. How is Martin Luther King like Tupac?

I'm using King and Tupac as figureheads, as honorary heads of their respective generations, viewpoints, and philosophies. When I compare King and Tupac, I'm suggesting that there was much more in common between the civil rights generation and the hip-hop generation than we heretofore have acknowledged. But Martin Luther King did have some similar characteristics with Tupac. And that doesn't mean, however, that King and Tupac were twins, and it doesn't mean that Tupac Shakur had the moral genius or the rhetorical capacity of King to make social change. Nor does it mean that they were morally equivalent or philosophically committed to the same ideals or principles. That's ridiculous.

I know that King is not Tupac, but having said that, Tupac doesn't have to be Martin Luther King to be accepted, struggled with, and to be viewed as a worthy bearer of good news for young black people—even though it's contradictory that, on the one hand, he applauded black women and, on the other hand, he embraced vicious misogyny to make his point. He was a complex figure, and I'm paraphrasing: "You ought to be full of rage at the principles of racism and classism that make you poor, you ought to stand up against forces that make you poor, you ought to stand up against forces that beat up on you, like police brutality." For example, Tupac realized that after he was subject to police brutality, he was underwriting it: "So we payin' the pigs to knock the blacks out."

Well, you ain't got to be involved in Marxism 101 to understand that that's an astute analysis of the subsidization of our own oppression. Tupac understood that the tax base of [black] America was helping support the very policemen who were not protecting us, and that's a very sharp point that many people overlook. They simply see Tupac as a young man who went astray and got put in jail because of a rape charge (even though he was charged with one count of "forcibly touching the buttocks") and don't see the complex life he led outside of that. Even when he gave in to his worst side, there was more than enough evidence that here was a highly intelligent and gifted figure who was capable, at his best, of articulating the claims of rage, anger, and invisibility, or hypervisibility, from which young black men and women suffered.

Martin Luther King Jr. in his own time exposed to white America, and to some sections of black America, the rage that black America faced. He also tried to explain his understanding of how America's racial politics were fiercely harming young black people. Malcolm X had more ingeniously articulated the principles of black rage in a fashion that was enormously attractive to black youth, but Martin Luther King caught on later. And this is why, again, Martin Luther King began to promote an enlightened vision of black nationalism. He never succumbed to tribal loyalties that subverted the principles of fundamental equality and democracy for the citizenry of America. But he did embrace the need for black people to organize themselves for the purposes of black upward political and economic mobility, and not in a selfish way, but in a fashion that would enhance the collective standing of the race. So Martin Luther King ingeniously tapped into some of that rage and some of the angst that young black Americans felt.

What I mean by comparing Tupac and Martin Luther King—no disrespect to Dr. King—is to suggest that many people overlook the same faults that King had in common with Tupac to announce King's genius, while refusing to see in Tupac some of the same characteristics that King evidenced—the ability to speak truth to power and to represent an entire generation's anxieties about the erosion of certain rights. They didn't do it in the same way, since Martin Luther King had much more training and much more rhetorical genius and political power in fighting the battle for black America. But that is no slight to Tupac—times have changed. Martin Luther King couldn't be Martin Luther King today because the political demands for representation have been shifted, partially at least, into the cultural realm. So politics is not simply about electoral votes and nonparliamentary pressures put by prophetic figures on existing politicians. It is also about the articulation of black rage in a cultural sphere. It's about hip-hop's expression of rebellion against black bourgeois capitulation to the status quo and its surrender of a prophetic voice. And I think Tupac represents that in a very powerful and direct fashion.

Speaking of politicians and politics, in discussing Martin Luther King's sexual indiscretions, you mention President Clinton. You're very harsh on President Clinton, referring to his "destructive racial politics," "racial bad faith," and "evil political genius."

Many people, from Chris Rock to Toni Morrison, who claim that Bill Clinton is the first black president, that here is a figure who has been metaphorically "black-faced," certainly have a point. His red neck and red skin have been dipped into the demonizing pools of blackness and he has reemerged as an icon and a substitute representative of metaphorical blackness. Ain't nobody gon' deny that. On the other hand, it is just that facility with black America that Bill Clinton has evinced over the years, one that has made black people love him, that has also allowed him to be so manipulative. When Clinton signed the crime bill, when he signed the welfare reform bill, that was more than an implicit attack on blacks, it was a direct attack on very vulnerable regions of black America, including the working poor and the permanently poor. Even though a blue-ribbon panel he commissioned on the subject of crime urged him to politically oppose the disparity in sentencing for cocaine abuses—the mostly white figures who abuse $10,000 of powdered cocaine who got the same sentences as a black or Latino person who might abuse $25 of crack cocaine—he demurred, with the justification that crack cocaine was much more addictive and therefore much more lethal for black Americans than powdered cocaine. But that ultimately didn't stand up.

The reality is that the disparity in sentencing led to many more black people being locked up and stigmatized and tracked in the criminal justice system, many of whom ultimately had their voting privileges removed from them, so that, effectively, their citizenship was simultaneously curtailed. And then with recent reports that many more black and Latino youth are more likely to be locked up, or to be jailed, or to be viewed as suspicious, than their white counterparts, means that we're basically warehousing and incarcerating a huge segment of the younger generation, and taking them, from their early teens on, from the school grounds to the prison yard. And Bill Clinton's policy aided and abetted that process in a vicious and destructive fashion.

Furthermore, I think Bill Clinton has played both ends against the middle, so to speak. When it's to his advantage to signify to white suburbia, as he did in his first campaign, that he is with them, he will in a minute cut loose his black loyalty in deference to white solidarity. And he did that by going to Jesse Jackson's Rainbow Coalition and beating up on Sista Souljah, while striking against Jesse Jackson and embracing conservative and fearful white suburbia. It was an ingenious move, an evilly ingenious move, and that is destructive of the very racial politics that he wants to see rehabilitated in America. So I stand by my rather harsh but just criticism of our first "black president."

In your conclusion, you discuss the Rosa Parks/Outkast controversy, in which Parks sued the group for naming a song after her, and say the incident should be used to establish dialogue between the hip-hop generation and the civil rights generation. You address the "neo-separatism" and "self-segregationism" that has emerged in the hip-hop generation, and how that flies in the face of the civil rights generation's integrationism. How do you explain the rise of "neo-separatism" and the appeal of Louis Farrakhan?

A couple of things are paramount to such an explanation. First is the failure of the liberal remedies that have been embraced by black political leadership to really help the working poor and the black poor. That's an important failure, since a large segment of black America—a full one-third—continues to live below the poverty line, despite the fact that there has been an enormous expansion of the black middle class that [Henry Louis] Skip Gates and others have ingeniously talked about. The reality is that enormous segments of black America continue to be part of the working poor. They get up and work forty, fifty, and sixty hours a week and still can't make it above the poverty line. So I think that's one of the reasons for the high appeal of Minister Farrakhan, especially earlier on in the '90s, and the appeal of neo-separatism among African American communities. The racial remedies of liberalism and neo-liberalism, which have been pegged to integrationist philosophies and strategies and tactics, have failed to produce significant gains for those most vulnerable to economic rebuff and social stigma.

And, number two, I think what's important is to acknowledge that there is an aesthetic component to this appeal. That is, the celebration of blackness unapologetically is altogether and always appealing to black people who have been marginalized because of their skin color, because of their racial identities. Farrakhan and other neo-separatists' unswerving valorization of blackness as the primary symbol of pride, but also their understanding how it continues to be the basis of social oppression, means that they are at once captivating an audience by celebrating black identity, while understanding how it is continually being politically denigrated. I think that's very important in explaining how self-segregation and neo-separatist policies are appealing.

And, finally, the reality of self-segregation is captured in the by now familiar question, "Why are all the black kids sitting together?" You pass up twenty-eight tables of white kids sitting together to get to and question the twenty-ninth table of black folk sitting together. Self-segregation has always been stigmatized because black solidarity has always been viewed suspiciously in a white supremacist culture. And that is why, I think, black self-love is an extraordinarily political gesture, perhaps even unavoidably so, in the context of a culture that continues to heap suspicion and aspersion on the heads of those black folk who simply attempt to love themselves and embrace themselves without apology or restriction.

I've heard you defend Snoop Dogg and other hip-hop artists' lyrics and language. In fact, I believe the course you taught on hip-hop at Columbia University had a section titled, "Can You Say F—k and Still Be A Public Intellectual?" One of the things the civil rights generation most intensely dislikes about the hip-hop generation is the so-called crassness and foul language. . .

[Laughs] I'm a "'tweener." I'm in between the two generations. I'm not old enough to have participated in the civil rights generation, but too old to be hip-hop—even though an old man like me is still trying to represent for the peeps. [*Laughs*] But I understand both of those generations, being caught between them, and I understand some of the ideals, the identities, the images that prevail in each, and the moral and social aspirations that each nurtures at the heart of its existence. What I try to do is become a bridge between these two, while being critical of both.

It is true that the civil rights generation often says that you can't have hip-hop as a serious political answer to the destructive policies of Reagan, Bush—and we should throw Bill Clinton in at his worst, as is true with Gore and Bush the younger coming. We should add them at their worst as well. It's true in one sense that we do need sustained political activity in an organized and traditional sense to oppose the policies that have been enshrined in custom, convention, and law. Therefore we must seek a more immediate political remedy in the orthodox sense.

On the other hand, the shift from traditional and orthodox politics into a cultural realm may be seen as a decline of black imagination, politically and racially speaking. But it's also a mark of the times in which we live. Instead of blaming the failure on black youth who are insufficiently political, we have to suggest that the failure belongs equally, if not more so, with the older generation that failed to comprehend the shifted terrain, and that has failed to speak to the issues that young black people find themselves speaking to and being confronted with.

That's why rapper Mos Def can say:

You can laugh and criticize Michael Jackson if you wanna,
Woody Allen molested and married his stepdaughter
Same press kickin' dirt on Michael's name
Show Woody and Soon-Yi at the play-off game
Now just sit back and think about that
Would he get the same dap if his name was Woody Black?
OJ found innocent by a jury of his peers
They been f—kin' with that nigga for the last five years
Is it fair, is it equal, is it just, is it right?
Do we do the same thing if the defendant's face is white?
White boys doin' it well, it's success
I start doin' it well, it's suspect . . .
They say they want you successful
But then they make it stressful
You start keepin' pace
They start changin' up the tempo.

Well, I don't care what you say, that's a serious political analysis about the cultural denigration of a black icon—complex and conflicted as he is—while evoking the unconsciously white supremacist articulation of support, even if equivocating support, for a white icon. Even though that lyric is not about the maldistribution of resources, it is about the maldistribution of political and representative capital and that's so important in a society that is highly culturalized, including the means by which political denigration is articulated. To traditionalists, the politics of culture may not be equally significant as orthodox politics, but they are significant nonetheless, and orthodox politicians and traditional intellectuals have often underestimated and denied the valuable viewpoints these young people bring to bear.

On the other hand, I think there's legitimate room for critique of people who want to reduce into the cultural realm the struggles of black America. We know that the cultural and the political are simultaneous and convergent, and that means we have to take the cultural and political hand in hand and see how they influence and inform one another. And when older critics say, "well, black youth are not as politically involved as we were," the reality is that it takes a whole lot of nostalgia and amnesia on the part of black folk to suggest that 100 percent of the people involved in the civil rights movement were *physically* invested in defending the interests and principles and practices of black America. Only about 10 percent of black folk were physically involved, which is by no means a judgment on blacks, since there were all sorts of ways black folk could participate in liberation struggle.

When such a narrow view is evoked to denounce the ostensible apoliticism and ahistoricism of black youth, it just seems patently unfair. It ignores the broad spectrum of actions, ideas, beliefs, and behaviors that might be mobilized to articulate a racial politic. Still, there's no denying that a major reason we celebrate King, Malcolm, Paul Robeson, and Du Bois and Rosa Parks is that they put their bodies on the front line in defense of black principles and identities and images. But they were not typical of the masses of black people's physical investment. Instead, they represented black people symbolically.

Most black people who wanted to be involved were invested in ways they found tenable, and, as I said before, I'm not suggesting that all black people should have been physically involved. There are many ways of supporting black America—for instance, by giving money, by going to church, the temple, and the mosque to pray and rebel, by giving moral support to politically active figures, and so forth. But if that's the case, we can't beat up on young people who find alternative strategies for political investment, for political behavior and practice. There are all kinds of ways, cultural and political, for people to respond to and rebel against the denial of opportunity and the maldistribution of resources. I think that the hip-hop generation can certainly stand for some critique, but that critique is going on within hip-hop. But those who don't understand hip-hop culture, or who refuse to take the time to try and comprehend what they're doing, fail to see that critique.

They [the civil rights generation] are deeply sympathetic to a critique of aspects of hip-hop culture that have been so crassly materialized with the "bling-bling" and with the "back that thang up" booty-shakin' romanticization of the *gluteus*—emphasis on *maximus*—[such] that it has no time to pay attention to the brain or to the heart and soul. We have to make subtle and sophisticated moral distinctions that allow us to comprehend the genre's response and reaction to the forces of white supremacy and oppression, and therefore cede both to the hip-hop generation and to the civil rights generation legitimate authority within its own realm, without denigrating the other. Each of them has something interesting, important, and insightful to bring to bear on the struggle for black freedom in the new millennium.

How has your revisionist view of Martin Luther King been received by the older generation? I heard you on BET Tonight *with Tavis Smiley compare Dr. King to Puff Daddy, saying King "lifted, jacked, and sampled" his "I Have a Dream" speech. That must be blasphemous to older folk.*

[Laughs] Yeah, yeah, yeah—they think I'm crazy. A black man came up to me at a church in Los Angeles where I was doing a book signing and said, "Thank you, brother. Thank you for doing the white man's job for him." Now I must admit I'm usually on the other side of that equation—black people usually thanking me for defending them against the Ward Connerlys or the Armstrong Williamses or the Charles Murrays or the Linda Chavezes of the world. I understand what it means to defend black America and to be loved for that, but I have also understood what it means to be very critical of aspects of black America from the very beginning. That's my job as a social and cultural critic. In my first book, *Reflecting Black*, I talk about being an "oppositional" black critic, which means that we have to oppose viewpoints, visions, and insights that we think are destructive in black America, or somehow wrong.

My book [*I May Not Get There with You*] is in its fourth or fifth printing, thank you Jesus. They called me up and told me it's number one on the Blackboard best-seller list, which comes out in *Essence*. So I'm grateful, on the one hand, for black people receiving this book, reading it, and struggling with me, and for critiquing my book. How can I be a public intellectual and be offended by the very practice of critique by which I live?

On the other hand, I've met too many black people who've only heard what the book was about or heard me on a television program, and refuse to grapple with the book. They used to say, "If you want to hide something from black people, put it in a book!" [Laughs] That was racist and vicious, primarily because it was against the law for black slaves to read, and even after slavery, coerced illiteracy was a critical tool of the apartheid South. On the other hand, it might have been true for some of us who refuse to comprehend or struggle with an entire text. And we have to be honest about that. So, for me, some black people who have refused to struggle with the entire argument have certainly criticized my book. I don't think that anybody can honestly read my book and believe that I'm trying to assault or insult Dr. King. I call him the greatest American ever produced in the history of America—not the greatest black man, not the greatest black person, but the greatest American.

How has the King family reacted?

With deafening silence to me directly, but indirectly, through people who know them, they've been quite disappointed, and I can understand that to some degree. But the King family as well must understand, as the Mafia says, it's not personal, it's business. It's about bringing a critique to bear on some of their more unjust practices, while highlighting the very good things that they've done—and I've put both in my books. And I have been very critical of some of the actions of the King family because I think there is little question that it would not be immoral for the King family to make money off of King's legacy. But it would be immoral to pretend King would like it.

Here was a man who was absolutely, as [King's biographer] David Garrow says, as "uncommercial" a man as you might imagine, and his legacy is being bought and sold and distributed on the Internet . . . which can be a very edifying and helpful thing. It can also be destructive of the very empire of black integrity that he erected. I think the King family has been quite good, and in some instances has been quite bad. We must be unafraid to critique them even though they are the First Family of Black America. My job as a public intellectual is to be a paid pest. I get paid to pester myself, to pester my colleagues, to pester with ideas that I engage, and to receive criticism of my work. We should not engage in ad hominem assaults but in vigorous, just, and reciprocal review of our intellectual and artistic efforts.

Interview by Hisham Aidi
New York, New York, 2000

17

Prophetic Black Islamic Ethics

Malcolm X, Spiritual Warfare, and Angry Black Love

Could you explain to the readers of this special issue (of Religion and Literature*) how you are using the figure of Malcolm X in your book* Making Malcolm: The Myth and Meaning of Malcolm X*?*

What I'm trying to do with Malcolm is not a straightforward biography. I view him as a culturally significant figure whose striking achievements during a wonderful and complex career continue to generate interest. Malcolm's life has been shaped by myth and used by people for a variety of conflicting purposes. My book attempts to figure out how that myth is related to resonant intellectual and social traditions in African American culture. It also reflects on the fascination of Americans with radical figures who rebel against numerous forms of authority. Next, I examine how Malcolm is being used in African American popular culture, especially by hip-hop artists and black filmmakers, to extend their own obsessions with masculinity. In addition, I investigate how Malcolm has been used by cultural politicians to set themselves up as authorities within African American culture. That is, to be identified with Malcolm is to derive some sort of legitimacy within radical black politics to articulate the claims and concerns of black people.

Finally, I look at Malcolm's intellectual legacy. I examine the categories of interpretation that have been used to explain Malcolm's life. I aim to understand as clearly as possible what contributions Malcolm made to the intellectual life of the black movement in the late 1950s and early 1960s. I also discuss how his legacy has been interpreted, in turn, by intellectuals and scholars who have assessed his racial worth and cultural merit. So these varieties of interests were very much on my mind as I examined how Malcolm's myth was being shaped and remade. I argue that his past indeed has a future, and that we must continue wrestling with him as a cultural figure.

In your book, you try to complicate Malcolm's current reception within a general black, mostly male audience and extend Malcolm to a larger, more ethnically diverse population.

My ambition to complicate Malcolm X was driven by a desire to challenge perceptions that many folk have about who Malcolm X was. For instance, if you believe that he was merely a prophet of anger and rage, you've got to confront the enormous significance of Malcolm's latter-day humanistic philosophy, which allowed him to reach across the chasm of race and color to embrace all people as his spiritual kin. Had he lived longer, I can only hope that Malcolm would have reached out to those who were different by virtue of their gender and sexual preference as well.

One of my aspirations was to find a way to communicate a vision of the broadly humanitarian Malcolm who often gets lost when we celebrate his black revolutionary importance. I also wanted to communicate a complex vision of Malcolm to those who saw in him strictly an icon of black self-esteem and culture. I wanted to show that Malcolm was interested in traveling beyond the boundaries of African American life to interact with all sorts of people around the globe.

Much has been made about your own background: you began your career as a teenage father, a welfare recipient, a factory laborer in the ghettos of Detroit, and then you became an ordained Baptist minister and a Ph.D. with teaching positions in highly respected seminaries and universities. Do you see a parallel shift of your own from moving from the ghetto to interacting with a broader, more diverse audience?

I think that's an astute observation. Yes, in many ways I think that is true. My own odyssey began in the inner city of Detroit. I became a teen father and received food stamps. My wife was enrolled in the WIC (Women, Infants, and Children) program, and I had to stand in line to receive powdered eggs and milk to feed my son. I worked two jobs full time, barely making a sustainable wage. The enormous obstacles I faced certainly challenged my self-definition and identity as a black man.

On a personal level, I began to think about what I would do to reshape my life so that I could achieve a certain moral status within my own community. Having access to that tremendous narrative of uplift that is threaded throughout African American culture—from Martin Delaney and Alexander Crummel, Booker T. Washington, Ida B. Wells-Barnett, and down to W.E.B. Du Bois, Paul Robeson, Fannie Lou Hamer, Pauli Murray, and James Baldwin—helped me respond to those challenges.

Also, I was encouraged through my participation in the black church. The church I belonged to was named Tabernacle Missionary Baptist Church. My pastor, Dr. Frederick Sampson, is an extraordinary intellectual and spiritual figure, and he lent me tremendous support. I was fortunate to have many remarkable people, so-called ordinary people, to provide me the impetus to make that shift from ghetto life to a life where I might become an example of the ingenuity of black survival.

The unfortunate part of the ghetto experience, of course, is that material misery and economic deprivation bring psychic harm and spiritual hurt to so many black folk. For every person who gets out of the worst of ghetto situations, there are many more people who remain trapped in its punishing grip. I certainly don't romanticize poverty or the ghetto, although I understand how they have come to be mythologized in many black narratives of survival.

There is a parallel between my own existential situation—a move from one set of difficult conditions in the ghetto to another set of obstacles in my present life that are just as challenging in their own way—and Malcolm's constant reconstruction and self-reinvention. I think the paradigm of self-reinvention is so central to black autobiography because there's a powerful move toward transformation in black life. Those parallel moves between life and literature, between personal story and racial story, are quite essential in light of the *narrative* quality of black existence. We shape our lives through story, and through it we also reshape our self-understanding. Although our self-understanding is surely rooted in the *facts* of our real lives, those facts take on new meaning when seen in light of the moral possibilities opened up by telling the story of our lives in different ways, with different accents.

When we allow ourselves to see our lives in a different light, we are empowered to either bear the extraordinary consequences of our misfortunes or reinterpret them.

In my case, a religious narrative motivated me to reinterpret my suffering and transform it into something that spurred me on to greater achievement. My suffering was no longer an albatross weighing me down. I see a parallel movement in my own life and in Malcolm's shifts and transformations, as he moved from a ghettoizing to a catholic vision of life.

You speak of both self-reinvention and a move not to romanticize poverty. How can you link that to Malcolm's conversion to Islam and to his angry rhetoric?

I think that Malcolm's self-reinvention was greatly enabled by his conversion to Islam. One form of self-reinvention is conversion, the remaking of the ego and the ideal spiritual self in light of the religious narratives that are crucial to sustaining one's sanity and helping one to confront the evils of the world. Religious transformation helps us deal with those forces that have so much to do with determining the quality of our lives.

In looking at Malcolm's conversion, we should view the narrative of self-reinvention in tandem with the rhetoric of anger that he expressed. He could only have the kind of anger he unleashed against white racism *because* he went beyond the hustling ethic that had informed his earlier life. The move from street hustler to a minister for the Nation of Islam allowed him to be conscientious about fighting white racism.

Prior to his ministry, Malcolm did not have the requisite skills and tools to acknowledge or adequately analyze how white racism undermined the ability of many black folk to even understand how they were being abused. Some orthodox Marxists might call it false consciousness: there had been a distortion of Malcolm's self-understanding and therefore a denial of the reality of oppression that was right before his face.

In one sense, Malcolm's conversion to the Nation of Islam gave him both the consciousness and the capacity to confront white racist oppression. His conversion elicited in Malcolm the appropriate anger that wasn't available to him before his religious rebirth. Malcolm's reinvention allowed him to access that anger in a way that had been denied to him previously because of his hustling life. On the other hand, Malcolm's move beyond narrow forms of black nationalist rhetoric and his embrace of broader humanitarian values that he proclaimed near the end of his life was aided by a subsequent religious conversion, this time to orthodox Islam. It was another milestone in Malcolm's quest for self-reinvention.

Ironically, the second movement in the suite of reinventions in Malcolm's life emphasized a broad Islamic perspective that accented people's humanity and their capacity to overcome bias in asserting the brotherhood and sisterhood of all people. That second movement allowed Malcolm to reinvent himself according to a religious narrative that did not deify narrow racial divisions. However, Malcolm provided a historical context for that affirmation. His trip to Mecca permitted him to see many lighter-skinned and white Arabs who treated him as if he were a brother and fellow citizen. This experience gave Malcolm a vision of the possibility of existing beyond the narrow rule of race that prevailed in America.

However, when he returned to America, even after having written letters that testified to his tremendous transformation, he continued to insist that America was not Mecca. He understood that our nation perpetuated the political, cultural, and social expression of racism. However, I think his trip to Mecca had a radical effect on him. It transformed his self-understanding and strengthened his desire to relate to people of color who differed from him ideologically. It also positively affected his relation to white Americans, whom he now believed could at least go into their own communities—where Malcolm and other blacks might never be allowed to go—to take the message of racial salvation. So the relationship between Malcolm's self-invention and his rhetoric of anger had different functions in his life depending on what stage he was experiencing at the time.

I'm wondering about the role of violence in his rhetoric, too. Could this broader appeal, then, help eliminate some of the violent tensions that were arising over Malcolm and his ministry?

Yes, that's a very interesting point. On the one hand, much has been made about Malcolm's rhetoric of violence, which, for the most part, has been misunderstood or misrepresented. Malcolm's main point was that black people should be prepared to defend themselves in the face of white hostility. In Malcolm's view, America came into being because a group of citizens refused to be oppressed and exploited and violently defended their interests in war. Malcolm contended that the same logic must be applied to internal domestic disputes. Malcolm believed that violence was as American as apple pie, that it was central to the definition of American society.

Therefore, he felt it was hypocritical for whites to demand that black folk deny themselves their birthright as American citizens by not employing violence to defend themselves against those whites who were physically attacking us. On one view, Malcolm, like Martin Luther King, was appealing to the specific character of American identity to justify his beliefs. Of course the emphases, and results, were different. By using the rhetoric of Christian charity, Martin Luther King Jr. appealed to the conscience of white Americans to change their ways. He also articulated his religious and humanitarian concerns by partially grounding them in the documents that are central to American political self-definition: the Constitution and the Declaration of Independence.

On the other hand, Malcolm reminded us of the ugly, gritty history of how ideas of freedom and equality were implemented in real life. He emphasized resistance to oppression through war. Malcolm was saying that if what it means to be an American is to participate in democracy, then we have to talk about the consequences of blacks being denied democracy and how black Americans should defend themselves in the face of that denial. The rhetoric of violence for Malcolm X became a way of playing on a trope of American self-definition and identity. What Malcolm wanted to do was to remind Americans in a clever way of that dark side of democracy, that side that it didn't want to face up to.

Second, what's important to understand about Malcolm's rhetoric of violence is how he was not talking about going out and attacking white folk. His point was that when white people were lynching black folk, when they were shooting them, when the bicuspids and incisors of German shepherds were tearing into the flesh of black people in Birmingham, that we should have fought back, we should have defended ourselves. It was not proactive violence visited on white people. It was self-defense in the face of white hostility and evil. For Malcolm, violence was a reaction to a previously existing condition of spiritual and physical violence that threatened the selfhood and, literally, the safety of black people.

Third, however, there's no denying that Malcolm often rhetorically attacked white Americans and black leaders with whom he disagreed. The supreme irony, of course, is that the Nation of Islam mostly expressed violence within its own ranks. It didn't get violent with the white people it had verbally targeted. The famous picture of Malcolm peeping out of a window holding the curtain open with a gun in his hand has been mistakenly seen as evidence of his willingness to be violent with whites. It truth, it portrayed Malcolm lying in wait for the black men who, after his departure from the Nation of Islam and his criticism of the honorable Elijah Muhammad, were threatening to kill him.

The very rage that Malcolm's rhetoric helped unleash was prevented political expression because the Nation of Islam was forbidden from being involved in politics by the Honorable Elijah Muhammad. Not until Malcolm escaped Elijah Muhammad's grip could he express a broader vision of political insurgence and resistance by blacks. In sum, though, I think the more humane Malcolm can be used to attack the narrow bigotries that were expressed by the early Malcolm.

I'd like to compare the ethic of the Islamic puritanical, rigid assertion of racial difference and black identity against the ethic of Christian compassion that might be more universal and might have fit in better with the prevailing Christian ethic in the United States.

Well, it is true that the black moral Puritanism advocated by the Nation of Islam accorded with some principles of fundamentalist Islamic practice, despite the fact that the Nation of Islam was repudiated by many orthodox Muslims when it was at its height in the 1960s. Followers of orthodox Islam made it a point to distinguish themselves from the Nation's rigid racial beliefs.

Let me say right off the bat that we have to fight the enormous prejudice against Islamic belief that prevails in a nation like ours, where Islamic faith is associated with extremists. Islamic peoples are wrongly deemed incapable of coping with difference, and of being unable to adjudicate disputes in peaceful ways. This is simply not true. It is a caricature of Islamic belief. We have to be quite cautious in making blanket statements.

There is, I think, something at work in the fundamentalist Islamic ethic of self-assertion that, like its fundamentalist Christian counterpart, reveals a rigid understanding of the relationship between religious experience and texts, and personal behavior. The fundamentalist conception of this relationship is much more rigid than that found in a progressive Islamic or Christian ethic that asserts a less punitive relationship between belief and behavior. I think there's something at work in fundamentalist Christian and Islamic belief that challenges secular arrangements by which religion must cooperate with the state in order to survive at all in order to express itself. The division between church and state allows for the proliferation of religions and makes it possible for Christians, Muslims, Jews, and Buddhists to coexist in a secular arena that protects the religious liberties that all religions must observe in order to survive.

On the other hand, I think that the ethic of self-assertion at work in fundamentalist belief expresses the desire of its advocates to shape the state according to rigid religious ideas. Those religious ideas, when enacted in sectarian ways, often have disastrous political consequences. We see this in countries where the practice of fundamentalist religion is so closely identified with the state that we cannot discern the difference between the two because religion is officially sanctioned. The consequences to those who exist outside the logic and moral parameters of that religion are quite severe.

We would see an American version of this problem if the aspirations of people like Jerry Falwell or Pat Robertson were to be realized. Falwell and Robertson want to remake the American state according to a sectarian, Christian fundamentalist viewpoint. When we look at Malcolm and see how that ethic of self-assertion manifests itself in the rhetorical violence of his early stage, I think we get a different glimpse of how the state would be related to religious belief. Since Malcolm spurned the political arena early on, his notion of existing *in* but not *of* the state implicitly endorsed a protectionism provided within the logic and laws of liberal democracy. To not get involved in politics so that you can maintain your own religious liberty is a ringing endorsement of the political arrangement that permits such pursuits to occur.

This is where Malcolm's difference to King is sharply illustrated. King sought to transform American culture by appeals to a broadly shared set of beliefs that in some ways held national citizenship and identity together. But he neither sought to enshrine his religious beliefs as law (as Falwell and Robertson do), nor did he seek to avoid the necessary political engagement to reform American culture (early Malcolm). The ethic of self-assertion and narrow identity found in fundamentalist belief contrasts boldly to an ethic of compassion and universalism found in progressive Christian and Islamic beliefs.

I think that the severe ethical prescriptions and rigid beliefs promoted within fundamentalist communities works against the sort of humanitarianism that accepts difference, and that allows us to live with those differences in ways that are not violent or harmful. That's true for Christians and Muslims. Intolerance for those who are different because of gender, sex, or race must be opposed. Religious belief should help us combat the vicious bigotries which harm and hurt human beings. Instead, narrow Christian and Islamic communities reinforce such bigotries and undermine the affirmation of difference even within religious faiths.

It is true that the rigidity of the Nation of Islam was an attractive feature to people whose lives had descended into a chaos of immorality. For those who had led the hustling life or a life of prostitution, or who had been pimps, dope dealers, drug addicts, fallouts from society, the ethical demand of the Nation of Islam indeed worked to their advantage in terms of cleaning them up.

The problem, of course, is that once the ethic transformed their lives—converted them from hustlers to healers, from pimps to preachers—they were not as open to the possibility that human identity is a complex amalgam of failure and success, of ideal and reality. The complex interaction of ideal and reality often produces apparently hypocritical and sometimes contradictory behaviors that in a ramshackle way move human beings toward *relative* perfection. The rigid ethic of the Nation of Islam was quite literal and prevented a complex understanding of the human negotiations people must pass through in order to achieve any sense of solid ego identity or self-respect.

However, I think that the Nation of Islam was far superior to Christianity in terms of reconstructing people's lives who were on the periphery of society. The civil rights movement often overlooked, until its latter period, the urban strata of the ghetto poor. The Nation of Islam's ingenuity was that its ideology intuited the ethical needs of the poor black urbanite. The Nation understood the need that the poor and working poor had for a moral circumspection and reconstruction that was rigid and clear because sometimes their own moral lives were chaotic and dissembled.

On the other hand, once its members moved from the gutter to the glory of religious affiliation, the Nation of Islam was not as open, in principle, to other varieties of moral behavior. Consequently, their rigidity sometimes turned to violence. It was not simple physical violence. It was also the mental and spiritual violence that occurs within any sectarian religious organization that derives its energy from forms of moral community that draw such sharp distinctions between itself and the larger society.

The irony, of course, is that the Nation of Islam was, in many senses, prototypically American. The Nation's black moral Puritanism encouraged the group to contrast itself to the "degradation" of so much of the black community, a move often made by mainstream whites. The Nation of Islam's beliefs accent the degree to which many people of color, especially African Americans, are culturally and religiously conservative even while being politically progressive. They adhere to standard, very traditional conceptions of moral community, which gives the lie to claims by certain critics and politicians that black folk in the main are dissolute and morally reprobate.

The reality is that black folk are often puritanical people who buy hook, line, and sinker the "Protestant ethic and the spirit of capitalism." Or they practice very conservative Islamic principles of moral community. They've used both Christian and Islamic faith to reconstruct their identities according to religious narratives that uplift and valorize hard work, self-discipline, and sacrifice for the future of one's children. Unfortunately, ethical rigidity is often a concomitant. The social ethic of the best of black religious traditions accents personal liberty along with self-sacrifice and social participation toward the goal of transforming American culture.

You said that the Islamic religion has a larger belief in the authority of religious experience. I was wondering if that was a conversion experience or some other kind of experience. Also, you mentioned Islamic cosmology. Could you clarify some of those terms?

What I mean by the authority of religious narrative is how, for many people in countries where Islam is practiced, religion is collapsed into politics and politics is absorbed by religion. One's moral principles are regulated and buttressed by state law. It's not that American Christians don't seek to link their own political behavior to their personal belief. It's just that the state isn't officially backed by religion. I think that's the ingenuity of American political culture: *theoretically*, at least, democracy allows every religion to coexist.

Ironically, in American society the establishment of a secular state allows the proliferation of religious bodies and beliefs. The exclusive identification of law with religion doesn't often provide an ethical stance from which to criticize the one by means of the other. For instance, one of the virtues of American society in the 1950s was that America was not a Christian nation. It was precisely because it was a secular society that the state could intervene on behalf of one set of citizens, black Christians, to defend them from a variety of evils—including lynchings, burnings, stabbings, and shootings—committed by another set of citizens, white Christians. In countries where there's no distinction between law and religion that kind of possibility would not exist. To incur the wrath of the state is to incur the wrath of religion, which means that you are doubly undone. An Islamic cosmology asserts the authority of religious narratives and religious experience over secular ideas and society.

Given your critique of Malcolm and his reception in terms of his misogyny and the misogyny of black nationalism, I'm wondering why you focus so much on the reception of Malcolm by black men and the construction of black masculinity. Could you have extended his appeal to black women, in particular, through the figure of Malcolm's mother, a Garveyite and political activist, and his wife, Betty Shabazz?

Yes, unquestionably, and that's a fair and just criticism of my own take on Malcolm in my book, where I focus on the politics of masculinity and the ways Malcolm both energized those politics and embodied some of their worst manifestations. I think, given my desire to criticize the misogyny and sexism of Malcolm X, one of the ways I might have *structurally* done that within my book is to have accented, as you say, the importance of Malcolm's Grenadan mother. I might have more extensively discussed how her service as the recording secretary of the local UNIA exemplified a powerful instance of black women contesting the narrow gender politics that Malcolm subsequently adopted within the Nation of Islam.

Or I might have more broadly defined the role of Dr. Betty Shabazz, who left Malcolm after the birth of each of their first three children over disputes about the role that she should adopt as an autonomous moral agent and social activist apart from Malcolm. Even within the moral worldview that the Nation of Islam created, I think that there were already cracks in its cosmology with Dr. Shabazz's independent attitudes and activities. I think that I might have more skillfully employed Malcolm's mother and wife to criticize his own narrow gender politics.

I focus on men so much because I am trying to join in the furious debates about masculinity within African American culture. I am trying to struggle with issues of black manhood in a way that respects the integrity of those debates, that is, the way in which they deal with the real crises of young and old black males. However, by articulating the political, cultural, economic, and domestic consequences of black male suffering, I am by no means suggesting that black women are not suffering as well.

What I am suggesting is that the immediate consequences of the devastation that black men face amounts to a palpable threat to the survival and flourishing of black communities. I am trying to address those crises in a way that employs Malcolm's career as a metaphor for the possibility of moral reconstruction and social transformation. I also employ him as a prism through which we see the limitations of a narrow masculinist psychology. I see Malcolm as an example of how black men can be self-critical and constructively critical of others in order that black communities might truly flourish. I use Malcolm's complex evolution as a critical wedge underneath the hypermasculinist impulses within black society that squeeze out the possibility of black women's participation in the reconstruction of black life.

While you criticize black masculinity, you support black men by showing that some of their misogyny, the well-publicized condemnation of rap groups' lyrics and behavior, comes from ideologies within church and state institutions. You put them into a wider perspective and attempt to stop the victimization of these men who are caught in a web of constant violence and criminal behaviors.

Right. I think we have to avoid victimizing the least politically protected group in America: young black people, in this case, young black men, some of whom are rappers. To pretend that they are the sources for the most nefarious expressions of misogyny, sexism, and patriarchy in our culture is ludicrous. That is not to suggest that they don't need to be criticized. They certainly do. I think that when we look at the recent debacles of Tupac Shakur, Snoop Doggy Dogg, Dr. Dre, Slick Rick, and other prominent rappers—some of whom face murder charges, while others face sexual assault and drug charges—we can't romanticize their music or careers. Given his moral Puritanism, Malcolm X would have much to criticize in hip-hop culture. He'd have a lot of negative things to say about gangsta rap's moral infidelity to a more humane ethical community than that expressed within the narratives of many of its songs.

On the other hand, I think that it would be hypocritical for us to focus our moral outrage primarily on these young black people when we know that the synagogue, the mosque, and the church have promoted and preserved the social, religious, and cultural inferiority of women. Even more troubling, these institutions have generated narratives that legitimate women's oppression. These religious bodies often seduce women into identifying with religious narratives that curtail their quest for liberation. I think that it's wrong for us to deny that religious rhetoric and belief have justified and reinforced patriarchal and misogynistic tendencies much more effectively than hip-hop culture.

Can you talk a little about the tradition of the black church, its oratory, and the rhetorical resistance that is part of African American political tradition? How do you connect the role of the African American church and its oratorical strategies in the struggle for civil rights?

I think that during the civil rights movement the rhetorical strategies employed by a person like Martin Luther King Jr. were extraordinarily effective. One of the rhetorical strategies King and other church-based civil rights activists used was to accent the power of speech to transform human behavior. If you couldn't physically harm people or retaliate against white racist domination—as King certainly preached—then you could motivate white folk to change their hateful ways by speaking powerful rhetoric that led to concrete action.

Black religious speech also had the capacity to hearten black folk in the face of oppression and even death. Such rhetoric was linked to religious narratives that advocated transformation through moral trial, reinvention through self-examination, conversion through confrontation with the good, and redemption through suffering. For King and other religious figures, their rhetoric rung with moral authority because its claims and performance were inspired by imminent contact with a transcendent God. King often spoke of civil rights devotees enjoying "cosmic companionship." Thus their speech and social practices were never presumed to be theirs alone, but were motivated by a God who gave people the capacity to speak and act in the first place. The same God-given power that enabled King and others to speak and act could also change personal sentiments and thinking, and social structures. Religious rhetoric, and its translations in civil society, was an important vehicle and inspiration for such transformation.

This last part, in fact, is part of another rhetorical strategy employed by Martin Luther King Jr. and others: they fused the language, rhythms, and modes of black sacred rhetoric with civic rhetoric and civil religious symbols in American society. When Martin Luther King Jr. appealed to the Declaration of Independence and the Constitution, he did so with an eye to making religiously inspired uses of the secular documents that undergird civil society and that codify its basic beliefs about the character of American citizenship. He used those documents—along with the beliefs about democracy they encouraged and the rhetoric of equality they mobilized—as a vehicle to express his religious interpretations of justice, freedom, and equality.

Martin Luther King Jr. took his own religious convictions seriously. Time and again, he reminded us that he was a preacher first and foremost, and only then a civil rights leader. But that preacherly vocation was an extraordinary one because his congregation was American society, indeed the world. King's religious beliefs were the impetus for his translation of an ethic of *love as justice* in public discourse and practice. He made his ideas comprehensible to a broad variety of Americans who didn't necessarily share his religious beliefs. King linked his understanding of social transformation to the quest for the public good through the language of civic virtue and civil rights.

Their religious beliefs gave King and others the psychic, spiritual, and rhetorical armor to stand up to an American government that failed to practice the ideals of freedom and equality articulated in the Constitution and the Declaration of Independence. King made the tension between ideal and reality the opportunity to highlight, especially toward the end of his life, the sheer hypocrisy of American claims of justice for all its citizens.

That, too, is a rhetorical strategy honed in the black church: you signify on the limitations of the embodiment or practice of an ideal by proclaiming your dedication to the ideal as well. For King and many civil rights devotees in relation to the American government, it ran something like: "I believe in the ideal of freedom, justice, and equality that you've articulated, but you haven't done such a good job in living up to it." That's essentially what King said in his famous "I Have a Dream" speech in Washington, D.C. King's rhetorical strategy was to compel Americans to concede that there was indeed, as T.S. Eliot wrote about another matter, a shadow between the ideal of democracy and its reality. In so doing, King proved again that the meanings of these important documents are not fixed. He showed that these documents can be reinterpreted in light of historical experience and in light of moral issues that drive political conflict.

Finally, King and other freedom fighters recognized that oppressed communities had to literally describe their visions of social transformation in ways that would not immediately cause white Americans or people in power to further oppress or kill them. They had to engage in what James Scott calls "everyday forms of resistance," that is, to resist power in a manner that was small but significant, that was more cumulative than revolutionary.

Further, they had to use what Scott terms "hidden transcripts," public performances of speech that veil its real meanings, that hide its coded messages. During slavery, of course, spirituals sometimes functioned in this way. The double meaning of such songs often signaled to slaves when and where and whom they were to meet to escape north to freedom. White masters were being entertained, but black slaves were being emancipated. And all through the same vehicle, a song.

For King and other participants in the civil rights movement, *how* issues of justice, freedom, and equality were framed played an important part in how they were perceived, and received, in white society. Many times, King and other leaders masked their goal of radical transformation by arguing, at least initially, for incremental change or by going for symbolic victories that meant a lot to the people they affected. (I don't mean that black leaders always had radical goals that were masked in moderate rhetoric; initially, many of the goals of the civil rights movement were rather modest.)

The Montgomery bus boycott was such an example. It was a local case, and largely symbolic, but its symbolism ignited an entire freedom movement throughout the South that brought the giant of legalized segregation to its knees. But the ambitions of the civil rights movement were largely framed in a rhetorical context of passive resistance, of Christian love, of nonviolent protest, when in reality deeply racist ways of life and unjust laws were being undermined and destroyed. Such gestures of resistance—and the action they inspired—were rhetorically brilliant, philosophically cunning, and socially quite substantive at the same time.

To conclude, you end your book speaking about a "ministration of a daily political ethic of care for fractured black bodies and spirits." Is there a way to translate a fractured identity, a fractured society, in a way that can start to heal some of these divisions?

That's a powerful question. One of the ways we can do that is to constantly take up the kinds of issues that our deepest religious passions motivate us to be concerned about. For me, that means "the least of these," the people who are poor, the people who don't have access to institutions of higher education, those who are shut out of power or acceptance because of their gender or sexual preference. This daily ministration of a political ethic of care is about edifying expressions and public translations of Christian, Islamic, or Buddhist compassion. It is also about the expression of secular compassion.

I emphasize human compassion and the need to translate it into a broad politic that allows us to accent an ethic of care without being laughed at. The so-called politics of neocompassion are being scorned by the New Right and substituted by a brand of politics that deals with the so-called hard realities of life. The takeover of American politics by the hard right is unfortunate. It propels our society into a Hobbesian war of all against all that is indeed nasty and brutish, that pits the have-gots against the have-nots; and with the odds already stacked against the have-nots, we know in advance who's favored to win. I think that the problem with such politics is that they not only discourage our country from living up to the highest expressions of our moral traditions, but they also suppress the flourishing of our American democratic tradition at its best. One way to translate compassion into politics is to acknowledge—and to build programs around that acknowledgment—that many people have been fractured through no fault of their own. For instance, we must confront how our society has contributed to the social suffering and economic misery of people of color. We must simply stop demonizing poor black women, whose financial vulnerabilities make them easy symbols of the blights of the welfare society. We should have the basic decency to admit that we live in a country that in numerous ways has undermined the ability of people of color, and other poor folk, to make a decent wage.

We can no longer blame such folk for not having jobs without making substantive analyses of economic policies and forces that prevent their stabilization. The structural transformation of the American political economy has disproportionately disadvantaged people of color. The shift from manufacturing to service industries that has been talked about from a variety of commentators means that there has been a hemorrhaging of economic resources in those postindustrial centers where many black people live: New York, Philadelphia, Detroit, Los Angeles, Baltimore, Washington, D.C., and so on.

The prospect of high-wage, low-skill jobs has all but evaporated. The prospects of poor and working poor people have been even further damaged by the technologization of American industries. Further, the black working class has been literally squeezed out of its living spaces by processes of gentrification in the inner city where structures are overtaken by individuals and businesses with the means to rehabilitate marginal housing. The political ethic of care I'm talking about is not a sappy kind of love or compassion that doesn't pay attention to hard political realities. It is the demand for sophisticated social analysis, profound investigation of economic conditions, and strategic social intervention in American politics and social movements with an eye toward transforming American culture. It stresses the need to live up to a vision of radical democracy that embodies the best of our traditions of freedom and justice but also accents the possibilities of human beings to realize and preserve the rich meanings of their individual existence as well.

Another form of the political ethic of care I advocate is the translation of spirituality into American discourses about virtue. William Bennett's and Newt Gingrich's discussions of virtue often miss the political influences and social contingencies that nuance any conception of virtue, that permit and encourage virtue to thrive. We must take the best of recent virtue ethics (from Alasdair MacIntyre to Stanley Hauerwas or Jean Porter) and the best work in moral philosophy on "moral luck" (from Bernard Williams to the brilliant work of Martha Nussbaum) to understand the complex interplay of personal and social forces in determining how we view what's good and virtuous.

To paraphrase Dorothy Day, "I want to work toward a world in which it is *possible* for people to behave decently." Decent or virtuous behavior flourishes under those conditions where people's livelihoods are sustained and where their lives are not constantly *materially* threatened. We need to analyze the relationship between public and private virtue and between personal considerations of ethical reconstruction and their public consequences. We need to reconstruct the public polity to reflect our compassion for people while encouraging excellent behavior from them as well. Finally, my version of a political ethic of care promotes the centrality of tolerance and diversity to a democratic culture. I don't mean a weak ethic of tolerance that says, "whatever goes"; if you have weighty ethical considerations and serious moral principles, you're going to have limits and, inevitably, conflicts. What I'm aiming at is the notion that vigorous multiculturalism, in substance and procedure, is not the worst thing to happen to American culture. To accent difference and diversity is not to surrender standards or merit. It is to criticize how we construct standards and to rigorously examine how we understand the notion of merit. Standards and merits are really contingent goods. They do not exist in a cultural vacuum or historical void. Merit expresses the relationship between an ideal of excellence and its possibility of achievement. Merit always exists in relation to relative standards that we generate.

Multiculturalism, polyethnicism, and diversity express what I have elsewhere termed the edifying impurity of American identity—the way Americans are culturally and intellectually creolized and hybridized, always interacting across a number of boundaries. Those hybridities and creolizations are examples of how the character of American identity is constituted by a robust variety of "impure" ingredients. Not only does such a reality work wonders for our educational system, but its full realization would add considerably to American political culture as well.

Interview by Laura Winkiel
Durham, North Carolina, 1995

18

Homotextualities

The Bible, Sexual Ethics, and the Theology of Homoeroticism

Please elaborate on your theology of homoeroticism.

What I mean by theology of homoeroticism is a theology that is grounded in the biblical admonition to acknowledge sexuality as a crucial function of human identity, and as a symbol of the interpenetration of the divine and the human, signifying a fusion of planes. Since we are grounding our sexual ethics in a theology that speaks poignantly to human experience, it is natural to turn to the Bible to justify, legitimate, or sanction our beliefs. I believe that there is theological and biblical space for the articulation of a homoerotic instinct, homosocial ideas, and a homosexual identity. People who happen to be same-sex identified can certainly find support within our churches.

Furthermore, I sought, in my notion of a theology of homoeroticism to underscore an implicitly homoerotic moment within the ecclesiastical order of black Christendom. Think, for instance, of men claiming to love Jesus standing on their feet in fully enthralled ecstasy, emoting about their connection to a God who became flesh and dwelled among us, *as a man*. For men to publicly proclaim their intense, unsurpassed love for a God who became a man leaves the door open for homoerotic identification and communion within the liturgy of the black ecclesial universe. In short, the black church provides space for men and women to love their own gender in erotic ways with biblical and theological sanction. My conception of the theology of homoeroticism is an attempt to develop a theologically sound and biblically justified relationship of love that is the underlying ethic within any sensual order, regardless of one's orientation, whether it is bisexual, transsexual, transgendered, gay, lesbian, or heterosexual. The prevailing ethic in any sexuality ought to always highlight the precise function of love in the adjudication of competing erotic claims. Whenever there is a contest between destructive incarnations of lust and righteous expressions of erotic communion, love promotes the latter. That doesn't mean that lust or fantasy cannot embody an ethically justifiable sexual urge. But it does mean that we have to pay attention to how a relationship of justice is exercised within the context of a sexual ethic. Sexual relations are related to the theological and moral ideals to which we subscribe.

When I think about homosexuality or any sexual identity, the prevailing idea is not simply satisfaction of the erotic drive and the sexual urge, but the manner in which the human being is recognized as the center of one's sexual ethic. Corporeal identity, theologically speaking, should exist in relationship to the divine order that prescribes human activity. A homoerotic theology is an acknowledgment that there are legitimate means to express same-sexuality, and the fantasies and erotic desires that grow from it. It also holds that there's a way of theologically asserting love as the predicate of such unions, since love ought to be the central principle of any sexual orientation. The question should be, regardless of orientation: How does this relationship enable the flourishing of an ethic of self-concern and other-regard? If that basic test is met within a sexual ethic, then the content of one's sexual identity should not be dictated by traditional theological proscriptions of homoerotic union. Even in the black church we can affirm the sexual legitimacy of brothers and sisters who do not meet the heterosexual norm, and still support them as fellow members of a religious community.

A theology of homoeroticism points to the effort to embody the full expression of God's sexual gifts to us, and to find legitimate theological support for the articulation of a broad erotic order within the context of our religious beliefs. If we can't do it there then we can't do it anywhere. Sex and salvation should be seen as neither mutually exclusive nor identical.

However, they are often mutually reinforcing, since sexual union within a religious ethic is often a symbol of God's care and love for the other. Erotic unions at their best engender the salvific function of intimate contact between God and believer, a relationship often pictured as one between a lover and his beloved. In that light, a believer's sexual identity should be fully supported within an ecclesial context that embraces the erotic as a symbol of divine presence and affirmation.

A theology of homoeroticism combats recalcitrant prejudice against alternative sexualities—prejudices, by the way, that parallel bigotry against the black body in Western thought and culture. That makes it even more painful to observe the failure of the black church to embrace the full range of sexual identities that have been mobilized and manifested within our communities. In so doing, we have mimicked the sexual bigotry that has bedeviled us. I suppose such behavior is to be expected, since we have failed to be just and fair with gender relations in the black church. If the gendered character of heterosexual ethics has presented a profound challenge to the black church, God knows that homosexuality and homoeroticism present a formidable challenge. That's even the case for theologies of liberation that have been promulgated and, in limited form, adapted in the black church.

Of course, we can account for such resistance to a liberating sexual ethic by tracing it to the schism between body and soul that many black believers adapted in the face of feeling that they had to defend themselves against a charge of sexual profligacy, perversion, and impurity. Thus the black church bought into the division of the body and soul that the white church foisted on us to justify its psychic, moral, and material investments in chattel slavery and racial hegemony. The white church justified its assault on black humanity and its evil experiment in slavery by saying, "at least we're taking care of their souls," a goal they sought to achieve by containing and controlling the black body. In the minds of white Christians, the black body was a savage body. In a white Christian prism, the ethical end, the moral telos, of slavery was the social, psychic, and theological subordination of the African savage to European Christianity. This ideological matrix provided the crass ethical utilitarianism for European American Christianity's justification of slavocracy: "As long as we're addressing their soul's salvation, we can do what we will to their bodies." But this theological schizophrenia that rested on the artificial division of body and soul was more Greek than Hebraic, since the latter insists on the essential unity of corporeal and spiritual identity. Such theological schizophrenia introduced into our culture some vicious beliefs that have negatively impacted our racial self-perceptions, not only as subjects of our own sexuality but also as objects of the criminalization of our sexuality by white culture. The black church hasn't done a good job of resisting the worst elements of theological schizophrenia, leading us to suppress alternative, unconventional, and transgressive sexualities in the black church and beyond.

So that almost leads directly to my next question: Do you think that black homosexuals can use the Bible for sexual healing? If yes, how, and what kind of healing?

Black homosexuals can definitely use the Bible for sexual healing. They can do so because the biblical texts are a reflection of historical struggles with enlightened revelation. God has placed on the hearts and minds of human beings beliefs about how we should live our lives, even though such beliefs are fallible since they are mediated by the human voice and cognition. The Scriptures reflect the attempt of human beings to wrestle with divine revelation within the context of our particular histories, given cultures and local traditions. In interpreting biblical texts, we must always pay attention to what biblical scholars call the *Sitz im Leben*—the historical context within which scriptural revelations emerged.

Consequently, we must always be on the lookout for the political hermeneutic of a biblical text. What I mean by political hermeneutic is that the horizon of interpretation is always shaded by the social order in which readers and hearers discover themselves. We must remember that the Bible was compiled over the course of a few centuries. That means that there are an incredibly diverse array of identities, intentions, ethical limits, and political philosophies articulated within the discursive and theological perimeters that shape the interpretation of the Bible and God's revelation. Even though some of us think of the Bible as the inspired word of God—the transcendental truth of eternity mediated through written revelation—we must not forget the critical role of the amanuensis. Whether it was Matthew, Mark, Luke, or John, or the scribes of the Pentateuch, or one of the ostensible authors in the JEDP documentary hypothesis, the truth is, they were secretaries—or as Mary J. Blige might say, and I'll pronounce this phonetically, seck-uh-taries! And secretaries can get stuff wrong, sometimes by mistake! They can leave the i's undotted, the t's uncrossed, or they may occasionally impose on a document their own beliefs or shades of their own meaning.

Remember that Paul says at one point in the Scriptures—and I'm paraphrasing—"Now this is what God says, and this is what I'm telling you." So he at least tried to gesture toward a hermeneutical ethic that acknowledged the implicit human character that shapes the record of God's inspiration. He at least tried to distinguish between human interpolations and divine revelation—a notion that is fraught with peril, to be sure, since providence and revelation are concepts often manipulated by religious elites or those with claims to esoteric knowledge. Moreover, Paul metaphorically suggested the human limitations of comprehending divine revelation and the fallibility of interpreting God's word when he declared, "We have this treasure in earthen vessels."

I note all of this as a backdrop to saying, yes, as with any of us, I think gay, lesbian, transgendered, transsexual, bisexual, and all other-sexed black Christians can certainly turn to the Bible for sexual healing. After all, this is the great book of love that points to the appropriate ethical etiquette for our sexual behavior. As such, it points back to God. The mores, folkways, and moral traditions that shape us inevitably impinge on our consciousness and color our understanding of what we should do and how we should behave. Conscience is the product of a historical encounter with ethical ideals. One's conscience is always shaped by the culture in which one is reared. Therefore our beliefs about the Bible, about ethical behavior, about good and bad, and about how we should adhere to certain principles are unavoidably shaped by the political and social and moral contexts we inherit and create. Depending on how it has been deployed and interpreted, the Bible has been both the Ur-text and Err-text of black ethical existence. It has been the great, grand narrative thread that has been weaved throughout the collective history of African American people and through the individual consciousness of millions of blacks, even if they didn't officially join the church. "The Book" has been the dominant interpretive touchstone for the ethical behavior of African people in America and other parts of the black diaspora.

Black homosexuals can turn to the Bible for sexual healing, just as many of us heterosexuals have, because it tells us that God loves us, that God created us in God's image, and that we should learn to accept ourselves as we are. Of course, I realize that the process of self-acceptance is an index of our evolving spiritual maturity. It takes profound spiritual and moral wisdom to claim—with our own lives on full theological display—that what God made is good. We can make such a claim despite the critical modifications introduced into Christian thought through Augustinian themes of original sin and the ethical miasma that was its consequence in "the fall." We must accentuate the positive dimensions of human identity and self-conception as the admittedly distorted reflection of the *imago dei*. Still, we can affirm our recreated goodness through discourses of redemption open to *all* human beings. There is no asterisk in the biblical promise of redemption that excludes homosexuals. We have to reclaim the primordial goodness of God that ultimately took human form in Jesus. As they say in Christian circles, God didn't make any junk, and that means that whomever God has made, whether homosexual or heterosexual, is a good person.

I realize there are debates about biological determinism versus social construction in sexuality. I know there's a dispute about whether gay and lesbian sexuality, indeed all sexualities, reflect an inherent predisposition biologically implanted in the human genetic code that regulates sexual orientation, or if sexual identity is the result of human choice. I happen to believe that gays and lesbians can no more get up tomorrow morning and be heterosexual than heterosexuals can get up tomorrow morning and be gay or lesbian. I'm not gainsaying the fluidity of sexual identity, the elasticity of erotic urges, the changeability of passionate proclivities, or the broad continuum of sensual engagements and stimuli. And I'm not suggesting that biological urges are not socially constructed. After all, even homosexuals who grow up in a culture where their identity and self-perception is shaped in the crucible of heterosexism, internalize the belief that it is a sin or an unbearable stigma to be gay or lesbian. Thus they often suppress their sexual desires and erotic urges, whether they are conceived to be "natural" or constructed.

That is why the coming-out process is often especially volatile: it involves the painful irony of self-identification with the very sexual identity that has been culturally demonized. That's why there's so much self-hatred among gays and lesbians. The coming-out process must address the fact that the self has been artificially split off from self-consciousness, at least a self-consciousness that is socially supported. This accounts for why the homosexual ego is coerced into epistemic and ethical isolation, or the proverbial "closet." In the closet, one must subordinate one's "natural sexuality" to society's accepted sexual norms, to its entrenched mores. So the Bible should help Christians liberate the sexual urge from artificially imposed restrictions and repressions. In the case of homosexuals, such restrictions and repressions are fueled by heterosexist values, but these values, I believe, can be critiqued by an appeal to a progressive sexual ethic, an enlightened biblical hermeneutic, and a humane theological tradition. How can black homosexuals use the Bible for sexual healing? They can do as all Christians should do: express their sexuality in the context and pursuit of a right relationship with God, which is the predicate of all sexual ethics.

But critics who seek to proof-text their opposition to homosexuality often neglect to interpret such biblical passages in their larger theological meaning. For instance, the story of Sodom and Gomorrah is more about underscoring the necessity for hospitality to strangers than it is about homosexual perversion. In essence, the larger pericopes in which biblical texts are contained are either neglected, severed from their interpretive frameworks through theological axe grinding, or subject to hermeneutical myopia. Hence the practice of biblical interpretation reinforces the heterosexist culture from which the theological repression of sexual difference has emerged. What's fascinating about black Christian appeals to the Bible to justify suppression of homosexuality is that such appeals are quite similar to those made by whites to justify slavery. Then again, that was already a familiar hermeneutical move in black religious circles, since it had been employed to justify theological strictures against the ecclesial expression of female authority. Those of us promulgating a theology of homoeroticism must engage in hermeneutical warfare and interpretive battle, not only with the text but also with the heterosexist presuppositions that shaped the biblical narratives and their subsequent mainstream interpretation.

Finally, I think that Jesus states the bottom line when he says that all of the law and prophets were contained in his summary of the ethical aim of Christian belief: "Thou shalt love the Lord they God with all thy heart, and with all thy soul, and with all they mind. This is the first and great commandment. And the second *is* like unto it, Thou shalt love they neighbor as thyself. On these two commandments hang all the law and the prophets."

That means that we must embrace and affirm all brothers and sisters regardless of where we stand on the mysteries of sexual identity. Too often we have focused on a subsidiary accounting of sexual identity and thrust it into primary consideration to determine legitimate standing within the religious community. Being in right relationship with God and our neighbor is the crucial factor in our Christian existence. Once that issue is settled, then sexual orientation becomes subsidiary. Sacred orientation is more important than sexual orientation. When the Bible is read through that liberating lens and through the prism of self-acceptance in light of God's offer of the gift of love and affirmation, it can be read as a source of sexual healing for homosexuals.

One of the most crucial issues a liberating interpretation of the Bible can address is the culture of dishonesty that smothers alternative sexualities. Gays and lesbians, as well as all other-sexed people, often have had to deny to themselves they were homosexual. They denied their sexuality to others who might have perceived it even before they did, a perception that might have caused them great discomfort. They often have had to stay in an epistemological closet, a theological closet, a sociological closet, and to some degree, even a biological closet, because they didn't want to suffer the consequences of coming out. The culture of deceit imposed on gays and lesbians has to be relieved by the church's open affirmation of their legitimacy, so that they don't have a distorted consciousness and a bruised conscience about their own sexuality. In the final analysis, we are liberated into self-acceptance by a loving and forgiving God.

Okay. You are going to change everybody's mind.

We can hope.

Well, I think so. You've already largely answered my next question, but I'm going to ask it in case there is something you want to add. How do we reread the Bible as a guide to promoting complete and healthy homosexual relationships?

As I've stated, in order to skillfully interpret the Bible, we've got to get at the social, political, and ideological history of the time during which its constitutive texts emerged. By so doing, we get a sense of the philosophical reflections on race, gender, culture, class, and of course, sexuality as well, that penetrated the discursive frames and theological views of the Bible. Some of these reflections were egalitarian, but many more were authoritarian. Then, too, we've got to acknowledge that the culture in which we live shapes our self-understanding, as well as our understanding of our relationship to the Bible, and what role it should play in regulating our intellectual and moral lives. Our cultural situations even affect how we think we are capable of transforming our self-understanding through a new interpretation, perhaps even radical reinterpretation, of the Bible in light of the moral aspirations that we learn to claim as legitimate components of our individual and collective identities.

But it's equally important to understand there are multiple textualities within revelation's household. Of course, the Bible is the crucial, significant, and central text that shines on other texts interpreted in its light, and within the circumference of its ethical imagination. But a crucial implication of revelation is the belief in the variegated modalities through which it is articulated, which means that God speaks and is revealed to us in a number of ways. Even though the Bible is the hermeneutical ground of all textualities and modalities of revelation, it is not the exclusive or exhaustive medium of revelation. I think fundamental Christians in particular fail to comprehend this point, or at least they strongly disagree with this theological belief and interpretive principle. As a result, there is often in such circles a species of bibliolatry, or worship of the Bible. In my view, we should only worship the God who inspired the Bible. Bibliolatry is a way to foreclose wrestling with the complex demand of responsible assessment of the contradictory data of human experience in light of religious belief. Bibliolatry resolves all complexity, nuance, ambiguity, and so on.

Other Christians believe that we can't worship the Bible on the premise that God continues to speak. When we close the Bible, we have neither shut God's mouth nor closed God's mind. The radical openness of the mouth and mind of God means there is ongoing revelation in our times. It means that God is still speaking to us. That means that we have scriptural-like, biblical-like revelations that need to be taken seriously. The backdrop of such critical reflection is the understanding that the Bible is, besides a book of faith, also a book of history. It is a text that belongs to time and circumstance. Even though it claims to mediate eternal truth—a claim I take seriously—its medium is birthed in contingency. God's word is true, but the means by which we know it are limited, finite, and fallible. That means we've got to confront the historical conditions of biblical production. We've got to ask the questions: Why were all the books in the Bible written by men? Why was the canon largely shaped by masculinist sensibilities? In many ways, the canon reflects a patriarchal code rearticulated as theological necessity. In truth, historical contingency has been recapitulated as transcendental inevitability. Those of us believers who are skeptical, even suspicious of human claims of divine revelation, also believe that God continues to speak to liberated—and liberating—people.

Therefore, in spite of occasional biblical crankiness about (alternative) sexualities, one can conceive of the biblical worldview as an interpretive canvas on which to sketch a liberating ethical intentionality. We must account for the manner in which writers smuggled their biases into the biblical text, even as the biblical landscape accommodated the social perspectives and cultural norms of societies that shaped its construction. We must also take the risk of reinterpretation and posit the principle of extended canonicity. I think we have to appeal to the extrabiblical textualities—of experience, suffering, and oppression—that shape the lives of believers and affect the modalities and anatomy of revelation. It is extrabiblical revelation because it is not contained in the Bible, but the Bible is contained in the believer's arc of experience. But blacks, women, gays, lesbians, and other minorities have to risk reinterpreting the words of the Bible in light of the Word—to whom the text points and who legitimates the experience of these minorities.

That covers the Bible, but what about the Qu'ran *and other sacred Scriptures?*

Sure, the same applies to the *Qu'ran*, the Bhagavad-Gita, the Torah, and other holy texts by which religious believers abide. And what I say is significant for all religious communities, whether they believe God speaks through Moses or Muhammad.

I wrote a story years ago about a black man who was rescued by Jesus, and they made love. So basically, it was very erotic, with brown skin to brown skin. What is your reaction to that type of story?

I think that there's space in our fantasy lives for the fusion of autonomous human eroticisms and divinely ordered sexual identities, especially as we struggle to imagine the dynamic and complex nature of our relationship to God. We have to remember that the intimate relation between believers and God is deeply and profoundly erotic at points, a perception that is reinforced in biblical texts and in theological and religious literature of all sorts throughout the ages. It makes sense that erotic communion is the analogical predicate for the intimate relation between the divine and the human. After all, we start with what we know—intimate human communion—and analogize to what we imagine—God's identity. Since erotic relations that take place in the context of a committed relationship is one of the most profound unions on earth, it is the basis for understanding the intensity of God's presence.

I think that whether it's your story or the story I read once, I think, in the book, *Spirituality for Ministry*, by Urban T. Holmes, more than twenty years ago—where some nuns were either fantasizing about making love to Jesus or dreaming about him in a sexual fashion—the notion of erotic engagements with God appear to be honored by sacred precedent. Communion with God takes multiple forms. I don't think we can, in an a priori fashion, determine any sexual orientation per se as off limits when it comes to understanding our relationship to God. It's important in this context to view our erotic relations in a metaphoric vein, that is, as attempts to analogize the highest moment of human ecstasy in regard to the ecstatic communion with God. Penetration of the flesh, among other erotic gestures, becomes a vehicle for a realized spiritual communion. I think all forms of edifying, nondestructive erotic play can ultimately become true grist for the mill of our sexual imaginations and express true hunger for God.

Let me ask you this then: I shared this story with a friend of mine, and he was offended. He called it blasphemy and he didn't want to touch the story; he didn't want to finish it. It was almost as if he were being contaminated or getting the evil spirit from the story itself, almost like he was afraid of it. What do you think about that?

Beliefs or fantasies that are radically dissimilar to our normal beliefs, behavior, and identity are certainly dangerous. They're taboo. They are contaminating, but perhaps in a good sense. It conjures for me the title of Mary Douglas's magisterial work, *Purity and Danger*. In some religious communities, the sexual relation is never to be thought of in relationship to God; the purity of God's identity is not to be enmeshed in the passionate, erotic communion. And yet God creates human beings with sexual organs and orientations. I think it is very dangerous and disturbing for many of us to imagine a different sexual order than the one that supports and governs our everyday existence. Plus, let's face it, we often fear what we don't understand. Or as Stevie Wonder phrased it, "when you believe in things that you don't understand, then you suffer"—but he added a key phrase that the dominant society should take to heart: "Superstition ain't the way." We could replace superstition with hate, fear, intolerance, bigotry, and the like. America once feared blacks and oppressed us and, when forced to accept us, discovered either that we weren't so different or that we presented a valuable difference that the nation eventually learned to embrace. The inability to embrace sexual difference says more about a culture or tradition that strangles innovation and creativity in our relationships to one another and to God, than it says about the sinful character of the fantasy or imagination that might offend us. Beliefs and passions that fall outside of the norm often bring terror, perhaps even the terror of self-recognition, which may be the ultimate terror. The possibility that the very thing I despise may represent a suppressed fantasy is all the more cause to outlaw that fantasy.

How important is fantasy to our sexuality?

I think fantasy is extraordinarily important to sexuality. Fantasy draws from the collective or individual expressions of one's historically shaped erotic and sexual desire. Fantasy is the projection of a possible erotic or sexual engagement with another human being or entity that is driven by our socially constructed and biologically driven conception of what is desirable. So fantasy, in one sense, is indivisible from the political and historical contexts in which our identities are shaped. We learn to desire the things we're taught to believe are desirable. Sometimes desire cuts across the grain of the socially sanctioned and "appropriate" fantasy. Certain fantasies are ruled as legitimate and others as illegitimate and, unsurprisingly, the rules follow a broadly patriarchal and heterosexist vein. It's just fine for young men to want to make love to young women at the appropriate age, but it's reprehensible for men and women to gravitate to their own gender, regardless of age. This notion falls into the realm of permissible fantasy. Permissible fantasy is an index of the sexual relations that may not be explicitly or overtly encouraged, but are nonetheless tolerated because they fall within the realm of heterosexual erotic identity. I'm thinking here, for example, of illicit sex between a married man and a woman. Even though there is a taboo to such sex, it causes nothing like the fear or revulsion of homosexual relations. In fact, the notion of a same-sex union is so profoundly offensive that its very existence is thought to be the mark of perversion, while adultery is viewed as a "sin." At that level, homoerotic fantasy cuts across the socially constructed object of desire and becomes a subversive political gesture in a heterosexist universe.

Fantasy nurtures the erotic life and permits the idealization of possibly perfect unions. If fantasies are read as both political projections and individual assertions of unrealized potential, or even remembered achievement, they become more than neo-Freudian expressions of suppressed sexualities. Of course, fantasy is also a crucial philosophical plank in the argument over offensive, transgressive sexual behavior. For instance, in the Catholic Church right now, the scandal over pedophilic priests is linked in the minds of some critics with outlaw sexual fantasies of illicit sex between men and boys. The fact that at least one accused priest was actively involved in NAMBLA, the North American Man/Boy Love Association, only served to cement the belief in the minds of millions that priests were little more than closeted gay pedophiles out to seduce altar boys. The perception among many straight Catholics is that this is a homoerotic fantasy that needs to be restricted, that if the fantasy didn't exist then the sexuality couldn't flourish. And even if the fantasy exists, the behavior should be outlawed.

Sexual fantasies present a template for erotic desire that is reproduced in bodily behavior. The fantasy is literally the prelude to the kiss. If one can control the fantasy life of a human being, then one might control the behavior that issues from the fantasy. Still, one might reasonably question if there is strict causality between fantasy and fulfillment. One is reminded of Jesus' words of warning that to even imagine an act of adultery is to essentially commit it: "But I say unto you, that whosoever looketh on a woman to lust after her hath committed adultery with her already in his heart." Few critics of homosexuality are likely to remonstrate with equal passion against millions who have lusted after a woman in their hearts, and who have, by Jesus' standards, already committed adultery. (One thinks unavoidably here of Jimmy Carter's confession in the pages of *Playboy* that he had lusted in his heart and therefore sinned.) Jesus is aiming here not simply at causality, but at the necessity to discipline one's imagination according to the ethical standards of a monogamous, committed relationship.

Hence, it wasn't the sexual identity that was the cause of sin—after all, it was articulated within the logic of heterosexuality—but a sexual imagination or fantasy that subverted faithful relations. One supposes, therefore, that one's sexual orientation would not necessarily alter the ethical prescriptions that regulate one's fantasies when one is in a committed relationship. One's moral practice seems more important in the fantasy life than one's sexual orientation. But I do think that fantasies play a legitimate, even crucial, function in sexual identity by nurturing a vision of the ideal relations in one's mind that one may not ever live up to. In this positive sense, fantasy is the picture of perfection against which practices are measured. That can be quite punishing because in a heterosexual world, where erotic ideals of perfection crowd the fantasies of many men, the collective imaginary, politically speaking, is often a pornographic one. Most women cannot live up to that ideal and perhaps they shouldn't have to even try to reach that unattainable goal. (The reason for my qualification here is that I don't want to rule out all acts of pornography as problematic, such as those enjoyed within a healthy erotic relationship among committed adults.)

My comments and observations are equally applicable to gays and lesbians. Ironically enough, in the humdrum, mundane, quotidian relations among homosexuals, gays and lesbians end up depressingly similar in their lives to heterosexuals. The lion's share of that depression is experienced by close-minded heterosexuals who come to realize that in most regards, there's no big difference in gays and lesbians and straight folk in their day-to-day existence. They just happen to have sex differently and may have the same sexual fantasies as heterosexuals, just with different partners. I'm not suggesting that all fantasies are good, healthy, or edifying, but that has nothing to do with sexual orientation. When they occur in a context of erotic and sexual health, as well as ethical strength, fantasies are just fine.

On an individual level, do you think there are such things as illegitimate fantasies?

For anybody, any group, I think that there are obvious limits. If you are a gay or lesbian person and you fantasize about murdering somebody in the process of having sex, I think that's a deeply disturbing, perhaps even potentially destructive fantasy, just as it is for straight folk. So yes, there are always ethical norms and limits generated within the logic of a given sexual ethic. You don't have to step outside of gay or lesbian sexuality to find a restrictive norm that could be imposed as a legitimate one. Within all orientations, sexual liberty should be shaped by moral responsibility. However, I don't think responsibility is determined by an ahistorical and depoliticized appeal to a transcendental norm of respect for the other, although I'm not knocking Kantian ethics, just disagreeing with aspects of its description of how morality works. I think that responsibility is a highly nuanced ethical concept, shaped by an ethic of respect that finds expression in historically specific and culturally conditioned relations to others. It causes one to ask the questions: How can one seek one's best while acting in a way not to harm others? How can the flourishing of one's erotic desire be checked by a sense of community that respects the integrity of the other? For example, rape is wrong, period, and the fantasy of rape that one intends to act on is highly destructive, regardless of one's sexual orientation. So yes, I think that . . .

Let me step in. There are some fantasies that are not acted on. Or let's think about if a fantasy is one that imitates or plays out behavior that some find offensive, say a woman who might have a fantasy about being raped . . .

Oh sure, sure. I thought about that immediately, as soon as I made my comments on rape. When it comes to fantasy, the sky's the limit, and if you tell no one your fantasy, or if you share your fantasy with someone of like mind, or act on it with consenting partners in a noncoercive, nonviolent fashion, it's all good. I certainly think that it's important to acknowledge the irreverence and the transgressive potential of autonomous sexual desire and fantasy within one's own mind. I think that the landscape of the psyche should be scouted for fantasies that allow people to uninhibitedly embrace their healthy erotic identities. I suppose even so-called illicit fantasies of rape, or of being raped, within a nonviolent context of reciprocal affection—or as a solitary fantasy nurtured within one's solipsistic universe of erotic desire—may be fine as long as one doesn't act on that fantasy in a violent fashion. For instance, we've got to allow for the pantomime of rape by couples as an erotic stimulation within the moral boundaries of their relationship. But I'm rather more libertarian about these matters and believe in a kind of autonomous sexuality within the limits of fantasy that allows people to sustain a range of irreverent, transgressive beliefs as long as they don't turn violent.

Years ago I was at a party and I saw a black man walking through the party wearing a leash behind a white man. This was in the Castro, in San Francisco, which at the time was very white supremacist, was very white. And I remember I wrote about it, and it got a lot of reaction. One of the questions that came up was, Does sexual fantasy imitate reality, or does reality imitate fantasy?

It's a dialectical process, isn't it? It's a give-and-take. Can we really divorce Robert Mapplethorp's *Man in a Gray Suit*—is that the name of it?

Polyester suit.

Man in a Polyester Suit, right. I'm mixing up Mapplethorp and Gregory Peck, who starred in the film *Man in the Gray Flannel Suit* [which I'm actually conflating with a film he did a decade earlier, *A Gentleman's Agreement*], which was about another form of bigotry: anti-Semitism. Anyway, as erotically charged as *Man in a Polyester Suit* is, and as full of transgressions against the heterosexual norm as that photo is, can we really divorce Mapplethorp's imagination from the political context of a socially constructed black male sexuality, with the large black organ it features as the site and source of so much fantasy and fear within the white heterosexual world?

I read in Mapplethorp's biography that he had fantasies about the black male animal. So that shaped my view of his photography.

Right, right. Technically, that may be true as a precise term of the mammal—the animal—but we both know that "animal" signifies racial primordialism and a savagery of sorts within the context of an eroticized black masculine subjectivity. But even individual fantasies reflect the political context in which people are shaped and in which they mature. The same is true for homoerotic desire, even as it thrives on articulations of non-normative desire. So it's dialectical: fantasies shape behaviors and behaviors are shaped by fantasies, though I'd still resist the strict one-to-one correlation between the two, since it fails to account for other causative factors. Fantasies are related to politics, and politics to the articulation of not only the possible—as in politics is the art of the possible—but also to the ideal one holds in one's mind.

When I think of the black man being led around on the leash by the white man, I think of the Hegelian dimension of the master-slave dialectic—or the relationship between the dominant and the dominated—illustrating, in this case, that there's a reciprocity of means that promotes a mutual reinforcement of fantasy and its fulfillment. They feed each other and sustain each other, even if in unequal fashion. On the one hand, the white man has the power because he can pull the black man. On the other hand, if the black man is stronger, he can resist; so there's give-and-take. Even in a relation of inequality, there's tension. That's not only Hegelian, it's downright Foucaultian. Whereas traditional theories of power located authority in conventional spots of domination in a rigid hierarchical schemata, Foucault contended that power breaks out everywhere. Its locus classicus is not simply in an institution or in hegemonic power, but in varied and complex relations and negotiations among and between the powerless as well.

That having been said, there's no question that when white men dominate black men, even within a homoerotic context, that can certainly be the corollary of a white supremacist ethic, or perhaps its direct expression. White supremacist domination, or fantasies of domination, may fuse with homoerotic desires of union with black men. I'm not suggesting that white gays and lesbians cannot be white supremacists, or that they cannot derive benefits, pleasures, and perks from white skin privilege. In fact, their white supremacist fantasies can be projected onto black bodies. For instance, the big black dick can be sought by gay white men who possess vicious, stereotypical views of black sexuality, aping—pun intended, I suppose—the behavior of some white straight communities. The relations of power and domination, although eroticized within a same-sex framework, can nevertheless express a white supremacist fantasy that is prior to the sexual fantasy, or at least coterminous with it. I think this is relatively untheorized in certain white gay and lesbian communities. Still, I must add, without essentializing them, that white gays and lesbians seem more aware in general of the complex racial dynamics of both intimate and social relations than their heterosexual counterparts. That's not a law or rule, just an informal ethnographic observation about how one minority is sometimes sensitive to the plight of another minority—although the exact opposite is also true, since we know that in straight black communities and among gay and lesbian white communities, there's plenty of ignorance and bigotry to go around.

One thing I was thinking about was in terms of the black male's perspective, and his eroticizing of white supremacy . . .

Oh sure. If heterosexual blacks can internalize white supremacist views where we hate our big black lips, our broad noses, or our big behinds—although there ain't that much black self-hatred around that, thank God!—and seek to modify features of our God-given beauty through cosmetic surgery, then certainly gay black men can absorb a white supremacist identity that subordinates black sexuality to dominant white sexualities. There's no homosexual exemption to racial self-hatred. In fact, for the black other-sexed, there's an exacerbating effect of self-hatreds, an exponential increase in multiple self-abnegations: with the black self and the gay self in tandem, there are potentially more selves to despise, resent, even hate. (I'm not playing into the additive theory of multiple minority statuses, here where folk don't integrate their various constituent identities into a "person." I'm simply trying to highlight how, among those prone or vulnerable to self-hatred, there's more to hate of one's self when it integrates a variety of identities and fights a variety of battles.)

Thus there is a reinscription of a pattern first generated within the context of patriarchal heterosexism's sexual fantasies, so that gay white communities rearticulate dominant whiteness. Some gays get off on white supremacist fantasies, which could conceivably fuse with rough trade homoeroticism that may be a cognate of white supremacist domination of the other. I'm not suggesting that the two are necessarily the same thing, or that they share a reciprocal relationship. I am simply saying that the two can merge. Homosexuality has modalities that extend the white supremacist's desire to subordinate the black sexual identity to himself, and the acceptance of that by black men is no less problematic because it occurs in the context of a homoerotic union. Just because the white fist up your ass gives you pleasure doesn't mean that it's not meant to rip out your guts.

But is the black man's fantasy an illegitimate fantasy?

It's not necessarily illegitimate, it's just troubling. It is legitimately problematic, even self-destructive. One cannot, by entering a homoerotic union, escape the ethics of relationality that should govern any healthy relationship.

Now how about educated, successful black men who have prison fantasies?

Again, I don't think anything is off-limits in terms of the autonomy of desire within the context of fantasy, so I am not interested in restricting such fantasies, even for those who may subordinate themselves to white men because they have internalized a white supremacist worldview. To be sure, I would find such fantasies problematic and self-destructive, even if they are literally instrumental to one's erotic existence. I don't have any desire to impose an ontologically grounded black ethic of propriety on the homosexual mind. Still, if such fantasies ultimately prove to be dehumanizing to gay black men, it diminishes the community, and if it diminishes the community, it impacts all of us in some measure. Self-loathing often has social repercussions.

Yeah, but see, I'm thinking that when these black men have prison fantasies, a lot of times their fantasies remind me of inverted white supremacy, where they are taking the ideas of black masculinity being animalistic, and so on, and they are eroticizing that.

That's different. It's like the state of nature meets the myth of the black savage as Jean-Jacques Rousseau shakes hands with Carl Van Vechten, the gay white patron of black artists during the Harlem Renaissance. In many ways, Van Vechten was a great guy, and incredibly supportive of black writers like Langston Hughes. But at his worst (and remember, as with most of us, the best and the worst live on the same block, in the same house, and when you get one you get the other), he seemed to go trolling among the Negroes to get in touch with the primitive state of man that was signified in blackness. Indeed, the genealogy of the eroticized primitivism and fetishized animalism of black masculinity stretches back to our first moments on Western soil as slaves in 1619, down to educated gay black men seeking the ideal savage type and the archetypically most unreconstructed black masculinity available—the black prisoner.

What may be erotically attractive to educated gay black men, even in the straight black male prisoner, is the prospect of situational homosexuality, since at any moment in prison, heterosexual agency is redirected into homosexual channels, given the restricted erotic commerce available. By definition, prison sex in male prisons among prisoners is sex between men, excluding the occasional heterosexual alliance in various guises. In prison, the black heterosexual male is often transformed into a vulnerable or victimizing gay man, at least in provisional, situational terms, his body marked by ad hoc homoeroticism. The idealization of the prisoner as the black savage is nothing but the postmodern urban update of the state of nature primitive with a huge sexual organ grinding in the fantasies of an erotically omnivorous culture.

This is a deep conversation. One last topic. I'm thinking about the word "queer." In your essay on the black church and sexuality in Race Rules, *you mentioned "Afriqueermericans." Queer is a word that is really debated in the black gay and lesbian community. I see queers of color, younger gays and lesbians, and I guess they use that word because it's supposed to be coopting it, and it's not white, and it's not male. When I was growing up, the term queer was used by white people, and it was used in reference to boys—little boys were "queer." I don't know where I'm going with this . . .*

Where you are going with it, at least in my mind, is that the change in the use of queer points to the dynamic character of linguistic transformation, signifying that words change over space and time. Moreover, they mean one thing to one group, something different to another group, much like "nigger" or "bitch." Queer is not as demonizing as nigger, or as bitch for that matter, but it carries an ontological negativity that is mediated through its enthralling witness against the norm. Queer: not normal. The riot against normalcy that queer betokens makes it a highly explosive and useful weapon in the politics of publicity for gay and lesbian causes. I think here the hierarchy of race makes a huge difference even in gay and lesbian communities. Black gays and lesbians, as well as other-sexed people, have been caught in the crosswinds of seeking acceptance in predominantly white gay and lesbian communities that provide erotic and intellectual succor, but which may close them out culturally—or hunting for love in a black culture that provides familiar rituals of home while alienating, stigmatizing, and even demonizing them because of their sexual preferences. They've been caught betwixt and between; it has been especially difficult for minority gays, bisexuals, and lesbians to find an appropriate grammar of erotic identification and communion.

Although "queer" has the resonance of a specific time and cultural identification, it has interpretive flexibility and can be used to signify a transgressive, even playful, resistance to the term's negative connotations. Queer can be a terminological rallying point to galvanize multiple constituencies within gay and lesbian communities. There can be a postmodern sense of *jouissance* as well, as in, "Damned right, I'm queer," or "Damned right, I'm a fag"—the latter expression, perhaps, a more tolerable or racially resonant signifier among a certain generation of blacks. Such terms represent the articulation of ethical agency among gays and lesbians that says, "We refuse to be put off by your negative language; in fact, we are going to rearticulate it positively in our world in our own way." The same was done, of course, by some blacks with the word "nigger," and by some women with the word "bitch." Whether that works or not, I think, is an open question. I think it's more difficult to talk about among gays and lesbians of color because they have dramatically participated in multiple kinship groups in their quest for a home. Only when you find a home can you enjoy the leisure of self-parody or the luxury of grounding a derisive term in the history of your community's response to bigotry. There has not been, by and large, a stabilization of black gay and lesbian communities. Individual examples of success abound, but authentic homosexual community has been much more difficult to attain.

One thing that I think is different between the words "nigger" and "queer" is that, when I hear rappers use the word nigger, I don't think they are really changing its meaning. They are reinforcing and personifying what it means. Years ago, we couldn't point to what a nigger was. If someone called you a "nigger," you said, "Well I'm not a dumb person, I'm not a nigger." Now you have these black men acting ignorant, acting loud, cursing, swearing, and so on, and saying, "By the way, I'm a 'nigger' and I'm black." So they personify what "nigger" is. I think what "queers" are doing—even though I hate the word, it sounds nasty—is that they are at least projecting intelligence and projecting respect.

Right, right, right. That is a very interesting point. You've touched on one of the great contentions in black life, especially with the rise of hip-hop culture. Some critics, however, would disagree with you; they would say that there were dumb, ignorant people to whom we could point all along in black history. They would tell you that there have always been people who could justify the stereotype. But they will also tell you that "nigger" as an epithet never represented the complexity of black identity, and that to isolate a minor personality type—the so-called nigger—within the behavioral norms of blackness to justify the demonization of all black people was patently unjust. As a result, blacks questioned the legitimacy of the claim that the epithet was deployed by whites to define the behavior of people who fell outside the norm of good behavior. That's because every black person in the eyes of most whites was a nigger.

In that light, we might be able to concede the racial daring and subversive attempt among some blacks to appropriate the linguistic negativity of "nigger" and to recirculate, recontextualize, recode, refigure, refashion, and rearticulate the term for their purposes. At least now when it came to that word, the "niggas"—the term as it is baptized in black linguistic subversion—were in control, challenging whites and bourgeois blacks who could never consider using the term in any incarnation. In the eyes of the contemporary "niggas," bourgeois blacks do not exercise the same level of discretion over their rhetorical and linguistic self-representation as do the folk, say, in hip-hop.

So the argument could be made that there is indeed a flip, that the people who were supposed to be dumb are not dumb at all. Instead, they are playing the culture to the hilt. They are reinforcing certain stereotypes while challenging others. They're reaping economic remuneration from trying to parody and stigmatize what "nigger" is or saying, "Yeah, if you call me a nigger, I'm going to live up to that, I'm going to be a larger-than-life nigger, and I'll show you what that might mean." Or they might say, "I dare you to keep calling me 'nigger' in the face of my embracing this term in such a fashion as to not only reinforce the negative behaviors that you think characterize the term, but to deploy it as a rhetorical weapon against the white supremacy that seeks to deny black people the opportunity to choose their own destinies." So I think the use of "nigga" is much more complex than the either/or absolutism that bewitches too many black critics in their discussion of the term.

I understand your point in terms of queer. But your perception that "queers" are engaging in their linguistic subversion in an intelligent way has to do with the fact that gay and lesbian people have not been subject to the same stereotype of being unintelligent that blacks have been saddled with. For centuries now, blackness has signified stupidity and ignorance in the West. But gays and lesbians have not been perceived as intellectually inferior to heterosexuals. In fact, the opposite is true: gays have been tied, at least in the West, to the Greeks, who were viewed as exceeding intelligent. So what you face as a queer minority is the improbable complexity of black gay identities because you're dealing with both stereotypes collapsing on your head: dumb nigger and smart queer. Although I'm sure an exception is made for black queers, whose race may cancel out their sexual orientation, at least in the intelligence sweepstakes. How much more degraded and contradictory can one get in one body? So I think that black gays and lesbians would certainly be much more sensitive to the nomenclature of self-disclosure and self-description than even most white gays and lesbians might ever imagine.

One last topic: class issues. By most people's account, we would be considered bourgie. I think, like W.E.B. Du Bois's notion of "the talented tenth," we're leading the masses. Don't you feel that as such we should set an example . . .

Set an example for whom?

In general for the masses of African Americans, since we're going to be leaders. Say for instance, earlier you mentioned bourgie blacks, and it was kind of in a derogatory sense. In fact, I think most "bourgie blacks" are doing positive things.

Sure, sure. What I mean by "bourgie"—which is a pejorative term shortened from bourgeois—is not simply middle class. I mean by bourgie the construction of a self-determined persona that is hostile to, and scornful of, ordinary black people. You can be rich and not be bourgie. Class in black America has been less about how much money you make or how many stocks you have than the politics of style. Still, your overall point is well taken. I think that those of us who are privileged—and that includes gays and lesbians who have high levels of education—have an absolute obligation to "give back" to the less fortunate. I think we are bound by blood, history, and destiny to our brothers and sisters, especially to those who will never know the privilege or positive visibility that many in the middle class enjoy. And we should cross all lines—sexual, economic, religious, gender, geographical, generational—in speaking for the oppressed. For instance, that's why I think it's incumbent on me as a heterosexual black man to speak against the bigotry and injustice faced by my black brothers and sisters who are gay, lesbian, bisexual, and other-sexed. And it's equally important for educated, upwardly mobile blacks to not forget those who have been entombed in permanent poverty and miseducation.

It is part of the hidden courage of black gays and lesbians that despite the stigma they have endured, they continue to work within the arc of black identity and community in fulfillment of their sense of personal and political destiny. I think that's a beautiful thing. Being "queer" or "gay" is a tremendous struggle, but even before the enemies of black people see a fey snap of the wrist or the "butch" dress of lesbian women, they see black pigment. So pigment may trump sexual orientation in a manner that many black gays and lesbians intuitively understand in their bodies, even though deeply inscribed in their bodies at the same time is the recognition of their unalterable sexual identities that need to be sustained, affirmed, and prized. To the degree that black gays and lesbians struggle with the complex convergence of racial, sexual, gender, and class issues, they already represent courageous role models of negotiating differences in one body at one site. They represent to us what blackness will look like well into the twenty-first century.

What a beautiful ending.

Thanks, brother.

Interview by Kheven LaGrone
Chicago, Illinois, 2002

BIBLIOGRAPHY

BOOKS

Aaron, Hank. *Aaron*. New York: Crowell, 1974.

Adams, Joey, and Henry Tobais. *The Borscht Belt*. New York: Bobbs-Merrill, 1966.

Adams, Linda, and Keith Burns, eds. *James Dean: Behind the Scene*. New York: Carol, 1990.

Alexander, Paul. *Boulevard of Broken Dreams: The Life, Times, and Legend of James Dean*. New York: Viking, 1994.

Allen, Theodore W. *The Invention of the White Race*. Vol. 1, *Racial Oppression and Social Control*. London: Verso, 1994.

Ali, Drew. *The Holy Koran of the Moorish Science Temple of America*. N.p., 1978.

Ali, Muhammad, and Richard Durham. *The Greatest: My Own Story*. New York: Random House, 1975.

Anderson, Benedict R. *Imagined Communities: Reflections on the Origin and Spread of Nationalism*. London: Verso, 1984.

Angelou, Maya. *I Know Why the Caged Bird Sings*. New York: Random House, 1969.

______. *Just Give Me a Cool Drink of Water 'Fore I Diiie*. New York: Random House, 1971.

______. *Poems*. New York: Bantam, 1986.

______. *The Complete Collected Poems of Maya Angelou*. New York: Random House, 1994.

______. *Even the Stars Look Lonesome*. New York: Random House, 1997.

Anzaldúa, Gloria, ed. *Making Face, Making Soul (Haciendo Caras): Creative and Critical Perspectives by Feminists of Color*. San Francisco: Aunt Lute Foundation Books, 1990.

Archer, Jules. *Rage in the Streets: Mob Violence in America.* San Diego: Browndeer, 1994.

Arendt, Hannah. *The Human Condition*. Chicago: University of Chicago Press, 1958.

______. *Men in Dark Times*. New York: Harcourt, Brace & World, 1968.

______. *On Violence*. New York: Harcourt, Brace & World, 1970.

______. *Crises of the Republic: Lying in Politics, Civil Disobedience, On Violence, Thoughts on Politics, and Revolution*. New York: Harcourt Brace Jovanovich, 1972.

Armstrong, Louis. *Satchmo: My Life in New Orleans*. New York: Da Capo, 1986.

______. *Louis Armstrong, In His Own Words: Selected Writings*. Ed. Thomas Brothers. New York: Oxford University Press, 2001.

Baker-Fletcher, Karen. *A Singing Something: Womanist Reflections on Anna Julia Cooper*. New York: Crossroad, 1994.

Baraka, Imamu Amiri. *Blues People: Negro Music in White America*. New York: Morrow, 1963.

Barlow, William. *"Looking Up at Down": The Emergence of Blues Culture*. Philadelphia: Temple University Press, 1989.

Bascom, William Russell. *The Yoruba of Southwestern Nigeria.* New York: Holt, Rinehart & Winston, 1969.

Beath, Warren Newton. *The Death of James Dean*. New York: Grove, 1986.

Beauvoir, Simone de. *The Long March*. Cleveland: World, 1958.

______. *The Prime of Life*. Cleveland: World, 1962.

Becker, Ernest. *Beyond Alienation: A Philosophy of Education for the Crisis of Democracy*. New York: Braziller, 1967.

Bennett, Lerone. *Black Athena: The Afroasiatic Roots of Classical Civilization*. New Brunswick, N.J.: Rutgers University Press, 1987.

______. *Before the Mayflower: A History of Black America.* Rev. ed. New York: Viking Penguin, 1988.

Bernal, Martin. *Black Athena Writes Back: Martin Bernal Responds to His Critics*. Ed. David Chioni Moore. Durham, N.C.: Duke University Press, 2001.

Bernstein, Mary, and Renate Reimann, eds. *Queer Families, Queer Politics: Challenging Culture and the State*. New York: Columbia University Press, 2001.

Berry, Mary Frances, and John W. Blassingame. *Long Memory: The Black Experience in America*. New York: Oxford University Press, 1982.

Bhabha, Homi. *Nation and Narrative*. London: Routledge, 1990.

______. *The Location of Culture*. London: Routledge, 1993.

Black, Allida M. *Modern American Queer History*. Philadelphia: Temple University Press, 2001.

Blauner, Robert. *Alienation and Freedom: The Factory Worker and His Industry*. Chicago: University of Chicago Press, 1964.

Bloom, Harold. *Anxiety of Influence: A Theory of Poetry.* New York: Oxford University Press, 1973.

Bloom, Harold, ed. *Black American Prose Writers of the Harlem Renaissance.* New York: Chelsea House, 1994.

______. *Modern Black American Poets and Dramatists.* New York: Chelsea House, 1995.

Bloomfield, Morton W. *The Interpretation of Narrative: Theory and Practice.* Cambridge: Harvard University Press, 1970.

Bogle, Donald. *Dorothy Dandridge: A Biography.* New York: Amista/St. Martin's, 1997.

Boritt, G. S., and James McPherson, eds. *Why the Confederacy Lost.* New York: Oxford University Press, 1992.

Bradley, David. *Life and Letters.* New York: Oxford University Press, 1997.

Bradley, David, et al. *The X Factor.* New York: Oxford University Press, 1992.

Brahms, Johannes. *Johannes Brahms: Life and Letters.* Ed. Styra Avins. New York: Oxford University Press, 1997.

Brandon, George. *Santeria from Africa to the New World: The Dead Sell Memories.* Bloomington: Indiana University Press, 1993.

Brown, Jim, and Steve Delsohn. *Out of Bounds.* New York: Kensington, 1989.

Brunn, Harry O. *The Story of the Original Dixieland Jazz Band.* Baton Rouge: Louisiana State University Press, 1960.

Bunche, Ralph J. *Ralph J. Bunche: Selected Speeches and Writings.* Ed. Charles P. Henry. Ann Arbor: University of Michigan Press, 1995.

Burgan, Michael. *John Adams: Second U.S. President.* Philadelphia: Chelsea House, 2001.

Burnham, Kenneth E. *God Comes to America: Father Divine and the Peace Mission Movement.* Boston: Lambeth, 1979.

Burns, George. *100 Years, 100 Stories.* New York: Putnam, 1996.

Burns, George, and Hal Goldman. *Wisdom of the 90s.* New York: Putnam, 1991.

Butler, Judith. *Bodies That Matter: On the Discursive Limits of "Sex."* New York: Routledge, 1993.

______. *Excitable Speech: A Politics of the Performative.* New York: Routledge, 1997.

______. *Gender Trouble: Feminism and the Subversion of Identity.* New York: Routledge, 1999.

Cable, George Washington. *The Dance in Place Congo and Creole Slave Songs.* New Orleans: Faruk Von Turk, 1974.

Callas, Maria. *Callas at Julliard: The Master Classes.* Ed. John Ardoin. New York: Knopf, 1987.

Cannon, Katie G. *Teaching Preaching: Isaac Rufus Clark and Black Sacred Rhetoric.* New York: Continuum, 2002.

Cantin, Paul. *Alanis Morissette: A Biography.* New York: St. Martin's, 1998.

Carmichael, Stokely. *Stokely Speaks: Black Power Back to Pan-Africanism*. New York: Random House, 1971.

Carmichael, Stokely, and Charles V. Hamilton. *Black Power: The Politics of Liberation in America*. New York: Knopf, 1967.

Carnes, Mark C., ed. *Past Imperfect: History According to the Movies*. New York: Henry Holt, 1995.

Carter, Dan T. *From George Wallace to Newt Gingrich: Race in the Conservative Counterrevolution, 1963–1994*. Baton Rouge: Louisiana State University Press, 1996.

Caruso, Enrico, and Andrew Farkas. *Enrico Caruso: My Father and My Family*. Portland, Ore.: Amadeus, 1990.

Castro, Fidel, et al. *Revolutionary Struggle, 1947–1958*. Cambridge: MIT Press, 1972.

Cell, John Whitson. *The Highest Stage of White Supremacy: The Origins of Segregation in South Africa and the American South*. New York: Cambridge University Press, 1982.

Chafe, William Henry. *Remembering Jim Crow: African Americans Tell About Life in the Segregated South*. New York: Norton, 2001.

Chic Street Man, Zora Neale Hurston, and George C. Wolfe. *Spunk: Three Tales*. New York: Theatre Communications Group, 2000.

Ching, Barbara. *Knowing Your Place: Rural Identity and Cultural Hierarchy*. New York: Routledge, 1996.

Clement, Eaton. *A History of the Old Southern Confederacy: The Emergence of a Reluctant Nation*. New York: Macmillan, 1974.

Cobain, Kurt. *Incesticide*. Milwaukee: Hal Leonard, 1995.

______. *Journals*. New York: Riverhead, 2002.

Cohn, Lawrence. *Nothing but the Blues: The Music and the Musicians*. New York: Abbeville, 1993.

Cole, Michael D. *The L.A. Riots: Rage in the City of Angels*. Springfield, N.J.: Enslow, 1999.

Collier, James Lincoln. *The Making of Jazz: A Comprehensive History*. New York: Dell, 1978.

______. *Louis Armstrong: An American Genius*. New York: Oxford University Press, 1983.

______. *Jazz: The American Theme Song*. New York: Oxford University Press, 1993.

Collins, Patricia Hill. *Black Feminist Thought: Knowledge, Consciousness, and the Politics of Empowerment*. Boston: Unwin Hyman, 1990.

Columbus, Christopher. *The Log of Christopher Columbus*. Ed. Robert Henderson Fuson. Camden, Me.: International Marine, 1987.

Cone, Cecil Wayne. *The Identity Crisis in Black Theology*. Nashville: AMEC, 1975.

Cone, James H. *Black Theology and Black Power*. New York: Seabury, 1969.

______. *God of the Oppressed*. San Francisco: Harper San Francisco, 1975.

______. *Risks of Faith: The Emergence of a Black Theology of Liberation, 1968–1998*. Boston: Beacon, 1999.

Cooper, Anna J. *The Voice of Anna Julia Cooper: Including 'A Voice from the South' and Other Important Essays, Papers, and Letters*. Ed. Charles C. Lemert and Esme Bhan. Lanham, Md.: Rowman & Littlefield, 1998.

Copeland, Kenneth. *The Force of Faith*. Forth Worth, Tex.: KCP Publications, 1983.

______. *Honor: Walking in Honesty, Truth, and Integrity*. Tulsa: Harrison House, 1992.

______. *A Journey of Faith*. Fort Worth, Tex.: Kenneth Copeland Publications, 1997.

Cosby, Bill. *Time Flies*. New York: Doubleday, 1987.

Crane, Hart. *The Poems of Hart Crane*. Ed. Marc Simon. New York: Liveright, 1986.

Crowther, Bruce. *Gene Krupa: His Life and Times*. New York: Universe Books, 1987.

Dalton, David. *James Dean: American Icon*. Ed. Ron Cayen. New York: St. Martin's, 1984.

Daniels, Jessie. *White Lies: Race, Class, Gender, and Sexuality in White Supremacist Discourse*. New York: Routledge, 1995.

Davies, William David. *Invitation of the New Testament: A Guide to Its Witness*. Ed. David Duabe. New York: Doubleday, 1966.

Davis, Francis. *The History of the Blues: The Roots, the Music, the People: From Charlie Parker to Robert Cray*. New York: Hyperion, 1995.

Davis, Miles, and Quincy Troupe. *Miles: The Autobiography*. New York: Touchstone, 1990.

DeGeneres, Ellen. *My Point: And I Do Have One*. New York: Bantam, 1995.

DeLong, Thomas A. *Pops: Paul Whiteman, King of Jazz*. New York: New Century, 1983.

Dewey, John. *John Dewey on Education*. Chicago: University of Chicago Press, 1983.

Dillard, J. L. *Black English: Its History and Usage in the United States*. New York: Random House, 1972.

Dingle-El, Timothy. *The Resurrection: Moorish Science Temple of America*. Baltimore: Gateway, 1978.

Dodd, C. H. *More New Testament Studies*. Grand Rapids, Mich.: Eerdmans, 1968.

______. *The Founder of Christianity*. New York: Macmillan, 1970.

Dor-Ner, Zvi, and William Scheller. *Columbus and the Age of Discovery*. New York: Morrow, 1991.

Douglas, Ann. *Terrible Honesty: Mongrel Manhattan in the 1920s*. New York: Farrar, Straus & Giroux, 1995.

Dovidio, John. *Prejudice, Discrimination, and Racism*. San Diego: Academic Press, 1986.

Dowdey, Clifford. *The Land They Fought For: The Story of the South as the Confederacy, 1832–1865*. Garden City, N.Y.: Doubleday, 1955.

Drewal, Henry John. *Yoruba: Nine Centuries of African Art and Thought.* Ed. John Pemberton and Allen Wardwell. New York: Center for African Art/H. N. Abrams, 1989.

D'Souza, Dinesh. *The End of Racism: Principles for a Multiracial Society.* New York: Free Press, 1995.

Du Bois, W.E.B. *The Souls of Black Folk.* New York: Penguin, 1989.

______. *Black Reconstruction in America.* Rev. ed. New York: Harcourt, Brace & Company, 1992.

Dyson, Michael Eric. *Reflecting Black: African-American Cultural Criticism.* Minneapolis: University of Minnesota Press, 1993.

______. *Making Malcolm: The Myth and Meaning of Malcolm X.* New York: Oxford University Press, 1995.

______. *Between God and Gangsta Rap: Bearing Witness to Black Culture.* New York: Oxford University Press, 1996.

______. *Race Rules: Navigating the Color Line.* Reading, Mass.: Addison-Wesley, 1996.

______. *I May Not Get There with You: The True Martin Luther King Jr.* New York: Free Press, 2000.

______. *Holler If You Hear Me: Searching for Tupac Shakur.* New York: Basic Civitas, 2001.

Earl, Riggins Renal. *Dark Symbols, Obscure Signs: God, Self, and Community in the Slave Mind.* Maryknoll, N.Y.: Orbis, 1993.

Egan, James. *Authorizing Experience.* Princeton: Princeton University Press, 1999.

Epstein, Lawrence J. *The Haunted Smile: The Story of Jewish Comedians in America.* New York: Public Affairs, 2001.

Ewen, David. *The Life and Death of Tin Pan Alley: The Golden Age of American Popular Music.* New York: Funk & Wagnalls, 1964.

Fallaize, Elizabeth, ed. *Simone de Beauvoir: A Critical Reader.* London: Routledge, 1998.

Farrakhan, Louis, Lenora Fulani, and Al Sharpton. *Independent Black Leadership in America: Minister Louis Farrakhan, Dr. Lenora B. Fulani, Reverend Al Sharpton.* New York: Castillo International, 1990.

Festenstein, Matthew. *Pragmatism and Political Theory: From Dewey to Rorty.* Chicago: University of Chicago Press, 1998.

Fine, Michelle, et al., eds. *Off White Readings on Race, Power, and Society.* New York: Routledge, 1996.

Foner, Eric. *A House Divided.* New York: Norton, 1991.

Foner, Philip Sheldon, ed. *The Black Panthers Speak.* Philadelphia: Lippincott, 1970.

Foy, David M. *Great Discoveries and Inventions by African-Americans.* Edgewood, Md.: APU Publishing Group, 1998.

Frankenberg, Ruth. *White Women, Race Matters: The Social Construction of Whiteness.* Minneapolis: University of Minnesota Press, 1993.

Franklin, C. L. *Give Me This Mountain: Life History and Selected Sermons*. Ed. Jeff T. Titon. Urbana: University of Illinois Press, 1989.

Franklin, Robert Michael. *Another Day's Journey: Black Churches Confronting the American Crisis.* Minneapolis: Fortress, 1997.

Frazier, Edward Franklin. *The Free Negro Family: A Study of Family Origins Before the Civil War*. New York: Arno, 1968.

______. *On Race Relations: Selected Writings*. Ed. G. Franklin Edwards. Chicago: University of Chicago Press, 1968.

______. *The Negro Church in America*. New York: Schocken, 1971.

______. *Black Bourgeoisie*. New York: Free Press, 1997.

Frye, Marilyn. *Willful Virgin: Essays in Feminism, 1976–1992*. Freedom, Calif.: Crossing, 1992.

Gabel, Leona C. *From Slavery to the Sorbonne and Beyond: The Life and Writings of Anna J. Cooper*. Northampton, Mass.: Smith College, 1982.

Gardiner, James J., and J. Deotis Roberts, eds. *Quest for a Black Theology.* Philadelphia: Pilgrim, 1971.

Garvey, John, and Noel Ignatiev, eds. *Race Traitor.* New York: Routledge, 1996.

Gates, Henry Louis. *Signifying Monkey: A Theory of Afro-American Literary Criticism.* New York: Oxford University Press, 1988.

______. *Loose Canons: Notes on the Culture Wars.* New York: Oxford University Press, 1992.

Gates, Henry Louis, and Cornel West. *The African-American Century: How Black Americans Have Shaped Our Country*. New York: Free Press, 2000.

Giddins, Gary. *Visions of Jazz: The First Century*. New York: Oxford University Press, 1998.

Gillespie, Dizzy, and Al Fraser. *To Be, or Not . . . to BOP: Memoirs*. Garden City, N.Y.: Doubleday, 1979.

Giovanni, Nikki. *Black Feeling, Black Talk, Black Judgment.* New York: Morrow, 1970.

______. *Racism 101*. New York: Quill, 1994.

______. *Selected Poems of Nikki Giovanni.* New York: Morrow, 1996.

Giroux, Henry. *Border Crossings: Cultural Workers and the Politics of Education.* New York: Routledge, 1992.

______. *Counternarratives.* New York: Routledge, 1996.

______. *Channel Surfing: Race Talk and the Destruction of Today's Youth.* New York: St. Martin's, 1997.

Gitlin, Todd. *The Sixties: Years of Hope, Days of Rage*. New York: Bantam, 1987.

______. *The Twilight of Common Dreams: Why America Is Wracked by Culture Wars.* New York: Metropolitan, 1995.

Goldberg, Isaac, and Edward Jablonski. *Tin Pan Alley: A Chronicle of American Popular Music*. New York: F. Ungar, 1961.

Gooding-Williams, Robert, ed. *Reading Rodney King: Reading Urban Uprising.* New York: Routledge, 1993.

Goss, Clay, and Chico Hall. *Bill Pickett: Black Bulldogger.* New York: Hill & Wang/Random House, 1970.

Gourse, Leslie. *Unforgettable: The Life and Mystique of Nat King Cole.* New York: St. Martin's, 1991.

Hancock, Sibyl. Illustrated by Lorinda Bryan Cauley. *Bill Picket: First Black Rodeo Star.* New York: Harcourt Brace Jovanovich, 1977.

Handler, Edward. *America and Europe in the Political Thought of John Adams.* Cambridge: Harvard University Press, 1964.

Hanes, Bailey C. *Bill Pickett, Bulldogger: The Biography of a Black Cowboy.* Norman: University of Oklahoma Press, 1977.

Haraway, Donna. *Simians, Cyborgs, and Women: The Reinvention of Nature.* New York: Routledge, 1991.

Hartogs, Renatus. *Four-Letter Word Games: The Psychology of Obscenity.* New York: M. Evans, 1967.

Hartogs, Renatus, and Lucy Freeman. *The Two Assassins.* New York: Crowell, 1965.

Hasse, John Edward, ed. *Ragtime: Its History, Composers, and Music.* New York: Schirmer, 1985.

Hayes, E. Nelson, and Tanya Hayes, eds. *Claude Levi-Strauss: The Anthropologist as Hero.* Cambridge: MIT Press, 1970.

Herndon, Booton. *The Sweetest Music This Side of Heaven: The Guy Lombardo Story.* New York: McGraw-Hill, 1964.

Herrnstein, Richard J., and Charles A. Murray. *The Bell Curve: Intelligence and Class Structure in American Life.* New York: Simon & Schuster, 1996.

Hill, Mike. *Whiteness: A Critical Reader.* Ed. Mike Hill. New York: New York University Press, 1997.

Hochschild, Jennifer. *Facing Up to the American Dream: Race, Class, and the Soul of the Nation.* Princeton: Princeton University Press, 1995.

Holley, Val. *James Dean: The Biography.* New York: St. Martin's, 1995.

hooks, bell. *Black Looks: Race and Representation.* Boston: South End, 1992.

Horowitz, Tony. *Confederates in the Attic.* New York: Pantheon, 1998.

Hughe, Langston. *The Collected Poems of Langston Hughes.* Ed. Arnold Rampersad and David Roessel. New York: Knopf, 1994.

Hume, David. *The Philosophical Works of David Hume.* 4 vols. Edinburgh: Printed for A. Black and W. Tait, 1826.

Hurston, Zora Neale. *I Love Myself When I Am Laughing . . . and Then Again When I Am Looking Mean and Impressive: A Zora Neale Hurston Reader.* Ed. Alice Walker. Old Westbury, N.Y.: Feminist Press, 1979.

Hutchinson, Louise Daniel. *Anna J. Cooper: A Voice from the South*. Washington, D.C.: Smithsonian Institution Press, 1981.

Ignatius, Noel. *How the Irish Became White*. New York: Routledge, 1995.

Irons, Peter H. *May It Please the Court: The First Amendment: Transcripts of the Oral Arguments Made Before the Supreme Court in Sixteen Key First Amendment Cases*. New York: New Press, 1997.

Isaacs, Stan. *Jim Brown: The Golden Year 1964*. Englewood Cliffs, N.J.: Prentice-Hall, 1970.

Jackson, Robert B. *Earl the Pearl: The Story of Earl Monroe*. New York: H. A. Walck, 1974.

Jacobs, Jim. *Our Thing Is Drum!* Detroit: Black Star Printing, 1970.

James, C. L. R. *American Civilization*. Cambridge, Mass.: Blackwell, 1993.

Jasen, David A. *Tin Pan Alley: The Composers, the Songs, the Performers, and Their Times: The Golden Age of American Popular Music from 1886 to 1956*. New York: D. I. Fine, 1988.

Jasen, David A., and Trebor Jay Tichenor. *Rags and Ragtime: A Musical History*. New York: Dover, 1989.

Jefferson, Thomas. *The Portable Thomas Jefferson*. Ed. Merrill D. Peterson. New York: Viking Penguin, 1975.

Jensen, Arthur Robert. *Educability and Group Differences*. New York: Harper & Row, 1973.

Jones, Mary Ellen. *Christopher Columbus and His Legacy: Opposing Viewpoints*. San Diego: Greenhaven, 1992.

Kanfer, Stefan. *A Summer World: The Attempt to Build a Jewish Eden in the Catskills from the Days of the Ghetto to the Rise and Decline of the Borscht Belt*. New York: Farrar, Straus & Giroux, 1989.

Kant, Immanuel. *The Philosophy of Kant: Immanuel Kant's Moral and Political Writings*. Ed. Carl J. Friedrich. New York: Modern Library, 1949.

Kaplan, John, and Jon R. Waltz. *The Trial of Jack Ruby*. New York: Macmillan, 1965.

Katz, William Loren. *Black People Who Made the Old West*. New York: Crowell, 1977.

Kaufman, Walker, ed. *The Portable Nietzsche*. New York: Viking, 1988.

Kelley, Robin D. G. *Race Rebels: Culture, Politics, and the Black Working Class*. New York: Free Press, 1994.

______. *Yo' Mama's Disfunktional! Fighting the Culture Wars in Urban America*. Boston: Beacon, 1997.

King, Alan, and Chris Chase. *Name Dropping: The Life and Lies of Alan King*. New York: Scribner, 1996.

King, B.B., and David Ritz. *Blues All Around Me: The Autobiography of B.B. King*. New York: Avon, 1996.

King, Coretta Scott. *My Life with Martin Luther King Jr.* New York: Holt, Rinehart & Winston, 1969.

King, Edward. *The Great South.* Ed. W. Magruder Drake and Robert Jones. Baton Rouge: Louisiana State University Press, 1972.

Kipnis, Laura. *Bound and Gagged: Pornography and the Politics of Fantasy in America.* New York: Grove, 1996.

Kivel, Paul. *Uprooting Racism: How White People Can Work for Racial Justice.* Philadelphia, Pa.: New Society Publishers, 1995.

Klauber, Bruce H. *World of Gene Krupa: That Legendary Drummin' Man.* Ventura, Calif.: Pathfinder, 1990.

Kochman, Thomas. *Black and White Styles in Conflict.* Chicago: University of Chicago Press, 1981.

Kozol, Jonathan. *The Night Is Dark and I Am Far from Home.* Boston: Houghton Mifflin, 1975.

______. *Savage Inequalities: Children in America's School.* New York: Crown, 1991.

Kristeva, Julia. *Desire in Language: A Semiotic Approach to Literature and Art.* Ed. Leon S. Roudiez. New York: Columbia University Press, 1980.

______. *The Kristeva Reader.* Ed. Toril Moi. New York: Columbia University Press, 1986.

______. *Black Sun: Depression and Melancholia.* New York: Columbia University Press, 1992.

Kromkowski, John A. *Race and Ethnic Relations 98/99.* Guilford, Conn.: Dushkin/McGraw Hill, 1998.

Kübler-Ross, Elisabeth. *On Death and Dying.* New York: Macmillan, 1969.

______. *On Children and Death.* New York: Macmillan, 1983.

Lees, Gene. *You Can't Steal a Gift: Dizzy, Clark, Milt, and Nat.* New Haven: Yale University Press, 2001.

Leonard, William T. *Masquerade in Black.* Metuchen, N.J.: Scarecrow, 1986.

Lewis, Jerry, and Herb Gluck. *Jerry Lewis, in Person.* New York: Atheneum, 1982.

Lipsitz, George. *Time Passages: Collective Memory and American Popular Culture.* Minneapolis: University of Minnesota Press, 1990.

Litchfield, Jack. *The Canadian Jazz Discography.* Toronto: Toronto University Press, 1983.

______. *Toronto Jazz: A Survey of Live Appearances and Radio Broadcasts of Dixieland Jazz Experienced in Toronto During the Period 1948–1950.* Toronto: J. Litchfield, 1992.

Lomax, Alan. *Three Thousand Years of Black Poetry.* Greenwich, Conn.: Fawcett Crest, 1971.

______. *Mister Jelly Roll: The Fortunes of Jelly Roll Morton, New Orleans Creole, and "Inventor of Jazz."* Berkeley: University of California Press, 1973.

______. *The Land Where the Blues Began.* New York: Pantheon, 1993.

Lombardo, Guy, and Jack Altshul. *Auld Acquaintance.* Garden City, N.Y.: Doubleday, 1975.

Long, Charles H. *Alpha: The Myths of Creation.* Chico, Calif.: Scholar Press/American Academy of Religion, 1963.

______. *Significations: Signs, Symbols, and Images in the Interpretation of Religion.* Philadelphia: Fortress, 1984.

Lott, Eric. *Vision, Tradition, Interpretation: Theology, Religion, and the Study of Religion.* Berlin: Mouton De Gruyter, 1987.

______. *Love and Theft: Blackface Minstrelsy and the American Working Class.* New York: Oxford University Press, 1993.

Louis, Joe, Art Rust, and Edna Rust. *Joe Louis: My Life.* New York: Harcourt Brace Jovanovich, 1978.

Love, Nat. *The Life and Adventures of Nat Love, Better Known in the Cattle Country as "Deadwood Dick."* Lincoln: University of Nebraska Press, 1995.

Lutz, Catherine, and Lila Abu-Lughod. *Language and the Politics of Emotion.* New York: Cambridge University Press, 1990.

Lutz, Catherine, and Jane Lou Collins. *Reading National Geographic.* Chicago: University of Chicago Press, 1993.

Lyotard, Jean Francois. *The Postmodern Condition: A Report on Knowledge.* Minneapolis: University of Minnesota Press, 1985.

______. *Signed, Malraux.* Minneapolis: University of Minnesota Press, 1999.

Madison, D. Soyini, ed. *The Woman That I Am: The Literature and Culture of Contemporary Women of Color.* New York: St. Martin's, 1994.

Malcolm X. *Malcolm X: The Last Speeches.* Ed. Bruce Perry. New York: Pathfinder, 1989.

______. *Malcolm X on Afro-American History.* New York: Pathfinder, 1990.

______. *Malcolm X: Speeches at Harvard.* Ed. Archie Epps. New York: Paragon, 1991.

Malcolm X and George Breitman. *By Any Means Necessary: Speeches, Interviews, and a Letter.* New York: Pathfinder, 1970.

Malcolm X and Alex Haley. *The Autobiography of Malcolm X.* New York: Ballentine, 1992.

Marable, Manning. *Black American Politics.* New York: Verso, 1993.

______. *Beyond Black and White: Transforming African-American Politics.* New York: Verso, 1995.

Márquez, Gabriel García. *One Hundred Years of Solitude.* New York: Harper & Collins, 1998.

Marquis, Donald M. *In Search of Buddy Bolden, First Man of Jazz.* Baton Rouge: Louisiana State University Press, 1978.

Massey, Douglas S., and Nancy A. Denton. *American Apartheid: Segregation and the Making of the Underclass.* Cambridge: Harvard University Press, 1993.

Mays, Willie, and Lou Sahadi. *Say Hey: The Autobiography of Willie Mays.* New York: Simon & Schuster, 1988.

Mazrui, Ali al-Amin. *The African Condition: A Political Diagnosis.* New York: Cambridge University Press, 1980.

______. *The Africans: A Triple Heritage.* Boston: Little, Brown, 1986.

McCarthy, Jenny, and Neal Karlen. *Jen-X: Jenny McCarthy's Open Book.* New York: Reaganbooks, 1997.

McCulloch, Warren S. *Embodiments of Mind.* Cambridge: MIT Press, 1965.

McIntosh, Peggy. *White Privilege, Male Privilege: A Personal Account of Coming to See Correspondences Through Work in Women's Studies.* Wellesley, Mass.: Wellesley College, Center for Research on Women, 1988.

McKeon, Richard, ed. *Introduction to Aristotle.* Chicago: University of Chicago Press, 1974.

McLuhan, Marshall. *Understanding Media: The Extensions of Man.* New York: McGraw-Hill, 1964.

______. *Culture Is Our Business.* New York: McGraw-Hill, 1970.

McMillan, Terry. *Waiting to Exhale.* New York: Viking, 1992.

McPherson, James M. *The Struggle for Equality: Abolitionists and the Negro in the Civil War and Reconstruction.* Princeton: Princeton University Press 1972.

______. *Drawn with the Sword: Reflections on the American Civil War.* New York: Oxford University Press, 1996.

Meyer, Stephen Grant. *As Long as They Don't Move Next Door: Segregation and Racial Conflict in American Neighborhoods.* Lanham, Md.: Rowman & Littlefield, 2000.

Monroe, Marilyn. *My Story.* New York: Stein & Day, 1974.

Moore, Marianne. *The Complete Poems of Marianne Moore.* New York: Macmillan/Viking, 1967.

Moraga, Cherríe, and Gloria Anzaldúa. *This Bridge Called My Back: Writings by Radical Women of Color.* New York: Kitchen Table Women of Color Press, 1983.

Morgan, Garrett A. *Garrett A. Morgan Papers, 1894–1970.* Cleveland: Western Reserve Historical Society, 1994.

Morison, Samuel Eliot. *Admiral of the Ocean Sea: A Life of Christopher Columbus.* New York: Time, Inc., 1962.

Morrison, Toni. *The Bluest Eye.* New York: Washington Square Press, 1970.

______. *Sula.* New York: Knopf, 1974.

______. *Song of Solomon.* New York: Knopf, 1977.

______. *Tar Baby.* New York: Knopf, 1981.

______. *Beloved: A Novel.* New York: Knopf, 1987.

______. *Jazz.* New York: Knopf, 1992.

______. *Playing in the Dark: Whiteness and the Literary Imagination.* Cambridge: Harvard University Press, 1992.

______. *Paradise.* New York: A.A. Knopf, 1998.

Morrison, Toni, ed. *Race-Ing Justice, En-Gendering Power: Essays on Anita Hill, Clarence Thomas, and the Construction Of Social Reality.* New York: Pantheon, 1992.

Mother Divine. *The Peace Mission Movement: Founded by M.J. Divine, Better Known as Father Divine.* Philadelphia: Imperial, 1982.

Mudimbe, V. Y. *The Invention of Africa: Gnosis, Philosophy, and the Order of Knowledge.* Bloomington: Indiana University Press, 1988.

______. *Before the Birth of the Moon.* New York: Simon & Schuster, 1989.

______. *The Surreptitious Speech.* Chicago: University Of Chicago Press, 1992.

______. *The Idea of Africa.* Bloomington: Indiana University Press, 1994.

Murphy, Joseph M. *Santería: An African Religion in America.* Boston: Beacon, 1988.

Murray, Charles A. *In Pursuit: Of Happiness and Good Government.* New York: Simon & Schuster, 1988.

______. *What It Means to Be a Libertarian: A Personal Interpretation.* New York: Broadway Books, 1997.

Muse, Benjamin. *Ten Years of Prelude: The Story of Integration Since the Supreme Court's 1954 Decision.* New York: Viking, 1964.

Naison, Mark. *Communists in Harlem During the Depression.* Urbana: University of Illinois Press, 1983.

Newitz, Annalee, and Matt Wray, eds. *White Trash: Race and Class in America.* New York: Routledge, 1997.

Niebuhr, H. Richard. *The Social Sources of Denominationalism.* New York: New American Library, 1975.

Nietzsche, Friedrich Wilhelm. *The Philosophy Of Nietzsche.* New York: Modern Library, 1954.

______. *The Will to Power.* Ed. Walter Arnold Kaufmann and R. J. Hollingdale. New York: Vintage, 1968.

Nin, Anaïs. *Cities of the Interior.* Chicago: Swallow, 1974.

______. *A Woman Speaks: The Lectures, Seminars, and Interviews of Anaïs Nin.* Ed. Evelyn J. Hinz. Chicago: Swallow, 1975.

______. *Delta of Venus: Erotica.* New York: Harcourt Brace Jovanovich, 1977.

______. *The Novel of the Future.* New York: Swallow, 1990.

Novak, Michael. *The Rise of the Unmeltable Ethnics: Politics and Culture in the Seventies.* New York: Macmillan, 1972.

Nussbaum, Martha Craven. *The Quality of Life.* Oxford, U.K.: Crandon; New York: Oxford University Press, 1992.

______. *The Therapy of Desire: Theory and Practice in Hellenistic Ethics.* Princeton: Princeton University Press, 1994.

______. *Cultivating Humanity: A Classical Defense of Reform in Liberal Education.* Cambridge: Harvard University Press, 1997.

______. *Sex and Social Justice.* New York: Oxford University Press, 1999.

______. *Upheavals of Thought: The Intelligence of Emotions.* New York: New York University Press, 2001.

Oakeshott, Michael. *Experience and Its Modes.* New York: Cambridge University Press, 1978.

______. *The Voice of Liberal Learning: Michael Oakeshott on Education.* Ed. Timothy Fuller. New Haven: Yale University Press, 1989.

______. *On Human Conduct.* New York: Oxford University Press, 1993.

O'Connor, Carroll. *I Think I'm Outta Here: A Memoir of All My Families.* New York: Pocket Books, 1998.

Ogbu, John U. *The Next Generation: Ethnography of Education in an Urban Neighborhood.* New York: Academic Press, 1974.

______. *Minority Education and Caste: The American System in Cross-Cultural Perspective.* New York: Academic Press, 1978.

______. *Schooling in the Ghetto.* Newark: University of Delaware, School of Education, 1981.

______. *Cultural Models and Educational Strategies of Non-Dominant Peoples.* New York: City College Workshop Center, 1991.

Ogbu, John, and Margaret A. Gibson, eds. *Minority Students and Schooling: A Comparative Study of Immigrant and Involuntary Minorities.* Reference Books in International Education, vol. 7. New York: Garland, 1991.

Oliver, Melvin L., and Thomas M. Shapiro. *Black Wealth/White Wealth: A New Perspective on Racial Inequality.* New York: Routledge, 1995.

Oliver, Paul. *The Story of the Blues.* Philadelphia: Chilton, 1969.

Omi, Michael, and Howard Winant. *Racial Formation in the United States: From the 1960s to the 1980s.* New York: Routledge, 1994.

Ondaatje, Michael. *Coming Through Slaughter.* New York: Penguin, 1984.

Ong, Walter J. *Orality and Literacy: The Technologizing of the Word.* London: Methuen, 1982.

Onyeberechi, Sydney. *Critical Essays: Achebe, Baldwin, Cullen, Ngugi, and Tutuola.* Hyattsville, Md.: Rising Star, 1999.

Orwell, George. *Animal Farm.* New York: Harcourt, Brace, 1946.

______. *Nineteen Eighty-Four.* New York: Harcourt, Brace & World, 1949.

______. *The Collected Essays, Journalism, and Letters of George Orwell.* Ed. Ian Angus and Sonia Orwell. New York: Harcourt, Brace & World, 1968.

______. *Orwell: The Lost Writings.* Ed. W. J. West. New York: Arbor House, 1985.

Osofsky, Gilbert. *Puttin' On Ole Massa: The Slave Narratives of Henry Bibb, William Wells Brown, and Solomon Northup.* New York: Harper & Row, 1969.

Owens, Chandler D. *Preaching COGIC Style.* Memphis, Tenn.: Publishing Board of the Church of God in Christ, 1996.

Patterson, Orlando. *Freedom*. New York: Basic, 1991.

______. *Rituals in Blood: Consequences of Slavery in Two American Centuries.* New York: Basic, 1998.

Paz, Octavio. *Claude Levi-Strauss: An Introduction.* Ithaca: Cornell University Press, 1970.

Perry, Theresa, and Lisa D. Delpit, eds. *The Real Ebonics Debate: Power, Language, and the Education of African-American Children*. Boston: Beacon, 1998.

Pfeil, Fred. *White Guys: Studies in Postmodern Domination and Difference*. London: Verso, 1995.

Pinn, Anthony. *Why Lord? Suffering and Evil in Black Theology.* New York: Continuum, 1995.

______. *Varieties of African American Religious Experience.* Minneapolis: Fortress, 1998.

Poe, Edgar Allan. *The Purloined Letter.* New York: F. Watt, 1966.

Pollock, Della. *Exceptional Spaces: Essays in Performance and History*. Chapel Hill: University of North Carolina Press, 1998.

Popper, Karl Raimund. *The Open Society and Its Enemies.* Princeton: Princeton University Press, 1966.

______. *Objective Knowledge: An Evolutionary Approach.* New York: Oxford University Press, 1972.

______. *The Logic of Scientific Discovery.* New York: Routledge, 1999.

Porter, Cole. *Cole.* Ed. Brendan Gill and Robert Kimball. New York: Holt, Rinehart & Winston, 1971.

Porter, Jean. *Moral Action and Christian Ethics.* New York: Cambridge University Press, 1995.

______. *Natural and Divine Law: Reclaiming the Tradition for Christian Ethics.* Grand Rapids, Mich.: Eerdmans, 1999.

Pound, Ezra. *Pound/Joyce: The Letters of Ezra Pound to James Joyce, with Pound's Essays on Joyce.* Ed. Forrest Read. New York: New Directions, 1967.

______.*Selected Prose, 1909–1965*. Ed. William Cookson. New York: New Directions, 1973.

Pound, Roscoe. *The Development of Constitutional Guarantees of Liberty.* New Haven: Yale University Press, 1967.

Powell, Colin L., and Joseph E. Persico. *My American Journey.* New York: Random House, 1995.

Powell, Linda C., et al., eds. *Off White: Reading on Race, Power, and Society.* New York: Routledge, 1996.

Presley, Elvis. *Elvis in His Own Words.* Ed. Pearce Marchbank. London: Omnibus, 1977.

Quinn, Vincent Gerald. *Hart Crane.* New York: Twayne, 1963.

Raboteau, Albert J. *Slave Religion: The "Invisible Institution" in the Antebellum South.* New York: Oxford University Press, 1978.

Reed, Adolph L., ed. *Race, Politics, and Culture: Critical Essays on the Radicalism of the 1960s.* Westport, Conn.: Greenwood, 1986.

______. ed. *Without Justice for All: The New Liberalism and Our Retreat from Racial Equality.* Boulder: Westview, 1998.

______. *Class Notes: Posing as Politics and Other Thoughts on the American Scene.* New York: New Press, 1999.

______. *Stirrings in the Jug: Black Politics in the Post-Segregation Era.* Minneapolis: University of Minnesota Press, 1999.

Reed, Willis, and Phil Pepe. *A View from the Rim: Willis Reed on Basketball.* Philadelphia: Lippincott, 1971.

Rich, Adrienne. *Dark Fields of the Republic, Poems, 1991–1995.* New York: Norton, 1995.

Richman, Irwin. *Borscht Belt Bungalows: Memories of Catskill Summers.* Philadelphia: Temple University Press, 1998.

Roberts, J. Deotis. *A Black Political Theology.* Philadelphia: Westminster, 1974.

______. *Black Theology Today: Liberation and Contextualization.* New York: Mellen, 1983.

______.*Liberation and Reconciliation: A Black Theology.* Philadelphia: Westminster, 1994.

Robertson, Pat, and Bob Slosser. *The Secret Kingdom.* New York: W Publishing Company, 1992.

Robeson, Paul. *Paul Robeson Speaks: Writing, Speeches, Interviews, 1918–1974.* Ed. Phillip Sheldon Foner. Seacaucus, N.J.: Citadel, 1978.

______. *Here I Stand.* Boston: Beacon, 1988.

Rodman, Dennis, and Tim Keown. *Bad as I Wanna Be.* New York: Delacorte, 1996.

Roediger, David. *Towards the Abolition of Whiteness (Up From Whiteness).* New York: Norton, 1994.

Rogin, Michael. *Blackface, White Noise: Jewish Immigrants in the Hollywood Melting Pot.* Berkeley: University of California Press, 1996.

Rorty, Richard. *Philosophy and the Mirror of Nature.* Princeton: Princeton University Press, 1979.

______. *Contingency, Irony, and Solidarity.* New York: Cambridge University Press, 1989.

Rotberg, Robert I., and Ali Al-Amin Mazrui, eds. *Protest and Power in Black Africa.* New York: Oxford University Press, 1970.

Rousseau, Jean-Jacques. *The Social Contract, and Discourses.* New York: Dutton, 1950.

Royce, Josiah. *The Letters of Josiah Royce.* Ed. John Clendenning. Chicago: University of Chicago Press, 1970.

______. *The Philosophy of Josiah Royce.* Ed. John K. Roth. New York: Crowell, 1971.

Russell, Bertrand. *Portraits from Memory and Other Essays.* New York: Simon & Schuster, 1956.

______. *The Autobiography of Bertrand Russell.* Boston: Little, Brown, 1967.

Russell, Bill, and Taylor Branch. *Second Wind: The Memoirs of an Opinionated Man.* New York: Random House, 1979.

Russell, Bill, and William Francis McSweeny. *Go Up for Glory.* New York: Coward-McCann, 1966.

Said, Edward W. *Covering Islam: How the Media and the Experts Determine How We See the Rest of the World.* New York: Pantheon, 1981.

______. *The Question of Palestine.* New York: Random House, 1992.

______. *Culture and Imperialism.* New York: Knopf/Random House, 1993.

______. *Out Of Place: A Memoir.* New York: Knopf, 1999.

______. *Power, Politics and Culture: Interviews with Edward E. Said.* Ed. Gauri Viswanathan. New York: Pantheon, 2001.

Sakolsky, Ron, ed. *Sounding Off: Music as Subversion/Resistance/Revolution.* Brooklyn, N.Y.: Autonomedia, 1995.

Saldivar, Jose. *Border Matters: Remapping American Cultural Studies.* Berkeley: University of California Press, 1997.

Sánchez, Sara M. *Afro-Cuban Diasporan Religions: A Comparative Analysis of the Literature and Selected Annotated Bibliography.* Coral Gables, Fla.: Institute for Cuban and Cuban-American Studies, School of International Studies, University of Miami, 2000.

Sanchez, Sonia. *Home Coming: Poems.* Detroit: Broadside, 1969.

______. *We A Baddddd People.* Detroit: Broadside, 1970.

______. *Love Poems.* New York: Third Press, 1973.

______. *A Blues Book for Blue Black Magical Women.* Detroit: Broadside, 1974.

______.*Homegirls and Handgrenades.* New York: Thunder's Mouth, 1984.

______. *I've Been A Woman: New And Selected Poems.* Chicago: Third World Press, 1985.

______. *Under a Soprano Sky.* Trenton: Africa World Press, 1987.

Santayana, George. *The Birth of Reason and Other Essays.* Ed. David Coy. New York: Columbia University Press, 1968.

______. *Physical Order and Moral Liberty: Previously Unpublished Essays of George Santayana.* Ed. John Lachs and Shirley Lachs. Nashville, Tenn.: Vanderbilt University Press, 1969.

______. *The Last Puritan: A Memoir in the Form of a Novel.* New York: Scribner's, 1989.

Sartre, Jean-Paul. *The Age of Reason.* New York: Vintage, 1992.

______. *Being and Nothingness: A Phenomenological Essay on Ontology.* New York: Washington Square Press, 1993.

Saxton, Alexander. *The Rise and Fall of the White Republic: Class Politics and Mass Culture in Nineteenth-Century America.* London: Verso, 1990.

Schafer, William John, and Johannes Riedel. *The Art of Ragtime: Form and Meaning of an Original Black American Art.* Baton Rouge: Louisiana State University Press, 1973.

Schiesel, Jane. *The Otis Redding Story.* Garden City, N.Y.: Doubleday, 1973.

Schopenhauer, Arthur. *On the Basis of Morality.* Indianapolis: Bobbs-Merrill, 1965.

______. *The Will to Live: Selected Writings.* Ed. Richard Taylor. New York: F. Ungar, 1990.

______. *Prize Essay on the Freedom of the Will.* Ed. Günter Zoler. New York: Cambridge University Press, 1999.

Scott, Cathy. *The Killing of Tupac Shakur.* Las Vegas: Huntington, 1997.

Segrest, Mab. *Memoir of a Race Traitor.* Boston: South End, 1993.

Shakespeare, William. *The Tragedy of King Richard the Second.* Ed. Robert T. Peterson. New Haven: Yale University Press, 1957.

______. *The Tragedy of Antony and Cleopatra.* Ed. Michael Neill. New York: Oxford University Press, 1994.

Shakur, Tupac. *The Rose That Grew from Concrete.* New York: Simon & Schuster, 1999.

______. *The Tupac Shakur Collection.* Musical Score. Miami: Warner Bros., 2002.

Sharpton, Al, and Anthony Walton. *Go and Tell Pharaoh: The Autobiography of the Reverend Al Sharpton.* New York: Doubleday, 1996.

Shaw, Arnold. *Black Popular Music in America: From the Spirituals, Minstrels, and Ragtime Soul to Disco and Hip-Hop.* New York: Schirmer, 1986.

Shils, Edward. *Life or Death: Ethics and Options.* Portland: Reed College, 1968.

______. *The Intellectuals and the Powers, and Other Essays.* Chicago: University Of Chicago Press, 1974.

Shockley, William. *Shockley on Eugenics and Race: The Application of Science to the Solution of Human Problems.* Washington, D.C.: Scott-Townsend, 1992.

Simone, Nina, and Stephen Cleary. *I Put a Spell on You: The Autobiography of Nina Simone.* New York: Pantheon, 1991.

Simpkins, Daphne. *Nat King Cole: An Unforgettable Life of Music.* Montgomery, Ala.: New South, 2001.

Smith, Anna Deavere. *Twilight—Los Angeles, 1992 on the Road: A Search for American Character.* New York: Anchor, 1994.

Spillers, Hortense. *Comparative American Identities: Race, Sex, and Nationality in the Modern Text.* New York: Routledge, 1991.

Spivak, Gayatri Chakravorty. *The Post-Colonial Critic: Interviews, Strategies, Dialogues.* Ed. Sarah Harasym. New York: Routledge, 1990.

Stannard, David E. *American Holocaust: The Conquest of the New World.* New York: Oxford University Press, 1992.

Stevens, Wallace. *Collected Poems.* New York: Vintage, 1990.

______. *Letters of Wallace Stevens.* Berkley: University of California Press, 1996.

Stout, Jeffrey. *The Flight from Authority: Religion, Morality, and the Quest for Autonomy.* Notre Dame, Ind.: University of Notre Dame Press, 1981.

______. *Ethics After Babel: The Languages of Morals and Their Discontents.* Boston: Beacon Press, 1988.

Sullivan, Clayton. *Rethinking Realized Eschatology.* Macon, Ga.: Mercer University Press, 1988.

Sullivan, Randall. *Labyrinth.* New York: Atlantic Monthly Press, 2002.

Teilhard de Chardin, Pierre. *The Future of Man.* New York: Harper & Row, 1964.

______. *The Appearance of Man.* New York: Harper & Row, 1965.

______. *The Making of a Mind: Letters from a Soldier-Priest, 1914–1919.* New York: Harper & Row, 1965.

______. *The Phenomenon of Man.* New York: Harper & Row, 1965.

Temple, William. *The Church Looks Forward.* New York: Macmillan, 1944.

______. *Religious Experience, and Other Essays and Addresses.* London: J. Clarke, 1959.

______. *What Christians Stand for in the Secular World.* Philadelphia: Fortress, 1965.

______. *Christianity and Social Order.* New York: Crossroad, 1977.

Thompson, Becky. *Names We Call Home: Autobiography on Racial Identity.* Ed. Becky Thompson and Sangeeta Tyagi. New York: Routledge, 1996.

Thurman, Howard. *The Search for Common Ground: An Inquiry into the Basis of Man's Experience of Community.* New York: Harper & Row, 1971.

______. *For the Inward Journey: The Writings of Howard Thurman.* San Diego: Friends United Press, 1984.

______. *Jesus and the Disinherited.* Boston: Beacon, 1996.

______. *The Luminous Darkness: A Personal Interpretation of the Anatomy of Segregation and the Ground of Hope.* New York: Friends United Press, 1997.

Tillich, Hannah. *From Time to Time.* New York: Stein & Day, 1973.

Tillich, Paul. *Love, Power, Justice.* New York: Oxford University Press, 1964.

______. *The Future of Religions.* Ed. Jerald C. Brauer. New York: Harper & Row, 1966.

______. *On the Boundary: An Autobiographical Sketch.* New York: Scribner, 1966.

Toll, Robert C. *Blacking Up: The Minstrel Show in Nineteenth-Century America.* New York: Oxford University Press, 1974.

Tomasky, Michael. *Left for Dead: The Life, Death, and Possible Resurrection of Progressive Politics in America.* New York: Free Press, 1996.

Trachtenberg, Alan, ed. *Hart Crane: A Collection of Critical Essays.* Englewood Cliffs, N.J.: Prentice-Hall, 1982.

Van Vechten, Carl. *Keep A-Inchin' Along: Selected Writings of Carl Van Vechten About Black Art and Letters.* Ed. Bruce Kellner. Westport, Conn.: Greenwood, 1979.

______. *Letters of Carl Van Vechten.* Ed. Bruce Kellner. New Haven: Yale University Press, 1987.

______. *Generations in Black and White: Photographs.* Ed. Rudolph P. Byrd. Athens: University of Georgia Press, 1993.

Voeks, Robert A. *Sacred Leaves of Candomblé: African Magic, Medicine, and Religion in Brazil*. Austin: University of Texas Press, 1997.

Walker, Margaret. *For My People*. New Haven: Yale University Press, 1942.

______. *Prophets for a New Day*. Detroit: Broadside Press, 1970.

______. *This Is My Century: New and Collected Poems*. Athens: University of Georgia Press, 1989.

______. *On Being Female, Black, and Free: Essays by Margaret Walker, 1932–1992*. Ed. Maryemma Graham. Knoxville: University of Tennessee Press, 1997.

Wallace, Michele. *Black Popular Culture/ A Project by Michele Wallace*. Ed. Gina Dent. Seattle: Bay Press, 1992.

Walser, Robert. *Keeping Time: Readings in Jazz History*. New York: Oxford University Press, 1999.

Ward, Brian. *Just My Soul Responding: Rhythm and Blues, Black Consciousness, and Race Relations*. Berkeley: University of California Press, 1998.

Ware, Vron. *Beyond the Pale: White Women, Racism, and History.* New York: Verso, 1997.

Washington, James Melvin. *Frustrated Fellowship: The Black Baptist Quest for Social Power.* Macon, Ga.: Mercer, 1986.

Watts, Jill. *God, Harlem U.S.A.: The Father Divine Story*. Berkeley: University of California Press, 1992.

Weil, Simone. *Crusade for Justice: The Autobiography of Ida B. Wells.* Chicago: University of Chicago Press, 1970.

______. *Oppression and Liberty.* Amherst: University of Massachusetts Press, 1973.

______. *The Simone Weil Reader.* New York: McKay, 1977.

______. *Lectures on Philosophy.* Cambridge: Cambridge University Press, 1978.

______. *Selected Works of Ida B. Wells-Barnett.* Ed. Trudier Harris. New York: Oxford University Press, 1991.

Wells-Barnett, Ida B. *On Lynchings: Southern Horrors, a Red Record, Mob Rule in New Orleans.* New York: Arno, 1969.

Welsing, Frances Cress. *The Isis Papers*. Chicago: Third World Press, 1991.

West, Cornel. *Prophesy Deliverance! An Afro-American Revolutionary Christianity.* Philadelphia: Westminster, 1982.

______. *The American Evasion of Philosophy: A Genealogy of Pragmatism*. Madison: University of Wisconsin Press, 1989.

______. *The Ethical Dimensions of Marxist Thought.* New York: Monthly Review Press, 1991.

______. *Race Matters.* Boston: Beacon, 1993.

West, Dorothy. *The Living Is Easy.* New York: Feminist Press, 1975.

______. *The Richer, the Poorer: Stories, Sketches, and Reminiscences.* New York: Doubleday, 1995.

______. *The Wedding.* New York: Doubleday, 1995.

Wheatley, Phillis. *The Poems of Phillis Wheatley.* Ed. Julian D. Mason. Chapel Hill: University of North Carolina Press, 1989.

White, Armond. *Rebel for the Hell of It: The Life of Tupac Shakur*. New York: Thunder's Mouth, 1997.

Whitman, Walt. *Leaves of Grass.* Modern Library Series. New York: Random House, 1993.

Wickham, DeWayne. *Bill Clinton and Black America*. New York: Ballantine, 2002.

Wideman, John Edgar. *Brothers and Keepers.* New York: Holt, Rinehart & Winston, 1984.

______. *Fatheralong: A Meditation on Fathers and Sons, Race and Society.* New York: Pantheon, 1994.

Wiener, Norbert. *Cybernetics; Or, Control and Communication in the Animal and the Machine.* New York: MIT Press, 1961.

______. *God and Golem, Inc.: A Comment on Certain Points Where Cybernetics Impinges on Religion*. Cambridge: MIT Press, 1964.

Wilentz, Sean, ed. *Major Problems in the Early Republic, 1781–1848, Documents and Essays.* Boston: Houghton Mifflin, 1992.

Wilford, John Noble. *The Mysterious History of Columbus: An Exploration of the Man, the Myth, the Legacy*. New York: Knopf, 1991.

Williams, Armstrong. *Beyond Blame: How We Can Succeed by Breaking the Dependency Barrier.* New York: Free Press, 1995.

______. *Letters to a Young Victim: Hope and Healing in America's Inner Cities.* New York: Free Press, 1996.

Williams, Bernard Arthur Owen. *Moral Luck: Philosophical Papers, 1973–1980.* Cambridge: Cambridge University Press, 1981.

______. *Ethics and the Limits of Philosophy.* Cambridge: Harvard University Press, 1985.

Wilson, Woodrow. *The Politics of Woodrow Wilson: Selections form His Speeches and Writings*. Ed., with an introduction, by August Heckscher. New York: Harper, 1956.

Wittgenstein, Ludwig. *Remarks on Colour.* Ed. G. E. Anscombe. Trans. Margarete Schattle and Linda L. McAlister. Berkeley: University of California Press, 1990.

______. *Philosophical Investigations: The English Text of the Third Edition.* Trans. G. E. M. Elizabeth Anscombe. New York: Prentice-Hall, 1999.

Wolfe, George C. *The Colored Museum.* New York: Grove, 1988

Wolfe, George C., et al. *Jelly's Last Jam.* New York: Theatre Communications Group, 1993.

Wolff, David. *You Send Me: The Life and Times Sam Cooke.* New York: Quill, 1996.

Woolf, Virginia. *Collected Essays.* Ed. Andrew McNeille. New York: Harcourt, Brace & World, 1966.

______. *The Letters of Virginia Woolf.* New York: Harcourt Brace Jovanovich, 1975–1980.

______. *The Essays of Virginia Woolf.* Ed. Andrew McNeille. San Diego: Harcourt Brace Jovanovich, 1987.

Wright, Richard. *American Hunger.* New York: Harper & Row, 1977.

______. *New Essays on Native Son.* Ed. Kenneth Kinnamon. New York: Cambridge University Press, 1990.

______. *Rite of Passage.* New York: HarperCollins, 1994.

______. *Native Son.* Intro. Arnold Rampersad. New York: Harper Perennial, 1998.

Young, Coleman A., and Lonnie Wheeler. *Hard Stuff: The Autobiography of Mayor Coleman Young.* New York: Viking, 1994.

Zuberi, Tukufu. *Thicker Than Blood: How Racial Statistics Lie.* Minneapolis: University of Minnesota Press, 2001.

JOURNAL ARTICLES

Allmendinger, Blake. "Deadwood Dick: The Black Cowboy as Cultural Timber." *Journal of America Culture,* Winter 1993, 79.

Baraka, Amiri. "Margaret Walker Alexander." *Nation* 268 (1999): 32.

Beasley, Conger. "In the Belly of the Beast." *North American Review,* May-June 1996, 10.

Bennett, William J. "A Symposium: Is Affirmative Action on the Way Out? Should It Be?" *Commentary,* March 1998, 19.

Biles, Roger. "Richard J. Daley: Politics, Race, and the Governing of Chicago." *Peace Research Abstracts* 36 (1999).

Bloom, Harold. "The Necessity of Misreading." *Georgia Review,* Winter-Spring 2002, 69.

Boundas, Constantin V. "Transgressive Theorizing: A Report to Deleuze." *Man and World* 29 (1996): 327.

Brodie, James Michael. "Feel Good History." *Black Issues in Higher Education,* April 18, 2000.

Brown, Ronald. "Beyond Black and White: Transforming African-American Politics, by Manning Marable." *Journal of Politics* 59 (1997): 267–270.

Clinton, Bill. "Racism in the United States. Address, October 16, 1995." *Vital Speeches of the Day* 62 (1995): 75–79.

Cone, James H. "Whose Earth Is It Anyway?" *Cross Currents*, Spring 2000, 36.

Connerly, Ward. "The GOP's Black Problem . . . and the Blacks' GOP Problem." *National Review*, December 18, 2000, 40.

______. "Don't Box Me In: An End to Racial Checkoffs." *National Review*, August 16, 2001, 24.

Damon, Maria. "The Jewish Entertainer as Cultural Lighting Rod: The Case of Lenny Bruce." *Postmodern Culture* 7 (1997).

"Dorothy Day Didn't Want to Fight Poverty: She Wanted to Help Poor People." *American Enterprise*, November-December 1995, 85.

Dei, George Jerry Sefa. "'Why Write Back'?: The Role of Afrocentric Discourse in Social Change." *Canadian Journal of Education*, Spring 1998, 200–208.

DeWitt, Lynda. "Spotlight on—Bill Cosby." *National Geographic World*, February 2002, 8.

D'Souza, Dinesh. "Pride and Prejudice: The Errors of Afrocentrism." *American Enterprise*, September-October 1995, 51–54.

Early, Gerald. "Adventures in the Colored Museum: Afrocentrism, Memory, and the Construction of Race." *American Anthropologist*, September 1998, 703–711.

Frank, Henry. "African Religions in the Caribbean: Santeria and Voodoo." *Caribe*, Spring-Summer 1982, 34–36.

Gingrich, Newt. "The Agenda for the U.S. House of Representatives—Race, Drugs, and Ignorance—Newt Gingrich—Speaker of the United States House of Representatives from Georgia." *Vital Speeches of the Day* 63 (1997): 231–233.

Glenn, Linda. "Robert McAfee Brown: Presbyterian, Theologian, Activist." *American Presbyterians*, Spring 1994, 49.

"Increasing Faith: The Price Is Right. Pastor F. Price." *Christianity Today*, October 1995, 102.

Kerr, Philip. "Silly Billy." *New Statesman*, October 15, 2001, 43–44.

Konstan, David. "Not Out of Africa." Review of *Not Out of Africa: How Afrocentrism Became an Excuse to Teach Myth as History*, by Mary Lefkowitz. *History and Theory*, May 1997, 261–269.

Kushnick, L. "Beyond Black and White: Transforming African-American Politics by Manning Marable." *Race and Class* 37 (1996): 107.

Lambert, Gregg. "Deleuze and the 'Dialectic' (a.k.a. Marx and Hegel)." *Strategies: Journal of Theory, Culture, and Politics* 15 (2002): 73–78.

Leahy-Dios, Cyana. "On Simone de Beauvoir." *European Legacy* 6 (2001): 81–83.

Lefever, Harry G. "When the Saints Go Riding In: Santeria in Cuba and the Untied States." *Journal for the Scientific Study of Religion*, September 1996, 318–330.

Lemelle, Anthony J., Jr. "Oliver Cromwell Cox: Toward a Pan-Africanist Epistemology for Community Action." *Journal of Black Studies* 31 (2001) 325–347.

Loury, Glenn C. "The Return of the 'Undeserving Poor.' Welfare Reform During the Clinton Administration." *Atlantic Monthly,* February 2001, 545.

Luconi, Stefano. "Mafia-Related Prejudice and the Rise of Italian Americans in the United States." *Patterns of Prejudice* 33 (1999): 43–57.

Manning, Marable. "After the March: The Success of the Million Man March." *New Statesman Society,* October 27, 1995, 14–18.

May, Todd. "The Ontology and Politics of Gilles Deleuze." *Theory and Event* 5 (2001).

Maynard, Kevin. "Ellen and Ellen: Two Movie Roles Showcase Ms. DeGeneres' Post-Ellen Big Screen Career." *Advocate,* April 27, 1999, 73.

McFadden, Margaret T. "'America's Boy Friend Who Can't Get a Date': Gender, Race, and the Cultural Work of the Jack Benny Program, 1932–1946." *Journal of American History,* June 1993, 113–134.

"Michael Dyson Heading for New York as a Visiting Professor in African-American Studies at Columbia University." *Black Issues in Higher Education,* December 26, 1996, 33–34.

Newman, Mark. "Manning Marable, Black Leadership." *Journal of American Studies* 36 (2002): 151–198.

Oxford, Edward. "Mr. Television: Milton Berle. A Chat with One of the Pioneers of Television Comedy." *American History,* February 1, 1996, 32.

Patterson, Orlando. "The David Riesman Lecture on American Society: The America View of Freedom: What We Say, What We Mean." *Society* 38, no. 4 (2001): 37–46.

Reid, Anthony. "Benedict Anderson, Imagined Communities: Reflections of the Origin and Spread of Nationalism." *Australian Journal of Politics and History* 40 (1994): 134.

Reinstein, Robert J. "Completing the Constitution: The Declaration of Independence, Bill of Rights, and Fourteenth Amendment." *Temple Law Review,* Summer 1993, 361.

Rosen, Gary. "'Bush v. Gore' and the Conservatives." *Commentary,* March 2002, 10–24.

Rushton, Richard. "What Can a Face Do? On Deleuze and Faces." *Cultural Critique* 51 (2002): 219–237.

Scheurer, T. E. "The Beatles, the Brill Building, and the Persistence of Tin Pan Alley in the Age of Rock." *Popular Music and Society* 20 (1996): 89.

Temple, Johnny. "Hip-Hop Politics on Campus." *Nation,* May 15, 2000, 16.

Torzilli, P. "Reconciling the Sanctity of Human Life, the Declaration of Independence, and the Constitution." *Catholic Lawyer* 40 (2000): 197–226.

Vintages, Karen. "'Must We Burn Foucault?' Ethics as Art of Living: Simone de Beauvoir and Michel Foucault." *Continental Philosophy Review* 34 (2001): 165–181.

Yescavage, Karen, and Jonathon Alexander. "What Do You Call a Lesbian Who's Only Slept with Men? Answer: Ellen Morgan. Deconstructing the Lesbian Identities of Ellen Morgan and Ellen DeGeneres." *Sage Family Studies Abstracts* 21 (1999).

MAGAZINE ARTICLES

Barras, Jonetta, et al. "What Clinton's Year-Long Rap on Race Left Out." *American Enterprise,* November-December 1998, 85.

"Bill Cosby." *People Weekly*. Special Anniversary Issue. March 15, 1999, 205.

"Bill Cosby and Phylicia Rashad Continue to Give Viewers Family Values on 'Cosby' Show." *Jet,* April 3, 2000, 60–64.

"C. Delores Tucker Crusades Against Gangsta Lyrics, Giving Record Companies a Bad Rap." *People Weekly,* December 25, 1995, 71–73.

"C. DeLores Tucker Wants Time Warner to Pull the Plug on Some of Its Best Selling Rap Artists." *People Weekly,* June 26, 1995, 105–108.

Chavez, Linda. "Hispanics and the American Dream." *St. Croix Review,* February 1, 1997, 34.

______. "The Racemonger: Gore at His Worst." *National Review,* August 14, 2000, 36.

Chavez, Linda, and Connerly Ward. "Up from Preferences: Creating Equal: My Fight Against Racial Preferences." *National Review,* 2000, 66.

Chideya, Farai. "All Eyez on Us: It's Time for the Hip-Hop Generation to Get Real." *Time,* March 24, 1997, 47.

Clifton, Lucille. "Wishes for Sons." *Ms.*, 2002, 65.

"Dear Billy . . . Al Franken, Jon Stewart, and Other Wits Suggest Killer Lines for Billy Crystal." *TV Guide,* March 22, 1997, 52.

Dowling, Claudia Glenn. "So Long, Archie." *People Weekly,* July 9, 2001, 56–59.

"Ellen DeGeneres Finds Love, as Well as Liberty, When She Opens the Door to Her Closet." *People Weekly,* December 29, 1997, 56.

Gergen, David. "To Have and Have Less: Income Disparity Grew During B. Clinton's Presidency." *U.S. News & World Report,* July 26, 1999, 64.

Gest, Ted. "Popgun Politics: Misrepresentation of Crime and Drug Issues by Presidential Candidates." *U.S. News & World Report,* September 30, 1996, 30–34.

Huntington, Samuel, et al. "The Special Case of Mexican Immigration." *American Enterprise,* 2000, 20.

Leavy, Walter. "Eddie Murphy, Richard Pryor, Redd Foxx: Three Generations of Black Comedy. The Movie *Harlem Nights* Brings Together Three of the Funkiest Comics." *Ebony,* January 1990, 102.

Lemann, Nicholas. "Second Thoughts About Integration." *Gentlemen's Quarterly*, December 1, 1997, 266.

"Mos Def, Making It Happen in Music & Film." *Jet,* May 6, 2002, 46.

Solotaroff, Ivan. "Gangsta Life, Gangsta Death." *Esquire,* December 1, 1996, 78.

"The Steve Harvey Show: Black America's Favorite TV Series." *Jet,* August 16, 1999, 60.

"Television's Coming-Out. Gays Are TV's Favorite Sidekick. Will Ellen DeGeneres Be Our Lead?" *Advocate,* January 1997, 103.

Ward, Francis. "Black and White Blues." *Emerge,* June 30, 1996, 50.

Wolff, Alexander. "The Sky's the Limit. Tar Heel Rasheed Wallace Heads a Squadron of Remarkable First-Year Big Men." *Sports Illustrated,* November 29, 1993, 34.

NEWSPAPER ARTICLES

Hall, Corey. "Bronzeville Blues Tour Explores 'Heaven' and Beyond." *Chicago Weekend,* April 29, 1999, 3.

McKeough, Kevin. "Living Legend Still Has Touch; B.B. Is Still the King, but Other Acts Past Prime." *Chicago Tribune,* August 17, 2002, North Final ed., 27.

SOUND RECORDINGS

2pac. *Me Against the World*. Interscope, 1995.

______. *All Eyez on Me*. Death Row Records/Interscope Records, 1996.

______. *2pacalypse now*. Interscope Records, 1997.

Ali, Muhammad, Joe Louis, Max Schmeling, Jessie Owens, James J. Braddock, and Tony Galento. *Speech at Michigan State University, Circa 1970*. Sound cassette. J. Fred McDonald, 1987.

Armstrong, Louis, and King Oliver. *Lois Armstrong and King Oliver*. Milestone, 1992.

Bacharach, Burt. *What the World Needs Now Is: Bacharach & David*. Reader's Digest Association, 1997.

______. *The Look of Love.* Rhino, 1998.

Beiderbecke, Bix. *Bix Beiderbecke*. LP. Time-Life Records, 1979.

______. *Bix Beiderbecke.* Vol. 1, *Singin' the Blues*. Legacy Records, 1990.

______. *Bix Beiderbecke.* Vol. 2, *At the Jazz Band Ball*. Legacy Records, 1990.

Bilal et al. *1st Born Second*. Interscope, 2001.

Bland, Bobby. *First Class Blues*. Macaco Records, 1987.

______. *Greatest Hits: The Duke Recordings*. Vol. 1. MCA Records, 1998.

Blige, Mary J. *My Life*. MCA, 1994.

______. *Mary*. MCA Music, 1999.

Blige, Mary J., et al. *No More Drama*. MCA, 2002.

Burns, George. *George Burns and Gracie Allen*. Audiocassette. The Mind's Eye, 1985.

______. *Burns and Allen*. Audiocassette. Metacom, 1989.

Callas, Maria. *Maria Callas: The Voice of the Century*. Angel Classics, 1998.

Carmichael, Stokely, and Huey P. Newton. *Stokeley Carmichael Speaks*. Audiocassette. Cornell University Library, 1976.

Caruso, Enrico. *Caruso in Song*. EMG/RCA, 1993.

Cleveland, James. *Old Time Religion et al*. Audiocassette. Power Pak, 1974.

______. *Love of God*. Black Label, 1992.

______. *The King of Gospel*. 601 Records, 1997.

Coltrane, John. *A Love Supreme*. GRP Records, 1963.

______. *Blue Train*. Blue Note, 1985.

______. *Giant Steps*. Atlantic, 1987.

______. *Live in Antibes, 1965*. Esoldun, 1988.

______. *My Favorite Things*. Atlantic, 1990.

Common. *One Day It'll All Make Sense*. Relativity Records, 1997.

______. *Like Water for Chocolate*. Universal, 2000.

Cooke, Sam. *The Man and His Music*. RCA, 1986.

______. *The Rhythm and the Blues*. RCA, 1995.

______. *The Man Who Invented Soul*. RCA, 1957, 2000.

______. *Keep Movin' On*. Tracey Records, 1959, 2001.

Copeland, Kenneth. *Personal*. Audiocassette. Kenneth Copeland Ministries, 1986.

Davis, Miles. *Bitches Brew*. Columbia Jazz Masterpieces, 1987.

Davis, Miles, et al. *Kind of Blue*. Columbia/Legacy, 1981.

Elliott, Missy. *Supa Dupa Fly*. Elektra/Asylum, 1997.

______. *Miss E . . . So Addictive*. Elektra/Asylum, 2001.

Franklin, C. L., and New Bethel Baptist Church (Detroit) Choir. *Only a Look*. Jewel Records, 1972.

______. *The Eagle Stirreth in Her Nest*. Paula/Jewel, 1996.

Goodman, Benny. *King of Swing*. Time-Life Music, 1986.

______. *Benny Goodman's Collector's Edition*. Savoy, 1990.

______. *Feels Like Rain*. Jive, 1993.

Guy, Buddy. *Buddy Guy Live at the Checkerboard Lounge, Chicago, 1979*. JSP Records, 1980.

Harlem Ramblers. *Dixieland with the Harlem Ramblers*. PolyGram Records AG, 1981.

Lombardo, Guy. *The Sweetest Music This Side of Heaven.* ASV Living Era, 1995.
King, B.B. *Blues Summit.* MCA, 1993.
______. *Blues on the Bayou.* MCA, 1998.
KRS-One. *Edutainment.* RCA, 1990.
Kweli, Talib, and Hi Tek. *Reflection Eternal.* Priority Records, 2000.
Mau Maus et al. *Bamboozled: Original Motion Picture Soundtrack.* Motown, 2000.
Montgomery, Wes, Don Sebesky, and Deodato Eumir. *Down Here on the Ground.* A&M, 1968.
Morissette, Alanis, and Glen Ballard. *Jagged Little Pill.* Maverick/Reprise Records, 1995.
Mos Def. *Black on Both Sides.* Rawkus, 1999.
Mos Def and Talib Kweli. *Mos Def and Talib Kweli Are Black Star.* Rawkus, 1998.
______. *Hip Hop for Respect.* Rawkus, 1999.
Multiple Artists. *Blues from the Montreaux Jazz Festival.* Malaco Records, 1991.
Nelly et al. *Hip-Hop Hits.* Vol. 4. Special 2000 Millennium Ed. Def Jam Recordings, 2000.
Norvo, Red, et al. *Congo Blues.* New World Records, 1976.
Notorious B.I.G. *Ready to Die.* Arista, 1994.
______. *Life After Death.* Bad Boy Records, 1997.
______. *Born Again.* Bad Boy Records, 1999.
Oliver, King. *King Oliver and His Creole Jazz Band, 1923–1926.* Classics, 1992.
Oliver, King, and Louis Armstrong. *King Oliver's Jazz Band.* Smithsonian Collection, 1975.
Original Dixieland Jazz Band. *The Original Dixieland Jazz Band.* RCA Victor, 1970.
Outkast. *Aquemini.* LaFace Records, 1998.
Porter, Cole. *The Cole Porter Songbook.* Verve, 1985.
Rawls, Lou. *It's Supposed to Be Fun.* Blue Note, 1990.
______. *Anthology.* Manhattan, 1993.
Redding, Otis. *The Very Best Of Otis Redding.* Atlantic/Rhino, 1992.
Rodgers, Richard, et al. *Waiting to Exhale.* Arista, 1995.
Scott, Jill, et al. *Experience: Jill Scott 826+.* Hidden Beach Recordings, 2001.
Scott-Heron, Gil, and Brian Jackson. *The Revolution Will Not Be Televised.* BMG Music, 1988.
Seinfeld, Jerry. *I'm Telling You for the Last Time.* Universal Records, 1998.
Simone, Nina. *The Best Of Nina Simone.* PolyGram, 1990.
______. *Nina Simone.* Verve Records, 1994.
Sinatra, Frank. *Gold.* EMI/Capitol Records, 1992.
Slick Rick. *The Great Adventures of Slick Rick.* Def Jam Recordings, 1988.
______. *The Ruler's Back.* Def Jam Recordings, 1991.
______. *The Art of Storytelling.* Def Jam Recordings, 1999.

Taylor, Koko. *Koko Taylor: Queen of the Blues.* Alligator, 1985.

______. *Jump for Joy.* Sound disc. Alligator, 1990.

Taylor, Koko, Criss Johnson, Jeremiah Africa, Jerry Murphy, Ray Allison, Brady Williams, and Buddy Guy. *Force of Nature.* Alligator, 1993.

Temptations. *Anthology.* Motown, 1973.

______. *For Lovers Only.* Motown Records, 1995.

______. *The Ultimate Collection.* Motown, 1997.

Various Artists. *Deep Detroit.* Vol. 1, *Techno-soul.* Pow Wow Trans, 1993.

Various Artists. *Say It Loud! A Celebration of Black Music in America.* Rhino, 2001.

Vaughn, Sarah. *How Long Has This Been Going On?* Pablo, 1978.

Washington, Dinah. *What a Diff'rence a Day Makes.* Mercury, 1984.

______. *The Dinah Washington Story: The Original Recordings.* PolyGram Records, 1993.

______. *Dinah Washington.* Blue Note, 1997.

Whiteman, Paul. *Paul Whiteman at Aeolian Hall.* Smithsonian Collection, 1981.

Williams, Robin. *A Night at the Met.* CBS, 1986.

______. *Reality: What a Concept.* Casablanca Record and FilmWorks, 1979.

FILMS AND VIDEO RECORDINGS

All in the Family. Performed by Carroll O'Connor et al. Columbia Tri-Star Home Video, 2002.

Batman. Videodisc. Twentieth Century-Fox Home Entertainment, 2001.

Bill Cosby, Himself. Directed by Bill Cosby. Videocassette. Twentieth Century-Fox Video, 1996.

Black Athena. Directed by Christopher Spencer. Videocassette. California Newsreel, 1991.

Boyz 'n the Hood. Directed by John Singleton. Videocassette. Columbia TriStar Home Video, 1992.

Burns, Ken, Geoffrey Ward, Lynn Novick, and Keith David. *Jazz.* Episode 5, *Swing: Pure Pleasure.* Videocassette. PBS Video, 2000.

CBS News. *The Chicago Riots.* Films for the Humanities and Science, 2002.

Celebrating the Life, Ida B. Wells-Barnett. DePaul University, BIP Studio 101, 1999.

Chris Rock: Bring the Pain. Performed by Chris Rock. Dreamworks Records, 1996.

Crystal, Billy, Alan King, and JoBeth Williams. *Memories of Me.* Videocassette. Metro-Goldwyn Mayer, 1989.

Dyson, Michael Eric. *Michael Eric Dyson at Pacific Lutheran University.* Pacific Lutheran University, 1997.

———. Martin Luther King Jr. Memorial Convocation panel discussion for the UCSC community, featuring Michael Eric Dyson. Santa Cruz: University of California, 1999.

Good Will Hunting. Directed by Gus Van Sant. Videocassette. Miramax Home Entertainment, Distributed by Entertainment, 1997.

Jerry Maguire. Directed by Cameron Crowe. Videocasette. Columbia TriStar Home Video, 1996.

Jerry Rice: The Ultimate Receiver. Videocassette. Quality Video/All Pro Sports, 1996.

John Coltrane. Directed by Jean-Noel Cristiani. Rhino, 1995.

The Journey of the African-American Athlete. Produced by Leslie D. Farrell et al. HBO Sports, 1996.

Long Jump. Performed by Igor Ter-Ovanesyan and Ralph E. Boston. Universal Education & Visual Arts, 1972.

Lutz, Catherine, and Roy Park. *Home Front*. C-SPAN (Television Network) Archives, 2002.

Miss Evers' Boys. Directed by Lorna Littleway. Videocassette. HBO Home Video, 1997.

Mr. Saturday Night. Performed by Billy Crystal et al. Videocassette. MGM Home Entertainment Inc., 1992, 2002.

Muhammad Ali: The Greatest Collection. Performed by Muhammad Ali et al. Videocassette. HBO Home Video, 2001.

Nganga Kiyangala: Congo Religion in Cuba. Produced by Luis A. Soto and Tato Quiñones. Televisión Latina, 1991.

Panther. Directed by Mario Van Peebles. Videocassette. PolyGram Video, 1995.

Pryor, Richard, and Michael Blum. *Live & Smokin'*. Videocassette. Vestron Video, 1985.

Raw. Performed by Eddie Murphy, Robert Townsend, and Keenan Ivory Wayans. Videocassette. Paramount Pictures, 1988.

Shaft. Directed by Gordon Parks. Videocassette. Metro-Goldwyn Mayer, 1971.

Spirer, Peter. *Rhyme & Reason*. Videocassette. Buena Vista Video, 1997.

Taking Back Detroit. Directed by Kenneth V. Cockrel et al. Videocassette. Icarus Films, 1981.

The Vigil (for Kurt Cobain). Directed by Justin McGregor. Vanguard, 1998.

Understanding Creation. Produced by Kenneth Copeland and Carl Baugh. Kenneth Copeland Ministries, 1995.

United States Congress. *USIA Film, Wilma Rudolph Olympic Champion: Report (To Accompany H.R. 6949)*. Washington, D.C.: USGPO, 1975.

University of California, Santa Cruz Fifteenth Annual Martin Luther King Jr. Memorial Convocation, featuring Michael Eric Dyson, University of California, Santa Cruz, Media Services, 1999.

Waiting to Exhale. Directed by Forest Whittaker. Videocassette. Twentieth Century-Fox Video, 1995.

DISSERTATIONS

Berest, Ina M. "The Fairy Tale in the Theories of Erikson, Bettleheim, Montessori, and Piaget." Ph.D. diss., Chicago State University, 1977.

Dyson, Michael Eric. "Uses of Heroes: Celebration and Criticism in the Interpretation of Malcolm X and Martin Luther King, Jr." Ph.D. diss., Princeton University, 1993.

Farguheson, Ivy. "Black Feminism, Womanism, and the Million Man March." Ph.D. diss., University of North Carolina, 1997.

Hunter, Herbert Marshall. "The Life and Work of Oliver C. Cox." Ph.D. diss., Boston University, 1981.

Kennedy, Darren. "Hip-Hop Culture: The Effect on White Youth of Black Role Models." Ph.D. diss., Hampshire College, 1993.

Lott, Eric. "The Seeming Counterfeit: Blackface Minstrelsy and Working-Class Culture in America." Ph.D. diss., Columbia University, 1991.

Norman, Gary Alfred. "A Critique of C. H. Dodd's View of 'Realized Eschatology.'" Ph.D. diss., Abilene Christian College, 1967.

Perry, Margaret. "A Bio-bibliography of Countee P. Cullen, 1903–1946." Ph.D. diss., Catholic University of America, 1959.

Pinn, Anthony B. "I Wonder as I Wander: An Examination of the Problem of Evil in African American Religious Thought." Ph.D. diss., Harvard University, 1994.

Spillers, Hortense J. "Fabrics of History: Essays on the Black Sermon." Ph.D. diss., Brandeis University, 1974.

Stout, Jeffrey. "Religion, Morality, and the Justification of Moral Knowledge." Ph.D. diss., Princeton University, 1976.

Strait, Kevin Michael Angelo. "The Jazz Artist as a Response to Minstrelsy: James Baldwin, Miles Davis, and the 'Protest Traditions' of the Early to Mid Sixties." Master's thesis, George Washington University, 2002.

Washington, James Melvin. *The Origins and Emergence of Black Baptist Separatism, 1863–1897*. Ph.D. diss., Yale University, 1979.

Acknowledgments

As usual, I would like to thank Liz Maguire, my editor and intellectual soulmate. This makes six books we've done together, and it just gets better with time. I would also like to thank Will Morrison for his timely and wonderful assistance. And I'd like to thank Kay Mariea for her expert care and shepherding of the manuscript, and the fine editorial work of Chrisona Schmidt.

I want to thank all the scholars, journalists, and intellectuals who interviewed me, including: Sidney J. Dobrin, Lana Williams, Ronald E. Chennault, Jonathan Smith, Maria Agui Carter, Calvin A. Lindsay, Jr., George Roy, Abby Lynn Kearse, Marc Vogl, Tonelius Oliver, Yanko Damboulev, Frank A. Thomas, Hisham Aidi, Laura Winkiel, and Kheven La Grone.

I want to send a serious shout out to Mark Anthony Neal, the brilliant young critic who wrote the foreword for this book. I thank him for taking time from his busy schedule to place my work in a critical and cultural context, and thus, to help me understand what it is that I do. I would also like to thank Kim Ransom and Crystal Conway for their help on the bibliography.

I am grateful to my new academic family at the University of Pennsylvania, whose support has already given a boost to my scholarship. I would like to thank Tukufu Zuberi, a brilliant and engaging scholar and the director of the Center for Africana Studies at Penn, and his equally gifted wife, Akilah, a brilliant intellectual and wisewoman in her own right. Their friendship has been a great boon. I would also like to thank Judith Rodin, the amazingly talented, energetic, and exceptionally smart president of

Penn, whose support of Africana studies has breathed new life into a much-needed program. Her friendship is precious and endearing to me.

I also want to thank Sam Preston, the bright and capable dean whose support of me and our department has facilitated its strengthening as a first-rate center for intellectual inquiry. His friendship is a wonderful asset. I also want to thank my wonderful new family in Religious Studies, including Ann Mater and Steve Dunning, whose sharp minds, and encouraging souls, and friendship have been incredibly heartening. Finally, but not least, I want to thank Gayle Garrison, Onyx Finney, Carolyn Davis, and Marie Hudson for being a wonderful support staff. Their eagerness to help, and their considerable intellectual gifts, and their friendship as well, have already left a profound mark on me.

Finally, I want to thank my family, including my mother, Addie Mae Dyson, and my four brothers, Anthony, Everett, Gregory, and Brian. I also want to thank my children, Maisha, a fine actress, Mwata, a fine physician, and Michael II, my main man, homeboy, and a fine student. (Pops Dukes loves you all.)

And to Rev. Marcia Louise Dyson, I am extraordinarily grateful for all your help, love, nurture, and support—and for reading every word of this book, and for working so diligently on whipping the bibliography into shape. Without your providing a space for me to work, this book wouldn't exist.

INDEX